NO LESS THAN MYSTIC

A History of Lenin and the Russian Revolution for a 21st-Century Left

John Medhurst

Repeater

Published by Repeater Books
An imprint of Watkins Media Ltd
19-21 Cecil Court
London
WC2N 4EZ
UK

www.repeaterbooks.com

A Repeater Books paperback original 2017
1

Distributed in the United States by Random House, Inc., New York.

Cover design: Johnny Bull
Typography and typesetting: Josse Pickard
Typefaces: Bembo/Futura

ISBN: 978-1-910924-47-1
Ebook ISBN: 978-1-910924-48-8

*To my Mum and Dad
and to the Isle of Dogs 1982-1988, where I learnt
to argue about the Russian Revolution.*

Contents

The Marxist doctrine is omnipotent because it is true

—V.I. Lenin, *The Three Component Parts of Marxism*, 1914

No less than mystic is the concept of a political
form that, by virtue of its particular character, can
surmount all economic, social and national conditions

— Julius Martov, *The State and the Socialist Revolution*, 1920

And Azrael, among scales of crippled wings,
threading his difficult way,
takes by its high art,
the defeated sky

— Osip Mandelstam, *Poems*, 1922

Because It's True

The aim of this book is to present a history of Lenin and the Russian Revolution that is relevant to today's democratic, libertarian left, especially those born since the fall of the Soviet Union. Although it broadly covers the period 1903 to 1921 and seeks to explain why the Bolshevik Revolution degenerated so quickly into its apparent opposite, it is not simply a work of history. It continually examines the Russian Revolution through the lens of a 21st-century, non-Marxist, participatory socialism, and draws parallels with recent anti-capitalist struggles, attempting to open up the past to the present and points in between. It suggests that corporate capitalism should be opposed not with a set of revolutionary formulations which were questionable one hundred years ago and have even less relevance now, but with popular social movements built on people's needs and experience.

As a result, it is kinder to Russia's non-Leninist socialists than are most histories. Although not blind to the many faults of the Russian Mensheviks, Socialist Revolutionaries and Jewish Bundists, I seek to rescue them from a century of disrespect. In doing so I do not assume the knowledge of the subject that many Russian Revolution hobbyists take for granted, nor show much deference to those icons of Bolshevism, Lenin and Trotsky, still common today on the left. In the end I suggest that anti-capitalist writers and campaigners such as Murray Bookchin, Noam Chomsky, Naomi Klein, Michael Lowy and Paul Mason have more constructive options to offer the left today than do the sages of Bolshevism.

Some will ask why, outside of academic history, this should be of any interest. The modern left does not look to the events of the French Revolution of 1789–95 for guidance, so why scrutinise and debate the Russian Revolution? The Russian Empire of the Romanov dynasty was a semi-feudal, multi-national monstrosity that collapsed as a result of total European war. We will not see that specific historical conjunction again. But for all that, the Bolshevik Revolution was still the first "modern" revolution – i.e. led by the urban working class and with a socialist objective – in an era dominated by global capitalism. As a result, it remains a key issue and point of contention from which subsequent arguments about capitalism and its alternatives derive. Its centenary in 2017 has generated new exhibitions of its popular art and imagery, commentary in the liberal media and documentaries on BBC2. There are competing retrospectives seeking to establish a firm consensus for future generations on the lessons of the Bolshevik experiment.

Most of these assessments fall in to two camps: a general condemnation of the revolution, and by extension all revolutionary change; or a defence of Bolshevism with an admission that because of civil war and the failure of the

European proletariat to also rise up it degenerated into bureaucratic tyranny. This book adopts neither of those perspectives. It argues that the real revolution of 1917 took place in February not October, and was led by a wide alliance of socialists, trade unionists, peasants and populists in which the Bolshevik Party played only a minor role. Despite the enormous difficulties involved in creating a durable democratic framework after the February Revolution, it contained great potential for social and cultural liberation and a far better future for the Russian people than they had suffered under three hundred years of Tsarism or would endure under Leninism and Stalinism.

This revolution, and many of its key players, had much within it that today's anti-capitalist campaigners should re-examine. Whilst it is true that some elements of the Bolshevik Revolution, most notably its attempts to provide greater freedom for women and a short-lived libertarian attitude to social and educational experimentation, were bold and emancipatory, that revolution soon established a power structure as monumental and oppressive as the Tsarism it replaced. Within a few months (in some cases days and weeks) of the Bolsheviks taking power in October, most of the democratic freedoms offered by the February Revolution were swiftly curtailed. For a variety of reasons, not least the undemocratic and authoritarian nature of Leninist doctrine, the Bolshevik Revolution had little to no chance of achieving a genuine socialist transition in Russia, much less in the rest of Europe.

This argument is not in itself new. It could even be said to fall under the rubric of the "continuity thesis", i.e. that the policies of the Bolshevik government from October 1917 laid the groundwork for the Stalinist dictatorship of the 1930s. But I do not advocate the simplistic version of continuity, which is that the decisions and policies of the Bolsheviks led in linear fashion straight to the Gulag Archipelago. There were many forks in the road where a radical but democratic socialist alternative could have been taken. Some of these alternatives were argued for by prominent Bolsheviks in both the moderate tendency in the party in 1917-18, and the Workers' Opposition grouped around Alexandra Kollontai and Alexander Shliapnikov in 1920-21, and even, to a lesser extent, the Bukharinite "right-wing" Bolsheviks of the 1920s. Most crucially, the history told here does not absolve capitalist society then or now for its terrible inequalities and oppressions simply because the so-called alternative, an inherently authoritarian socialism, would be even worse. It denies that this is the alternative.

In his own time, certainly before 1914, Lenin was part of the broad European socialist and labour movement, more dogmatic and uncompromising than many but still firmly within that political family. After 1917 the philosophy and practice of Leninist parties, underpinned by arguments and strategic programmes of great appeal far beyond the established Communist parties, indeed often replicated in all but minor details by the Trotskyist groups supposedly opposing them, dominated much of the intellectual left.

This is not surprising. Lenin was a powerful thinker, a forceful polemicist and, within strict boundaries, an adroit leader of both the Bolshevik Party and the Soviet Union. Nor was he simply an authoritarian, although that was a core element of his personality and politics. Even in *What Is To Be Done?*, the iconic and justly-famous case for discipline and hierarchy within the revolutionary Russian left, he argued that "The Social Democrat's ideal must not be the secretary of a trade union, but a people's tribune". At that point, and up to *The State and Revolution* in 1917, many of Lenin's broader ideas were progressive and emancipatory. But they were infected and over-ridden by his deeper political and organisational philosophy, a philosophy that led in time to party-state officials exercising a monopoly of power, functionaries who were nothing at all like a people's tribune and infinitely worse than the worst trade union secretary.

Lenin's defenders argue that the corruption of the revolution arose from the intolerable pressure of external events. But significant though these were, I would argue that the primary causative factor was the inherent logic of Leninism. Once certain precepts central to Lenin's vision of socialism—i.e. the leading role of a vanguard of professional revolutionaries who represent the advanced working class; contempt for "formal" democracy; disregard for universal civil rights and cultural freedoms; and acceptance of temporary repression during transition to a future utopia—were accepted, then the larger goal of liberation was already and inevitably lost.

Many on the left who make confident references to the Russian Revolution in political discussion, social-media debate etc., are often much less informed on the subject than they suppose.[1] Part of the reason for this is the simplistic bias of most primers and summaries. There is a need for a new history, unambiguously of the left, that nevertheless rises above the old dichotomies and stereotypes. The Marxist historian Christopher Hill opened his superb history of Britain in the 17th century, *The Century of Revolution 1603-1714* (1961), with the statement: "History is not a narrative of events. The historian's difficult task is to explain what happened".[2] This is true up to a point, although these are not mutually exclusive. A proper accounting of "what happened" requires a fusion of narrative and explanation.

This book has the surface format of a narrative history, but it interweaves explanation – social, political, cultural – within the narrative to broaden understanding of what occurred and why. It is not a work of Marxist historiography, although it utilises Marxist economic categories where they are useful. I do not offer a grand theoretical synthesis, being naturally sceptical of such things, although woven into the commentary and conclusion are observations on socialist strategy and suggestions for what Paul Mason has called "revolutionary reformism". Its final conclusion, presented with as much fealty to the historical evidence as I can summon, is that the legacy of Lenin and the Bolsheviks is one the contemporary left should reject.

That being said, I hope it gives the Bolsheviks their due. Between February and October 1917, especially after Lenin's return to Russia in April, the Bolshevik Party became stronger and more significant as it took root in the Soviets (Workers Councils) of the major cities and campaigned for Peace, Bread and Land. In this period, the same one during which Lenin produced his supreme example of revolutionary theory, *The State and Revolution*, the Bolshevik Party undoubtedly spoke for the majority of the workers in the cities. However, this phase of the party's work and the principles of *The State and Revolution* were comprehensively rejected once the Bolsheviks took power in October.

From here the Soviets and other manifestations of democratic workers' power were swiftly curtailed and real decision-making power was removed to the Supreme Council of People's Commissars (Sovnarcom) and the Supreme Economic Council (Vesenka). Political and press freedom went the same way within weeks of October. Whilst the "bourgeois" parties were immediately outlawed, even other socialist parties did not last long once Sovnarcom had firmly established its power. The Socialist Revolutionaries, the Mensheviks and the anarchists were tolerated for a while after the insurrection, but for a far shorter time than is commonly supposed. Most of their newspapers were instantly suppressed. They were then persecuted, censored and finally banned as the Bolshevik Party became inextricable from the organs of state.

Rosa Luxemburg distrusted the theory and mentality of Leninism from its first appearance in 1903. Once it assumed power her worst fears were confirmed. In 1918, writing of the limits and shortcomings of all institutions including democratic ones, she concluded, "But the remedy that Lenin and Trotsky have found is worse than the disease it is meant to cure". Having seen the Bolsheviks' strangulation of political and press freedom and the suppression of internal democracy in the Soviets, Luxemburg wrote, "Freedom only for the supporters of the government, only for the members of one party—however numerous they may be—is no freedom at all". She found that under Bolshevik rule the only "active element" was the bureaucracy, and that therefore Bolshevik rule was "at bottom a clique affair—a dictatorship, to be sure, not the dictatorship of the Proletariat however but only the dictatorship of a handful of politicians".[3]

From a different perspective, but equally unafraid to state honestly what he observed, Bertrand Russell, in *The Practice and Theory of Bolshevism* (written in 1920 after a long visit to Russia and interviews with Lenin, Trotsky and Gorky), found that the Soviets had long died out as living democratic institutions because "no conceivable system of free elections would give majorities to the Communists, either in town or country".[4] This was hardly surprising given that the social and political system created by Lenin and the Bolsheviks was

> a slavery far more complete than that of capitalism. A sweated wage, long hours, industrial conscription, prohibition of strikes, prison for slackers, diminution of already insufficient rations in factories where production falls below what the authorities expect, an army of spies ready to report any tendency to political disaffection and to procure imprisonment for its promoters—this is the reality of a system which still professes to govern in the name of the proletariat.[5]

This centralised state capitalism, presided over by a small political elite that denied political expression to any outside its own ranks, was not created by Stalin in the late 1920s and 1930s—Stalin simply added the physical liquidation of the Old Bolsheviks and a massive increase in the apparatus of state terror. On the contrary, this *was* the work of the Old Bolsheviks.

The best informed critique of Bolshevik authoritarianism

came from the Russian left itself. Most especially the always present alternative best represented by the Mensheviks, led by Julius Martov, Lenin's great opposite and antagonist since 1903 when the Russian Social Democratic and Labour Party (RSDLP) had split into Bolsheviks and Mensheviks. Martov remained Lenin's most articulate and principled Marxist opponent until his death in 1923. In the 1920s his acute and honest accounts of the new regime were forgotten as Stalinist ideological orthodoxy clamped itself on the thinking of the Western left. For those with ears to listen, though, Martov had already in 1919 laid out the bare truth of life in Bolshevik Russia and the betrayal of the hopes and promises of October 1917. "Reality has cruelly shattered all these illusions," he wrote:

> The Soviet State has not established in any instance electiveness and recall of public officials. It has not suppressed the professional police. It has not done away with social hierarchy in production [...] On the contrary, it shows a tendency in the opposite direction. It shows a tendency towards the utmost possible strengthening of the principles of hierarchy and compulsion. It shows a tendency toward the development of a more specialized apparatus of repression than before.[6]

Martov's passionate critiques were a permanent reminder that a different and finer form of Russian Marxism existed. There were, of course, other political traditions that spoke and acted for the revolution and for the political freedom it had briefly offered. The broad anarchist and anarcho-syndicalist movement was one. Two of the most outstanding representatives of that movement, Alexander Berkman and Emma Goldman, returned to Russia in 1919 after having been deported from the US in the "Red Scare". At first they wished to work for and assist the Bolshevik Revolution. By 1921, when the Bolsheviks crushed the Kronstadt rebellion, they had been cruelly disillusioned and had little choice but to leave the country.

Berkman's *The Bolshevik Myth* (1925) was a powerful indictment of the Bolshevik regime and its brutal suppression of trade union, socialist and anarchist opposition, soaked in vivid detail and *saeva indignatio*.[7] Goldman's *My Disillusionment in Russia* (1924) did much the same, detailing her travels to Kharkov, Poltava, Kiev and Odessa, her encounters with rigged Soviets, harassed unions, forced labour and relentless persecution of any and all opposition. She freely admitted that "The strongest of us are loath to give up a long cherished dream"[8]; yet give it up she eventually did, the final severance coming after the mass slaughter at Kronstadt. From then she considered the Bolsheviks "the most pernicious enemies of the revolution".[9] Goldman's and Berkman's books were widely available on the left in the 1920s and 1930s and helped form the thought of anti-Leninist socialists like George Orwell.

For many of today's anti-capitalist campaigners the legacy of non-Leninist, libertarian socialism has found its best expression in the positions taken by Noam Chomsky since the 1960s. Chomsky's forensic and damning indictments of US foreign policy are rooted in his anti-authoritarian politics. He is also one of the few outstanding left intellectuals to unambiguously reject Leninism and Bolshevism as not just misguided but fundamentally *anti-socialist*, and "in my view counter-revolutionary". Speaking of "incipient socialist institutions" such as Soviets, Factory Committees and workers' cooperatives that emerged in the period after the February Revolution, Chomsky observed that "Lenin and Trotsky pretty much eliminated them as they consolidated power". He conceded there are arguments about the pressures and justifications for doing so (i.e. the need to win the civil war) but believed that "the incipient socialist structures in Russia were dismantled *before* the really dire conditions arose".[10] More detailed studies, such as Maurice Brinton's analysis of Workers' Control in the period 1917-1921, confirm this.

Chomsky's general critique derives from "Council Communists" such as Anton Pannekoek and Sylvia Pankhurst, anarcho-syndicalists such as Berkman and Rudolf Rocker, and an underlying and long-established anti-statist radicalism best expressed by Michael Bakunin, the great seer and leader of 19th-century anarchism. Lenin himself added credence to their analyses through his political activities and philosophy—from his clearly stated belief that the working class was "incapable on its own of developing anything more than a trade union consciousness", and required political leadership "from without", to his blunt admission shortly after October that "socialism is nothing but state capitalist monopoly made to benefit the whole people". Diane P. Koenker, in a study of labour relations in the post-October period, summed up what this meant for ordinary Russian workers: "In the shops where one-man management (Lenin's own preference) replaced collegial management workers faced the same kinds of authoritarian management they thought existed only under capitalism".[11]

Against this critical interpretation one must measure an equally valid argument about the initial attraction and mass base of the Bolshevik Revolution, best expressed in Trotsky's magnificent *History of the Russian Revolution*. In the academic sphere this case has been substantiated by Alexander Rabinowitch's outstanding work on the Bolshevik Party during the crucial period from mid-1917 to mid-1918, specifically his conclusion that

> The October Revolution in Petrograd was less a military operation than a gradual process rooted in popular political culture, widespread disenchantment with the results of the February Revolution and, in that context, the magnetic attraction of the Bolsheviks' promises of immediate peace, bread, land for the peasantry, and grass roots democracy exercised through multiparty soviets.[12]

Whilst this is true, it must be seen in the context of the Bolsheviks' rapid backtracking on their main slogans from an early stage after October, a backtracking that raises suspicion that the slogans were short-term tactical necessities rather than firm political principles. This book details the scale and speed of that backtracking, which included the suppression of the Soviets as genuine vehicles of grassroots democracy, the crushing of press and political freedom, the replacement of workers' control by one-man management, the establishment of a secret police apparatus far more extensive and brutal than the Tsars', the dismissal of the Constituent Assembly whose defence and convocation had been one of the justifications for October, the militarisation and control of the trade unions by the state and, finally, the mass murder of socialist activists at Kronstadt who had been instrumental in October, for the crime of abiding by its initial ideals.

Despite this there has been, and still is, a strong tradition on the left of exculpation of the Bolsheviks. Outside of a handful of serious works this rarely goes into detail, but broadly asserts that the period from 1917-21 was the original essence of the October Revolution. After that, it concedes, the Revolution began to falter due to a "counter-revolution" fed by the decimation of the Bolsheviks' best cadres in the civil war and the rise of a bureaucratic structure controlled by Stalin. As Lenin fell ill and died, and Trotsky was marginalised and replaced, the counter-revolution gained power and strength, reversed most of the liberatory social and political initiatives of October (though not the nationalisation of the economy) and clamped down on political freedom. The process culminated in the Great Terror of the 1930s and Stalin's emergence as Dictator.

This has been the general view of the left since the public discrediting of Stalinism that followed Khrushchev's 1956 "Secret Speech". Often without acknowledgment, it reflects Trotsky's analysis of the degeneration of the Bolshevik Revolution as expounded in *The Revolution Betrayed* (1936). It found a particularly loud expression in the works of Tony Cliff, the intellectual guru of the British Socialist Workers Party (SWP), whose three-volume biography of Lenin is the *ne plus ultra* of Leninist hagiography.

Cliff's work had its counterpart in more sophisticated authors such as Isaac Deutscher and Marcel Leibman, who themselves followed a line of intellectual defence of Leninism first expounded by the Hungarian Marxist philosopher Georg Lukács in *Lenin: A Study on the Unity of His Thought* (1924). Lukács' short book is an ingenious if disreputable justification of Lenin, whom he regarded as "the greatest thinker to have been produced by the revolutionary working class movement since Marx". Cloaking Lenin's every strategy and tactical maneuver in the armour of "dialectics", Lukács asserted that criticism of Leninism as elitist and undemocratic arose from "the undialectical concept of the 'majority'", and lamented that "Many workers suffer from the illusion that a purely formal democracy, in which the voice of every citizen is equally valid, is the most suitable instrument for expressing the interests of society as a whole".[13]

Lukács ridiculed the "mechanistic rigidity of undialectical thought" that drew attention to the Bolsheviks' betrayal of many of their pre-October promises. To free critics from their mechanistic rigidity, Lukács explained, "the Russian Communist Party's policy, Lenin's policy, is only contradictory in so far as it seeks and finds the dialectically correct solution to the objective contradictions of its own social existence".[14] Lukács' book was re-released by Verso in 2009 as part of its Radical Thinkers series with the publisher's recommendation that it "remains indispensable to an understanding of the contemporary significance of Lenin's life and work".

A far better defence of Leninism can be found in Deutscher's classic three-volume life of Trotsky.[15] Written with flair and passion and rooted in a serious Marxist analysis utterly devoid of Lukács' theoretical verbiage, Deutscher's intention was to provide a redemptive account of Trotsky's role in the revolution and, especially, as Stalin's great antagonist, the holder and heir of the "Classical Marxist" tradition. He wished to show Trotsky as a man of consistent principle, vital to the success of October and the Bolsheviks' victory in the civil war, a historical and literary critic of the first rank and the man who maintained the heroic ideal of October while nearly all other Bolsheviks either capitulated to or were eliminated by Stalin. Deutscher achieved all this. His trilogy is intellectually stimulating and politically engaging and yet it is, ultimately, an apologia for Leninism and therefore, tragically and unintentionally, for Stalinism.

At the close of Deutscher's first volume, taking Trotsky's life to 1921, he acknowledges the immense problems that economic collapse and the civil war had created but concludes that "the Working Class had not come to regret the revolution". Although true in a general sense – the working class did not wish for a restoration of Tsarism – this frames the argument to equate "revolution" with one-party rule by the Bolsheviks. It thereby misrepresents working-class resistance to that rule and is untrue to the period. To take one example, Deutscher casually observed that "In three years the Socialist Revolutionaries and Mensheviks had been completely eclipsed and hardly dared raise their heads", omitting to mention that the primary reason they hardly dared raise their heads was relentless legal and physical persecution.[16] He also ignored the inconvenient fact that in 1918 and 1919 the Mensheviks made a notable comeback in the few Soviet elections not rigged by the Bolsheviks.

The belief that the Bolsheviks had *by definition* conducted a socialist revolution, and therefore all their actions were justifiable expedients to defend it, undermines Deutscher's entire analysis. Whilst intensively examining the pressures of economic crisis and civil war he hardly mentions the suppression of Soviet democracy from an early stage after October, the rise and suppression of the Extraordinary Assembly of Delegates from Petrograd Factories and Plants (EADS), and the liquidation of the Kronstadt rebellion, to which he devotes three pages which completely avoid the issues raised by the rising. After a quick reference to the rising being "led by anarchists" (it was in fact led by veterans of 1917 who wished to return to democratic Soviet power), Deutscher's hurried account of the rebellion is a brief and unsatisfactory summary of events, lacking any of the deep analysis he brings to other subjects. He does not even mention the mass strikes convulsing Petrograd and Moscow at the time, which ignited the Kronstadt revolt, nor the imposition of martial law to crush them.

The less ideologically committed work of E.H. Carr (whose fourteen-volume *History of Soviet Russia* from 1917 to 1929 was a groundbreaking study, soaked in Namierite "objectivity" that evoked much admiration within British historiography) provided a similar whitewash, such was his admiration for the scale of the economic transformation attempted and achieved by Soviet planners. This admiration led him to conclude that not only was Lenin a figure of "unique greatness"—quite true, in the sense of his effect on world history—but that "his genius was far more constructive than destructive".[17] Given Lenin's record, this is an astonishing conclusion and demonstrates that for all its impressive academic rigor Carr's work lacks moral or cultural sensitivity. It is undeniable that Lenin constructed a massive and historically unprecedented edifice upon the ruins of revolution and civil war, but he greatly contributed to those ruins in the first place and the edifice was so defective that it rotted from within.

Deutscher's skillful justification of Leninism, added to and indirectly supported by Carr's monumental research, was highly praised and influential. Lesser writers, such as the Italian Marxist Lucio Colleti, followed in its wake. A leading figure of the post-war Italian Communist Party and a key thinker of the 1960s New Left, Colleti's *From Rousseau to Lenin* (winner of the Isaac Deutscher Memorial Prize in 1972) considered the meaning and relevance of Lenin's *The State and Revolution* in comparison to the work of the more "evolutionary" Marxist Karl Kautsky, and concluded that "for Lenin, the revolution is the end of all masters; for Kautsky, it is merely the arrival of a new master".[18] Yet nothing in either man's work justifies this. All Lenin's actions post-October, and his own unequivocal statements about the paramount need for authority, control, direction from the top and one-person management, demonstrate that the revolution he actually led (as opposed to the one he wrote about in *The State and Revolution)* was about the arrival of a new master.

A similar level of self-delusion is found in the work of Belgian Marxist economist and theorist Ernest Mandel, which had some vogue within the left of the 1960s and 1970s. Mandel considered that the Leninist theory of organisation created the "Marxist science of the subjective factor", i.e. it provided a theoretical justification and guide to practical actions – although one could say the same of Bernstein's

Revisionism, implying that it was the subjectivity rather than the science that concerned Mandel. For Mandel, what he called "comprehensive political activity" would "answer all questions of internal and external class relations" and thereby would "train the masses", who were otherwise "limited to the confines of the trade union or the factory".[19] This was written in 1970, apparently unaware that many working-class men and women already had lives and dreams beyond the confines of the trade union and the factory. Many, indeed, had never set foot in a factory.

Marcel Liebman's highly successful *Leninism under Lenin* (1975) offers a more substantial argument. Liebman, whilst defending and justifying Lenin's basic record before and after the Bolshevik Revolution, acknowledged that he never solved (or even tried to solve) the problem of how to organise a meaningful democracy within the "socialist dictatorship" that he and Trotsky openly admitted was their aim, and that "the limitations of his thinking about western capitalist society"[20] were so serious that he utterly misread the role of reformism within those societies. Precisely because of Liebman's honesty in examining these weaknesses, his carefully argued conclusion that in the final analysis Leninism "gave back to the working class movement a revolutionary content that corresponds to the alienated situation of the proletariat in capitalist society"[21] was superficially persuasive.

Enthusiasm for Lenin – based partly on reading Deutscher, Liebman and Cliff, but also (and perhaps mainly) on unquestioning acceptance by middle-class students of a simplistic radical image of unyielding revolutionary integrity, aided by numerous posters, T-shirts and badges – grew out of the political turmoil of the 1960s and 1970s, and abated somewhat in later decades. But recently it has come back into intellectual fashion, as demonstrated by the works of Lars Lih, Slavoj Žižek, Paul Le Blanc and Tamas Krausz. Lih's work, in particular his massive exegesis *Lenin Rediscovered: What Is To Be Done? in Context* (2006) and his shorter primer *Lenin* (2011), has laid the groundwork for a redefinition of Lenin for the Occupy generation. Lih considers Lenin more of a romantic revolutionary activist than a puritanical Marxist intellectual. In an important sense this is right, although not in the manner Lih intends.

Whilst Lenin and the doctrine he created are soaked in revolutionary voluntarism and have given *carte blanche* to impatient socialists to launch a series of ambitious programmes with little attraction to the working class, this has not led to significant victories in the sense of building durable socialist democracies. Where Leninist parties gained power in the 20th century, whether in China, Eastern Europe, Africa or elsewhere, they have without exception introduced one-party police states. In European democracies, Leninism has been the bedrock of small political sects incapable of building alliances with other socialists, let alone securing mass working-class support. Lih's attempt to humanise Lenin and to place his interpretation of Marxism within the context of Russian culture is historically revealing, but it fails to address the inherent problems of Leninist practice.[22]

Kevin Murphy's *Revolution and Counter Revolution: Class Struggle in a Moscow Metal Factory* (2005) faces these issues head on, if with one eye closed. Drawing on new archival sources, it is a rich and detailed account of the daily life and politics of workers in a complex of metal factories in Moscow from the 1890s to the early 1930s. But even though it illuminates many areas of the life of the Russian proletariat that more traditional works have ignored – what workers did in their leisure hours, their domestic lives, etc. – it still tends to hue to the broadly accepted paradigm on the left for the Russian Revolution. Murphy begins by covering the years from 1890 to February 1917, before moving to the crucial February-October period, providing many examples of how, to quote the Menshevik historian N.N. Sukhanov, "Bolshevism began blossoming luxuriantly and putting forth roots throughout the country", the deepest roots being in the large factory complexes of the capital and Moscow.

The remainder of the book is a compelling account of how workers in the Hammer and Sickle Metal Factory in Moscow weathered the storms of civil war, the New Economic Policy, stringent and repressive labour laws, and Stalinism. Significantly, though, the book skips lightly over the period between October 1917 and the beginning of the civil war in June 1918. Remarkably for such a thorough and conscientious work, it does not even mention the Extraordinary Assemblies and the extent to which anti-Bolshevik socialists within the factory were persecuted long before the start of the civil war. On the contrary, Murphy claims that during this period (roughly to 1923), "Rather than state repressions, strike actions were avoided by trade union intervention".[23]

As a summary, this is untrue. During 1917–23 Russia was convulsed by strike action against the Bolshevik regime, for a variety of reasons ranging from protests against food shortages and privileges for party officials to solidarity with Soviets and Factory Committees suppressed by the Red Guards and the Cheka. One outstanding study of socialist opposition to Bolshevik rule finds that workers' demands in 1918–19 centered not only on matters like food distribution and working hours, but also on demands for "free elections to the Soviets, release of all political prisoners, and freedom of political activity for the Mensheviks and Socialist Revolutionaries".[24] Most of these strikes were violently suppressed. In 1918 workers at the Obukhov and Putilov works in Petrograd took strike action against food shortages and the suppression of their Factory Committees (in an echo of the action of the battleship *Aurora* in October 1917, militant sailors in the Baltic Fleet docked a destroyer alongside the plant to express support for the workers). In June 1918 the Obukhov workers ejected management and took control of the plant, demanding that the EAD declare a strike across Petrograd in protest at the suppression of the Soviets. Eventually martial law was declared and they were arrested.

In early 1919 mass strikes broke out in Petrograd, Tula, Briansk, Tver and many other cities. In Tula the Cheka occupied factories on strike and arrested 1,000 strikers. In Petrograd the Putilov strikers were treated even more harshly. After fighting between Red Guards and strikers

the strike was suppressed and the Cheka went to work, holding summary trials. Many executions followed, taking place in a remote locality called Irinovka [...] The procedure was to line up the victims against the wall, blindfolded, and to shoot them down in batches by machine-gunfire.[25]

31

Murphy doesn't consider these events, except to add that groundbreaking studies of early Soviet labour, such as those of Jonathan Aves and Diane P. Koenker, "attempt to explain the demise of working class militancy by echoing continuity arguments with grossly inflated estimates about early state repression, concentration camps and coercion".

Nowhere does he justify this. Instead he concludes that on the key issues of October and Stalinism, "The Marxists got it right".[26] He does not specify *which* Marxists got it right, but it seems safe to assume he does not mean Marxists like Martov, Axelrod and Kautsky, who foretold that the October insurrection would lead to a bureaucratic police state, and who actually did get it right.

A different approach was adopted by *Lenin Reloaded: Towards a Politics of Truth* (2007).[27] A dense collection of essays by a stellar line-up of neo-Marxist and post-Structuralist academics such as Slavoj Žižek, Etienne Balibar, Alain Badiou, Frederik Jameson and Terry Eagleton, *Lenin Reloaded* offers pearls of wisdom such as "A Leninist Gesture Today: Against the Populist Temptation" (Žižek); "Lenin as reader of Hegel: Hypothesis for a reading of Lenin's Notebooks on Hegel's *The Science of Logic*" (Kouvalakis); "One Divides Itself into Two" (Badiou); and "Lenin and Revisionism" (Jameson). The essays vary in quality from marginally interesting to pretentious and irrelevant, but they all argue that Leninism provides vital and necessary guidance to today's anti-capitalists. The editors believe in "a return to Lenin" and a re-invention of the Leninist revolutionary project. They find the source of Lenin's originality in his "externality" from European Marxism and call any assertion that Leninism is a perversion of classical Marxism "part of the standard western racist argument against Lenin". The book's summary of its political project promises that "Such a project would be 'Leninist' in its commitment to action based on truth and its acceptance of the consequences that follow from action".

Lenin Reloaded should have derailed the trend to rehabilitate Lenin, yet socialist writers such as Paul Le Blanc have not only carried on much of its argument but praised it specifically. In *Unfinished Leninism* (2014),[28] Le Blanc offers a clearer case for Lenin's contemporary relevance than do the academics of *Lenin Reloaded*, although he avoids delving too deeply into Lenin's atrocious political record post-1917. Conceding that some of the contributors to *Lenin Reloaded* retain "traces of Stalinist residue", he finds that these traces can be dealt with "in a comradely tone" and are preferable to the "sterile anti-Leninist consensus". On behalf of the contributors of *Lenin Reloaded* he apologises for the fact that whilst they argued that Lenin must be translated into the distinctive political realities of our time, because of "space limitations" they could not "illustrate what such efforts might look like". Le Blanc concludes his review of *Lenin Reloaded* with praise for the "rich, diverse contributions" it offered and considers them "a challenge for all serious intellectuals and activists of our time".[29]

This is the antithesis of serious and challenging. It also ignores the real advances made in understanding the Russian Revolution in the last three decades. The "Social History" school of Soviet historians that emerged in the 1980s, most especially the work of Diane P. Koenker, William Rosenberg and Ronald G. Suny, has produced a corpus of groundbreaking studies that recreates and gives dignity and agency to Russian workers and peasants as political actors. Two decades before Murphy's work on the lives of Moscow metal workers—much praised by Marxist academics because it reinforced the Leninist thesis of the revolution—the Social Historians had been to the archives and rediscovered the Russian worker and his/her social experience. Their focus on the shopfloor, the canteen and the Factory Committee, rather than the statements and actions of political leaders such as Kerensky, Lenin and Trotsky, shook up and redefined Soviet historiography much to its benefit.

Astonishingly, Koenker's and Rosenberg's *Strikes and Revolution in Russia 1917* (1990) was the first systematic study of strikes and industrial actions in 1917 that not only linked them to the broader Revolution, but examined the social identities and perceptions of Russian workers outside of parties and Soviets. Koenker and Rosenberg concluded that rather than the leadership of the Vanguard Party, it was, in fact, factory-centred strike activism within the context of social and economic breakdown that led workers to assume a temporary "revolutionary" perspective. With the exception of a hardcore of party members, most Russian workers gave their support to the Bolsheviks in October 1917 for specific, provisional reasons, rather than because they suddenly realised, in a Pauline conversion, that they were soldiers of the Vanguard all along.

This Social History does not ignore the political dimension (led, as ever, by bourgeois intellectuals), but it balances it with the independent actions and wishes of the working class, in particular through re-emphasising the centrality of the

Factory Committees to the revolutionary process. It finds that it was the Committees that had the most organic connection to working-class struggle, that best expressed workers' desire for economic democracy and self-management. This approach has been attacked by both mainstream and Leninist historians, who while ostensibly opposed share some common assumptions. They both demonstrate disdain for the untutored Russian masses and admiration for Lenin, frequently respected by bourgeois-conservative historians for his "realism" and no-nonsense approach to leftist utopians. Some of the most iconic studies of Lenin have merged on this front. On the right, Adam Ulam's sympathetic biography of Lenin (1965) exemplified this approach. On the left, Tony Cliff's trilogy (1972-75) matched Ulam exactly in its dismissal of "left-wing infantilism" and anarcho-syndicalist industrial experiments.

What does this matter now? Leninist theorists such as Cliff and Mandel have passed away, and their work has not stood the test of time. Carr's volumes are themselves a historical monument. Academic study of the period from 1917-24 is vastly more sophisticated than during their heyday, deepened and enriched by the school of Social History. But I am not primarily interested in the halls of academe. It is the broad, politically literate left public that I am concerned with. In this world, the "soft Leninist" tradition of Deutscher, Liebman, Lih, Murphy, Le Blanc, etc. still set the parameters of debate about the Russian Revolution, and after a period of decline seem to be doing so more than ever. They command broad intellectual respect and are widely reviewed and analysed (comparatively and retrospectively) in numerous left journals and blogs. They convey to the politically engaged – or those wishing to become so, but unsure of their moorings – an impression that the left is indulgent, even supportive, of Lenin and Bolshevism. In my view this needs to be countered to ensure that a democratic, libertarian, anti-Bolshevik tradition, with a much better claim to represent radical socialism, is not forgotten or ignored.

Many Marxists and socialists still expend time and effort on championing and defending the Bolshevik Revolution, on special pleading to exonerate its denial of civil liberties, repression of democratic opposition and recourse to state terror, and on attempting to uncover a libertarian diamond buried under the rough of Stalinism and Cold War demonology. But the historical record, stripped of ideological distortion and willful blindness, is clear. There never was a diamond.

CHAPTER ONE
The Spark

In 1883, several members of the "Land and Freedom" populist revolutionary party who had recently become Marxists—the first to do so within the Russian revolutionary movement—reassessed the best route to the overthrow of autocracy in their homeland. Led by George Plekhanov, "the father of Russian Marxism", they formed a small group called the Emancipation of Labour. This group rejected Russian "exceptionalism" (the theory that Russia, because of the unique communal nature of Russian village life, might skip the full development of capitalism and instead advance straight to socialism) and stated bluntly that a revolution in Russia could only take place if it was based on a fully developed industrial proletariat. The Emancipation of Labour group sought to lead the infant Russian working class from Switzerland. They had hardly any connection to the Russian labour movement and limited resources. Many of the group's books and pamphlets were regarded by Russian state censors as so esoteric and boring that they allowed them to be officially published. Not for the first or last time the Russian authorities made a historic and suicidal mistake.

The Emancipation of Labour group was the seed of the Bolshevik Party, but it was itself the inheritor of a unique Russian revolutionary tradition. Given the nature of Russian society, this had of necessity been a tradition of revolution from above, and one could argue that the Bolshevik Party did not, ultimately, depart from this. The Romanov dynasty was established in 1613 as a result of a shifting of dynastic fortunes, with Mikhail Romanov offered the throne by the Zemsky Sobor, a feudal Estates parliament, after a "Time of Troubles" which saw the fall of the Rurik dynasty. Although the Zemsky Sobor was summoned annually for a while under Mikhail I, it was soon abandoned.

Since then, all attempts at radical reform, let alone revolution, had been instigated from the top, from the modernising programme of Peter the Great to the liberal aristocratic "Decembrists" of 1812. Only the unruly mass rebellions of Stenka Razin in 1671-72 and Yemelyan Pugachev in 1773-74 had deviated from that pattern, being movements of discontented peasants led by renegade Cossacks. Significantly, these rebellions, the only truly mass-based "revolutionary" initiatives before 1905, had fought for ethnic and peasant autonomy rather than political liberalisation.

The gravitational centre of Russian politics from 1613 to 1917 was Tsarist absolutism. The growing governmental and police apparatus (including the infamous Third Section of the Imperial Chancellery, a political police that was the precursor of the Okhrana, Cheka and KGB) existed to serve the Tsar alone and not, as in Western Europe, a growing professional middle class. This top-heavy bureaucracy was directed by an aristocratic, landowning elite. Underneath it rested a massive, mostly illiterate peasantry that up until 1861 were literally serfs. There was no breeding ground for a Russian variant of John Stuart Mill's philosophical radicalism or Gladstone's political and economic liberalism.

The most likely candidate for the role of Mill and/or Gladstone in 19th-century Russia, Alexander Herzen, set the template for the Russian political exile and for the "intelligentsia", a nebulous social category that had no real equivalent in Western Europe. The intelligentsia did not correspond to either the aristocracy (which with some notable exceptions supported the Tsar) or the bourgeoisie (which was miniscule before the second half of the century), but was a particular coalescence of critical intellectuals whose signature was its "impulse to criticise and oppose the fundamental iniquities and occasional barbarities of Tsarism".[1] Although its members came invariably from the bourgeois professions – writers, artists, doctors, teachers and lawyers – by no means all (or even a majority) of these professions were part of the intelligentsia. Yet those within its ambit would instinctively know where they stood in relation to each other and to the power structures of autocracy. Priests, Cossacks and policemen despised them, and were despised back.

The role of the intelligentsia as the unofficial opposition within Tsarist Russia arose from the failure of the 1812 Decembrist rebellion. As a young man, Herzen, who revered the memory of the Decembrist martyrs, wrote a few mild condemnations of police corruption. He was arrested, harassed and eventually driven to exile, where he had little option but to put his literary ability to use in advocating a complete overthrow of Russia's autocratic state. From this grew his establishment of the Free Russian Press and the beginning of decades of work to guide and instruct the opposition to Tsarism, mainly through the influential *The Bell*, a political periodical that for a while after the accession of Alexander II in 1855 had a hearing even within Russia itself. *The Bell's* combination of ethical socialism and practical reform ensured it was loathed by autocrats and reactionaries, but it was also attacked by a growing revolutionary sub-culture that saw progress only in violent revolution based on the peasantry. Herzen, a romantic liberal at heart, could not tolerate the violent terrorist actions of the new revolutionary groups Young Russia and Land and Freedom, lauded by his great contemporary Nikolai Chernyshevsky.

Chernyshevsky's writing was designed to stir emotions and incite action rather than analyse issues and suggest solutions. He came to prominence as the author of impassioned attacks on the Tsarist state in the pages of *The Contemporary*, a vibrant literary magazine established by the socialist writer Vissarion Belinsky and the radical poet Nikolai Nekrasov. Although nominally within the same revolutionary current as Herzen and a great admirer of his earlier work, Chernyshevsky and his comrades at *The Contemporary* took their political cues from French utopian socialism. From this they forged "Narodism" and its political vehicle the Land and Freedom party, the first and most authentic expression of Russian radical populism.

The course of Russian agrarian populism has much to teach today's left about developing durable campaigns with indigenous and rural populations. In an era of globalised neoliberalism it is often native indigenous peoples that are at the sharp end of economic exploitation. Amongst examples of mobilised indigenous resistance are the Yaruro Indians of Venezuela, whose culture Hugo Chavez incorporated into the project of Bolivarian Socialism, and the Quechua and Amarya peoples of the Andes and Altiplano regions of South America, whose political militancy resulted in the creation of the Movement Towards Socialism (MTS) and the election of the first indigenous President of Bolivia, the radical eco-socialist and former *cocalero* trade union activist Evo Morales.

In deprived towns like El Alto, the Aymara utilised their social and kinship networks to create a Federation of Neighborhood Committees, a mixture of an informal local government and a political campaign network. In 2003 the Committees were the focus of an uprising that ousted the corrupt President Gonzalo Sánchez de Lozada. This built on earlier struggles in Cochabamba where unionised water irrigators and cocoa growers, aided by urban-based anarchist activists, mobilised against the multi-national company Bechtel. As soon as it won the contract for Bolivia's privatised water utilities, Bechtel hiked charges and prosecuted those who collected rainwater in buckets. Having turned off the rain, it threatened the same to the water supply of those who could not pay the increased water bills. In 2000 protestors called a general strike in Cochabamba and demanded that the privatisation be reversed. The protests spread to the capital La Paz and were joined by teachers and students. Faced with an incipient revolution the government reversed water privatisation. This successful campaign led to the creation of the Movement Towards Socialism and the election of Morales as President in 2005.

These and other manifestations of indigenous resistance arise from a philosophy of "*Comunalidad*". Broadly, this revolves around four pillars of native life: communal governance via a popular assembly; communal territory, or land held in common; communal celebration, or feast days; and communal work for the benefit of the whole. These models of self-governing communities fundamentally challenge the Western model of economic growth advanced by the IMF and World Bank in favour of models of local sustainability that do not mindlessly exploit the environment or its resources with no regard for social consequences. In Noam Chomsky's summary, "Many don't see any particular point in having their culture and lifestyle destroyed so that people can sit in traffic jams in New York".[2]

One of the most useful effects of *Comunalidad* has been the erosion on the left of an unhelpful divide between urban and rural, working class and peasantry, and a recognition that the marginalised and exploited poor of the global south – and those of the supposedly more affluent BRIC countries of Brazil, Russia, India and China – do not easily fit into 19th- and 20th-century Marxist categories. And that the packaging of them into these, with the explicit assertion that one category (the urban proletariat) was the only one that really mattered, has prevented the emergence of global anti-capitalist movements with common aims.

19th-century Russian revolutionaries had none of this experience to draw upon. In 1874, the first stage of the Populist insurgency took the form of a "Pilgrimage to the People", in which young Narodniks from privileged backgrounds went to live and work amongst the villages of the Russian countryside. Their aim was to relate to the peasants as fellow human beings, working with them, learning from them, and thus generate a truly mass-based revolutionary culture. Some tried to actually become peasants, whilst some sought to put their educational, technical and medical skills at the service of peasant communities. With a few exceptions the crusade did not go well. Most of the young idealists were met with suspicion and even hostility. After several summers of repeated but pointless endeavor the vast majority of them were disenchanted with the peasants and their lack of revolutionary fervor.

From this fiasco grew the more hardened freedom fighters of the Zemlya I Volya (the People's Will), a splinter group from Land and Freedom. They did not spend their energies trying to teach illiterate peasants the theory of evolution. They targeted the most prominent and powerful men in society for assassination. For a few years in the late 1870s and early 1880s the idealistic terrorists of the People's Will engaged in a series of actions that defied the mighty Third Section and reached the pinnacle of aristocratic power around the Tsar. In 1881 they finally succeeded in murdering the "Tsar Liberator" Alexander II.

The assassination led to the complete opposite of its stated aims. On the eve of his murder, Alexander II approved reforms which might have opened a road to the kind of pluralist, democratic state the Narodniks wished to see. The newly appointed liberal Minister of the Interior, Loris-Melikov, had proposed a limited constitution to be implemented through a Supreme Commission consisting of appointed experts and representatives elected by rural and city Councils. The Commission would put legislative proposals to the appointed Council of State, which would have a new tier of fifteen delegates directly elected by the public. It was a toe in the water of representative democracy.

However, the assassination of his father led Alexander III to follow the lead of ultra-conservatives who opposed these reforms. They wished to strengthen the landed nobility and weaken aristocratic liberals such as Prince Georgy Lvov, who sought to increase the powers of the Zemstvos – elected rural local councils introduced by Alexander II in 1864. Although their franchise was weighted to give landowners and rural magnates greater power than the peasants and the merchants of the towns, in the context of 19th-century Russia the Zemstvos were a great step forward.

The hostility of Tsarist governments to the Zemstvos arose from the growing number of semi-urban professionals, such as doctors, teachers and agronomists, who worked within them. These were known as the "Third Element", to distinguish them from the First and Second Elements (the governors and the elected Deputies) who were drawn from long-established landowning families. The Third Element, however, had worked their way up from peasant or lower-class backgrounds and their politics were brusquely democratic. In response to their growing influence, the Ministry of the Interior introduced reforms to Zemstvo procedures in 1890 that denied Jews or landowning peasants the right to be elected to the assemblies, and gave direct control of Zemstvo policies and personnel to provincial governors who answered only to the Ministry. The possibility of local democracy promised by the Zemstvos slammed shut.

At the turn of the century, approximately 80% of the citizens of the Russian Empire were classified as peasants, and the majority of these were illiterate (although by 1914 a growing number of rural primary schools were bringing literacy to the villages). The urban proletariat itself was still half peasant—many were seasonal workers whose main attachment was to their families back in the village. Even so, between 1865 and 1917 the urban population of the Russian Empire grew from 7 million to 28 million. By 1914 half of St Petersburg's population of 2.2 million people had arrived there in the previous twenty years.[3] In the capital, and even more so in socially conservative Moscow, these workers initially kept to the patterns of life and cultural traditions of the peasantry. So did the vast army of migrant labour which in autumn and winter headed to the cities to find factory, transport or construction work, returning to their villages in the spring.

The Russian bourgeoisie, in turn, lacked the collective ethos of the politically assertive middle class of Victorian England. This only started to appear after the great famine of 1891. After a terrible crop failure, a famine began in the Volga region which spread rapidly to the Urals and the Black Sea. Had the government directed grain to the affected regions it might have been curtailed but it did nothing, not even banning export of grain, and by 1892 half a million peasants had starved to death. This led to fierce public criticism of the government's slow and incompetent reaction. After first denying the existence of a famine and censoring newspapers who reported it, the government finally authorised the creation of voluntary bodies to coordinate famine relief. The result was the emergence in Russia's political life of an organised civil society, disgusted and angry with the official organs of its own state.

Meanwhile, the Russian government set out on a grand industrial experiment, the building of the Trans-Siberian Railway between 1892 and 1903, that would define the efforts of the progressive bourgeoisie to drag the country out of its feudal past. As conceived by Count Witte, the most intelligent and far-sighted Minister to serve under Alexander III and Nicholas II, the Trans-Siberian Railway was one element of a conscious industrial strategy by the Ministry of Finance. The overriding necessity for economic growth was a stable financial climate. To this end the ruble was linked to gold in 1897. At the same time taxation was raised to ensure the state had enough reserves to fund and support projects such as railway modernisation.

Foreign investors were granted generous tax concessions and subsequent investment from Britain, France and Germany provided the impetus to new industries like oil, chemicals, metallurgy, rubber and electrical engineering. Between 1865 and 1890, the number of enterprises employing more than a hundred workers had already grown from 706,000 to 1,432,000. Aided by a growing railway network, Russian industry took off in the 1890s. In the decades before the First World War the production of coal in Poland and the Donetz Basin, iron and steel in Ukraine, and oil in Azerbaijan increased ten-fold. But this did not mean a national capitalism. By 1913, out of a total 5.25 billion rubles invested in Russian industry, about a third was foreign capital.

Many of these new industries were on the semi-colonial fringes of the Empire. The Russian Empire had a social and administrative core – Greater Russia – but it also encompassed the "national territories" of Poland, Finland, Belarus, Latvia, Estonia, Lithuania, Ukraine, Georgia, Bessarabia, Armenia, Azerbaijan and numerous Muslim provinces in Central Asia. By the reign of Nicholas II non-Russians formed more than half the population of the Russian Empire. In response the Russian state imposed a policy of "Russification", the persecution of non-Orthodox religions and the banning of non-Russian native languages from schools, literature, newspapers, street signs and other public displays. Russification invariably provoked movements for political and cultural independence within the territories it dominated. It made little difference if these were "political" or not. Faced with an inflexible Russian state, they all assumed revolutionary characteristics.

Ukraine and Poland were the largest "nations" trapped within the Empire. In 1863 Polish nationalists were provoked to armed revolt after the Tsar's government forcibly conscripted young Polish men into the Russian army. This led to the "January Uprising", a massive revolt across what was known as the Polish-Lithuanian Commonwealth. The rising was led by student radicals, Polish-Lithuanian army officers and elements of the Catholic Church. It took Russian troops sixteen months to crush the rebellion, after which its leaders were executed and 80,000 men and women exiled to Siberia. But the lesson was not forgotten. Poland's next challenge to the Russian Empire would not be led by a ragtag collection of bourgeois nationalists, but by Josef Pilsudski's Polish Socialist Party.

Similarly, the refusal of the Russian state to concede any autonomy to Ukrainian nationalism (it would not even allow public use of the word "Ukraine") stoked rebellion. Kiev became a centre of cultural ferment based on Ukrainian language and literature. The widely read Ukrainian-language newspaper *Fatherland* spread nationalist sentiment throughout Ukrainian society, from peasant villages to the clubs of the capital. Since the Emancipation Edict, Ukrainian landowners (three quarters of whom were "foreign", i.e. Russians or Poles) had enclosed common fields and pastures used by peasants. Ukrainian nationalists in Kiev decried this as an example of Great Russian oppression. Georgia and Azerbaijan added socialism to the brew. In the later 19th century peasant labour flocked to Tiflis and Baku to work in the booming new oil industry, forming a young working class receptive to social-democratic politics.

Some did not think Russia should industrialise at all. The Narodniks and other populists believed that it need not expand into a full-blown urban capitalism or go through what some Narodniks labeled a "very foul purgatory" before reaching socialism, but instead develop its agriculture on the basis of democratically controlled small-scale production.[4] After Emancipation the peasants were in theory assured of their own allotments, but these were in fact held in title by the *Obschina* or *Mir*, the village commune, and they could not do with them as they pleased. If this system prevailed over that of private landlordism, then a very different economic future for Russia—one of "popular production" based on local peasant agriculture and communal control – might beckon.

Vasily Vorontsov's *The Fate of Capitalism in Russia* (1882), "one of the most influential books to appear in Russia in the second half of the 19th century",[5] denied that Russia must automatically follow England's economic path, i.e. the complete disappearance of the peasantry and its absorption into the proletariat. Vorontsov suggested that Russia demonstrated a number of conflicting modes of production, that Russian capitalism was an "imitation" and a "transplantation" of real capitalism. He believed the Mir, although neglected by governments and decomposing as a voluntary alliance, was still "a group of persons forcibly bound together by mutual responsibility"[6] and could still be used by an interventionist government to meet the peasants' aspirations half-way and avoid the tragedy of class war. Even Marx, in a letter of 1881, had said that the rural commune might, in the right conditions, become "the starting point for the regeneration of Russia".[7] In his last published writing, Marx suggested, "If the Russian Revolution becomes the signal for a Proletarian Revolution in the West, so that both complement each other, the present Russian common ownership of land may serve as the starting point for a communist development".[8]

This was wishful thinking. Russia was moving away from communalism. Its industrial expansion was deliberate and state-led, heavily assisted by massive foreign investment. Its by-product was the formation, growth and solidification of a permanent working class in the cities of the Russian Empire. With some exceptions such as printers and metal workers, who could command higher wages for their skills, the conditions in which this primitive proletariat lived were appalling. They were jammed tight into the tenements of St Petersburg, Moscow, Kharkov and Kiev, in which there were hardly any sewage systems, running water or electricity. In 1909, 30,000 of them died in a cholera outbreak in St Petersburg that could have been prevented if the Tsarist government had instituted basic urban hygiene.

Despite its dazzling intelligentsia and world-class novelists (the latter half of the 19th century saw Turgenev, Chekhov, Tolstoy and Dostoyevsky at their zenith), Imperial Russia had a stunted civil society, hardly any democratic institutions, and a trade union movement with no legal means of expression. Consequently, the Marxism that took shape within that society was simplistic and inflexible. In Western Europe, Marxism, although the official creed of the mighty German Social Democratic Party, had begun to reform itself in reaction to social and economic developments, and some of the socialist movement's bolder intellectuals, such as Eduard Bernstein, began to state the obvious.

As the 19th century drew to a close, Bernstein suggested that the European working class could now wrest significant improvements in its social and working life from the capitalist state. He therefore advocated proceeding along these lines rather than preparing for violent revolution. His controversial *Evolutionary Socialism* (1899) not only questioned the realism of a revolutionary strategy by reference to how European socialist parties actually conducted themselves, but also criticised several of Marx's core concepts. He pointed to the complexity of modern techno-industrial society and the great variety of social strata and economic forms found within it. His conclusion – that capitalism might not end in a vast entropic implosion after which socialism would rise from its ashes, but would, like all previous societies, evolve and transform over time – profoundly shocked the faithful.

In later years, the Polish philosopher Leszek Kolakowski, whose three-volume *Main Currents of Marxism* (1976-78) remains the most intellectually rigorous examination of Marxist philosophy and economics, forensically identified logical flaws in Marx's work. Amongst other concepts, he questioned Marx's theory of value, i.e. that it is the amount of "labour-power" put into a product that gives it its value, and therefore any profit from that product above the wages given to the labourer is surplus value taken by the capitalist owner. Kolokowski argued that it is impossible to identify where that value exists and how it could be separated from other elements that go into the final "exchange-value" of a product (such as the pre-existing labour and value inherent in tools and machinery, capital investment to bring labour and tools together, the effect of sales techniques, the fluctuations of supply and demand and other determinants of price). Given this, Marx's theory of value "provides no way of empirically confirming or refuting what it says".[9] This has never bothered most socialists, for whom it is a moral condemnation of wage and wealth inequality rather than an empirical theory in the real sense of the term.

Despites its impact on the European labour movement, Marxist economic theory was seldom examined seriously by mainstream economists. *Capital* volumes I to III, and its theoretical development by Marxist economists from Rudolf Hilferding to Paul M. Sweezy, was sidelined by the academic establishment outside the Soviet Union until the 1970s. A notable exception was the Keynesian economist Joan Robinson's *An Essay on Marxian Economics* (1942). Robinson's work was an early trailblazer of modern perspectives on Marxist economics, which after the crash of 2008 has seen renewed advocacy by the likes of Amartya Sen and Meghnad Desai. Robinson found "many pointers in *Capital* to a theory of effective demand", and lauded Marx for producing a "long-run dynamic analysis" of capitalism. In her view, Marx had useful things to say about the process of capital accumulation and its development into monopoly capital. Less useful were his contradictory analyses of the labour theory of value and the falling rate of profit. Of the former Robinson wrote, "The concept of *value* seems to me to be a remarkable example of how a metaphysical notion can inspire original thought, though in itself it is quite devoid of operational meaning".[10]

These conceptual flaws were not lost on those who broadly agreed with Marx's analysis of capitalism and the class exploitation on which it rested. This led dissident Marxists and other left-libertarians, many of whom saw no need to repeat *pro infinito* every proposition of an economic theorist who died in 1883, to revise, update and refine the doctrine. The work of writers such as Murray Bookchin, Rudolf Bahro, André Gorz, Michael Albert and Michael Lowy is far removed from the hyper-theorised edicts of Marxist Structuralists like Althusser or philosophical Leninists like Žižek and Badiou. Whilst these writers do not form a doctrinal school they do share a refusal to endorse outdated theories simply because they have become sacrosanct. Taken together they offer a lively revision of Marxism that retains its fundamental questioning of capitalism as an economic model.

There was always criticism of Marxism and Leninism from the left—most obviously the anarchist critique from Bakunin to Rocker—but it was only from the 1960s that it began to merge with a broader left-libertarian current. One of the prime movers of this new synthesis was Murray Bookchin, a Trotskyist union organiser in the 1940s who moved away from Marxism to anarchism. Although fully engaged with the US New Left of the 1960s, he was dismayed at the ease with which some of its leaders fell back into Marxism-Leninism, which he felt was a regressive step from the inclusive radicalism of its early days. In 1969 he penned a blistering attack on these tendencies called "Listen, Marxist!", a *cri de coeur* for leftists who saw no future in democratic centralism and the Vanguard Party. It formed part of his *Post-Scarcity Anarchism* (1971), which with *The Ecology of Freedom* (1982) advocated a "Social Ecology" that fused practical anarchism and eco-socialism and was a guiding influence on the new German Green Party.

In "Listen, Marxist!", Bookchin took aim not only at the record of Lenin and the Bolsheviks but at "the historical limits of Marxism". He found that work that was "liberating a century ago" was a straitjacket today. Basing himself on the student protest movement against the Vietnam War, he criticised an exclusive focus on the working class as the sole agent of revolutionary change "at a time when capitalism visibly antagonises and produces revolutionaries among virtually all strata of society, particularly the young". He pointed out that by 1960 capitalism, through nationalisation of public utilities and welfare provision, implemented policies which used to be regarded as socialist – although he did not foresee how these would be reversed by right-wing neoliberal governments in the near future. Whilst he acknowledged that traditional classes had not disappeared, and nor had class struggle, he argued that its terms and geography had changed. It was now "the physiology of the prevailing society, not the labour pains of birth".[11] These were to be found elsewhere, in new forces of resistance and in a rejection of all hierarchies of oppression, including those of the traditional left.

While radical *soixante-huitards* like Bookchin and Daniel Cohn-Bendit disinterred and re-invigorated libertarian socialism, Michael Albert developed a systematic alternative to both market and statist economics. Albert's *What Is To Be Undone* (1974) emerged from the intellectual ferment of 1968 but, unlike leftists who took a detour into Structuralism and Critical Theory, it remained firmly anchored to concrete strategies to transform capitalism. It and his later *Unorthodox Marxism* (1978) attempted, in the words of Stanley Aronowitz, to fulfill "a long-needed critique of contemporary Marxist orthodoxy", specifically that "socialism requires a theory that takes into account not only capitalism's economic dynamics, but its social and cultural aspects as well".

In *Parecomic* (2013), an engaging and accessible graphic novel about Albert's life and thought, the writer Sean Michael Wilson presents the young Albert's view that

Marxism had too much about hours of work and not enough about sex and celebration. Marxism didn't explain the better things in life. Nor did it explain rape, lynching, denigration or sectarianism. People don't solely sleep, eat, and work, as

Marxism seemed to assume. On paper, Marxism was too pat, too confident, and too narrow. In practice, it was too centrist, statist and authoritarian.[12]

Albert advanced a strong critique of the record of Lenin and the Bolsheviks after the October Revolution, reformulating the criticisms of Rosa Luxemberg, Emma Goldman and Maurice Brinton about the denial of democratic rights to socialist and anarchist opponents of the Bolsheviks. He stated bluntly that "no matter what Lenin and Trotsky sometimes said about power in the Soviets, they no longer believed in it as a first principle and they had no intention of ever allowing it to come about". He concluded that the Leninist model "is perhaps not so bad if one wants a transfer of power in an environment of chaos, or if one merely wants to run a bourgeois factory effectively. But for an all-sided revolution or any kind of broadly humanitarian endeavour it is terrible".[13]

While Bookchin, Albert and others such as Chomsky were attempting to lead the American left away from an authoritarian and schematic Marxism, Rudolf Bahro and André Gorz blazed a similar trail in Europe. As a dissident in East Germany Bahro published *The Alternative in Eastern Europe* (1977), which E.P. Thompson called "one of the few necessary, original and truly significant contributions to the political thought of Europe in the post-war years". Although not overtly critical of Lenin, Bahro concluded that in 1917 Russia had not been economically advanced enough to manage the transition to socialism, which was why the attempt had ended in the mass industrialistion of the 1930s. His conclusion that the Soviet Union was still not a socialist society and needed a cultural revolution before it could become one led to an eight-year prison sentence (later commuted to two).

Bahro's real influence lay in his work after he moved to the west, in books such as *Socialism and Survival* (1982) and *From Red to Green* (1984). In these he developed the first "Red-Green" theoretical programme, identifying—decades before Lowy and Klein—the threat the capitalist economic model posed to the eco-sphere, and questioning the role of the trade unions and working class in resisting it. He did not assign to the working class alone the task of transforming capitalism when there were many others, driven by concern for the environment and the wider "species-interest" of humanity, who were prepared to challenge the system and offer viable alternatives beyond simply wage struggle. With some justice he found that "If there is anything today that really does deserve the label of a single-issue movement, it is the institutionalised wage struggle which is ultimately subordinated completely to the overall process of capitalist reproduction".[14]

Bahro acknowledged a great debt to the Austrian (naturalised French) Marxist André Gorz. Gorz's youthful Existentialism made him naturally sympathetic to the resurgence of interest in the 1960s in Marx's early work and the re-discovered *Grundisse*, a neglected Marxist classic which stressed the humanist mission of socialism as the overcoming of alienation and abolition of wage labour. From the late 1960s Gorz explicitly identified himself as a "revolutionary-reformist" with a particular interest in political ecology. His focus on "post-industrial capitalism" and how to achieve it separated him from a French left still sunk in freeze-dried Marxist orthodoxy.

Gorz's books *Farewell to the Working Class* (1982), *Paths to Paradise* (1985) and *Critique of Economic Reason* (1989) questioned, like Bookchin, if the working class was any longer an agent of revolutionary change. He suggested the necessary transformation of capitalism "can only come from areas of society which embody or prefigure the dissolution of all social classes, including the working class itself".[15] To that end he sought to build a radical ecological alternative to capitalist productivism, based on the liberatory use of technology and a Guaranteed Basic Income. Gorz was accused by stern ideological commissars of apostasy, yet his ecologism remained fundamentally anti-capitalist, rooted in the young Marx and the *Grundisse*.

The work begun by Bookchin and Gorz has been extended by Marxist eco-socialists such as Michael Lowy, Joel Kovel and John Bellamy Foster. Four decades before Naomi Klein's *This Changes Everything* (2014) explicitly situated climate change and environmental degradation as the primary arena in which the self-destructive contradictions of capitalism could be challenged and overcome by public ownership of natural resources, Bookchin's *Our Synthetic Environment* (1962) had done the same, and proposed similar solutions. Bellamy Foster expresses Bookchin's argument in a Marxist idiom. He highlights a "metabolic rift" between humanity and nature, based on Marx's observation in *Capital, Volume III* that the unregulated development of capitalism will inevitably produce an "irreparable rift in the interdependent process of social metabolism".[16]

This often-overlooked strand of Marx's work was a continuation of his early thinking in the *Philosophical and Economic Manuscripts of 1844*, which was concerned with the perversion of the "species-being" of mankind by the development of capitalist relations of production, as well as its ruinous effect on the environment in which the species lived. Marx himself said of the planetary eco-sphere that society must "hand it down to succeeding generations in an improved condition". It was an insight that fused romantic anti-industrialism with a cold economic analysis of capital. It is the basis of Lowy and Kovel's vision of a socialism which consciously distances itself from the productivist varieties of the 20th century that led, in one iteration, to the Soviet Union's satellite states Czechoslovakia and East Germany holding the record for emission of greenhouse gasses per inhabitant. It was this vision that inspired the Belem Declaration, an Eco-Socialist Manifesto discussed and signed by thousands of anti-capitalist activists and writers at the World Social Forum in Belem, Brazil, in 2009.

As humanity races towards the second quarter of the 21st century it is now clear that to have any chance of not *exceeding* a 2°C increase in global temperature – an increase in itself now virtually inevitable, and which will produce severe environmental and social crises especially in sub-Saharan Africa and coastal areas – two-thirds of fossil fuel reserves will have to remain in the ground. At the same time, we must move rapidly to a post-carbon energy infrastructure with radically new forms of transport. Fracking, supported by some trade unions because it creates jobs, is an enormous backward step. If unions are to play any role in shaping and saving the future, they must urgently promote re-skilling and publically-funded jobs in renewable energy rather than act as compliant footmen to capital's exploitation of natural resources and human labour. As John McDonnell put it in *Another World is Possible: A Manifesto for 21st Century Socialism* (2007), "We cannot tackle climate change unless we address the system that has caused it".

The redefinitions of Marxism suggested by Bookchin, Albert, Bahro and Gorz, and latterly by Lowy, Kovel and other eco-socialists, emerged from the failure of Leninism to produce a democratic socialism or to transcend capitalism's productivist economic model. In the late 19th century Bernstein, without fully understanding what he was doing, laid the groundwork for such a revisionist critique. To the fury of dogmatic Marxists he attacked the theory at its point of pride – that it was a science akin to Darwinism, a unique paradigm shift amounting to a separate academic discipline. Bernstein denied this was so and claimed that a rigorous reformist socialism – i.e. a programme based on realistic plans for economic regulation – was in fact more scientific than the abstractions of Marxist political economy.

The utility and necessity of reformist socialism arose from the industrialised and urbanised capitalism of Europe and America at the beginning of the 20th century. But Imperial Russia was several decades behind this process and openings for political reform did not exist. Resistance to the gross inhumanity of early capitalism in Russia was a mixture of ferocious trade union organising and the occasional riot in the face of brutal state repression. The Russian labour and trade union movement may have been in its infancy, but it was already following Marx's prescriptions for resistance to working inhumanely long hours in unhealthy and unsafe conditions.

In *Capital, Volume I,* Marx pointed out that although there may seem to be a voluntary exchange of contracts between worker and owners in a free market, the imbalance of power was such that workers were inevitably exploited. The first step to resistance therefore had to be securing strong employment regulation and restrictions on working time. As Marx wrote in the "Working Day" chapter:

> The labourers must put their heads together and, as a class, compel the passing of a law, an all-powerful social barrier that shall prevent the very workers from selling, by voluntary contract with capital, themselves and their families into slavery and death. In place of the pompous catalogue of the 'inalienable rights of man' comes the modest Magna Carta of a legally limited working day, which shall make clear when the time which the worker sells is ended, and when his own begins.[17]

One of the most significant examples of this kind of trade union organising arose from the General Union of Jewish Workers, known as the Bund.

In the mid-19th century most of the four million Jews within the Russian Empire's borders were confined to the Pale of Settlement, which stretched from Poland and Lithuania to Ukraine and the Black Sea. In the 1860s and 1870s, Alexander II began to reform the Empire's oppressive anti-Semitic laws by allowing certain categories of Jews (merchants, doctors, craftsmen and ex-soldiers) to move beyond the Pale. Jews were allowed to enter the civil service and attend universities, and Jewish communities began to appear in St Petersburg and Moscow. But the accession of Alexander III saw a reappearance of mass pogroms, a ban on Jews working for the government and a restriction of the number of Jewish students.

The most significant change was a ban on Jews working the land. This inevitably pushed them into the cities of the Pale and created a large Jewish working class. By 1897 there were an estimated 105,000 Jewish urban workers in the Russian Empire, mainly in the big cities of Warsaw, Vilno, Lodz, Minsk, Grodno and Białystok. Between 1897 and 1910, the total Jewish urban population leapt to over three million. The result was the creation of the Bund, a trade union and political party which was an "organic emergence out of existing working class networks"[18] in those cities.

The Bund had its own democratic structures, a popular newspaper and paid full-time organisers. It was one of the founding bodies of the Russian Social Democratic and Labour Party (RSDLP) in 1903. It also rejected Zionism, which it called "emigrationism", and the idea that there was a World Jewry with common problems. At the same time, it insisted that the issues faced by the Jewish proletariat within the Empire must be addressed primarily by Jewish organisations. There was an obvious contradiction here. On the one hand the Bund dismissed the idea that it had a common interest with, say, rich French Jews, but it considered all Russian Jews a nationality and it wanted a Russian Revolution to deliver autonomy for all the Empire's oppressed nationalities, including its own. Yet for a time it led the way in providing a model of grassroots industrial organising for *all* the Russian working class.[19]

In late-19th-century Russia this kind of activism arose from the work of Jewish trade unionists in Vilno that became known as the Vilno Programme. At the end of the 19th century Jews comprised nearly 60% of the urban population of Poland, Lithuania, Latvia and Belarus. In 1891 Alexander III expelled all Jews from St Petersburg and Moscow, leading to an upsurge of radical political organisation in cities such as Vilno, Warsaw and Riga. In 1892 the disparate socialist groups in Poland came together to form the Polish Socialist Party. This would attract far more support from Polish workers (both Jewish and Catholic) than would the Marxist Social Democracy of Poland and Lithuania group, formed in 1893 on Rosa Luxemburg's initiative, which denied the necessity of a separate struggle for Polish independence.

The Bund adopted a socialist political programme which sought to improve the lot of Jewish workers inside the Empire. It campaigned for the recognition of Yiddish, full legal and cultural rights for Jewish citizens, and political liberalisation. The Vilno Programme, which pre-dated the creation of the Bund, derived from the efforts of Jewish social democrats such as Alexander Kremer to break out of propagandising for Marxism with small groups of "advanced workers" and to bring their ideas to the mass of common workers. To do this they decided to drop abstruse discussion of Marxist philosophy and concentrate on agitating for legal reforms and employment rights.

One of the key figures behind the Vilno Programme

was the 22 year-old Marxist revolutionary Julius Martov. Although the basic ideas were those of the older *Praktiki* (practical men) Kremer and Gozhansky, Martov wrote them up in a pamphlet called *On Agitation*. The pamphlet quickly "acquired the status of a handbook of social-democratic action".[20] For the first time it placed the politically conscious worker at the *centre* of events, rather than as the recipient of academic wisdom handed down to him by bourgeois intellectuals. Its goal was to link political analysis to the everyday needs of the urban worker, and by doing so "destroy his faith in a paternalist employer and his subservience to a paternalist state, and to turn him into a conscious and organised enemy of both".[21] To achieve this, revolutionaries should immerse themselves in the life of the worker in factory, dock or train yard, and be acutely aware of specific industrial struggles around pay and conditions.

In taking concrete steps to implement such a programme, Martov was far ahead of the other Marxists in St Petersburg and Moscow still sunk in the academic grind of the "study circles". In the aftermath of the 1891 famine even Plehkanov had argued for a shift of political work to agitation. In *On the Tasks of Socialists During the Famine in Russia* he wrote that Marxists must take up demands of more immediate relevance to the working classes, and "all — even the most backward workers — will be clearly convinced that the carrying out of socialist measures is of value to the working class".[22] At the time the Marxists of St Petersburg ignored his call. It was in the heavily Jewish parts of the Russian Empire such as Poland and Lithuania that it found a receptive audience, where working-class trade union organisation was far in advance of St Petersburg. Even in 1907, two years after the revolution of 1905, only 7% of St Petersburg's workers were organised in trade unions, whereas in Vilno it was 24%, in Minsk between 25-40%, and in Gomel over 40%.[23]

In 1893 Martov moved to St Petersburg, where he met other young Marxists, amongst whom was a brilliant lawyer from Samara named Vladimir Ilyich Ulyanov. Under the influence of the Vilno Programme this small group formed the Combat Union for the Emancipation of the Working Class, formerly an adherent of the Emancipation of Labour Group. Ulyanov begun to emulate Martov and was soon writing strike leaflets and providing legal advice to workers and their families.

From 1893 to 1896 the Combat Union established trust and a certain level of leadership with workers in some of the huge factory complexes in the city, such as the Thornton wool factory and Putilov engineering works, and were one of the contributory factors to the strikes that convulsed the city at that time.[24] In May 1896 a strike of spinners and weavers in the city, prompted by the refusal of factory owners to pay workers for the days lost to mark the new Tsar's Coronation, drew in 35,000 workers. It spread to encompass the entire city and led to the government's reluctant concession of a maximum 11.5-hour day.

Retribution was swift. The Okhrana (the secret police) arrested the leaders of the Combat Union, who were sentenced to internal exile. The well-connected and moderately wealthy Ulyanov used his family name to ensure he was exiled to the "Italian Siberia" of Minusinsk, where he was a local celebrity and was kept well-informed of political developments. Using the library and resources of the town doctor he wrote his first substantial Marxist work, *The Development of Capitalism in Russia* (1899), in which he utterly rejected Voronstov's thesis that Russia could avoid capitalism and argued that the Russian economy, rural as well as urban, was already well embarked on a process of capitalist accumulation. Martov, meanwhile, was singled out for harsher treatment and spent his three years at Turukhansk in the sub-Arctic Circle. Both men learnt the hard way that no serious revolutionary movement could be conducted by leaders who could be arrested at any moment. Upon their release in 1900, Martov and Ulyanov left Russia to join the leaders of the Emancipation of Labour Group in Geneva.

Although there were differences of personality between the older leaders Plekhanov, Vera Zazulich and Pavel Axelrod, and the younger activists Martov, Ulyanov and Alexander Potresov, they agreed that the essential first step was the creation and regular dissemination of a party newspaper. In 1900-01, with help from activists and correspondents inside Russia, they set up this newspaper, with the intention that it would help bring all Russian Marxists together into one united Social Democratic Party. They called it *Iskra*—Russian for "Spark". On 24th December, 1901 the first issue was printed in Munich. In January 1902, after much hard work and clandestine organising, *Iskra* arrived in Russia and was widely distributed in the larger cities and towns. The Spark was ignited.

CHAPTER TWO
Mensheviks and Bolsheviks

By 1901, much of the Marxist programme as explained by Marx, Engels and Plekhanov was looking outdated. In Western Europe class struggle had assumed different forms, and in Russia more relevant alternatives were about to arise. The 1890s saw the formation of various revolutionary Marxist groups in Russia, primarily but not exclusively in St Petersburg. These were the froth on a churning sea of labour struggle, particularly the great strike wave of 1896-97, which found its theoretical expression in what came to be known as "Economism". This advocated the solution of working-class oppression through reforms dragged out of the state by political and industrial campaigning instead of as an offshoot of revolutionary activity. It was not, initially, non- or anti-Marxist in the manner of, for example, the British labour movement. On the contrary, it flowed from the work of Marxist theorists such as Nikolai Berdyaev, Mikhail Turgan-Baranovsky and, most significantly, Peter Struve, who had drafted the initial programme of the Russian Social Democrats in 1898.

These were termed "Legal Marxists" because they lived legally, i.e. not under aliases and not as part of an underground network. They were primarily economists who had reached similar conclusions as Bernstein about Marx's analysis of capitalism. Struve, whom Lenin held in high regard because he praised and prioritised capitalist industrial development over the "popular production" theories of Vorontsov, later became an intellectual ringmaster for Russian liberalism. Had Russian society democratised in the manner of British, French and German society in the 19th and early-20th century, these trends would undoubtedly have led to the growth of a major trade union movement and Labour Party. Instead, 1901 saw the creation of a radical political party as significant as the RSDLP, which for the first twenty years of the 20th century spoke for the majority of Russia's population in a way that the Bolsheviks did not.

The Socialist Revolutionary Party (known as the Socialist Revolutionaries, or SRs) was formed from a number of neo-populist agrarian socialist bodies, the most important of which was the Northern Union of Socialist Revolutionaries. Inheritors of the Narodnik mantle, they adapted the Narodnik programme to make it attractive not just to the peasantry but to the semi-urbanised, seasonal proletariat. The SRs began to coalesce in the 1890s after exiled Narodniks such as Catherine Breshkovsky, Mark Natanson and Gregory Greshuni returned to European Russia. The party's primary theorist and leader, Victor Chernov, is the great "lost leader" and neglected historical actor of the Russian Revolution.

In the 1890s, Chernov attempted to organise the peasants

of the Samara province, for which he was imprisoned in the infamous St Peter and Paul Fortress. A Marxist theorist in his own right, he developed SR policy around Marx's suggestion that the Russian village commune might contain the seeds of a specifically Russian socialism that could avoid the ugliness and alienation of industrial capitalism. In the SRs he forged a mass party advocating progressive taxation, land re-distribution and agrarian socialism. In all contested elections held between 1906 (the first *Duma*) and 1918 (the first and last All-Russia Constituent Assembly, of which he was President), the SRs received the majority of votes of Russian workers and peasants. From 1901 to 1918 they indisputably held the most legitimate mandate to speak for the Russian masses.

The SRs offered an attractive package of radical reforms to a wide base of peasant and worker supporters. Francis King's history of the SRs during 1917 considered that in the light of today's indigenous peoples' movements the agrarian policies of the SRs "deserve more serious attention on the left".[1] From their earliest days, the SR's believed "the coming revolution would be national in character, expressing the aspirations of workers, peasants and intellectuals".[2] Their call for immediate socialisation of the land without compensation and its redistribution to peasant small holders was immensely popular. The SRs based themselves on educational activity and support to the peasantry such as Sunday Schools for adult literacy and Committees for the Elimination of Illiteracy (these efforts were frowned upon by the Ministry of the Interior, who saw no benefit in a literate peasantry).[3] This activity "played a considerable part in achieving the rapprochement between the peasantry and the intelligentsia which was a prerequisite for successful revolutionary work in the countryside".[4]

The particular type of "intelligentsia" attracted to the SRs were not the highly educated lawyers and philosophers of the RSDLP. They tended to be village schoolteachers, medical assistants and nurses, and were often the sons and daughters of peasants themselves. This gave them a deeper insight in to the lives and concerns of the peasants than the urban-based Marxists. Because of this organic connection to their members the SRs supported the local consumer and producer cooperatives promoted by peasant radicals such as Sergei Semenov, who wished to escape the often-chaotic allocation of narrow strips of land by the Mir for a more rational system of land management.[5] At the same time the SRs' violent retaliatory actions against repressive police and Land Captains secured the emotional sympathies of peasants looking for swift class justice. Not surprisingly the SRs were subject to fierce attacks by the Social Democrats. Struggling to forge a united Marxist party, the last thing the Social Democrats needed was a populist socialist alternative that tapped into the gut instincts of the mass of worker-peasants.

The SRs practiced a populist rural socialism not dissimilar to that offered by the Mexican Zaptatista movement in response to the North Atlantic Free Trade Agreement (NAFTA) in the 1990s. The preconditions for Mexico entering NAFTA was the revoking of Article 27 of the Mexican Constitution which forbad selling communal land – the *Ejidos*, half of all Mexican land – held and used by indigenous people. NAFTA forbad any obstacle to "free" investment in the US, Canada and Mexico, and thus granted an unrestricted right to large American corporations to buy privatised state assets. It turned legal tenants into illegal land-squatters and made their communities informal settlements. On the day NAFTA became law, 1st January, 1994, the Zapatista National Liberation Army (EZLN), a collection of agrarian radicals and indigenous rights activists, took over land and vacant estates in the Chiapas region and announced they would march on Mexico City.

The EZLN emerged from self-defence brigades set up to protect peasants from the terrorism of Chiapas' coffee barons and cattle ranchers. Their statement of intent proclaimed:

> We are a product of 500 years of struggle: first against slavery, then during the War of Independence against Spain [...] then to avoid being absorbed by North American imperialism, then to promulgate our constitution and expel the French empire from our soil [...] Later the dictatorship of Porfirio Diaz denied us the just application of the Reform laws, and the people rebelled and leaders like Villa and Zapata emerged, poor men just like us.

In reality they did not attempt to overthrow the government but settled on occupation of their land. When the government of President Salinas threatened to eject them, the central square of Mexico City was flooded with Zapatista supporters, and Chief Advisor of Chase Manhattan Bank's Emerging Markets Group Riordan Rhett sent an instruction to President Salinas: "The government will need to eliminate the Zapatistas to demonstrate its effective control of the national territory and of security policy".[6]

Commentators on right and left expected the Zapatistas

to attempt to overthrow the government, but they refused to indulge what would have been a suicidal power play. Instead the Zapatista's iconic spokesperson "Subcommandante Marcos"—whose identity to this day is in dispute, and may even have been what the Zapatistas called a "hologram", a PR construct—declared at the National Democratic Convention in the Lacandon jungle in August 1994, that the Zapatistas rejected "the doubtful honour of being the vanguard of the multiple vanguards that plague us". He explained that unlike Leninist elites who imposed political programmes on workers and peasants, "The moment has come to say to everyone that we neither want, nor are able, to occupy the place that some hope we will occupy, the place from which all opinions will come, all the answers, all the truth. We are not going to do that".[7]

Following US orders the Mexican government attempted to crush the EZLN militarily—once in January 1994 and again in February 1995. Both times the government had to back off in the face of massive protests in Mexico City and around the world. In 1996, the government was forced to meet with EZLN leaders and negotiate the San Andrés Accords, which established local autonomy for indigenous peoples in Mexico, as well as new educational, social and cultural rights. They required changes to the law and the Mexican constitution, and committed the Mexican government to eliminating "the poverty, the marginalisation and insufficient political participation of millions of indigenous Mexicans". The commitments have not been fully honoured, but the Zapatistas continue to fight for the rights of the indigenous rural population against the legalised predation of US corporations and agri-business.

The challenge to Tsarism offered by the SRs might have developed along similar lines had they not had to contend with a fiercely urban-centred social-democratic alternative. While the SRs were gaining support amongst the peasantry, the Social Democrats were using *Iskra* as "a weapon to build a centralised all-Russian organisation".[8] Central to this work was *Iskra*'s primary strategist and organiser, Vladimir Ulyanov, now beginning to use the alias by which he would become famous – V.I. Lenin. Only Plekhanov was regarded as more senior and his eminence derived solely from his philosophical and theoretical writing.

Personally, Plekhanov was vain, prickly and difficult, and he did not contribute to the administrative grind behind the production and distribution of *Iskra*. This was left to the younger generation of Lenin, Martov and Potresov. Plekhanov regarded Lenin as a forceful polemicist, although crude and simplistic. But as one of Lenin's more critical biographers conceded, "Lenin wrote only to influence the actions of men. If his writing was often repetitious and over-simplified, he nevertheless hammered out what he wanted to say very effectively. And if his words did not always appeal to refined intellects, they carried wider appeal for the larger mass at which they were aimed".[9] Unlike Plekhanov, Lenin rarely adopted a revolutionary pose or militant attitude he did not genuinely believe. When Peter Struve moved across to liberalism in the early years of the 20th century, Lenin labeled him a renegade and a traitor in *Iskra*. He was criticised for this by a fellow Marxist who feared that Lenin's words might inflame someone to assassinate Struve. "He deserves to die", replied Lenin.

It is impossible to imagine his friend and collaborator Julius Martov saying such a thing. Although both men had worked closely together since their time in the St Petersburg Combat Union in the 1890s, they were temperamentally very different. Where Lenin was "hard", disciplined and implacable, a man who in the opinion of his own wife was "quite unable to write about the ordinary side of life", Martov was his polar opposite—a disheveled, warm-hearted idealist, widely liked and respected for his innate decency and honour. Like Lenin he was a convinced Marxist, but he was far more "classical" and European in his interpretation of the doctrine.

Martov had lived with and learnt from specific industrial struggles in Vilno. Lenin, although in 1895 under the influence of Martov and *On Agitation* he had begun to concern himself with the conditions in St Petersburg factories and to write leaflets and guidance to workers about them, emerged from a much more scholastic Marxist background and was never to lose its taint. His tendency to issue instructions to the masses was revealed with compelling clarity in his most important and influential work *What Is To Be Done?*, published in 1902 and named after Cherneshevky's novel of 1863.

What Is To Be Done? made up in blunt-force impact what it lacked in literary panache. In an iconic passage Lenin asserted:

> The history of all countries shows that the Working Class, exclusively of its own efforts, is able to develop only trade union consciousness, i.e. the conviction that it is necessary to combine in unions, fight the employers, and strive to compel the

government to pass necessary labour legislation, etc. The theory of socialism, however, grew out of the philosophical, historical and economic theories elaborated by educated representatives of the propertied classes, by intellectuals.[10]

Lenin was clear that socialism must be brought to the masses by the intelligentsia. He was adamant that "...the development of an independent ideology amongst the workers, as a result of their own struggle, is out of the question" and therefore "Class political consciousness can be brought to the workers only *from without*" (his emphasis). On their own workers could, at best, formulate trade unionism, "and trade unionism signifies the mental enslavement of the workers to the bourgeoisie".[11]

Lenin was not alone amongst *Iskra's* editors in wanting a united Russian Marxist party with a consistent message and a centralised leadership to direct the strands of activity within the Empire. With the ever-present threat of the Okhrana, it made sense that the party's Central Organ be small and based abroad. But Lenin pushed further into centralisation with his proposal that the Local Committees of the party should be composed exclusively of "fully convinced Social Democrats who should devote themselves entirely to Social Democratic activities". There should be no part-time members or those who worked for a living elsewhere. These stable mini-centres should direct all other subordinate bodies (factory branches, discussion circles, literary circles) and their decisions should be binding on those bodies. No one but the full-time professional revolutionaries would set policy.

This was the *Ur-text* of the Vanguard Party—a concept which Eric Hobsbawm rightly called "Lenin's formidable contribution to Twentieth century politics".[12] He meant it positively, but the concept of the Vanguard Party was one of the most disastrous things ever to befall the socialist ideal, one reason it was opposed from the start by most Russian socialists. They saw immediately that Lenin's plan was a radical departure from the large and growing socialist parties of Europe, most of which were formed between 1885 and 1905, and which for all their flaws were organically rooted in the working class and the trade unions.

Reflecting Germany's position as the new industrial powerhouse of Europe, the largest and most significant was the German Social Democratic Party (SPD). By 1914 it had over one million members and an entire support structure for them — libraries, choirs, youth clubs, crèches, health benefits, financial loans, occupational training, etc. Even Finland's Socialist Party, formed in 1899, followed the model of the German SPD, despite Finland being a territory of Imperial Russia. The Belgian Labour Party, formed in 1885, called the first general strike in European history in 1893 to demand universal male suffrage. Its victory meant that by 1911 it had grown to 276,000 members and was a major force in Belgian politics. By 1904 the Italian Socialist Party, created in 1892, had secured a fifth of the national vote. Even the United States had a mass socialist party with roots in the trade unions and a popular leader, Eugene V. Debs. In Australia a reformist labour (but not socialist) party formed the federal government in 1912.

The picture was not uniform. Although the German SPD was relatively united, Italian and French socialists were torn between syndicalism and parliamentarianism. The leadership of the French Socialist Party was contested by the passionate syndicalist Jules Guesde and the radical parliamentarian Jean Jaures. The British Labour Party, founded in 1906 and not to adopt any kind of socialist creed until 1918, emerged over decades out of the cooperative movement, Chartism and single-issue campaigns like the Land and Labour League. These coalesced eventually into the Independent Labour Party, founded in 1893 and led by Kier Hardie, and finally into the Labour Representation Committee/Labour Party. The drawn-out formation of the Labour Party, and its ambiguous and contested relationship to socialism ever since, has been a true reflection of its working-class base — class conscious but non-ideological, politically collectivist but personally individualistic, periodically militant but culturally conservative.

Russia was very different. With secretive, conspiratorial methods justified by the conditions of Tsarist autocracy, Lenin ploughed on. His strongest asset was the time he devoted to the concerns of *Iskra's Praktiki* back in Russia. This gave him a loyal following within the activist base and deflected the concerns of those who felt he was becoming too dictatorial. For these reasons Martov and other leaders of the nascent RSDLP did not openly attack *What Is To Be Done?*. Despite the fact that its language was brutal, it described and recommended what most RSDLP activists were already doing. Martov and others did not realise that whilst they saw the paper as "a bearer of propaganda and agitation and to a lesser extent as a mutual information bulletin for Social Democrats",[13] for Lenin it was something else. For him the paper was useful not only to propagandise for his conception of a highly centralised party run by professional revolutionaries, but also as the means to create that party.

In 1903, revolutionaries and socialists of all kinds were dependent on the newspaper, the agitational leaflet and the political meeting to reach, inform and mobilise potential supporters. Today these methods of communication and organsation are almost irrelevant, replaced by the Networked Individual and Networked Social Movements, which through creative use of social media have fundamentally changed the rules of political engagement. All mainstream political parties now utilise social media (websites, Twitter feeds, etc.), but these are still messages from on high. At the grassroots are independent activists who use digital and social networks – Facebook, Twitter, Tumblr, YouTube, Indymedia – to create and sustain independent, ad hoc anti-capitalist campaigns and actions.

Far removed from printed pamphlets smuggled past border guards and passed hand to hand, these new networks are, in the description of the sociologist Manuel Castells, "the fastest, most autonomous, interactive, reprogrammable and self-expanding means of communication in history".[14] They create and foster civic cultures of democratic dissent and debate. They were central to the revolutionary self-activity that led to the Arab Spring of 2010–12 and other mass anti-capitalist actions such as the *Indignados* campaigns in Spain and Greece, and the occupations of public spaces such as St Paul's in London and Zuccotti Park in New York by the Occupy movement.[15]

Governments and security agencies are keenly aware of the power of social media and the Internet. As Edward Snowden's revelations about the US National Security Agency (NSA)'s monitoring of private citizens' online activity demonstrated, they devote enormous resources to tracking and controlling these networks. They also seek to control and limit file sharing and Open Source technology. Yet the genie is out of the bottle. During the first days of the Egyptian revolution of 2011 and the occupation of Tahrir Square—events which were propelled by anti-Mubarek activists posting provocative videos on YouTube and then going viral on Twitter—the Egyptian government attempted to "switch off" Internet access and mobile phone networks within the country. On 27th January, 2011 it blocked text and Blackberry messaging. The next day it ordered Egypt's biggest Internet Service Providers (ISPs) to turn off their connections. The ISPs then used ISP routers to access and delete most of the IP addresses connected through that provider. Ninety-three percent of Egypt's internet traffic was disabled.

In response a global community of hackers, cyber-anarchists, Open Source activists and libertarians rallied to reconnect Egypt to the World Wide Web. Instructions to circumvent the blockages, to use dial-up by mobiles or laptops, were sent via fax and ham radio. These were blogged, re-blogged and tweeted. ISPs outside the country set up new channels to connect to Egypt. Google and Twitter set up a new system that converted voicemail messages into tweets. With Twitter accounts in Egypt blocked, Twitter created a new account called @twitter-globalpr which handled this traffic. Al Jazeera fed satellite news to telephones on the ground, which brought more protestors on to the streets. Within five days the attempted disconnection was circumvented and the Egyptian government, which had lost $90 million due to loss of telecommunications and Internet business, restored the ISPs.

The government had been defeated by a mass counter-power to the traditional military/state/media machine on which ruling elites have long relied. This counter-power is based on autonomous social networks difficult to isolate and shut down (although individual activists and groups can of course be suppressed) and it is used by activists who share its anti-authoritarian ethos. It is not sufficient on its own. The occupation of Tahrir Square by students and other militants was the beginning, not the end, of the Egyptian revolution. In February workers formed new trade unions separate from Mubarek's corrupt state-run unions and threatened strike action against the regime, followed by Women's Rights groups who marched in Cairo demanding an end to discrimination and violence against women. All these formed a critical mass of opposition that led the military to turn against Mubarek. Without the workers' and women's protests it is doubtful if the student revolt on its own would have succeeded. But it was that revolt—and its planning and dissemination on Facebook, Twitter and YouTube—that laid the groundwork.

The development of networks of free information and collaborative working has enormous political implications, even though social-media networks are heavily constrained by corporate ownership and the cultural logic of late capitalism. Networked individuals are still individuals. They have to *want* to access networks and find politically useful and incendiary information. Stoking that desire is the job of socialist parties, trade unions and other campaigning groups. The liberatory potential of social media is only tapped when it is politicised and weaponised in mass campaigns with clear goals and strategies. Ultimately, as the radical cultural theorist Jeremy Gilbert has suggested, huge global tech monopolies like Apple and Microsoft should be brought under democratic public ownership and run as mutuals or cooperatives by workers and users, empowered and regulated to provide a truly free and open social network.[16]

Even without public ownership, Castells makes the essential point that "Mass self-communication is based on horizontal networks of inter-active communication that, by and large, are difficult to control by government or corporations".[17] *Iskra*, by contrast, was far easier to control. Krupskaya later admitted that Lenin did not show Martov and the other editors all the correspondence he sent out and received. They did not sense that *What Is To Be Done?* was not simply an attack on wavering Economists, whose reformism Martov also rejected, but that it heralded an entirely new approach to revolutionary organisation and strategy. Between 1900 and 1903 these differences were obscured in Lenin's and Martov's mutual struggle to outmaneuver Plekhanov and to produce *Iskra* on a regular basis. But the elements of a major confrontation between them were stirring.

Lih and other defenders of Lenin maintain that "latter-day readers of *What Is To Be Done?* have removed Lenin's book from its context and thereby fundamentally distorted its spirit and impact".[18] But many of Lenin's contemporaries who were acutely aware of its context made their criticisms of it *at the time*—and because of these criticisms Lenin's formulation of party membership, based on *What Is To Be Done?*, was rejected by a majority at the Second Congress of the RSDLP. This congress, held mainly in London in August 1903, has become the stuff of legend.[19] The Second Congress of the RSDLP was in all but name the First Congress, its founding moment and crucible (the actual First Congress had been in Minsk in 1898, attended by nine self-mandated delegates and swiftly dispersed by the police). It was the culmination of years of work by Social Democrat leaders and activists, and was meant to form one united all-Russian Marxist revolutionary party around an agreed constitution and programme.

The Organisation Committee, which *Iskra* dominated, planned the conference, authorised numbers of delegates and sent out credentials. As a result, the Economists had only three delegates, the Jewish Bund (although much larger than *Iskra*) only five, with six unaligned. The remaining thirty-three delegates were all from *Iskra*. *Iskra*'s careful preparation was not entirely a response to reformism within the Russian left. The Bund was as committed to a socialist transformation of Russian society as the Social Democrats. It also wished to create an RSDLP. Its leader, the Marxist revolutionary Mark Liber, was the third most frequent speaker at the congress after Lenin and Trotsky, passionately making the case for the Bund to have the sole right to represent the Jewish proletariat within the Russian Empire (as part of a wider alliance within the RSDLP). This position was rejected by both Martov and Lenin.

The violent schism that would develop between Lenin and Martov arose from their definition of "party member". In reaction to *What Is To Be Done?*, Martov formulated a detailed constitution for a future RSDLP, which indicates that he had had serious concerns about Lenin's centralism before the Second Congress. His draft constitution followed an article he wrote in April 1903 for Rosa Luxemburg's *Social Democratic Review* in which he sketched the concept of a flexible, less centralised party. In the article Martov posed the key question before Russian Marxists as "how to reconcile the urgent need for conspiracy with the yearning for the creation of a broadly-based social-democratic party of the working masses".[20] He suggested that as long as the party was united by revolutionary theory it should encourage initiative and relative autonomy amongst its constituent elements.

Martov's draft attempted to do several things. It widened the membership criteria; the rights and independence of local committees and organising bodies was explained in detail, with the power of the central control organs to co-opt and to close down local bodies restricted; and rights were given to national and regional bodies to allow for the integration into the party of semi-autonomous bodies such as the Polish social-democrats and the Bund. The relative independence of the two main bodies of the party – the Central Organ (the ideological centre, located abroad) and the Central Committee (the organisational centre, located inside Russia) – was established, to allow freedom of thought and policy formulation. That Martov, never the fanatical organiser that Lenin was, took the trouble to map this out reveals his unspoken concerns for the Congress. His draft "was meant to cater for the widening and growing of the party; it would enhance local initiative of the committees and thus make for a certain weakening of centralisation".[21]

Lenin produced a shorter counter-draft and mocked the

length and verbosity of Martov's. But Martov's was necessarily longer as it sought to protect the rights of members and local committees against central *diktat*, and provide an appeals process. Lenin's was shorter because central *diktat* trumped all else. At the time, Martov was not inclined to formally challenge Lenin. Although irritated by the "hypertrophy of centralism" of Lenin's plans, his primary focus for the Congress was the same as Lenin's—to ensure that a united party emerged on the basis of *Iskra*'s programme. Other differences seemed secondary. Martov, acknowledging Lenin's eminence in organisational matters, withdrew his draft and allowed Lenin's to go before the Congress. He merely told Lenin that he would probably query some of the membership criteria.

Although there were disagreements with the Economists and the Bund, the *Iskra* delegates had a clear majority and carried the day on the party programme. Having agreed this, the Congress moved to the precise formulation of a member. Lenin proposed a definition, which was "Anyone who accepts the party's programme and supports it by personal participation in one of the party's organizations is to be considered a member of the Russian Social Democratic Workers' Party". Martov proposed a slightly different wording, which was "Anyone who accepts the party's programme, supports the party by material means, and renders it regular personal assistance under the guidance of one of its organisations is to be considered a member of the Russian Social Democratic Workers' Party". On the face of it there was hardly any difference, and members not privy to the prior disagreements between Lenin and Martov were astonished that the Congress divided so sharply on the issue.

If the issue was the two formulations alone, it would have been absurd. But it was not. As Martov told the conference, revealing publicly the differences between them:

> I agree with Lenin that in addition to organisations of professional revolutionaries we need 'loose organisations' of various types. But our formula is the only one to reflect our aim to have the organisation of professional revolutionaries linked with the masses by a series of other organisations. In our view, the workers' party does not consist solely of the organisation of professional revolutionaries, but of the latter plus all the leading active elements of the proletariat.[22]

Lenin responded that under Martov's definition "absolutely anyone could be a member". Martov replied, "Yes, if you like".

After a heated debate a vote was taken. Lenin's formulation was rejected by 28 votes to 23. On the crucial question of party membership, Martov had won. This was a bitter blow to Lenin. Having lost this important battle Lenin knew it was essential that he retain control of *Iskra*'s editorial board, and he threw everything into doing so. It was in *this* battle, and the tactics Lenin employed to get his own way, that the newly formed party cracked wide open.

Having lost on the membership, Lenin demanded that his personal supporters form a majority on the Central Committee. Martov refused, and in response Lenin used his agents to spread rumours about Martov's personal and political weaknesses. Only a few days old, the party was already dividing into "hards" and "softs", with men like Bauman, Krasikov and Shotman (who threatened to beat up a delegate who switched from Lenin to Martov) reveling in macho postures of revolutionary extremism.[23] Because of the animosity now infecting the Congress, some of the delegates, principally the Economists and the Bundists, departed. The Bundists under Liber also had major disagreements with the *Iskra* faction's attempt to annex the Jewish proletariat to the RSDLP. Aside from this issue, they had generally supported Martov.

With the Bundists gone Lenin now secured a majority to reduce the *Iskra* editorial board from six to three (removing Axlerod, Zazulich and Potresov, thus leaving Lenin and Plekhanov to outvote Martov on all major issues—or so Lenin supposed). As the Congress broke up in acrimony Lenin was quick to dub his own supporters "Bolsheviks" (Russian for "Majoritarians") and Martov's "Mensheviks" (Russian for "Minoritarians") on the basis of the final vote for the editorial board, ignoring entirely the bigger, more representative and significant vote on the membership clause, which he had lost. Martov made the almost incredible political mistake of letting the labels go unchallenged.

So the RSDLP appeared to split on the minor matter of the composition of *Iskra*'s editorial board. But that was deceptive. As the future Menshevik leader Theodore Dan put it in his magnum opus *The Origins of Bolshevism*, although Lenin and Martov had appeared united on key issues at the beginning of the congress, it became clear over the course of the congress that it was not a matter of different shadings of view "but of two tendencies of organisational thought and practice that were hard to reconcile".[24] Lenin was his doctrine personified. In his manipulation of delegates, his bullying and slandering of opponents who had until the Congress been his comrades and friends, his will to dominate regardless of the consequences, he had alienated many in the party. It was not very long before a key participant, Pavel Axelrod, went public with the underlying philosophical divergence between Bolshevism and Menshevism.

In an *Iskra* article "The Unification of Russian Social Democracy and its Tasks", Axelrod proudly acknowledged that "the triumph of revolutionary social democracy over other trends in our party was officially confirmed and proclaimed at our second congress", but went on to ask what the party must do to bring that triumph to the Russian masses. In doing so, he attacked those who were "fetishists of centralisation". He argued that it was not possible to develop a politically conscious working class "when the party members have been turned into so many cog-wheels, nuts and bolts, all functioning exactly as the centre decides".[25] Axelrod's article established a key element of Menshevism, namely that "Russian social democracy must be converted into a mass party controlled from below and composed of politically mature workers".[26]

Leninism—as Lenin's general philosophy and strategy for revolution can legitimately be called from 1903 onwards—had a different focus. It did not, at least initially, seek a mass party at all. The party it aspired to create was controlled from above and based on the assumption that most workers could not develop political initiative without a trained elite to show them how. Its fatal flaw was a lack of empathy with the workers it claimed to speak for. In the later analysis of the American socialist Irving Howe, Lenin's conception of the Vanguard Party and its relationship to the working class "assumes a homogeneity of interest and outlook in that class which is rarely present, and thereby it diminishes the claims of other radical parties to be authentic representatives of the working class or portions of it".[27] The conception, though, was *meant* to be divisive. Whatever its ultimate intentions, it was a charter for command, control and hierarchy.

The debacle of the Second Congress did not go unnoticed by European social democrats. Rosa Luxemburg, in *Organisational Questions of Russian Social Democracy* (1904), acknowledged the particular problems facing the Russian party by the conditions of autocracy, and that in those conditions it had to adopt clandestinity and centralisation, but she questioned the *degree* of centralisation advocated by Lenin. She noted that Lenin defined a revolutionary social democrat as "a Jacobin joined to the organization of the proletariat, which has become conscious of its class interests". To this she responded:

> The fact is that Social Democracy is not *joined* to the organization of the proletariat. It is itself the proletariat. And because of this, Social Democratic centralism is essentially different from Blanquist centralism. It can only be the concentrated will of the individuals and groups representative of the working class. It is, so to speak, the 'self-centralism' of the advanced sectors of the proletariat. It is the rule of the majority within its own party.

Her concern was that Lenin's scheme for a Vanguard Party would downgrade working-class self-activity.

Luxemburg wrote one year before the Russian Revolution

of 1905 and thirteen years before the revolution of February 1917, both of which were mass popular uprisings in which the Bolsheviks played a small, negligible and in some respects negative role. Already, she had discerned:

It is a mistake to believe that it is possible to substitute 'provisionally' the absolute power of a Central Committee (acting somehow by 'tacit delegation') for the yet unrealisable rule of the majority of conscious workers in the party, and in this way replace the open control of the working masses over the party organs with the reverse control by the Central Committee over the revolutionary proletariat.

She also sensed a deeper problem. "The ultra-centralism asked by Lenin is full of the sterile spirit of the overseer", she wrote. "It is not a positive and creative spirit. *Lenin's concern is not so much to make the activity of the party more fruitful as to control the party — to narrow the movement rather than to develop it, to bind rather than to unify it*". She concluded, "Stop the natural pulsation of a living organism and you weaken it, you diminish its resistance and combative spirit [...] The proposed means turn against the end they are supposed to serve".[28]

In the same year, Luxemburg wrote a pamphlet called *Leninism or Marxism?*, in which she identified the danger of giving the leadership of a revolutionary socialist party sweeping powers that "would multiply artificially and in a most dangerous measure the conservatism which is the necessary outgrowth of every such leadership". She concluded:

There is nothing which so easily and so surely hands over a

still youthful labour movement to the private ambitions of intellectuals, as forcing the movement into the straight-jacket of a bureaucratic centralism which debases the fighting workers into the pliable tools of the hands of a 'committee'.[29]

It was not only Luxemburg who foresaw the future. On arrival in London in 1902 after escaping Siberian exile, Leon Trotsky initially gravitated to Lenin. But Lenin's intolerance and hyper-centralism revolted him. When the split came Trotsky sided with the Mensheviks, although his allegiance would be highly quixotic (several times he tried to meld the two sides of Russian Marxism back together but the divisions went too deep). After the Congress he wrote a pamphlet, *Our Political Tasks*, in which he analysed Lenin's plans for a centralised party in which only full-time professionals had initiative and command. He criticised Lenin for setting up an "orthodox theocracy" in the party and came out for a conception of the party similar to that of Martov and Luxemburg. Lastly, he predicted what would occur if Lenin's schemes were fully implemented. "Lenin's methods", he wrote,

> lead to this: the party organisation at first substitutes itself for the party as a whole; then the Central Committee substitutes itself for the organisation; and finally a single dictator substitutes himself for the Central Committee.

Trotsky would live to see every part of his prediction come true.

CHAPTER THREE

1905 – The First People's Revolution

RSDLP workers who risked prison and exile to distribute *Iskra* were baffled by reports of a massive schism at the London Congress. The young worker Pianitsky echoed many activists on the ground when he recalled, "I could not understand why petty differences kept us from working together". Even Lenin's acolyte, the Bolshevik engineer Krzhizhanovky, admitted that when he heard the criticism leveled at Martov by supporters of Lenin, "the thought of Comrade Martov's opportunism seemed particularly far-fetched".[1] After the Congress, having been defeated on the criteria for membership, Lenin also lost control of the editorial board. Plekhanov, appalled at the split and at the manner in which he had forfeited the support of his old comrades for a man he could not abide, reversed himself rapidly and took against Lenin. Without his support Lenin no longer controlled *Iskra*.

Despite claims from his latter-day defenders that Lenin was reluctant to pursue the split, his actions speak otherwise. In his account of the Congress, *One Step Forward, Two Steps Back*

(1904), Lenin claimed that differences on organisational points reflected a deeper and more significant divide. Referring to Martov's off-hand remark that Lenin's centralised schema would turn members in to "serfs", he wrote that this revealed a strain of bourgeois individualism unworthy of a proletarian revolutionary. "To the individualism of the intellectual", he wrote, "which already manifested itself in the controversy over Paragraph 1, revealing its tendency to opportunist argument and anarchistic phrase mongering, all proletarian organisation and discipline seems to be serfdom".[2] Instead of working within the newly formed RSDLP and contributing to its official newspaper, *Iskra*, he opted to create a separate newspaper, *Vyperod* (Forward), and began to organise his own parallel organisation of activists to distribute it. Almost alone he set out to organise a new Congress which hardly anyone else in the party wanted.

Although the majority of the party's new Central Committee were Bolsheviks, even they did not wish for the split to continue. Five of the six members of the Central Committee then in Russia wrote publicly that they did not approve of Lenin's actions. They made clear that they wished to reconcile with the Mensheviks who ran *Iskra* and reforge party unity. As even Tony Cliff admits, "resistance to the split was wide-spread amongst the rank and file".[3] Yet Lenin was determined that the most constructive thing he could do to further the cause of socialism in Russia was pursue it to its bitter end. "It took months of Herculean effort", Cliff noted admiringly, "actually to put in to effect the break between Bolsheviks and Mensheviks in a number of Russian cities".[4] The final break in Moscow did not take place until May

1905, just in time to prevent united social-democratic action in the 1905 Revolution.

Almost unnoticed by the émigré Marxists, Russia was moving ever closer to revolution. A period of relative economic prosperity, based on the state-led economic expansion of the 1890s, had come to an end, and unemployment had rocketed. In similar fashion to the UK in 2010-11, the first mass protests against unbearable conditions arose not from the trade unions but from a radicalised student movement. Between 1860 and 1914 the number of university students in Russia grew from 5,000 to 69,000, and the number of newspapers shot up from a paltry thirteen (almost all in St Petersburg and Moscow) to 856. This produced an increasingly politicised intelligentsia.

The trade unions, emboldened by mass student demonstrations, followed suit. On 1st May, 1900 there was a general strike in Kharkov in which, for the first time, explicitly political demands were made. From 1901 workers in other cities such as Moscow, Kiev and Tomsk began to participate in student demonstrations. When a "general strike" of 30,000 students took place during winter 1901-02, workers in Moscow joined in and helped to fight off armed Cossacks sent to disperse it. In 1903 a wave of political strikes spread throughout the Ukraine and Georgia–Baku, Tiflis and Odessa saw mass demonstrations and street fighting.

Even middle-class liberals began to organise. In 1903 the Union of Liberation was founded by senior members of the intelligentsia, led by the liberal academic Paul Miliukov. It relied heavily on Peter Struve, who formulated a political programme for constitutional reform in Russia. Under the influence of his journal *Liberation*, published in Germany, the Union adopted reformist policies, including the introduction of universal suffrage, self-determination for the nationalities of the Empire, and a variety of progressive social reforms such as unemployment and health insurance. Many radical students gravitated to the Union. Many also joined the SRs and the RSDLP. Although democratic reforms were clearly necessary, the Tsar and reactionaries such as Interior Minister von Plehve clung to the principles of autocracy.

In 1904 Russia declared war on Japan over a disputed territory, Port Arthur, in Manchuria, mainly because von Plehve wanted "a small, victorious war to stem the tide of revolution". When Japan attacked Port Arthur, Russia's military commanders assumed a quick victory over a nation they held in racist contempt. But the Baltic Fleet, having sailed halfway around the world to meet the enemy, was promptly sunk at the battle of Tsushima, losing eight battleships and 5,000 men to Japanese losses of three torpedo boats. A month later, when the SRs assassinated von Plehve, most of the country openly celebrated and the "Zemstvo Men" revived their call for a National Zemstvo Assembly.

Von Plehve's successor, Prince Mirsky, a liberal reformer, wrote to Nicholas, "It is imperative to make peace, or else Russia will soon be divided into those who carry out surveillance and those who are under surveillance, and then what?" Upon taking up his post, Mirsky relaxed censorship, abolished corporal punishment and brought back Zemstvo men whom von Plehve had banished. Blocked at Court, he decided to convene a Zemstvo Assembly on his own authority and thus present the Tsar with a *fait accompli*.

On 6th-9th November, 1904 the Assembly, consisting of delegates from regional Zemstvos, met in several addresses around the capital and began to draw up plans for a new legislative body. It proved impossible to keep this a secret and messages of support flooded in. Mirsky presented the Tsar with a summary of the proposals of the Assembly, most important of which was the call for elected delegates from the Zemstvos to sit on the State Council (which Alexander II was considering just before his assassination) and a national Constituent Assembly with legislative powers. Nicholas' response was that whilst he might expand the powers of the Zemstvos, he would never countenance a representative form of government.

The Social Democrats now had a choice. They could maintain socialist purity and refuse *any* working alliance with the liberals and the Zemstvo movement, or they could recognise the reality of Russia's semi-feudal society and work towards a democratic capitalism, which as Marxists they still saw as the essential precondition for socialism. In November 1904, *Iskra* summed up the dilemma in a letter to party organisations. It admitted that in the Zemstvo liberals they had to "deal with the enemies of our enemy, who are not however willing or able to go as far in the struggle against him as is required by the interests of the proletariat", but concluded that "within the limits of the struggle against absolutism, and particularly in its present phase, our attitude towards the liberal bourgeoisie is defined by the task of imbuing it with more courage and impelling it to join in those demands being put forward by the Proletariat led by Social Democracy".[5]

Axelrod explained that this meant working on joint campaigns and demonstrations with Zemstvo liberals and sitting on the Zemstvo Assembly to advance the demands and goals of a liberal–democratic revolution. As against Lenin's demand that socialists must not in any circumstances work with the liberals, the Mensheviks' tactics were relevant policies for the time and place. If successful they might have strengthened the opposition and led to the establishment of a progressive republic like France or a constitutional monarchy like Britain. At the very least they would have avoided the pitfall of a divided opposition and the rallying of the forces of autocracy.

One of the autocracy's more subtle ideas had been to establish "Police Unions", i.e. to create the façade of a trade union themselves, secretly resourced and run by the police. Yet the "Zubatov unions" (named after the Okhrana Chief who initiated them) escaped control. One of these, the Assembly of Russian Factory and Plant Workers, was run by the Russian Orthodox priest Father George Gapon, who was unaware he was a mere pawn of the Okhrana. Although Zubatov was dismissed in 1903 when one of his unions organised a general strike in Odessa, the wheels he had set in motion refused to be halted. By 1904 Gapon's union had 11,000 members, more than the entire RSDLP. He was in contact with Zemstvo liberals, who advised him to present a petition to the government. In his memoirs he recorded, "But I did not think that such a petition would be of much value unless it were accompanied by a large industrial strike".[6] In perhaps the greatest example of blowback in history,

Gapon organised his followers to take part in a march to the Winter Palace to beseech the "Little Father" – the Tsar – for help in their distress.

In January 1905 over 120,000 workers were on strike in St Petersburg. Despite instructions to desist, on 7th February, 1905 thousands of protestors followed Gapon to the Winter Palace to present the Tsar with a "Humble and Loyal Address" asking him to remedy their many grievances. Organised by Gapon and a group of union activists and SRs, women and children were placed at the front to ensure that troops did not fire on the demonstration. This had no effect on the Cossacks sent to stop the march. As the procession approached the Narva Gates the cavalry charged the demonstration and killed 40 people. The demonstration then surged into the Nevsky Prospect, by now an angry crowd of 60,000. The troops guarding the Winter Palace panicked and fired, mowing down men, women and children. Over 200 were killed and nearly 800 wounded. As the protestors staggered away from the bloodbath, the refrain heard from hitherto loyal peasant-workers was, "There is no God, there is no Tsar". The 1905 Revolution had begun.

The blood had barely dried before a wave of strikes broke out in the Empire's major cities, especially in the west where the leading anti-Tsarist organisation was the Jewish Bund. The Bund "threw its entire apparatus into the building of the revolution [...] it put itself at the centre of the revolution and was largely recognised for it".[7] As a result its membership leapt to approximately 40,000. In Lodz, where nearly a third of the population was Jewish, it created nine new trade unions and organised radical student groups. The entire province of Lodz, which included other large towns, was soon brought to a standstill as over 100,000 workers took strike action to demand a democratic Constituent Assembly. Later, when the revolutionary tide receded, Tsarist and anti-Semitic groups would take their revenge on the province in a series of pogroms from which many fled to the US (where Bundists working in the heavily sweated New York garment trades helped form the International Ladies Garment Workers Union, one of the largest and most militant American labor unions).

The unrest was not confined to the cities. The sailors of the Black Sea Fleet Battleship *Potemkin* mutinied, cast off their officers and sailed to the revolutionary hotbed of Odessa. There they joined with striking workers before the Tsar's forces moved in and carried out the infamous massacre on the Odessa Steps. Peasants, scenting the weakness of the traditional landowning class, staged rent strikes and illegal land seizures. By summer nearly 3,000 houses were destroyed and "Witnesses spoke of the night sky lit up by the blaze of burning manors and lines of horse-drawn carts moving along the roads, loaded with plundered property".[8]

In 1905-06 a rural revolution escalated across the Empire, with peasant unions and cooperatives springing up to take power from the landowners and their enforcers, the Land Captains. In Markovo and Suny autonomous "Republics" were proclaimed that constituted "free territories" of peasant self-rule. Some of these established new schools, food co-operatives and reading clubs. But not all peasant rebellion was progressive. Class violence was cathartic but undisciplined. The SRs worried that without a firm socialist consciousness to guide it the peasant revolution would peter out in vandalism and theft. Victor Chernov wrote in the SR journal in May 1905 that the party's slogan should not be simply to "take the land" but to socialise it. He urged that after peasants took possession of the fields they ensured they were ploughed by the commune in an organised manner. He insisted:

> The possession of the land, however, should consist not in the arbitrary seizure of particular plots by particular individuals, but in the abolition of the boundaries and borders of private ownership, in the declaration of the land to be common property, and in the demand for its general, egalitarian and universal distribution for the use of those who work it.[9]

A giant step towards the "abolition of boundaries and borders of private property" was taken in July 1905 when the first congress of the All-Russia Peasant Union was held in Moscow, attended by over a hundred peasants from the provinces of European Russia, as well as delegates from the SRs and the RSDLP. The congress passed a resolution demanding the convocation of a Constituent Assembly elected by direct and universal suffrage, which would then finally settle the land question on an equitable basis.[10] The peasants, through a mixture of their own independent initiative and the political direction of the SRs, had entered the political arena.

The parallels with the land and estate seizures of the Zapatistas, and before them of the rural guerilla campaigns of the Nicaraguan Frente Sandinista de Liberacion Nationale (FSLN or Sandinistas) and the El Salvadoran Farabundo Marti National Liberation Front (FMLN) in the 1980s, are striking.

In Nicaragua, the Sandinistas adopted a strategy known as "Prolonged Popular War" (GPP). The GPP was centred on the central mountain zone of the country and focused on building a popular peasant support base in preparation for rural guerilla warfare. In opposition to this strategy, Marxist intellectuals such as Jamie Wheelock – the aspirant Lenin of the FSLN's "Proletarian Tendency" – argued that economic development had turned Nicaragua into a nation of factory workers and wage-earning farm labourers, and that a revolutionary strategy should be based on the working class and led by a vanguard party.

This was a dead end in a country like Nicaragua. A third faction sought to fuse the best elements of the opposing strategies. This Insurrectional Tendency, led by Daniel Ortega, his brother Humberto and Victor Tirado Lopez, called for tactical alliances with non-communist democrats in a Popular Democratic Front against the Somoza regime. It did not shy away from attacking the National Guard directly and it fought bravely to defend its own territory. But at the same time it built up support in the towns and in the capital Managua (as much as, in 1956–58, Castro's July 26th Movement and the guerilla forces of the Sierra Maestre worked in tandem with trade unions and other democratic forces in Santiago, Santa Clara and Havana). This flexible, inclusive popular front tactic led to the erosion of Somoza's internal support and the eventual triumph of the Sandinistas in July 1979.

Russia in 1905 saw a similar level of alienation between government and people. A combined wave of rural, urban and military rebellion was clearly a precursor to revolutionary upheaval. In September 1905, Moscow printers came out on strike and immediately linked up with radical students making wider political demands. In October a variety of strikes by transport workers, bank workers, hospital staff, academics and telegraph operators all merged into one mass strike against the structures of the autocracy itself. On 25th October all railways across the Empire ground to a halt. Moscow and St Petersburg were plunged into nightly darkness as electricity failed. As strikers fought police and Cossacks on the streets, their separate demands coalesced into the call for convocation of a Constituent Assembly – a national Parliament – elected by universal suffrage. This was no economic strike. The workers had transcended that limitation without the assistance or leadership of professional revolutionaries.

They had done more. The workers of St Petersburg had created a "Soviet" (Russian for council) of workers' representatives from the different industries, factories and offices taking part in the strikes, to oversee and coordinate activity. The St Petersburg Soviet, and the entire Soviet movement so central to the 1905 and 1917 Revolutions, began on 17th October, 1905 when 562 factory delegates assembled in the Free Economics Institute and elected a central committee of fifty people, which included seven delegates each from the Mensheviks, the Bolsheviks and the SRs. The radical Menshevik lawyer Krustelev-Noser was elected Chair, with fellow Menshevik Trotsky and the SR Nicholas Avksentiev as Vice-Chairs. The Soviet was far more than a strike committee. It had its own newspaper, and it ensured that food and other essential supplies were distributed throughout the city.[11]

Within two weeks Soviets had sprung up in nearly

every city across the Empire. It was the beginning of the revolution the Bolsheviks claimed to predict and support. Yet as Marcel Liebman admits, the Bolsheviks met the creation of the Soviets with "scepticism, incomprehension, and even sometimes outright hostility". This was not surprising given that its origin and conception not only "clashed with the political creed of Lenin's supporters", but complimented that of the Mensheviks, whose goal was to create "a party that should be as large as possible and in which workers' initiative and spontaneity should be given full play".[12]

As a result, throughout the 1905 Revolution the Mensheviks were the prime representative of the Russian proletariat and the leading force for social democracy. It was therefore crucial they establish a clear position on whether the working class, through the Soviets, should lead the revolution or merely support a "bourgeois democratic" revolution as orthodox Marxist theory dictated. The RSDLP conference of April–May 1905 (which the Bolsheviks boycotted) grappled with this problem. It declared that in principle it was not opposed to an armed uprising of the masses but it stressed that before it could be attempted more propaganda and educational work needed to be done. It adopted Martov's strategy of calling for "a network of organs of revolutionary self-government throughout Russia in the hope that these would ultimately amass enough strength to launch an assault on the central government".[13]

Some Mensheviks even began to consider whether Russia might transcend a bourgeois revolution and proceed straight to a socialist one. In Russia, those Mensheviks closest to the St Petersburg Soviet—Trotsky, Theodore Dan and Alexander

Martynov – created a new newspaper, *Nachalo*, which was far more militant than the Bolshevik paper and published articles which prefigured the theory of "Permanent Revolution". This led to differences with Axelrod and Martov, who whilst committed to revolutionary activity to overthrow autocracy were not willing to forego the central precept of Marxism, i.e. that the relations of production of a bourgeois capitalist system must be fully developed before it could begin a transition to socialism.

The Bolsheviks were even more confused. *What Is To Be Done?*, the bible on which the "hards" around Lenin had taken their stand in the split of 1903, had let them down. Worse, the Mensheviks were in the vanguard of a working class that had not waited for instruction or guidance from either faction of the RSDLP. The St Petersburg Bolshevik Committee passed a resolution condemning the Soviet and stating that it would "hold back the proletariat at a primitive level of development". Some members advocated joining it and then "exploding the Soviet from within".[14] As late as October 1905, when the Soviet was clearly the centre of working-class resistance to the autocracy, Alexander Bogdanov, the senior Bolshevik at the time after Lenin, insisted the Soviet accept the Bolshevik programme and submit itself to the Bolshevik Central Committee. When the Bolshevik delegate Krasikov put this to the Soviet, "the debate was very brief" and it dismissed the proposal with contempt. Just before Lenin returned to Russia in November 1905, the Bolshevik paper *Novaya Zhizn* published an article on the Soviets. It conceded that whilst social democrats might support the Soviet as an executive organ of working-class activity, they "must now no less vigorously combat all attempts on its part to become the political leader of the working class". That role was reserved for the party alone.[15]

Lenin himself now shifted his position. In an article the editors of *Novaya Zhizn* refused to publish he acknowledged the Soviet as "the embryo of a provisional revolutionary government" and suggested that the party should not be counter-posed to the Soviet. In this he was groping his way to a fresh, final conception of the 1905 Revolution. This would not lead, in his view, to a progressive bourgeois regime but to what he called a "revolutionary democratic-dictatorship of the proletariat and peasantry". This reflected Lenin's belated recognition of the potentialities of a revolution that he admitted the Bolsheviks had misjudged.

Writers such as Liebman and Lih have argued that under the pressure of the events of 1905 and the creation of the Soviets, Lenin demonstrated his innate creativity by jettisoning much that he had stood for up to that point and embracing the Soviets as the means through which to deliver socialism. In Liebman's opinion this showcased Lenin's "exceptional genius" and capacity to appreciate the "dialectical potentialities" of real life, in this case the obvious reality that the development of the 1905 Revolution contradicted the organisational strategy he had advocated only two years before. Yet at a separate Bolshevik Congress of April 1905 the overriding theme was the Bolsheviks' deep suspicion of the Soviets. Faced with the reality of Bolshevik "committee-men" who had taken his every word to heart, Lenin wrote in frustration to a St Petersburg Bolshevik activist, "Take a lesson from the Mensheviks, for Christ's sake!"[16]

Meanwhile, although the role of the Bolsheviks in the upheavals of 1905 was, in the opinion of E.H. Carr, "slight and undistinguished",[17] the Soviets—most especially the St Petersburg Soviet—plowed ahead with revolutionary activity. On 28th October it ordered that all shops and factories in St Petersburg be shut down or face "the people's vengeance". A few days later St Petersburg lay in darkness as electricity and telegraph systems were cut off and all courts, schools, restaurants and theaters were closed. With the German Kaiser offering him refuge and his chief advisors urging conciliation, Nicholas finally appointed Witte as Prime Minister.

For a brief period Witte held in his hands the concentrated power of the Tsar. He drew up and insisted the Tsar issue a proclamation known as the October Manifesto which, at least on paper, promised full civil and political liberties, an end to censorship, a consultative Duma (a Parliament) elected by universal male suffrage, and a Cabinet government under a still powerful but constitutional monarch. Nicholas had to declare that henceforth no laws emerging from his government, which would still be appointed by him, would be promulgated without the approval of the Duma. It was not the Constituent Assembly that Russian progressives had been demanding for decades, but it was a first step towards it.

The Soviet pressed on. It demanded a legally established eight-hour day, immediate pay rises in the industries of St Petersburg, an amnesty for all political prisoners and a promise of a full Constituent Assembly. A demonstration in the capital on 3rd November led to a bloody clash with the "Black Hundreds", gangs of anti-left, anti-Semitic thugs who enjoyed the toleration of Court and police. On 8th November the naval base at Kronstadt, a socialist stronghold, mutinied and joined the Soviet. Tsarist forces arrived swiftly to crush it and after brief fighting the leaders of the rebellion faced summary execution. In solidarity the Soviet called another general strike.

Lenin was adamant that the working class should initiate its own revolution independent of bourgeois liberals who, he suspected, were content to stop at the October Manifesto and build from there. But it was not simply Lenin pushing for insurrection. The Mensheviks under Dan and Trotsky, intoxicated by the atmosphere of revolutionary defiance that animated the St Petersburg Soviet, also favoured armed revolt. It was a terrible misjudgment. The social democrats, with a few exceptions such as Martov and Axelrod, did not consider whether the mass of working people would actually support armed revolution, whether the military was sufficiently alienated from the regime to disobey its orders, or how an attempted insurrection immediately after the October Manifesto would splinter any prospect of a successful popular front in opposition to Tsarism.

For Lenin this was irrelevant. "To say that because we cannot win we should not stage an insurrection", he wrote in November, "that is the talk of cowards". Even before he returned to Russia he had written to the St Petersburg Bolshevik Committee: "Organise at once and everywhere fighting brigades among students, and particularly among workers. Let them arm themselves immediately with whatever weapons they can obtain – a knife, a revolver, a kerosene-soaked rag for setting fires". Demanding "two to three hundred squads in St Petersburg in one to two months", he urged,

> Some can assassinate a spy or blow up a police station. Others can attack a bank to expropriate funds for insurrection. Let every squad arm, if only by beating up police. The dozens of sacrifices will be repaid with interest by producing hundreds of experienced fighters who will lead hundreds of thousands tomorrow.[18]

This had no relevance at all to working-class activists within Russia struggling to build a viable political machine, run strike committees and influence the Soviet.

Armed revolution began and ended in Moscow. On 3rd December the leaders of the St Petersburg Soviet were all arrested and the Soviet disbursed. The workers of St Petersburg did not rise in its defence. On 12th December barricades were erected throughout Moscow and the railway stations and bridges were seized. But the rebels did not march on the Kremlin, preferring instead to put defences around working-class areas like the Presnia district that the authorities could afford to bypass whilst they re-took the strategic points. And, crucially, the army did not revolt or disobey orders to crush the insurrection. On 15th December, after fierce fighting throughout the city, the Moscow revolt ended with the almost total destruction of the Presnia district under heavy shelling. Thousands of workers were killed, including many children, and the socialist parties were once more made illegal. For Lenin, for whom "victory does not matter", this was beside the point. He slipped quietly out of

Russia as soon as defeat was obvious.

In the strictest sense, the 1905 Revolution failed.[19] It failed because it did not replace autocracy with a fully functional liberal-democratic regime. Had all opposition parties been united on that goal it might have been achieved. But despite the mutiny on the *Potemkin* and some instances of refusal to obey orders, the prerequisite for a successful revolution – the subversion and dissolution of the army and navy, whose lower ranks comprised mainly peasant conscripts – had not occurred. Nevertheless, the political landscape of Tsarist Russia was irretrievably altered. Despite political repression after 1905 and the gerrymandering of the franchise and powers of the Duma, the genie could not be put back in the bottle. The Tsar had been forced by mass pressure to cede some of his absolute prerogatives, the disaffected working class and middle class had experienced political and intellectual freedom they would not soon forget, and the Duma, though not an "executive" in the Western sense, provided opportunities for legal oppositional activity.

There were other openings. The press was less censored and civil society less shackled. In March 1906 the first legal Russian Trade Union Congress met in Moscow. Although there were only approximately 245,000 trade union members across the entire Russian Empire, these were tightly concentrated – about a quarter in Poland and the Caucasus, with an estimated 52,000 in St Petersburg, 48,000 in Moscow, 12,000 in Baku and 10,000 in Odessa.[20] Many of these were the Jewish working class organised by the Bund. Now the unions advised their members to exploit whatever new legal opportunities existed to organise and grow.

One of the most important results of the new political freedom was the formation of the Constitutional Democrats. The party *par excellence* of bourgeois liberals, the Constitutional Democrats – or Kadets as they were henceforth known – formed in October 1905 in response to the issuance of the October Manifesto. Its membership was a wide and not always cohesive assortment of the leading bourgeois professions. Progressive academics such as Miliukov wished to democratise the Russian state, but "liberal" landowners, though ostensibly in agreement, were equally concerned to protect their property. Not surprisingly the Kadets could not agree on a meaningful social programme, preferring instead to focus on constitutional reform, universal suffrage, civil rights and increased autonomy for the territories of the Russian Empire. If the Kadets were the relatively enlightened liberals of Russian politics, then the Octobrist Party, formed at the same time, were its Tories. Based on the richer landowners, businessmen and senior government officials, the Octobrists did not support universal suffrage and only wished for limited reform of the autocracy as a means to defend their class interests.

The RSDLP also evolved. Under the pressures of revolution, with a radicalised working class taking matters into its own hands and creating proto-revolutionary organs like the Soviets, many of its activists simply ignored the factionalism of their leaders and begun to work together as they had done before 1903. Lenin himself wrote in 1905, "It is no secret that the vast majority of social democratic workers are exceedingly dissatisfied with the split in the party and are demanding unity".[21] With a new political situation calling for new strategies, the full RSDLP met in Stockholm between 23rd April and 3rd May 1906 at a "unity congress". Significantly, it was at this congress that the Jewish Bund, led by Mark Liber and Abraham Gots, returned to the RSDLP, and put itself behind the general political programme of the Mensheviks.

The key issue at the Congress was whether to prioritise underground conspiratorial work, as the Bolsheviks wished, or legal trade union organising and working within the Duma, as the Mensheviks desired. Axelrod urged the party drop its boycott of the Duma, which had led to the RSDLP not standing in the first round of elections. He described the Bolshevik policy of violent insurrection as "a conspiratorial-insurrectionary mixture of anarchist and Blanquist tendencies, dressed up in the terminology of Marxism".[22] A large majority of the congress agreed to contest the second round of Duma elections. Lenin, surprisingly, sided with the majority. As the revolutionary tide receded he saw in the Duma new opportunities for propaganda, and he formed a temporary alliance with the Mensheviks to agree that approach.

Lenin's biggest setback at Stockholm was the overwhelming condemnation of the Bolsheviks' most notorious policy—the "expropriations" (armed bank robberies) used to fund the separate Bolshevik political organisation within the RSDLP. The Congress unreservedly condemned the expropriations and demanded that they cease. Lenin gave vague assurances this would happen but had no intention of giving up a source of funding for his shadow structure within the RSDLP. Nor would he abandon those Bolsheviks who carried out the actions (including the notorious Georgian bandit "Koba", later to take on the revolutionary alias "Stalin"). As a result of these defeats, Lenin's authority took a severe blow and the Bolsheviks were reduced to three seats on the party Central Committee to the Mensheviks' seven.

But the most serious and existential threat to the revolutionary left—whose central message was that it offered the only possible response to an immovable, autocratic semi-feudalism—was that presented by the policies of the last great statesman of Tsarist Russia, Pyotr Stolypin, Prime Minster from 1906 to 1911. As Governor of Grodno Province, Stolypin had set up field court martials to arraign and summarily execute peasants who participated in land seizures during the 1905 Revolution. As Prime Minister he oversaw a ruthless suppression of radical parties and trade unions during 1907 which jailed up to 60,000 people. Despite this, he was intelligent enough to see that only innovative and meaningful reforms would provide the autocracy with the social base it needed to survive future challenges.

Stolypin's agrarian reforms were designed to abolish the powers of the communal Mir—which for all its flaws allocated strips of land according to familial and social criteria in the manner of the Open Field System long-since vanished in England and France—in favour of private land holdings. To assist the process, he created a Peasant Bank to make loans to peasants who wished to remove themselves from the Mir and own their own plots. This was accompanied by other measures to tie the peasants to Russian capitalism. Stolypin proposed, but never fully implemented, an extension of legal rights including participation in the Zemstvos based on individual property ownership, a reformed police force and improved local schooling. He was described by a contemporary as "an enlightened absolutist"[23] who combined far-sighted practical reforms with autocratic methods. But these methods lost him the support of the Kadets, whilst conservatives saw him as a provincial upstart who wished to overturn the accepted rural order.

The threat that Stolypin's reforms might attract liberal and peasant support and defuse the possibility of revolution symbolised the RSDLP's greatest dilemma in the pre-war years. The defeat of the 1905 Revolution raised painful questions. Would the Russian Revolution really be a classic Bourgeois Revolution? Would the relatively tiny Russian proletariat have to assume the leading role and begin a socialist revolution which would then spread to heavily industrialised Europe? Lenin felt this was the obvious conclusion. But although he was an intelligent man who lived for many years in London, Paris and Geneva he remained in many ways a provincial Russian intellectual. When living in European capitals he seldom engaged with their cultural life or made any attempt to play a role in their trade union or socialist movements. As such he had little to no feel for Western Europe's social and political reality in the decades before the First World War.

That reality was complex. It was not that there were no battles left to fight. The European ruling class – aristocratic, landowning, industrial, mercantile or a mixture of all these – did not concede political or economic power without a struggle. The 1893 Belgian General Strike, in which soldiers shot dead twelve strikers, had demonstrated that. Other battles such as the Italian General Strikes of 1904 and 1906 and the brutal Dublin lock-out of 1913 would demonstrate it again. France gained a Sunday rest law and the beginnings of old-age pensions in 1900 only over the bitter resistance of French employers, and from 1906 Clemenceau's radical government dispatched troops to break strikes with as much alacrity as its conservative predecessor. This was pure class warfare and it could not be fought without the brave and selfless work of dedicated activists within the socialist and labour movement.

Yet there was a profound contradiction at the heart of this movement. In theory, European socialist parties believed in the desirability and inevitability of social revolution, as explained by Marx and Engels and elaborated by the great Marxist theorists of the Second International Karl Kautsky, August Bebel, Rudolf Hilferding and George Plekhanov. But in practice the labour movement could not and did not confine itself to preparation for revolution, for "as a movement on behalf of the working class it needed working class support, which could only be obtained by showing practical results".[24] Hence the chosen compromise of most European socialist parties, including the German SPD, which paved the way for all the rest – a Maximum Programme of revolutionary demands which functioned as an ideal, and a Minimum Programme of social and economic reforms to be wrested from the state by mass agitation and political campaigning. Despite the revolutionary rhetoric of its leaders and official journals of Marxist theory devoted to fine points of philosophy, it was the Minimum Programme into which the socialists put most of their effort and that motivated the majority of working-class supporters.

The socialist and trade union movements had their

revolutionaries, but were not themselves revolutionary. It was so in 1880 and it is so now. Though socialists may wish it otherwise, the vast majority of union members do not see trade unions as vehicles for political action. Union leaders know this and often use the lack of revolutionary sentiment amongst members to defuse *any* radical trade unionism or *any* effective fight to protect rights, terms and conditions. They cite the failure of those rare attempts to use industrial action politically, i.e. not just to resist attacks on working conditions but to alter the wider political landscape – most especially the British Miners' Strike of 1984-85 – as a reason to take no stand against oppressive, anti-labour governments at all.

To this day, British socialists and trade unionists find it hard to acknowledge that the 1984-85 Miners' Strike was badly led and an almost inevitable disaster for the NUM and the wider union movement. Many feel that even to suggest this shifts the blame for the destruction of the NUM and of mining communities from where it belongs – Margaret Thatcher's government – and disrespects the sacrifices of the miners and their families during the strike. But the blame is and always will be on Thatcher. The miners fought like heroes in what Paul Foot called "the greatest act of sustained defiance in the history of British labour".[25] The government's case that it needed to shut uneconomic pits was revealed as utter hypocrisy when, after the strike, it proceeded to close fully economic pits as well. Its strategy was to engineer a strike and then use new anti-union laws to crush the miners and their union. Having provoked a strike when coal stocks were high, it then denied striking miners' families benefits in an attempt to starve them back to work. It used the police as a para-military attack force, sealing off pit villages and assaulting miners and their supporters with impunity. At Orgreave the police launched a mass attack on pickets, the footage of which a compliant BBC reedited to infer that the miners had attacked first.

It should not have been a surprise to a Marxist trade union leader like Arthur Scargill that the British ruling class and its political front, the Tory Party, were cruel and ruthless, or that they had a deliberate strategy to defeat the NUM and reduce the mining industry. This strategy, carried out in its entirety in 1984-85, had been laid out in the "Ridley Plan" of 1977 and leaked to the press. Given the clear forewarning an intelligent and responsible trade union leadership should have prepared accordingly, i.e. *not* take the bait when Cortonwood colliery was threatened with closure in March 1984, *not* rush to a strike when coal stocks were so high, *not* alienate public opinion by refusing to hold a national ballot which, with time and organisation, it could have won. Instead it simply launched a mass strike as if it was the "glorious summer" of 1972, not 1984 with a different kind of government and a culturally and politically fragmented working class far less likely to demonstrate industrial solidarity.

Although the NUM Executive endorsed his strategy, the ultimate responsibility for the misjudgments rested with Scargill. Even in the 1980s he was an unrepentant Stalinist (in 1981 he defended the Soviet Union's invasion of Poland and its crushing of the independent trade union Solidarity) with almost no conception of modern Britain and its workforce beyond the mining industry. His dogmatic politics and parochial thinking were instrumental in the defeat of the strike—as more intelligent officials such as the Scottish communist Mick McGahey knew, although he kept to trade union discipline and voiced his criticisms in private. The refusal to hold a national ballot, instead substituting a series of Area ballots, was not just a PR disaster but wrong in principle for what was an obvious national action. If a trade union thinks it cannot win a national ballot of its members it should either work to convince a majority to vote for one, or not launch national action.

In the social and political atmosphere of 1984-85 there was very little chance that a miners' strike like those of the early 1970s would succeed, or that an appeal to collective working-class solidarity—such as had been successful at Saltley Gates in 1972—would produce the same result. The subsequent discrediting of Scargillism in the wider labour movement gave perfect cover to those amongst the trade union bureaucracy who shy away from any fight—principled, smart, innovative or otherwise—with the Tories or with powerful employers. The most shameful example of this kind of defeatism came in November 2011 when major public-sector trade unions the GMB, Unison, PCS and the NUT took one-day national strike action to defend public-sector pensions and a decent retirement age. The strike was a mini-General Strike with nearly two million workers out. It could have heralded a mass anti-austerity movement to defend the welfare state and basic employment rights, of the kind that French trade unions had successfully carried out in opposition to the French government's plan to the raise the retirement age to 62.

In Britain things played out differently. After the one-day

national action on 11th November, 2011, as many within the unions and anti-austerity campaigns called for escalation against a clearly rattled government, the leaders of the GMB and Unison simply surrendered, conducting secret negotiations of their own with government ministers and then signing the "Heads of the Agreement" that provided for a rise in the retirement age to 67 on a reduced pension. The surrender left more militant unions like PCS and the NUT exposed and unable to carry on the fight on their own. The supine General Secretary of the GMB who led the climbdown, Paul Kenny, was rewarded by the Tories with a Knighthood, which he accepted "on behalf of his members". Sir Paul went on to endorse fracking and attack Jeremy Corbyn for his anti-Trident policy.

The Leninism of Scargill and the abject defeatism of Kenny are two sides of the same coin – unimaginative, inflexible strategies imposed by arrogant trade union leaders convinced they speak for their members. If British trade unions are to lead successful campaigns to defend jobs and conditions, much less to participate in broader anti-capitalist struggles, they have to transcend both. This will involve making alliances with a variety of organisations and campaigns such as the National Campaign Against Fees and Cuts, UK Uncut, Sisters Uncut, Frack-Off, the Anti-Bedroom Tax, the Benefit Justice Federation and others. In doing so they will have to move away from the sectional mentality and bureaucratic procedures that have defined them since the creation of the TUC in 1868 and embrace the principles and methods of Social Movement Unionism.

One hundred years before the Miners' Strike, the German

SPD was similarly tested. It had gone through the persecution of Bismarck's Anti-Socialist laws in the 1880s and emerged stronger for it. In 1890 it secured 1,400,000 votes and won 35 seats in the Reichstag. Its 1892 Erfurt Programme, drafted by Kautsky, was essentially the Maximum Programme, predicting the inevitable demise of capitalism because of its inherent contradictions. Throughout his life Kautsky maintained that if the development of the productive forces of a capitalist society was partial or insufficient, if its proletariat was "immature" or lacked political cohesion, then the efforts of socialists to introduce a socialist programme could not succeed. But by 1914 he considered the productive forces and the labour movements of Western Europe and America *had* reached this level, and that therefore the key element in these circumstances was the "*political* result of the *conquest of political power by the proletariat* and not of the automatic collapse of the capitalist mode of production".[26]

As early as 1892, Kautsky had supplied a commentary to the Erfurt Programme that filled the gap between the Maximum and Minimum Programmes. Of the "overthrow" of capitalism, he wrote:

A social revolution is not something that must be resolved in one fell swoop. Indeed, it may be doubted that this has ever happened. Revolutions are prepared in the course of political and economic struggles which last for years and decades, and occur through continuous modifications and oscillations in the relationship of forces between the particular parties and classes, often interrupted by counter-attacks of long duration (periods of reaction).[27]

The SPD would meanwhile exploit the expanded franchise of Imperial Germany to advance a programme of immediate demands to improve the lives of the working class. In 1892, Engels noted with approval the political progress of the SPD and its use of the democratic franchise to increase its support, which he considered "a model for the workers of all countries". He concluded, "we are thriving far better on legal methods than on illegal methods and revolt".[28]

Eduard Bernstein, with characteristic lack of cant, summed up the unarticulated beliefs of the majority of "practical" reformers and trade unionists across Europe who reserved flights of Marxist rhetoric for highdays and holidays. Writing in the SPD's theoretical magazine *Neue Zeit* in 1898, he presented these beliefs with blunt honesty. "I frankly admit", he wrote

> that I have extraordinarily little feeling for, or interest in, what is usually called the 'final goal' of socialism. This goal, whatever it may be, is nothing to me, the movement is everything. And by movement I mean both the general movement of society, i.e. social progress, and the political and economic agitation necessary to bring about this progress.[29]

Although this was the wide-spread belief system of most socialists in Western Europe, it was *terra incognita* for Lenin. Politically and intellectually marginalised on the edge of Europe, raised and formed within a state that had more in common with China than with Germany, he had no intuitive understanding of these developments. For him Bernstein and the reformists were simply cowards and criminals. This mentality led to an overestimation of the chances of violent social revolution in Western Europe and a widening of the gulf between Bolsheviks and Mensheviks in the RSDLP.

As part of their project to create a politically literate Russian working class able to assume political leadership, the Mensheviks increasingly prioritised non-party activity such as building trade unions, mutual assistance funds, cooperatives and reading clubs. Hence in 1906 they proposed a "Worker's Congress", a gathering of representatives from all socialist and trade union bodies to agree a common approach to building a popular socialist challenge inside Russia. It sought to break down barriers between trade unionists and socialists, *Praktiki* and intellectuals, the centre and activists. Lenin denounced it as a "chaotic idea" which would reduce working-class political activity, an ingenuous criticism as the Bolshevik faction of the RSDLP was not supported by the voluntary contributions of working-class members. It was kept going by money from the armed "expropriations", such as the infamous Tiflis bank job of 1907, that Lenin kept hidden from party scrutiny. Even after the RSDLP's 1907 Congress again condemned the expropriations by a large majority (170 to 35), Lenin continued to squirrel away the proceeds from the robberies to fund the secret Bolshevik "Centre".[30]

The differences between Bolsheviks and Mensheviks were best expressed in their approach to the Duma. The Duma Electoral Law was not as generous as the October Manifesto had promised. It weighted the franchise towards landowners and peasants, with the working class and urban middle class under-represented. The Duma could draft laws but it could not legislate. The Tsar still appointed Ministers who were responsible to him alone. The Fundamental Laws which created the new constitutional settlement could not be amended by the Duma, only by the Tsar.

Nonetheless, and to the shock of Tsar and Court, even the gerrymandered franchise produced significant gains by all parties who opposed autocracy. Of 478 deputies elected to the first Duma, the Kadets had nearly 50% (the initial absence from the ballot of the SRs and RSDLP increased their vote substantially). The Trudoviks – a group of moderate labour socialists who had split from the SRs over standing in the Duma – held 97. The conservative parties held only 16. When the second round of voting, in which the RSDLP stood candidates, was complete, the "united" RSDLP secured 18 seats and formed a socialist bloc with the Trudoviks.

The Tsar was compelled to enter into negotiations with Kadet leader Miliukov about forming a government based on a majority in the Duma. Faced with this opportunity, Plekhanov urged working-class parties to temporarily shelve their differences with the liberals and work with them to embed democratic freedoms into Russian society. Lenin disagreed, arguing that "the demand to appoint a ministry responsible to the Duma only serves to fortify constitutional illusions and to debauch the revolutionary consciousness of the people". Calling the Duma an "unsuitable institution" for ensuring the victory of revolution, he claimed,

> Only an all-popular Constituent Assembly elected by universal, equal, direct and secret ballot of all citizens without distinction of sex, religion or nationality, and possessed of the

full extent of state power – only it is capable of bringing about complete freedom.[31]

And yet the Duma quickly became a cauldron of democratic debate, "a rhetorical battering ram against the forces of autocracy".[32] On 8th July, 1906, following Kadet proposals for agrarian reform including confiscation and reallocation of the biggest landed estates, the Tsar dissolved the Duma, with new elections called for February 1907. The Kadets, shocked at the sudden termination of the institution in which they had placed so much hope, responded with an illegal conference in the Finnish town of Vyborg. The Vyborg Manifesto called for revolt against the dissolution of the Duma and for a campaign of mass resistance, including non-payment of taxes. But this was not 1905. There were no strikes and no uprisings. The Kadets had overplayed their hand. Over one hundred of their representatives were arrested for signing the Vyborg Manifesto.

But the second Duma was even more troublesome. The "centre" collapsed from 185 seats to 99, to be replaced by stronger left and right blocs. The Octobrists went from 13 to 44 seats and the proto-fascist Black Hundreds had 10. But the most significant shift was on the left. The Trudoviks secured 104 seats, and together the RSDLP and SRS 122 (of the RSDLP's 65 seats only 18 were pro-Bolshevik). This not only gave the left a majority but confirmed that the peasant vote, which the right had always assumed was supportive of Church and Tsar, was more likely to go left than right if it could support parties who advocated land redistribution.

On 7th June, 1907 Okhrana agents entered the Tauride

Palace and announced to assembled deputies that the Duma was again dissolved, to be re-elected in November. During the interregnum trade unions were suppressed and the franchise severely restricted. The number of deputies was cut from 542 to 442. Non-Russian provinces had their representation reduced or removed. The cities, which tended to return liberal or socialist deputies, were merged with provincial constituencies. As a result, the composition of the third Duma was heavily conservative, with the Kadets reduced to 52 seats and the RSDLP and Trudoviks to only 14 each. The Duma still existed, but its use as a democratic institution was confined solely to that of a propaganda platform.

For Lenin it had never been anything else. During the first and second Dumas, the Mensheviks had harbored hopes that a working alliance between socialists and liberals might provide the grounding for a genuine parliamentary regime. Martov's biographer Israel Getzler identifies Martov's preference for this strategy as recognition that "the mere fact of transfer, even temporarily, of executive power from a feudal-bureaucratic clique to bourgeois politicians would be an event of first-rate importance, pregnant with revolutionary changes".[33] Martov's strategy of creating an RSDLP-Kadet alliance within the Duma to effect fundamental reform of the Russian state received its final death blow when Stolypin dissolved the second Duma and shut down the socialist press.

Between 1907 and 1912, as a result of Stolypin's repression and disillusionment amongst its activists with the incessant in-fighting within the party, many RSDLP cells and committees ceased to function. In these years—the nadir of the RSDLP and of hopes for revolution in Russia—Lenin waged unrelenting war on a series of "traitors" and "opportunists" within the party. First and foremost were the Mensheviks, who Lenin accused of wishing to "liquidate" the RSDLP. Right up to the outbreak of war in 1914 he attacked all manner of "Liquidators"–political, cultural and theoretical. But there were also enemies within the Bolshevik organisation itself. The "Otzovists" (Re-Callists) wanted to boycott the Duma and the legal trade unions, and accused Lenin himself of being a closet Menshevik. The "Ultimatists" held off on complete recall of the Bolshevik deputies but demanded they be given ultimata to advocate the full Maximum Programme at all times and to never work with the Kadets.

Although Lenin had to discipline ultra-left Bolsheviks who saw no merit at all in legal agitation, he reserved his fiercest fire for the "Conciliators", i.e. Bolsheviks who wished to reunite with the Mensheviks. In this period, he revealed the hard core of his personality and his political philosophy, and how negative it ultimately was. As a result, he grew more and more politically isolated. Short of a titanic social convulsion in Russia that created entirely new political opportunities, there seemed little chance he would ever emerge from this isolation.

CHAPTER FOUR

Stop the War

In 1909, Alexander Bogdanov, the only Bolshevik with the intellectual ability to challenge Lenin, in partnership with the future Soviet Commissar for Education Anatoly Lunacharsky and the socialist author Maxim Gorky, opened a school for Marxist education on the island of Capri. This attracted a number of intellectually ambitious Russian workers. Bogdanov, Lunacharsky and Gorky became the leaders of an informal faction within the Bolshevik Party, a bohemian fringe allowed to formulate (or at least dabble in) new thinking in sociology and cultural politics. This small group of free-thinkers were bound to come up against Lenin, who in his struggles against Liquidators and Conciliators demonstrated what even a sympathetic writer like Liebman described as "a deliberate striving to transform the party into a monolithic bloc".[1] When Bogdanov began to revise Marxist philosophy Lenin sensed great political danger.

Like many Russian intellectuals battered by the defeat of the 1905 Revolution, Lunacharsky and Bogdanov were looking for a way to integrate the intelligentsia's political agenda with the deep religiosity of Russian peasants and workers. Lunacharsky's *Religion and Socialism* (1908) argued for an anthropocentric Marxist religion based on the deification of humanity. His definition of religion rejected the traditional concept of God and supernatural phenomena but accepted the most positive elements of religious faith – a sense of wider community, the desire to do good and be of service, the triumph over selfish individualism. In that sense the "God Building" of the dissident Bolsheviks produced a pantheistic religion with a political focus, not unlike the transcendental Buddhism that Russell Brand used as a vehicle to reach radical political conclusions in his best-selling *Revolution* (2014).

A mixture of personal experience, Buddhist philosophy and anarchist politics, *Revolution* identified and condemned the power structures of contemporary neoliberalism as destructive of economic, environmental and psychological health. It was also unashamedly "religious", not in the institutional sense, but in acknowledging that it was *spirituality*, specifically love and compassion, that motivated the author to seek a revolutionary transformation of capitalism. In his words, this would be defined by

> a sustained, mass-supported attack on the hegemony of corporations and the regulations that allow them to dominate us […] the radical decentralisation of power, whether private or state […] the return of power to us, the people, at the level of community […] the assertion of spirituality, of whatever form, to the heart of our social structures.[2]

Revolution's real achievement is not just to make the

transformation of corporate capitalism Brand advocates attractive in the basic sense (i.e. exciting, stimulating and enjoyable), but to boldly proclaim the ethical and spiritual motivation behind socialist agitation for a better world.

Lunacharsky's concept of a socialist religion was not new, although previously the socialism derived from the religion and not vice-versa. The libertarian essence of Christ's ministry had been recognised since the early Apostles. In the Middle Ages, religious dissidents such as the Lollards, Hussites and Anabaptists were persecuted by the Church and feudal aristocracy for daring to express it. It was the core of the Christian Socialist tradition expressed by John Ruskin's *Unto This Last* and Edward Bellamy's *Looking Backward*. Labour leaders Keir Hardie, George Lansbury and Tony Benn were driven by a Christian Socialist ethic, as were Martin Luther King and Hugo Chavez. In his *History of the World*, H.G. Wells wrote of Jesus that the rich elites of his own time, and subsequently, were discomforted by his message, for "He was like some terrible moral huntsman digging mankind out of the smug burrows in which they had lived hitherto. In the white blaze of this kingdom of his there was to be no property, no privilege, no pride and precedence; no motive indeed and no reward but love".[3] Or as Brand neatly put it, "Socialism is Christianity politicised".[4]

From this tradition and the school of Catholic social activism arose Liberation Theology, central to the revival of socialism and anti-imperialism in Latin America since the 1980s. Noam Chomsky described it as an attempt to return to the first three centuries of Christianity before the Nicene Creed of 325, when it was "a pacifist religion of the poor".

It arose from a conference of Latin American bishops at Medellin in 1968, after which many of its adherents refocused their missions towards social goals such as fighting poverty and a "preferential option for the poor". This option was inspired by passages in the Bible such as the excoriating attack on the rich in the New Testament, the Book of James 5, 1:6:

> Go now, ye rich men, weep and howl for the miseries that shall come upon you. Your riches are corrupted, and your garments are moth-eaten. Your gold and silver is cankered; and the rust of them shall be a witness against you, and shall eat your flesh as if it were fire. Ye have heaped treasure together for the last days. Behold, the hire of the labourers who have reaped down your fields, which is of you kept back by fraud, crieth: and the cries of them which have reaped are entered into the ears of the Lord.[5]

A radical and uncompromising Christianity was a challenge to the Catholic Church, with its vast riches and Vatican Bank, and to conservative hypocrites who professed Christianity in theory while ignoring it in practice. Catholic priests such as Samuel Ruiz, Bishop of Chiapas, increasingly came to see that the gold and silver of the Latin American elite was cankered and that as good Christians it was their duty to speak for "the labourers who have reaped down your fields". Ruiz supported the precursor of the Zapatista Army, the Maoist organisation Popular Politics (PP), and its model of community organising. Subcommandante Marcos praised him as one of the first twelve PP activists who relocated in Chiapas in 1983 to organise a guerrilla war. The PP operated under the protection of the local church, often accompanying priests on religious missions into rural areas. They demanded "work, land, housing, food, health, education, independence, freedom, justice and peace", and pledged to form a "free and democratic government". While they appealed to Mexican nationalism, they also spoke on behalf of Mexico's oppressed indigenous population.

Like Liberation Theology, the new rationalistic thinking of the early 20th century was inevitably subversive. Only in Russia was there a return to authority and tradition. A collection of essays called *Vekhi* (Landmarks) by several prominent Russian intellectuals, published in 1909, caused immediate controversy. The contributors were selected by Peter Struve, who now stood on the right of the Kadet party. With minor differences they all dissented from what to that point had been the central tenet of the Russian intelligentsia—its unwavering hostility to Tsarism and Orthodoxy. They argued that the intelligentsia's rationalism, utilitarianism and atheism had made it incapable of constructive political engagement, and this had led to the defeats of 1905 and the failure to establish a proper constitutional order.

Struve had moved away from Marxism because he felt it lacked a spiritual dimension and asked too much of its working-class base. He indicted all forms of rationalism and "scientism" and he condemned the Russian intelligentsia *tout court* as a frivolous, destructive opposition to whatever the Russian government attempted to do. But given that nearly all of the intelligentsia, from Marxist to Liberal, had taken part in the Duma experiment, and it was the government that closed it down and rigged its franchise, it is hard to see his logic. In the most notorious *Vekhi* essay the literary historian Mikhail Gershenzon criticised Marxists for dividing people into friends and enemies, and yet he did the same when he wrote that instead of union with the people "we ought to fear the people and bless this government which, with its prisons and bayonets, still protects us from the people's fury".[6]

Vekhi sought to isolate Russia from the cultural "degeneration" sweeping *fin-de-siècle* Europe at the pivot of the 19th and 20th centuries. It was a movement in which, to much surprise, Imperial Russia played a major part. Prior to 1890 Russia's chief claim to artistic fame was her glittering array of literary talent—a range of poets and novelists including Pushkin, Turgenev, Dostoyevsky, Chekhov and Tolstoy. Although their brilliance was universally acknowledged, it was not until the 1890s that an explosion of Russian artistic talent, in Camilla Gray's estimation, "began to make a serious contribution to western culture in general".[7] It was announced by the experimental watercolours of Mikhail Vrubel, a fusion of Byzantine art and erotic imagery that created a Russian version of *Art Nouveau*. Vrubel made his reputation in 1890 with *Seated Demon*, based on Lermontov's Romantic epic. He produced several paintings on different aspects of the Demon until the nihilistic, apocalyptic themes of his masterpiece *Demon Downcast* drove him to a nervous breakdown in 1902. But his work in the 1890s, in particular *The Dance of Tamara*, had opened the door to a flowering of Russian modern art which found its voice in the "World of Art" movement.

Established by the designer, producer and art critic Alexander Benois, the *World of Art* magazine ran from 1898 to

1904. It helped organise exhibitions as well as promoting and explaining Russian modernism to the world. After a while the entire enterprise fell under the control and direction of Sergei Diaghilev, the impresario and creative driver of the *Ballets Russes*, the most significant expression of the World of Art movement. The *Ballets Russes* never performed within Russia itself due to official censorship, but other manifestations of the World of Art had great impact on the cultural elite of Moscow, St Petersburg and Odessa.

Both the *World of Art* and its successor *The Golden Fleece* championed symbolist painting and verse as well as the early works of the emerging Cubist and Futurist movements. During those years, Moscow and St Petersburg were home to radical artists who used Futurist iconography in printing, calligraphy and poetry to challenge and destabilise bourgeois culture. In December 1912, the Russian Futurist movement issued a new manifesto titled *A Slap in the Face of Public Taste*, which consciously rejected the Grand Masters of Russian literature.

The birth of Russian modernism was bound to impact the revolutionary wing of the intelligentsia. Since the 1880s most Russian intellectuals regarded Marxism and philosophical materialism as the ultimate expression of progressive European culture. After 1905 that assumption was explicitly challenged by *Vekhi*. Even for those firmly committed to revolutionary politics, the emergence of a vibrant modernist culture within Russia itself – not simply transmitted from France and Germany – was a real alternative to the ABC of Marxism as explicated by Engels, Kautsky and Plekhanov. In 1908, Bogdanov, Lunacharsky,

Bazarov and other leading Bolsheviks published *Studies in the Philosophy of Marxism*, which sought to fuse Marx with the work of the neo-Kantians Avenarius and Mach. Even worse, for Lenin, the book was co-edited with the Mensheviks Yuskevich and Valentinov.

Sheila Fitzpatrick considered that the new "empirio-criticism" favoured by Bogdanov and Lunacharsky was "essentially a scientist's philosophy, seeking to eliminate unnecessary concepts and establish a framework for the rational organisation of empirical observations".[8] But Lenin was not interested in the rational organisation of empirical observations. He believed that "From the philosophy of Marxism, cast of one piece of steel, it is impossible to expunge a single basic premise, a single essential part, without deviating from objective truth, without falling into the arms of bourgeois reactionary falsehood".[9] To counter any deviation from objective truth, he set about intensive reading and research in London and Paris, the result of which was his one major philosophical work, *Materialism and Emperio-Criticism: Critical Comments on a Reactionary Philosophy* (1909).

Lenin's own philosophy, as expounded in this book and the later *Philosophical Notebooks*, was internally inconsistent. On the one hand he insisted, with all the exasperation of a bourgeois philistine, that human perception was an accurate copy of external reality. On the other he asserted the universal validity of "the Dialectic", an analytical method taken secondhand from Hegel and Marx. Dialectics is a philosophy of change and of the relationships that produce change. Its central formulation is the "conflict and unity of opposites", i.e. that the social, economic and physical forces that comprise human existence contain within themselves the seeds of radical transformation. The key to social development can therefore be found in the contradiction between the object/present we perceive and its embryonic subject/future, e.g. the capitalist economy gestates a proletariat that will supersede it once the relations of production outgrow the mode of production. Dialectics, applied skillfully, can justify numerous political compromises and betrayals by inferring that the surface level of events—the "facts"—are deceptive, concealing a dialectical truth that only the initiated can discern. Lenin would play this card often.

Materialism and Emperio-Criticism was only one part of a campaign to destroy Bogdanov politically. In late 1909 Lenin hastily arranged a "conference" of the *Proletary* editorial board in his Paris flat and had it summarily remove Bogdanov, although he had been appointed to his post by the full RSDLP party conference of 1907 and the editorial board had no power to remove him. In many ways the crushing of Bogdanov revealed the essential Lenin. No ideological deviation would be allowed within the Bolshevik faction. New ideas would be swept aside in a tide of scorn and insult. Those proposing them would be accused of deviating from "objective truth". They would then be subject to rigged internal procedures and expulsion.

For a hard-headed materialist Lenin was often driven by illusions. One of the most damaging was his belief in the honesty of the Bolshevik militant Roman Malinovsky. Malinovsky was General Secretary of the Russian Metalworkers Union and had transferred his allegiance from the Mensheviks. This, and his impeccable proletarian credentials, ensured that Lenin regarded him favourably, and he rose rapidly to become Head of the Russian Bureau of the Bolshevik Central Committee. Malinovsky appeared to be an exemplary class-conscious worker, but some noticed that activists who had dealings with him had a tendency to get arrested shortly after. Martov accused him of working for the Okhrana. Lenin brushed this aside and made Malinovsky leader of the six Bolshevik deputies in the fourth Duma of 1912-14.

But Malinovsky *was* working for the Okhrana and was instrumental in advancing their agenda to foment as much division between Bolsheviks and Mensheviks as possible. The RSDLP deputies in the Duma had achieved some success as visible tribunes of the working class and the trade unions, and their speeches played a role in igniting the industrial militancy that swept Russia from 1912. Malinovsky ensured this did not continue. He escalated Lenin's every attack on the Conciliators to make sure that the social democrats remained divided within the Duma. The Okhrana regarded him as its most important and successful agent.

Lenin's credulous belief in Malinovsky was part of a wider naivety. A world war was coming, but when it arrived no one was more surprised by the failure of the Second International to prevent it than Lenin. His surprise sprang from two massive misconceptions. Firstly, that the European socialist movement was starkly divided between revolutionaries and reformists and that all one's political actions would follow from which side of the divide one stood on. Secondly, that the rhetorical slogans and Maximum Programmes of the Second International, most especially those of the German Social

Democrats, were taken literally by its leaders (incorrigible reformists like Bernstein excepted).

Lenin might have had a better appreciation of the international scene and the likely response of the Second International to an outbreak of war had he not been engaged with yet more battles with Liquidators and Conciliators. At a Central Committee Plenum in 1910 the majority supported calls for reunification of the RSDLP. Lenin was ordered to shut down *Proletary* and return money that had been left as bequests to the whole party. A leading Bolshevik, Alexei Rykov, was sent to Russia to brief leading militants on the plans to reunite the party. Malinovsky immediately alerted the Okhrana, who shared Lenin's wish to avoid reunification and keep the social democrats locked in factional struggle. Rykov was arrested as soon as he arrived in St Petersburg and unification side-lined.

It was becoming clear to Lenin that he had no future as a leader in the RSDLP. His continuance of the secret Bolshevik Centre and misappropriation of money intended for the whole party to fund it, added to his refusal to condemn the expropriations or those who carried them out, had made him a pariah within the Second International. Years of such controversy had the result that "his reputation for even moderate political honesty vis-à-vis the rest of the party was now so compromised that there was little prospect of his being able to manipulate or maneuver within that sphere again".[10]

Accordingly, Lenin called a small meeting in January 1912 in Prague, which he labeled a party conference but from which the majority of the full RSDLP was excluded. The

Conciliators (i.e. the majority in both factions abiding by party policy), the Jewish Bund, the Polish social democrats and Trotsky's "centrists" were not invited to attend. The fourteen delegates who made up the "conference", two of whom were Okhrana agents, claimed to represent the majority of class-conscious Russian workers. On that basis they established the Bolshevik faction as a separate party and created a new Bolshevik newspaper, *Pravda*.

The final split of the RSDLP occurred just when the post-1905 retreat of the labour movement in Russia was coming to an end. A new wave of industrial unrest was beginning, ignited by a miners' strike in the Lena goldfields of northern Siberia in 1912, which ended with troops shooting down strikers. Upon hearing the news spontaneous strikes broke out in the major cities of European Russia. In November 1912, 15,000 strikers took action in Riga to support sailors who had been sentenced to death for mutiny in Sebastopol and in protest at the treatment of political prisoners. In the same month in St Petersburg six strikers were convicted of illegally organising a union in a "socially necessary factory". 100,000 workers in the city downed tools to protest for the right to organise unions wherever workers wanted them. Over 700,000 workers took part in strikes in 1912 alone. This rose to 900,000 in 1913 and to 1.3 million in the first seven months of 1914.[11]

Yet it was at this time, with the social democrats working together to publicise the demands of the trade unions and to agitate for greater political freedom, that Lenin instructed Malinovsky to effect an irreparable breach with Menshevik deputies in the Duma. Malinovsky put a demand to the head of the RSDLP deputies, the Menshevik Nikolai Chkheidze, that all the RSDLP deputies (six Bolshevik, seven Menshevik) follow Lenin's programme. Chkheidze rejected this and Malinovsky announced there was now a separate Bolshevik caucus of which he was Chair.

The Bolshevik paper *Pravda*, well-funded by the proceeds from the expropriations, launched a series of attacks on Menshevik deputies and trade union leaders. With Malinovsky's help the Okhrana targeted, arrested and imprisoned Menshevik trade unionists. As a result, the Bolsheviks, led inside Russia by an Okhrana agent, took control of many major unions. One of the Okhrana's senior officials, General Spiridovich, later wrote, "Malinovsky, carrying out the directives of Lenin and of the Police Department, achieved in October 1913 the final quarrel between the 'seven' and the 'six'".[12]

Such were Lenin's priorities in the last year of peace before Europe plunged into the First World War. In theory the Second International would stop its working-class members waging war on each other. A resolution of 1907 had committed it to take all means possible to prevent war should it be threatened. But although the International traced its ancestry back to the 1848 revolutions and the Paris Commune, the day-to-day work of the socialist parties now had very little in common with these struggles. The socialist parties of Western Europe now concentrated almost exclusively on reformist parliamentary politics, campaigning for an extension of civil rights and legal trade union work. This did not preclude serious political and industrial struggle, but the context in which these were conducted was that of reformism, not revolution.

The disjunction between Russian and Western European realities was demonstrated in 1907 when Austrian Social Democrats led by Victor Adler called a general strike to demand the granting of universal suffrage. With Vienna taken over by hundreds of thousands of workers the government conceded the demand, after which the Social Democrats returned to work. They had never seen the action as a precursor to violent revolution and neither had the vast majority of Austrian trade union members. Within the parties of the Second International the RSDLP was "almost the only one to treat the revolutionary traditions and watchwords with passionate seriousness and not as matter of mere decorum".[13] The RSDLP was therefore not prepared when in July 1914 a relatively insignificant Balkan assassination, that of the Austrian Archduke Franz Ferdinand by a Serbian nationalist, catapulted Europe into war. The system of national alliances created in the previous decade – the Triple Entente of Britain, France and Russia and the Central Powers of Germany and Austria-Hungary – led inexorably to disaster.

Some had seen it coming. Unlike most European socialist leaders, August Bebel, the veteran leader of German social democracy, came from the working class. He was the living embodiment of a militant worker who had transcended trade union consciousness (his book *Woman and Socialism* was a pioneering work of socialist feminism), but it was that very quality that meant he did not entertain illusions about his class. In 1907, at a congress held to consider the possibility of an international General Strike to prevent war, Bebel told an English delegate what the reaction of German workers would be if the Fatherland was in danger. "Do not fool yourself", he said, "Every Social Democrat will shoulder a rifle and march to the French frontier".[14]

They did. As did most French and English and Austrian workers. Caught up in the "extraordinary wave of patriotic enthusiasm"[15] which swept over their respective working classes as war was declared, the European socialist parties fell into line. The SPD held an internal vote in which Kautsky, Rosa Luxemburg and Franz Mehring (none of whom were Reichstag deputies) and 14 out of 78 deputies opposed voting for the war credits needed to mobilise the German military machine. But after the vote all the SPD's Reichstag deputies followed collective discipline and voted for the credits, with the sole exception of Karl Liebknecht who abstained.

The French Socialist party, after its leader Jean Jaures was assassinated days before the outbreak of war by an ultra-nationalist for trying to negotiate a common anti-war position amongst European socialists, also voted unanimously for war credits and even consented to join a wartime coalition government. The Austrian and Belgian socialists did the same. The British Labour Party did likewise, although Ramsay MacDonald and Kier Hardie resigned in protest. They were buried under a tide of calumny as the British working class—which did not need to be conscripted, such was its desire to get to the front—rushed to volunteer for service (750,000 did so in the first eight weeks alone, a further million in the first eight months).

Many illusions were shattered in August 1914, one of which was that the "Labour Unrest" of 1910-14 had effected a fundamental radicalisation of British workers. Although the industrial actions of the period had been dramatic and divisive, Donald Sassoon records the melancholy fact that "the wave of syndicalist unrest in the years leading up to the First World War did not make any serious inroad into the 'social-patriotic' mentality of most British workers".[16] Although socialist parties in neutral countries such as Italy and Denmark held out against the tide of militarism, those in belligerent countries were intimidated and overawed by the enthusiasm with which "the peoples of Europe, for however brief a time, went lightheartedly to slaughter and to be slaughtered".[1]

The reactions of the leaders of the apparently irreconcilable forces of "reformism" and "revolution" within the European left did not always conform to stereotype. Predictably most right-wing social democrats and trade union leaders became social-patriots. It was no surprise, for example, that the Belgian Labour leader Emile Vandevelde, who had been afraid to use the word "socialism" even in peace time, zealously supported the war. But it was a surprise that the fiery French Marxists Jules Guesde and Gustave Herve, who in the pre-war years had thundered denunciations of reformism and urged syndicalist strike action against the French state, became fervent patriots. So did H.M. Hyndman, leader of the Marxist Social Democratic Federation in Britain. So did the "Father of Russian Marxism" Plekhanov. So did the theorist of "Permanent Revolution" Parvus, from whom Trotsky took the initial concept. Yet the reformist parliamentary socialists Hardie and MacDonald in Britain, and Bernstein in Germany, resisted the rise of xenophobia and took public stands against the war. As did Jaures, who paid for his opposition with his life.

The exception was the Russian social democrats. The declaration of war by the Tsar on 3rd August, 1914 finally united the RSDLP. All party deputies in the Duma refused to vote for war credits and opposed the war. Such was Lenin's expectation that the Second International would abide by its slogans that when he read about the unanimous vote of the German Social Democrats in the Reichstag for war credits he refused to believe it. In contrast, the leading tribunes of Russian Marxism attained a kind of greatness in 1914. While nearly all the leaders of the European socialist parties betrayed the core principles of internationalism, Lenin, Martov, Axelrod and Trotsky stood firm. They ignored national sentiment in favour of working-class solidarity that, if acted upon, might have avoided the bloodbath of 1914-18. Virtually no other European socialist party did the same.

In September 1914, Martov set up an anti-war paper in Paris called *Golos* (The Voice), which was uncompromising in its condemnation of the war. Trotsky went to Paris in order to write for it. Lenin acknowledged that *Golos* was "at present the best socialist newspaper in Europe". He added, "The more often and the more strongly I dissented from Martov, the more categorically must I say he is now doing exactly what a social democrat ought to do". Martov in turn praised Lenin's new paper *Social Democrat* and said that in the light of the present crisis the pre-war controversies had lost significance. *Golos* was subject to severe censorship and harassment and only lasted until January 1915 when it was replaced by *Nashe Slovo*, a similar paper edited by Trotsky. It attracted the finest literary and journalistic talent of the former RSDLP, including Trotsky, Martov, Lunacharsky, Alexandra Kollontai and David Riazanov. But its passionate anti-war polemics concealed fundamental political differences amongst its contributors.

Martov was torn between his desire to condemn the war utterly and his comrades in the Menshevik party who had rallied to the defence of Russia. Although he fiercely disagreed with them and with the leaders of the Second International, he shrank from labeling them irredeemable traitors to the socialist cause, for had they not faithfully reflected the patriotic wishes of their working-class supporters? In November 1914 he wrote, "All governments, though not equally reactionary in their internal policies, were equally incapable in the sphere of international politics of fulfilling an emancipatory, progressive mission, all being carriers of grabbing, imperialist tendencies which derive from the basic conditions of the present stage of international capitalism".[18] He also saw the war differently than Lenin and Trotsky. For Lenin it was a great opportunity. It had armed the working classes and the longer it went on the more it would undermine the ruling elites of Europe and prepare the ground for social revolution.

At no point did Lenin experience Wilfred Owen's "pity of war". By vivid contrast, Rosa Luxemburg, imprisoned with Karl Liebknecht for opposing the war, wrote in the stirring *Junius Pamphlet* (1916):

> Gone is the first mad delirium. Gone are the patriotic street demonstrations, the singing throngs, the violent mobs. The show is over [...] Business is flourishing upon the ruins. Cities

are turned into shambles, whole countries into deserts, villages into cemeteries, nations into beggars, churches into stables; popular rights, treaties, alliances, the holiest words and the highest authorities have been torn into scraps [...] Shamed, dishonoured, wading in blood and dripping with filth, thus capitalist society stands. Not as we usually see it, playing the role of righteousness, or order, of ethics – but as a roaring beast, as an orgy of chaos, as a pestilential breath, devastating culture and humanity.[19]

This was an emotional register far beyond Lenin.

Like Luxemburg, Martov's stand against the war was driven not just by class politics but by revulsion at its destruction of civilised values and the sheer waste of human life. He called for the "speediest possible termination of the war and the most radical steps in the direction of disarmament". Lenin regarded such moralism as "contemptible pacifism" and preached a doctrine of "revolutionary defeatism", i.e. that Russian social democrats should agitate for the defeat of Tsarist Russia as this would inevitably lead to civil war and socialist revolution. Where Martov wrote articles demanding peace and disarmament, Lenin wrote in October 1914, "The slogan 'Peace' is not the right one at the moment. This is the slogan of priests and the petit bourgeoisie. The proletarian slogan should be 'Civil War'".[20]

With these crucial differences bubbling beneath the service, the anti-war left organised the only attempt during the First World War to create an internationalist front of socialists from combatant countries. With the International Bureau of the Second International actively stifling attempts to organise an anti-war conference, the Italian Socialist Party called a conference on its own. Martov and the leader of the Swiss Socialist Party, Robert Grimm, were instrumental in organising it and in securing the widest possible attendance. Anti-war socialists met at Berne to prepare the conference and to decide who to invite. Whilst Grimm and Martov wished the conference to be as inclusive as possible, Lenin wanted to exclude the German "centrists" Kautsky and Bernstein, who had taken a moral stand against the war but not broken with the SPD.

Lenin's proposals at Berne – to exclude the German centrists and to issue a manifesto calling on the soldiers of belligerent countries to mutiny – were rejected by a majority. Martov and most other delegates were attempting to form the broadest possible anti-war coalition, which meant working with all anti-war socialists whatever their other political positions. They pointed out that any delegates from belligerent countries who returned home advocating Lenin's manifesto would be arrested and possibly executed for treason (Lenin himself took no such risk as he lived in neutral Switzerland). The manifesto would also have been totally ignored. The worst bloodbaths of the Western Front had not yet begun and most of the European working class was still heavily patriotic.

On 5th September, 1915 anti-war delegates from the socialist parties of the Second International gathered at Zimmerwald in Switzerland to formulate a common position on the war. Germany was represented by several lesser members of the SPD who read out a message from Karl Liebknecht, imprisoned by the German government for his stand against the war; Italy by Angelica Balabanov, Morgari and Serrati of the Italian Socialist Party; Russia by Lenin and Zinoviev for the Bolsheviks, Martov and Axelrod for the Mensheviks, Trotsky for the *Nashe Slavo* group, Karl Radek for the Polish Social Democrats, and Victor Chernov for the SRs. Neutral countries such as Sweden, the Netherlands, Switzerland and Romania also sent delegates. Bruce Glasier and Frederick Jowett of the British Independent Labour Party sent fraternal greetings but could not attend because the British government refused them visas to do so. Although the delegates did not have specific mandates from their parent parties, what mattered was that they were meeting at all and that they were defying massive nationalistic sentiment in their countries. In the context of 1915 Zimmerwald was, in Isaac Deutscher's opinion, "an unheard of challenge to all warring governments".[21]

Internal divisions nearly derailed the conference. Although Martov wished to maintain relations with anti-war socialists within the Second International and was sensitive to their problems, he pushed for the conference's final resolutions to include a refusal to vote for further war credits. The majority felt this was asking too much of socialists still in the national legislatures of warring countries—although it is hard to see what being "anti-war" meant if it included voting for the funds needed to wage it. On this issue Martov and Lenin stood together and reflected the best of the anti-war left. But a separate minority led by Lenin wanted to go further and to explicitly advocate that socialists turn imperialist war into civil war. Lenin was frank that he did not care for the promotion of peace *per se*. "Much has been left in the world", he wrote in summer 1915, "that must be destroyed by fire and iron for the liberation of the working class".[22]

The majority statement that emerged from Zimmerwald condemned the war as imperialist, demanded peace without indemnities or annexations, and urged those who agreed with it to resist the war and fight for socialism. But it did not entirely repudiate the Second International or advocate "revolutionary defeatism". It was therefore more acceptable to those beyond the tiny confines of the "Zimmerwald Left" led by Lenin. It had an immediate effect in that in December 1915, 20 SPD deputies led by Hugo Haase refused to vote for war credits in the Reichstag, and Hasse and Kautsky followed this by calling on all European socialists to demand "Peace without Annexations".

In March 1916, Haase and 32 SPD deputies who supported him were expelled from the SPD Reichstag Party. They formed a "Socialist Working Group" within the SPD which led to their expulsion from the full party in 1917 and the creation of a radical Independent Social Democratic Party (USPD). But although the majority Zimmerwald Union set up a secretariat for those sympathetic to their aims, it still kept the door open to the Second International's International Bureau led by Vandevelde. The minority Zimmerwald Left therefore drafted a dissenting note that rejected all forms of pacifism and called for a new, revolutionary International.

Ultimately, despite its best efforts and the split within the German SPD, the Zimmerwald Union failed to build a mass anti-war movement. Lenin did little to help except saddle it with resolutions which made it impossible to reach out beyond the militant left and establish a popular front of potential supporters in the trade unions and liberal middle class. His position had a certain logic for it was undeniable that alliance with the "centrists" or anti-war liberals would channel anti-war activity into efforts to end the war on the most equitable basis and not to fundamentally destroy the bourgeois states that had started it. Others at Zimmerwald, like Grimm and Martov, did not feel that anything positive would emerge from the violent destruction of European society in war.

The war meanwhile reached its apotheosis in the mass slaughter of the Somme in July–November 1916 which, for their failure to turn their guns on their officers, Lenin felt the working class deserved. In September 1916, observing the bloodbath of the war thus far, he wrote, "An oppressed class which does not strive to use arms, to acquire arms, only deserves to be treated like slaves".[23] With the failure of Zimmerwald and the isolation of the "revolutionary defeatists", Lenin had never felt so marginalised. Uncharacteristically, he succumbed to pessimism and depression. In a public lecture on 22nd January, 1917 – a few weeks before a revolution broke out in Russia which overthrew the Tsar – the 46 year-old Lenin examined what appeared to him the dismal political prospects and declared, "We of the older generation may not live to see the decisive battles of this coming revolution".[24]

CHAPTER FIVE

February 1917 – The Second People's Revolution

The outbreak of war did not disturb a Russian *belle époque* of civilised ease and social peace (nor did it in Britain, which in summer 1914 was convulsed by industrial action, suffragette agitation and incipient civil war in Ireland).[1] On the 1913 anniversary of Bloody Sunday, 80,000 workers in St Petersburg took strike action in remembrance of 1905. In March 1914 thousands of workers struck in St Petersburg against government censorship of the socialist press. On May Day that year a quarter of a million Russian workers were on strike. The strikes, although large, were mostly confined to the big cities. By 1914 a fifth of Imperial Russia's total population lived in cities. Within this minority the four million or so workers of St Petersburg and Moscow (roughly two million in each) formed the core of the industrial working class. Particular workplaces such as the 30,000-strong Putilov Works in St Petersburg, dominated by Bolshevik militants, were the inner core. Other big cities such as Kiev, Odessa and Riga also had a significant working class.

Kevin Murphy records that at the heart of Moscow's

industrial proletariat—the Moscow Metal Works—sectarian differences between Bolsheviks, Mensheviks and SRS declined in the pre-war years, demonstrated by their working together to create a mutual strike fund. Murphy's micro-analysis of the metalworkers during this period finds that with Bolshevik and Menshevik activists decimated by the Okhrana, it was the SRS who "played a leading role in several large stoppages in the months prior to the war".[2] In April 1914 SR activists in the works led a mass strike to protest the expulsion of Metalworkers Union representatives from the Duma. In July 1914 St Petersburg was paralysed by a city-wide General Strike that led to barricades and scattered street fighting. 10,000 Moscow workers took solidarity action.

This seething unrest was swept aside in August 1914 in a surge of nationalism. Many on the socialist left, and nearly all liberals, rallied to the defence of Mother Russia. The RSDLP took a principled internationalist stand but there were a number of Mensheviks, and even Bolsheviks, who found reasons to support Russia's war effort. The SRS, who because of their closer connection to the ordinary Russian peasant-worker were always more prone to populist nationalism, gave in to the flood of social-patriotism. Although exiled leaders like Victor Chernov took anti-war stands and participated in Zimmerwald, most SR activists inside Russia gave temporary support to the war as "defence" against Imperial Germany. For a brief period, the industrial action that appeared unstoppable in early 1914 came to a halt. There were anti-German demonstrations on the streets and the German Embassy in the capital was ransacked. St Petersburg was renamed

Petrograd to give it a less Germanic, more Slavonic ring.

Despite the Tsar's belief that war would unify the nation, the initial outburst of social patriotism was mainly led by middle-class state functionaries. There are few records of cheering crowds and military bands waving conscripted peasant soldiers off to fight, reflecting the reality that "millions of peasants and workers who departed for the front felt little of the middle-class patriotism that had done so much to raise the Tsar's hopes".[3] Most of the peasants had very little conception of a Russian "nation" beyond their village and immediate locality. Their instinctive loyalty was to an idealised conception of God and Tsar, not to a concept of nationhood. The peasants' faith in those who ruled Mother Russia was thus much easier to shake and destroy. All it would take was privation and slaughter overseen by patently incompetent leaders.

By September 1915 the Ministry of War had mobilised 9.7 million soldiers, but this concealed a chronic lack of organisation, training, supplies and leadership. Russia's industrial base was too small and its supply lines too long to ensure that all its soldiers had even basic weapons. It was not unknown for the second and third ranks of Russian infantry to advance into battle without rifles, only to retrieve them from their comrades in the first rank once they had been mown down.[4] By January 1917 the Russian army had suffered nearly six million killed, wounded and missing. Wounded peasant soldiers returning to their villages told their families of the chaos at the front and were in turn told of the chaos at home.

In summer 1915 the Tsar assumed personal command

of Russian forces and relocated to Army HQ at the front, thus personally associating himself with every military disaster. The government was left in the hands of the Tsarina Alexandra, a fanatical neurotic under the sway of the charismatic priest Rasputin. As a result, the administration of the country virtually ground to a halt. Prime Minister Trepov tried to warn the Tsar about the poisonous influence of Rasputin and the damage inflicted by the Tsarina's disastrous meddling in government, but Nicholas refused to entertain any criticism of his wife or Rasputin. As transport of food and other supplies broke down there were severe shortages of bread and meat in the cities. Inflation rocketed and the basic staples of life, rare to find even on the black market, became unaffordable for most people.

In August 1914 the fourth Duma had voluntarily adjourned and the few anti-war deputies were arrested. In February 1916 the Duma was recalled and for the first time since 1907 began to seriously oppose the government. Under the leadership of President of the Duma and Octobrist Mikhail Rodzianko, Kadet leader Paul Miliukov, and Trudovik leader Alexander Kerensky, the "Progressive Bloc" watched aghast as the Tsar's government, run by utter mediocrities and riddled with corruption, literally self-destructed. From this point there was never a chance that monarchy, even a constitutional one, had a future in Russia, for "by stubbornly refusing to reach any *modus vivendi* with the Progressive Bloc of the Duma, Nicholas undermined the loyalty of even those closest to the throne and opened an unbridgeable breach between himself and public opinion".[5] The Romanov dynasty, three hundred years old, was in its death throes.

In October 1916 the head of the Moscow Political Police wrote to the Ministry of the Interior, "Privation is so great that not only are many people undernourished, but are actually starving. I am sure such bitterness and exasperation have never been witnessed before. Compared to conditions in 1905 the present state of affairs is of far greater portent to the government".[6] These reports were kept from the Tsar, but warnings of the imminent collapse of the government were relayed directly to Nicholas by Rodzianko and his uncle Grand Duke Nikolai, who told his nephew to his face, "Come to your senses before it is too late. Appoint a responsible ministry".[7] All warnings were ignored. The assassination of Rasputin by disaffected aristocrats in December 1916, though dramatic, had no impact on events.

The most radical element of the Progressive Bloc, the socialist Trudoviks, now openly called for the removal of the Tsar and a democratic government. The charismatic but mercurial Kerensky emerged as the leader of the anti-Tsarist forces in the Duma. His speeches were widely reported and he became an extremely popular figure with discontented peasants and workers. On 1st November, 1916 Miliukov, in a devastating and rapturously received speech, delivered a fatal blow to the government. Forensically listing the many instances of the government's incompetence, and playing to the wide-spread belief that the German-born Tsarina and highly placed Germanophiles within the government were actively sabotaging the war effort, Miliukov asked rhetorically after each example, "Is this stupidity, or is this treason?" Duma deputies bellowed back either "treason!"

or "stupidity!" or "both!" Miliukov himself thought it was mainly stupidity, but that was not how the speech played to the public, who devoured thousands of illegally printed copies. The Duma was now on a head-on collision course with the government and the Tsar.

Whilst the Duma argued, the initiative moved to the streets. Since 1915 strikes and work stoppages had been escalating. These were mainly protests against the privation of war and stagnation of wages rather than against the war itself. It was now apparent to all that the Duma's attempts to persuade the Tsar's government to address the situation were failing and that only force would bring change. In that sense, "the strikes that broke out in January and February 1917 were inspired primarily by economic motives"[8] and not by a desire to restructure society. On the contrary, marches by women workers in St Petersburg in February simply demanded cheaper bread. But although that was the immediate goal, the fact that female workers, the most economically and socially downtrodden part of the workforce, were no longer passively accepting their lot, said much about the fragility of the Tsarist social order.

By 1917, there were nearly 20 million women in the paid labour force of the Russian Empire, and one fifth of these worked in industry (i.e. factories, sales and services, communication and transportation) making up 40% of that part of the overall workforce.[9] Paid less than men and treated as social and sometime sexual serfs by male employers and factory managers, these women had seen their living standards plummet during the war. When they took to the streets to protest many male workers left their workplaces to join in.

In response the management of the Putilov Works locked out all its workers.

On 23rd February, International Women's Day, most of the 30,000 Putilov workers joined the women on a massive march through the city. This action was unsanctioned by the Bolshevik caucus at the factory. According to Trotsky, the Bolshevik committee in the Putilov met on the eve of the mass action on the 23rd and "since the committee thought the time unripe for militant action–the party not strong enough and the workers having too few contacts with the soldiers–they decided not to call for strikes but to prepare for revolutionary action at some indefinite time in the future".[10]

While they prevaricated the unofficial action escalated, epitomised in the experience of Alexandra Rodionova, a young tram conductress, who joined the women workers' march through a city in which trams had been halted and upended across the tracks. "I yelled along with everyone, 'Down with the Tsar' but when I thought, 'but how will it be without the Tsar?' my heart sank", she recalled years later. "Nevertheless I yelled again and again, 'Down with the Tsar!' I felt that all my familiar life was falling apart, and I rejoiced in its destruction".[11]

Workers like Rodionova did not wait for the vanguard and did not require its direction. As Trotsky himself conceded, "The fact is that the February Revolution was begun from below, overcoming the resistance of its own revolutionary organisations, the initiative being taken of their own accord by the most oppressed and downtrodden part of the proletariat–the women textile workers, among them no doubt many soldiers' wives".[12] For the first time demonstrators carried banners that read "Down with the war!" and "Down with the Tsar!" On 24th February, as 200,000 workers took to the streets to protest, the government sent Cossacks to beat them back. Although policemen fired from rooftops to disperse the strikers, the hitherto loyal Cossacks refused to charge the marchers. Two days later the soldiers of the Pavlovsky Regiment in St Petersburg (unpaid, maltreated and housed in barracks built for far smaller numbers) announced they would not fire on protestors. On 27th February, when ordered out of their barracks to do precisely that, they shot their commander and joined the strikers.

Bolshevik and Menshevik leaders were in exile or prison. In any case, they were not required, for "the street generated its own leaders—students, workers, cadets and NCOs, socialists whose names have never made it into history books".[13] The Bolsheviks joined in later but there is no evidence to support Trotsky's assertion (which contradicts his own analysis of how February began) that the February Revolution was "led by conscious and tempered workers educated for the most part by the party of Lenin".[14] The militant workers were as likely to be Mensheviks as Bolsheviks. The soldiers, as "peasants in uniform", inclined to the SRs and Trudoviks. Most were non-ideological, impelled by the simmering grievances of the army, instinctive solidarity with protesting workers and the passions of the moment.

On 26th February, infuriated by its relentless criticism of the government, the Tsar dissolved the Duma. The deputies refused to leave the building and began to organise the structure of a government without a Tsar, forming a "Provisional Committee" to run the country with the help of the ministries and Zemstvos. Rodzianko sent Nicholas a last message. He wrote, "The capital is in a state of anarchy. The government is paralysed. Transport and the supply of food and fuel have become completely disrupted. General discontent is growing. There must be no delay. Any procrastination is tantamount to death". Rodzianko made clear to the Tsar that the writ of the government in the capital no longer ran, and the only means to arrest revolution was to concede fundamental reforms immediately. "Tomorrow will be too late", Rodzianko finished.

Tomorrow was too late. On 27th February the tide turned decisively against the government when sailors of the Kronstadt garrison in the Gulf of Finland rose in armed mutiny. Long treated as uniformed serfs by their aristocratic officers, they rounded up and executed many of them on the spot. Militant sailors then crossed to the city and joined forces with disaffected soldiers. They stormed the Arsenal and liberated 40,000 rifles and 30,000 revolvers. With these arms they took over the telephone exchange and the railway stations. Soldiers and sailors fought pitched battles in the streets with the regime's last bastion, the police, who fired on the crowds from rooftops. Armed cars with red flags drove about the streets returning fire, but the only way to dislodge the police was to fight through to the rooftops and dispose of them there.

The crowds then turned on the most flagrant symbols of the dying regime – police stations, courts and prisons. Many of these were raided, ransacked and burnt down. The ultimate symbol of the old autocracy, the Peter and Paul Fortress which had held the old revolutionaries of the People's Will, was stormed by a vast crowd. When the red flag was raised over the Fortress a great cheer went out.

The eruption of mass rebellion and the speed with which the autocracy was overthrown prefigured the Tunisian and Egyptian revolutions of 2010 and 2011. The regime of Tunisian President Ben Ali was notoriously corrupt, a broker for the neoliberal economic agenda of the IMF and World Bank and a keen privatiser of Tunisia's national resources. In November 2010 WikiLeaks released secret US State Department cables revealing wide-spread corruption amongst Ben Ali's junta. A month later the "Jasmine revolution" began after the self-immolation of street vendor Mohammed Bouzizi as a desperate protest against police brutality. Bouzizi's suicide, the footage of which went viral, kickstarted protests and riots in his home town of Sidi Bouzid, 40 miles south of Tunis.

Vital to the revolt was "the existence of an internet culture made up of bloggers, social networks and cyber-activism"[15] that could quickly access and disseminate the WikiLeaks cables and the film of Bouzizi's death. This was followed by other symbolic suicides and riots throughout the country. On 27th December, 2010 independent trade unions organised protests in Sidi Bouzid, which resulted in the Tunisian Federation of Labour Unions supporting nationwide strikes. As with the refusal of the Pavlovsky Regiment to fire on strikers in February 1917, the turning point came on 11th January, 2011, when the Chief of Staff of the Tunisian Armed Forces refused to open fire on protestors. Three days later Ben Ali, the Tunisian Tsar, fled the country with his family.

The conventional wisdom of the Western political

class was that this was a one-off. After the fall of Ben Ali, Harvard Professor of International Relations Stephen M. Walt explained to the readership of *Foreign Policy* magazine "Why the Tunisian Revolution Won't Spread".[16] Within weeks it had spread to Egypt. Like the influential Tunisian blogging group Naawat.org, crucial to the dissemination of anti-Ben Ali messages during December 2010 and January 2011, Egyptian bloggers and social media ignited and escalated the Egyptian revolution, particularly the occupation of Tahrir Square. In Paul Mason's view, it was "a revolution planned on Facebook, organised on Twitter and broadcast to the world via YouTube".[17]

On 29th January the occupation and scattered other protests led to the withdrawal of the riot police from the streets, and with army units again refusing to open fire on protestors—more echoes of February 1917—there was a power vacuum on the streets of Cairo. This led to neighbourhoods setting up their own vigilante committees to defend themselves against the *baltagiya*, paid thugs employed by the Mubarek regime. At the same time Egyptian trade unions such as the Real Estate Tax Authority Workers and Suez Canal Port Authority Workers took illegal strike action to support protestors in Tahrir Square. Faced with this expression of mass solidarity, the army accepted the inevitable and swiftly expelled Mubarek.

Like Tunisia before, and Libya and Syria later, it was the struggle for power *after* the fall of the autocrat that really mattered. The army was an obvious power-broker, its effectiveness dependent on the extent to which it could maintain discipline and cohesion. In Egypt, the fall of Mubarek led to the emergence on the streets of the Egyptian trade unions and a fierce battle to determine the post-Mubarek regime. The urgent need was to create an organisational alliance between the young "networked individuals" who had led the initial protests – the 20 to 35 age group in Cairo, Alexandria and other urban centres, especially women, who wanted more from the revolution than simply the removal of Mubarek – and the traditional Egyptian working class.

Failure to build that alliance led to the emergence of the Muslim Brotherhood and the fracturing of the democratic front that had brought down a dictator. It need not have been that way. Castells' analysis of the revolution finds that "The Egyptian Revolution was not and is not an Islamic revolution, even if it may have created the conditions for a democratic way towards an Islamic-dominated polity in the country".[18]

The failure of the secular democratic revolutionaries of Tunisia and Egypt in 2010-11 to translate their rebellion into a permanent hold on power is in contrast to the success of the Georgian Social Democrats after February 1917. Like the other territories of the Russian Empire, Georgia had a strong independence movement, but unlike other regions such as Poland and Ukraine it was almost exclusively socialist. Ronald G. Suny's study of Georgia during the revolutionary period 1917-21 found that "The central political fact of Georgian life by the end of the first decade of the twentieth century was the absolute and almost unchallenged dominance of the Mensheviks". Menshevik leader Noe Zhordania was the *de facto* national leader and "Social Democracy had become the expression of an all-class national liberation movement of the Georgian people".[19]

Menshevik socialists formed a clear majority in the Soviets of Tiflis (and of Baku in Azerbaijan). Zhordania was clear from the start that for the Georgian revolution to put down roots and survive there needed to be unity between its three main elements—the working class, the revolutionary army and the progressive bourgeoisie. Despite disagreements about the redistribution of the landed estates this unity did not crack, and the Mensheviks' determination to maintain civil and democratic rights prevented complete social polarisation and internal civil war. In May 1918 an independent Georgian Republic was declared with broad support across the nation and only a Bolshevik minority dissenting.

In February 1917 the steam of revolution had been set free, but it needed to be directed and sustained if it was to have a lasting impact. Had the initiative stayed with anti-Tsarist politicians and military leaders, as it ultimately did in the Tunisian and Egyptian revolutions of 2010-11, the transfer of power would have been limited. It was essential that the socialists of Petrograd and other major cities create a vehicle to prevent this and ensure the revolution put down permanent roots. Luckily they had a precedent to hand. On 27th February, the day that Kronstadt rose and the police were defeated on the streets, the Petrograd Soviet of Workers' Deputies was formed. It consisted initially of about 50 "delegates", and was led by a hastily assembled Provisional Executive Committee. With senior Bolsheviks, Mensheviks and srs in exile, the Executive was led by relative unknowns. A leaflet was quickly drawn up, copied and sent out to the city's factories and larger workplaces asking for workers to elect deputies to the Soviet and send them to a plenary to be held at the Tauride Palace that evening.

The meeting was not particularly democratic. Most workers, soldiers and sailors were still fighting the remnants of the police or taking part in celebrations across the capital. The first session of the Soviet was essentially self-selected, resulting in an Executive of six Mensheviks, two Bolsheviks, two SRs and a few others. The two Bolsheviks, Molotov and Shliapnikov, were invited out of residual solidarity not because the Bolsheviks had played a significant role in the revolution. It is generally accepted that at the time the Bolsheviks' following amongst the politically conscious workers did not compare to that of the Mensheviks and Socialist Revolutionaries. By the next day the Soviet had expanded and become slightly more representative of the workers it claimed to speak for. Roughly 600 delegates packed into the Catherine Hall of the Tauride and elected a larger Executive with more representatives from the Bund, the Trudoviks and SRs, as well as Mensheviks and Bolsheviks.

The procedures of the Petrograd Soviet were intended to provide the opportunity for all to participate in mass democratic decision-making, but they often fell short of that ideal. In comparison, the General Assemblies of the Occupy movement have tried to avoid their mistakes, with mixed results. After a collection of anti-capitalist activists called Occupy Wall Street (OWS) occupied Zuccotti Park in New York on 17th September, 2011 and made broad demands about ending corporate power and wealth inequality, the media naturally looked for "leaders" and inner circles. But the main body for OWS's decision-making was the General Assembly, a forum which anyone at the occupation could attend. Initially these were held once a day, but as the occupation grew this became twice a week. Inevitably some activists ended up more prominent than others, but a real effort was made to provide open, democratic structures in which all could participate.

Outside the GA there were Working Groups which allowed more focus and reported back to the GA. Jose Whelan, a Buddhist anarchist and member of the Facilitation and Structure WG, found that the GA was "a great outreach tool but a very difficult medium for day-to-day logistical work".[20] The regular OWS organisers began to recognise the tension between the mass democracy of the GA and the need to meet quickly and get things done. The compromise reached at OWS was the creation of a "Spokescouncil" to which different Groups sent delegates. Despite this, Mark Bray, a core organiser of OWS's Press Working Group who saw the entire occupation from the inside, felt that OWS was driven by broad anarchist values, demonstrated in "directly democratic general assemblies and spokescouncils, the consensus decision-making process, a strategic focus on direct action and occupation rather than electoral politics, and a reluctance to settle for a few reformist demands".

One reason the general message of OWS was so powerful and popular was that it utilised bold new slogans created by the not-for-profit, anti-consumerist organisation Adbusters – who coined the "We are the 99%" meme that now defines populist anti-capitalism – delivered to an American public that was "generally receptive to many anarchist ideas but wary of their ideological trappings". Most importantly, ows was not crafting messages and demands that conformed to what Bray calls "the etiquette of communication with the elite". As a result, the mainstream media was constantly puzzled and wrong-footed by ows's tactics. "It never really occurred to them", writes Bray, "that perhaps our message was not directed at the bankers".[21]

The Petrograd Soviet of 1917, although at the time a massive advance on traditional working-class organsation, in other ways reproduced the hierarchies of those organisations. In some factories, elections to what would be a Petrograd Soviet took place as early as 24th February, but they remained localised until the Provisional Executive Committee, set up by Trudovik and Menshevik Duma deputies and trade union officials, called the main Soviet together and regularised its mandating procedures. Large factories could elect one deputy per 1,000 workers, but smaller factories could also send delegates. More significantly, military units could send one deputy per company (roughly 250 men), thereby unbalancing its political atmosphere. By mid-March there were approximately 2,000 soldier delegates to 800 worker delegates, even though the number of workers in Petrograd exceeded that of troops stationed in the city.

Inevitably, the Executive did the bulk of the work. The Soviet had to ratify the decisions of the Executive but this became a formality as few delegates had the information needed to consider alternatives. The Executive, in turn, was kept busy ensuring that food and other essential deliveries got through to factories and barracks. The primarily Menshevik Executive members generally regarded the urban working class as too small a social element to lead the revolutionary process. As they gazed out on a large plenary dominated by unruly soldier-peasants this view was only reinforced. By the time its procedures were revised to ensure a larger proportion of workers, Menshevik Soviet leaders like Mikhail Skobelev had moved on to participate in a reformed Provisional Government.

On 1st March the Executive issued a proclamation of immense importance and long-term impact, Order Number 1, which instructed soldiers and sailors to create Soviets within their regiments and units. These would be subject to the Petrograd Soviet's Soldiers Council. The Order commanded that all differences between officers and men be settled by the Soldiers' Soviets, and that formal signs of military discipline and hierarchy such as saluting be abolished. Point 4 of Order Number 1 made clear where the ultimate authority lay, stating bluntly, "The orders of the Military Commission of the State Duma shall be executed only in such cases as do not conflict with the orders and resolution of the Soviet and Soldiers' Deputies".

Order Number 1 was the real death knell of the autocracy. On 2nd March Nicholas abdicated in favour of his son, the Tsarevich Alexei, with his brother the Grand Duke Michael to serve as Regent until Alexei was of age. It was all irrelevant; nobody except the most rabid monarchists wished for the Romanov dynasty to continue and it was clear there could be no other. Grand Duke Michael turned down the dubious (and dangerous) honour and the Romanov family was removed to stay as guests of the Provisional Government at the Alexander Palace. That government had bigger problems than what to do with Nicholas and his family.[22] It had accrued a level of "legitimacy", in the traditionalist sense, through Grand Duke Michael's proclamation that he would transfer power to a Provisional Government chosen by the Duma until such time as a Constituent Assembly elected by all the Russian people decided the form of government they desired.

This meant nothing. The Provisional Government was not put in place by the last Romanov but by the leaders of the Soviet. On 1st March the three Bolsheviks and two of the SRs on the Soviet Executive demanded that instead of a government formed from the Duma there be a Provisional Revolutionary Government based on the Soviets. The majority of the Executive disagreed. It sent a delegation led by Chkheidze to meet Rodzianko, Miliukov and Kerensky to discuss the terms of a Provisional Government that would recognise the existence and authority of the Soviet. Miliukov and the left Menshevik journalist Sukhanov conducted most of the negotiations, out of which emerged an agreement that a Provisional Government formed from most of the parties of the Duma would assume temporary power.

Although the agreement imposed immediate legal reforms such as an end to state censorship, it did not propose policies to address land redistribution or the eight-hour day, issues of immense and pressing importance to the Soviet's peasant and worker supporters. This reflected the nature of the Soviet delegation. They were politicians of the second rank, mainly writers and journalists. At this crucial moment it needed the direction of leaders such as Martov or Chernov. But those leaders were still abroad. The SRs and Mensheviks decided not to accept ministerial office within the new government, although Kerensky went against that policy and became Minister of Justice. He then went to the Soviet, removing his frock coat and collar before addressing it, and passionately asked for its trust while he worked within the government to ensure that it kept its promises (he also switched parties from Trudovik to 'SR to ensure a wider base of support). The Soviet, swayed by his oratory, gave him a round of applause and endorsed an action he had already taken.

The Provisional Government was faced with a herculean task, made impossible by its refusal to countenance the one policy that would have secured it mass support and which was necessary for its survival – the withdrawal of Russia from the war. That aside, it was a government not without talent. The appointed Prime Minister, Prince Georgy Lvov, was an honest liberal nobleman, the leader of the "Zemstvo men" who had spent the last few decades trying to secure agrarian justice for the peasants. His weakness was that he focused solely on short-term practical measures and was content to leave a political settlement to the Constituent Assembly. His chief lieutenants Miliukov (Minister of Foreign Affairs) and the Octobrist Guchkov (Minister of War and Navy) were far more political. Guchkov wanted to protect landowners from mass expropriation. Miliukov, having removed the Tsar, reverted to the liberal imperialism of the right-wing Kadets. Shortly after he was installed as Foreign Minister he wrote a secret note to the Foreign Ministries of England and France to assure them that Russia would carry on the war and meet all its military commitments.

The only way the Provisional Government could have

consolidated power would have been to do a deal with the Petrograd Soviet, co-opt its leading members into the government, and above all end the war and redistribute the landed estates. It prevaricated on all these, although it took steps to remove the structures of autocracy and to institute full civic and legal rights. A day after the formation of the government it publicly announced its first policies, amongst which were a full and immediate amnesty on all issues political and religious, including terrorist acts, military uprisings and agrarian crimes; complete freedom of the press, trade unions, and other assemblies; the abolition of all hereditary, religious and national distinctions; replacement of the police with a public militia; elections to the Zemstvos to be on the basis of a universal, direct, equal and secret vote; and preparations for the convocation of a Constituent Assembly to determine the ultimate form of government.

This was a far more meaningful and democratic civil framework than Western European governments provided in 1917. Yet the Provisional Government gained little credit for it, at the time or subsequently. Isaac Deutscher's assertion that Lvov's government "strove to limit the revolution to the overthrow of Tsar Nicholas II and to restore, if possible, the monarchy" is unfair.[23] Lvov wished to address the issue of land redistribution through the Zemstvos, but conservatives such as Guchkov opposed him. It is indisputable that the government sought to continue the war in spite of the socialists' desire that it be concluded on the basis of no annexations and no indemnities. Octobrists and right-wing Kadets would not countenance Russia's withdrawal or "defeat" in the war. The liberal Kadets, Trudoviks and "revolutionary defencist"

Mensheviks felt that surrender or withdrawal would lead to a German occupation and the restoration of the Kaiser's cousin to the throne.

In this sense, the Provisional Government and many of its supporters *did* oppose a restoration of monarchy. With the exception of a left wing led by Martov, most of the Mensheviks were guided by two principles. Firstly, that the February Revolution was a bourgeois revolution in the classic sense, and that the relatively small Russian proletariat could not direct or control the transition to a socialist economy of a primarily agrarian society. Secondly, that defeat by Hohenzollern Germany would mean a giant step backward from the democratic gains achieved by the revolution. These were not dishonourable positions but they ignored two fundamental realities: that the Russian bourgeoisie was too afraid and disorganised to effect a substantial democratic revolution, existing as it did side-by-side with a militant socialist and labour movement; and that the prime driver of the revolution that had gifted them temporary power was mass disaffection with the war and a fervent desire to get out of it.

Although fragile and transitory, the political settlement that emerged in February-March 1917 was the Mensheviks' great historical opportunity. Yet the party's official position on the Provisional Government was astonishingly off the mark. On 7th March a Menshevik Party statement published in *Robochaia Gazeta* proclaimed:

It is *temporary*, i.e. it exists until the time when the Constituent Assembly creates a permanent one. It is *revolutionary*, i.e. it was created by a revolution in order finally to consolidate its gains

169

and to cast down the old regime. It is a *government*, i.e. it possesses the full power which is supported by the revolutionary army and the people.

The only part of this formulation that was true was that it was temporary.

At the time, the Menshevik party felt it had good reason to be satisfied with the first steps of the new government. Its statement made clear that the government's main task was "to destroy swiftly and decisively everything that remains of the old order", but its conception of the old order was strictly legal and juridical. It believed that in bolting a major extension of civil liberties onto the Provisional Government's first programme it had given the government "all the measures that are necessary for the establishment of democratic Russia". It considered that the revolutionary proletariat, during the February events and subsequently, had "demonstrated its readiness not to split, and to conduct the cause of the liberation of Russia together with the liberal bourgeoisie".[24]

This was a naïve assessment and a short-sighted strategy. The workers and soldiers who had overthrown Tsarism and formed the Soviets—which now existed in all of Russia's cities and many rural areas—no longer felt any deference to liberals or waited for them to introduce democracy over their heads. This was forcefully demonstrated in a wave of factory occupations and the emergence of Factory Committees that sought to introduce a form of Workers' Control in industry. In the first week of March, after the owners had disappeared or fled, Factory Committees spontaneously appeared in many cities. They were particularly strong in the state-owned metallurgical works run by the Artillery and Naval Departments. By April they existed in every large plant in Moscow and Petrograd. All major railway stations were overseen by a Workers' Committee. In Baku every plant had a Factory Committee.

Inevitably they were run in different ways, but as a general rule they answered to a General Assembly—a mass gathering of factory hands and white-collar workers. It was to the Assembly that the elected committees reported. At least 50% of workers in the factory had to participate in the election for it to be valid.[25] The Committee formed at the radio-telegraph Factory in Petrograd laid down rules for a minimum wage, the length of the working day, medical care at work, sick pay, a mutual fund, discipline procedures, food provision and hiring and firing of employees. Some committees went further and began to consider issues around production itself. In March and April, the owners returned to find their managerial prerogatives, and their claim to ownership itself, fundamentally challenged.

The Factory Committees were the most significant and innovatory bodies to emerge from the February Revolution. As early as 2nd March the Petrograd 1st Electricity Works elected a 24-person council to run the Works (even at this stage it included ten Bolsheviks, indicating that despite the hesitations of its leaders, the party's militants were more attuned to developments on the shop floor). On 7th March the Petrograd Soviet issued the instruction: "For the control of factory and shop administration, for the proper organisation of work, factory and shop committees should be formed at once. They should see to it that the forces of labour are not wasted and look after working conditions in the plant".[26] Although the impetus for this was practical – the workers needed to keep the plants going to ensure that machinery did not break down – Carmen Sirianni's comprehensive examination of workers' control and Soviet democracy in the period 1917-21 found that "the idea rapidly took root that workers control was the school for a system of self-management that would arise from the socialist revolution".[27]

Such was the unstoppable pressure of the new Factory Committees that on 10th March an agreement was signed between the Executive Committee of the Petrograd Soviet and the Petrograd Manufacturers Association in which the employers conceded the eight-hour day and formally recognised the Factory Committees as partners in negotiation.[28] The concession of the eight-hour day in a number of Petrograd businesses could not be contained. Workers in other factories and businesses simply took it for themselves and referred any complaints to the Soviet. Similar rank-and-file pressure led to the employers' reluctant concession of a national minimum wage. On 24th April, the Factory Committee of the Putilov Works declared: "While the workers of the particular enterprises educate themselves in self-management, they prepare themselves for the moment when private ownership of the factories will be abolished and the means of production will be transferred into the hands of the working class".[29]

The Putilov was not alone. A resolution passed by workers at the Old Parvianan metal and machine factory in Petrograd on 13th April, signed by its Chairman S. Ustinov, proclaimed that the workers of the factory, having assembled at a mass meeting of 2,500 men, had resolved:

1) To demand the removal of the Provisional Government, which has served only as a brake on the revolutionary cause, and to put power into the hands of the Soviet and Workers' and Soldiers' Deputies.
2) The Soviet of Workers' and Soldiers' Deputies, resting as it does on the revolutionary proletariat, must put an end to this war, which has benefited only the capitalists and landowners and has sapped the strength of the revolutionary people.
3) To demand from the Provisional Government the immediate publication of the secret military accords concluded between the old government and its allies.
4) To organise a Red Guard and arm the entire people.

There followed other demands about requisition of the bourgeois newspapers' printing presses and the immediate seizure of landed estates.[30] The Parvianan was more than usually assertive and political, probably reflecting the influence of Bolshevik militants within the factory, but in the context of April 1917 their demands were not exceptional.

This was the social ferment that the hastily assembled system of "Dual Power" was meant to contain – a combustible situation in which the Soviet held the power but not the responsibility, and the Provisional Government held the responsibility but not the power. It was an unstable compound that could not last very long.

CHAPTER SIX
Coalition Governments

The popular revolution of February 1917, like that of 1905, took Lenin entirely by surprise. Until early 1917 he had devoted the war years to two projects: the attempted creation of an internationalist revolutionary anti-war movement that resulted in the Zimmerwald Left, and an explanation of why that movement was required in an era of monopoly capitalism. Lenin's great work of these years, *Imperialism, the Highest Stage of Capitalism* (1916), is a necessary adjunct to *What Is To Be Done?* in that it seeks to explain how the working class of a highly developed capitalism had been diverted from the revolutionary activity Marx claimed was an inevitable by-product of that development. It drew heavily on the English liberal J.A. Hobson's *Imperialism* (1902), as well as Marxist analysis from the German Social Democrat Rudolf Hilferding and fellow Bolshevik Nikolai Bukharin.

Hilferding's *Finance Capital* (1910) analysed for the first time the transformation of classical *laissez faire* capitalism into the monopoly capitalism of the early 20th century, a transformation based on an unprecedented concentration of industrial capital. The core of Hilferding's analysis was the concept of "finance capital", i.e. bank capital that now functioned as a significant owner of industry in its own right. Arising out of this fusion of bank and industrial capital, Hilferding described what he termed "organised capitalism" or capitalism in which financial risk had been removed through the use of trusts, cartels and protective tariffs. This led to economic stagnation and attempts to overcome it. In this analysis, imperialism was the inevitable result of finance capital seeking profits overseas from new markets, by means of which it concentrated its ownership but expanded its production. Hilferding's work quickly became "the reference point for all left-wing debates about the future of capitalism for a century".[1]

In *Imperialism and World Economy* (published a few months before Lenin's work and from which Lenin lifted much of his own analysis), Bukharin openly addressed the uncomfortable fact that, as his biographer Stephen F. Cohen put it, "latter day capitalism was distressingly unlike the classical free enterprise system analysed in *Capital*".[2] Bukharin agreed that the finance capital described by Hilferding would develop into imperialism, but he rejected Hilferding's suggestion that capitalism might thereby avoid catastrophic implosion. Instead he called imperialism an "historic category" of modern capitalism bound to appear in its terminal stages. In much the same way, Antonio Negri and Michael Hardt, in their highly influential *Empire* (2001), advanced a theory of imperialism for the postmodern era.

Hardt and Negri argue that while the imperialism analysed by Lenin was driven forward by nation-states — whose interests could collide, thus producing war—modern imperialism is a supra-national process which they call "Empire". Empire is no longer competing for the world. It already owns it, presided over by the United States and the other G8 countries, who use their policemen, the IMF and World Trade Organisation to enforce their will on nation-states that are out of step. Occasionally, Empire convenes at Davos or elsewhere to coordinate its policies. The legal norms thus produced, such as the proposed Transatlantic Trade and Investment Partnership (TTIP) which gives transnational corporations more legal rights than national governments in the running of public services, are, in Hardt and Negri's terminology, "the material constitution of the new planetary order, the consolidation of its administrative machine, and the production of new hierarchies of command over global space".[3]

The Hardt-Negri thesis is a neo-Marxist vision of capitalism that sees it as quite literally a global entity requiring a similarly "total" response, an amorphous political resistance which they call the "Multitude". Their analysis moves beyond the categories of classical Marxism and suggests that anti-capitalist resistance now resides in a diverse range of campaigns, groups, alliances and peoples. Where Marxism-Leninism privileges the role of the working class in such resistance, Hardt and Negri assert that other forms of anti-Empire activity—environmental and student activism, direct action campaigns, the *Comunalidad*, etc.—are just as valid and important as working-class labour struggle, perhaps more so.

In their view, the Multitude "are also capable of autonomously constructing a counter-Empire, an alternative political organisation of global flows and exchanges".[4] The protests at Seattle and Genoa, the World Social Forum movement, the *Indignados* occupations, the Arab Spring and the global alliance against TTIP have all, to an extent, validated this theory, as has – in a negative sense – the Euro-Empire's crushing of Syriza's attempt to free Greece from its economic torture chamber. If that defeat proved anything it was that no matter how radical and populist it may be, a strictly national challenge based on a local democratic election is, to the forces of Empire, insignificant.

In 1914, Empire was still squabbling amongst itself. Following in Hilferding's and Bukharin's footsteps, Lenin analysed the political implications of this stage of capitalism. He repeated the argument that big business merged with financial institutions and together exported excess capital to colonial territories to reap "super-profits" through the use of cheap labour and raw materials, and that their need to do so was the primary reason for the acquisition of those territories. But his argument lacked nuance. For example, although German banks and big business worked together to advance a common agenda, in the largest Empire builder of all, Great Britain, the City tended to stay aloof from industry. It was mainly financial adventurers, not established plutocrats and banking houses, which led imperialist exploitation of colonial possessions.

Despite its methodological failings, the core argument caught a fundamental truth, i.e. that the social and cultural cloak of contemporary imperialism, "the white man's burden" and the romantic mythology associated with it, was hypocritical cover for economic self-interest and exploitation of new markets. That exploitation may not have been the most rational way for Western capital to seek returns, but that it did so, aided by a massive state-military apparatus of which it was an inextricable component, was one of the key and undeniable elements of early-20th-century capitalism. In Lenin's terms, it "emerged as the development and direct continuation of the fundamental characteristics of capitalism in general".[5] Although Lenin admitted his debt to the liberal economist Hobson (and grudgingly nodded to Hilferding), he did not concede that Karl Kautsky had preceded all of them and more accurately foreseen the broad trend of capitalist economic development.

A decade before Hilferding, Kautsky wrote that in advanced capitalism high finance "held government in a position of dependence, by virtue of public debt. But the modern kings of finance dominate nations directly through cartels and trusts and subject all production to their power".[6] Kautsky later considered that while imperialism was a definite stage in the development of capitalism, it was not the *final* stage, and that instead of heralding the terminal collapse of capitalism it might (in the summary of Massimo Salvadori) "consecrate the end of the primacy of Europe and the advent of the young and powerful United States as the dominant power on the world scene".[7] In an article written in 1914 entitled "Ultra-Imperialism", he predicted one vast global market designed by and for transnational corporations. Where Lenin saw only catastrophism, Kautsky saw globalism.

The global imperialism that emerged was less hypocritical than today's version, but in essentials it did not differ much from the neoliberal writer Thomas Freidman's 1999 hymn to market-based globalisation, in which he advised America "to act like the almighty superpower that it is". He openly admitted that

> the hidden hand of the market will never work without a hidden fist – McDonalds cannot flourish without McDonnell Douglas, the designer of the F15. And the hidden fist which keeps the world safe for Silicon Valley's technologies is called the United States Army, Navy, Air Force and Marine Corps.[8]

Aside from its crucial support to the US economy through defence contracts and R&D (most famously, the US Army's Arpanet communications network was the genesis of the Internet) the core mission of the US military machine is to protect and project US "Full Spectrum Dominance". In similar fashion in the pre-WWI period the US, British, French and German military carried out the larger geo-strategic policies of their civilian governments across "unclaimed" areas of the globe.

Eric Hobsbawm's synoptic history of the period from 1875 to 1914 examines the creation of a single global economy with a high level of technological development. This created a pressing need for new markets, as well as access to raw materials that were scarce or not available in America and Europe such as oil, rubber and copper. The US economy, in particular, urgently needed outlets for its massive agricultural and industrial surplus. This in turn meant interventions in the economies of the Middle East, Latin America and Africa, with ferocious exploitation of labour in the Congo and the Amazon (for rubber), in Latin America (for sugar and tobacco) and in South Africa (for gold).

In response a strain of moralistic anti-imperialism – seen in Britain during the Boer War and in the international outcry against Belgium's genocidal treatment of native labour in the Congo – became a part of Western liberal politics. For Lenin, imperialism produced far more important results than racist exploitation. In his view the level of super-profits reaped by monopoly capitalism "makes it economically possible to bribe certain sections of the workers, and for a time a fairly considerable minority of them, and win them to the side of the bourgeoisie of a given industry or a given nation against all others".[9]

This supported Engels' controversial theory of a "Labour Aristocracy", i.e. a particularly well-paid segment of the working class that as a result of relative prosperity internalised the values and priorities of the bourgeoisie, and through its strategic influence within the labour movement kept a cap on the more discontented elements of the working class. Reversing Marx, Lenin asserted that it was capitalism's very development that was responsible for the failure of a revolutionary proletariat to emerge. Something else was needed to break the log jam. That something else was revolutionary will.

If *Imperialism* was Lenin's most significant public contribution to Marxism, then his *Philosophical Notebooks*, written in private during the war, are an undeclared shadow doctrine and the secret driver of his actions. Marooned in Berne and Zurich he had more time than usual to devote to intellectual work. Whilst Europe burned he delved deeply into Marx's philosophical mentor Hegel, as well as

Aristotle and the classical philosophers. Until then Hegel's intellectual influence on Marx had been noted but politely ignored by most Marxists. In 1916 Lenin threw himself into Hegel's *Logic* and *Philosophy of History* and came to some surprising conclusions.

In his notebooks (which although subsequently published in Soviet Russia as the Philosophical Notebooks reflect their informal and unedited nature), he wrote:

> "Aphorism: It is impossible to obtain a complete understanding of Marx's Das Kapital [...] without having made a thorough study and acquired an understanding of the whole of Hegel's Logic. Consequently not one Marxist in the past half century has completely understood Marx".[10]

Aside from his astonishing claim that no Marxist except himself had understood Marx because they had not spent a few weeks in a Swiss library reading Hegel's *Logic*, he concluded, "Dialectics is the teaching which shows how opposites can be and how they happen to be (how they become) identical — under what conditions they are identical, become transformed into one another". Pursuing his theme, he asked himself "What distinguishes the dialectical transition from the undialectical transition? The leap. The contradiction. The interruption of gradualness. The unity, the identity of Being and not-Being".[11]

Intellectually Lenin was girding himself for a "leap", a "contradiction", a massive "interruption of gradualness". Yet Marx himself, foreseeing the temptations and limits of revolutionary adventurism, had warned in 1844, "The more one-sided, and thus the more perfect political intelligence is, the more it believes in the omnipotence of the will, the blinder it is to the natural and intellectual limits of the will, and thus the more incapable it is of discovering the sources of social evils".[12] Lenin might have done better, during his quiet war years, to restudy Marx rather than Hegel.

As soon as he received news of the February Revolution, Lenin was desperate to return to Russia. To do so he had to navigate across a war-torn continent. After a secret deal with the German government he and his entourage were allowed to traverse Germany in the infamous "sealed train", arriving at the Finland Station in Petrograd on 4th April. He returned to a Russia torn by internal strife. The new Prime Minister, Prince Lvov, who as leader of the Zemstvo Union had great experience of practical administration but very little of party politics, saw the February Revolution as the first step to a constitutional democratic order based on an extension of the franchise and civil rights. His government had already abolished capital punishment and overhauled the courts and legal system, as well as providing for elections to a Constituent Assembly. It had also abolished all existing anti-Semitic statutes and opened up massive new social opportunities for the Jews of the Empire, attracting at one stroke an intense level of loyalty and support from liberal and socialist Jews.

In March a delegation of Russian suffragettes met Lvov to plead for the right of women to vote in the elections to the reformed Zemstvos. They did not need to produce their carefully rehearsed arguments, for Lvov simply asked them, "Why shouldn't women be allowed to vote? I don't see what's the problem",[13] after which women were granted the right to vote in Zemstvos and city Duma elections. The issue of equal suffrage for the Constituent Assembly elections produced some reactionary opposition but the democratic momentum was unstoppable. In July a Special Conference for the Electoral Law for the Constituent Assembly proposed to give the vote to all adults over 20 years of age and the Provisional Government, then led by Kerensky, agreed to this. Russia thereby became the only belligerent in WWI with universal suffrage.

When Lenin arrived in Petrograd he found a Bolshevik Party that had adapted to this new reality. For a while the party in St Petersburg had been rudderless, but soon senior Bolsheviks such as Sverdlov, Stalin and Kamenev arrived from Siberian exile to take over from Molotov and Shliapnikov. They used *Pravda* to communicate with Bolshevik militants in the factories and Soviets. Faced with a popular revolution and the power of the Petrograd Soviet, Bolshevik leaders in Russia issued their first communication in the 28th March issue of *Pravda*. This urged: a) unification with the Left Mensheviks, and b) support for the Provisional Government as long as it carried out the programme agreed with the Soviet. It did not advocate Lenin's "revolutionary defeatism". On the contrary, now that a popular revolution had removed the Tsar's government the Bolsheviks edged towards the kind of "revolutionary defencism" advocated by Menshevik leaders such as Isaac Tseretelli. On this basis Tseretelli proposed complete unification of Bolsheviks and Mensheviks within one party. Many Bolsheviks were inclined to agree.

Lenin was not. After being greeted at the Finland Station

by a large crowd (all returning socialist leaders received a similar welcome) he immediately set to work to drag the Bolsheviks away from any support, however qualified, for the Provisional Government. His first speech to assembled Bolsheviks from the balcony of their temporary HQ assured them that working-class revolution was imminent in France, Germany and England. It was therefore in order for Russian socialists to push the bourgeois revolution of February into a socialist phase, secure in the knowledge that it would not be isolated and would act as an outlier for a larger Europe-wide revolution.

After this he went inside and brutally lambasted the leaders of the party. He completely repudiated any support for the Provisional Government and for the non-Bolshevik majority in the Soviet. "Only the Zimmerwald Left stands guard over the proletarian revolution!" he declared. The Menshevik historian Sukhanov, invited to attend the gathering as an observer, was perfectly placed to record the meeting. "I'll never forget the thunderous speech, startling not only to me, a heretic who had accidentally dropped in, but also to the faithful – all of them", Sukhanov later wrote. "It seemed as if all the elements of universal destruction had arisen from their lairs, knowing neither barriers nor doubts, personal difficulties nor personal considerations".[14]

The next day Lenin attended a conference at the Tauride Palace called to consider the unification of Bolsheviks and Mensheviks. He swept the initiative aside with contempt. He not only rejected a united RSDLP but also, for the first time in front of a non-Bolshevik socialist audience, explained his conception of the Russian revolution. He called for the replacement of the Provisional Government with a government of workers' and soldiers' deputies as the first step towards European revolution. His speech was received with amazement by most of the delegates, including the Bolsheviks. Many booed. Some laughed. Bogdanov, whom Lenin had removed from editorship of *Proletary* in 1909, shouted, "This is the delusion of a lunatic!"[15]

Other Bolsheviks accused him of abandoning Marxism for anarchism. At a meeting of the Bolshevik Central Committee Kamenev criticised Lenin for considering the situation in Russia to be like that of France in 1871, which had called forth the Paris Commune, "whereas we do not yet have behind us what was accomplished in 1789 and 1848". The general consensus was that Lenin was finished as a serious figure on the left. Lenin was undaunted. Two days later, on 8th April, *Pravda* published what came to be known as the "April Theses".

The April Theses, though only a few pages long, has a good claim to be Lenin's most significant work, in the sense of the direct effect it had on the future course of history.[16] It was perfectly pitched to its time, place and audience. The ten Theses flow smoothly from one to another. Because of the shortness of the text they are not hampered by details that might derail the momentum or logic of the argument. Thesis 1 is the clear assertion that under the Provisional Government the war "remains on Russia's part a predatory imperialist war" and that without overthrowing capital (i.e. the government) it is impossible to end the war with a truly democratic peace. Thesis 2 continues:

> The specific feature of the present situation in Russia is that the
> country is passing from the first stage of the revolution – which,
> owing to the insufficient class-consciousness of the proletariat,
> placed power in the hands of the bourgeoisie – to its second
> stage, which must place power in the hands of the proletariat
> and the poorest sections of the peasants.

The general argument proceeds from this, including no
support for the Provisional Government; a call to propagandise
for the Soviets to be "the only possible form of revolutionary
government", with a recognition that the Petrograd Soviet's
current majority had betrayed the revolution; the Soviets
to form "a republic of Soviets of Workers', Agricultural
Labourers' and Peasant Deputies throughout the country,
from top to bottom"; confiscation of all privately held land
and the creation of "model farms" by the rural Soviets;
unification of all banks into one National Bank controlled
by the Soviets; and a new International. Thesis 9 explained
that, "It is not our immediate task to introduce socialism,
but only to bring social production and the distribution
of products at once under the control of the Soviets of
Workers' Deputies". The caveat indicates that Lenin was not
entirely clear at which socio-economic model he was aiming,
although one of his explanatory notes adds that it would be
"a state of which the Paris Commune was the prototype".

The only member of the Bolshevik Central Committee
who agreed wholeheartedly with the April Theses was
Alexandra Kollontai. Before the war a Left Menshevik,

Kollontai now saw Lenin as the only revolutionary leader with the vision to actually deliver a proletarian revolution. Like many of his most ardent supporters on the Bolshevik left, such as the militant Vyborg Committee which mobilised young recruits fresh from the villages to the Putilov and other huge factory complexes, she did not consider whether Russia's fragile state and culture could sustain a proletarian revolution. She assumed that the workers, soldiers and sailors she daily addressed in an endless series of loud and passionate meetings were up to the task of socialist reconstruction, and that in any case the working class of Western Europe would soon rise up to support them.

If the Provisional Government had stabilised, Lenin would probably have remained a marginal political figure, rejected even by the Bolshevik Party. But while Lvov struggled to establish his government his conservative colleagues self-destructed. In April, Guchkov resigned as Minister of War because he could not work with the Soviet and its notorious Order Number 1. When it emerged that Foreign Minister Miliukov had secretly recommitted the new Russian government to the Tsarist government's war aims (i.e. the seizure of Constantinople and annexation of the Balkans) the subsequent public outrage meant he had to resign as well. He took with him many of his Kadet colleagues, and the party now shifted rightwards to side with Octobrists and landowners desperate to resist the confiscation of landed estates. With limited Kadet support Lvov had little alternative but to restructure his coalition to include the SRs, Trudoviks and Mensheviks who were running the Petrograd Soviet and who, for the moment, held the trust of the workers and soldiers.

As a result, the Provisional Government became in early May a coalition comprising ten Kadets and six socialist ministers. Tseretelli, leader of the Mensheviks now that Martov was aligned to the anti-war internationalists, became Minister of Posts and Telegraphs; his Menshevik colleague Skobelev became Minister of Labour; Victor Chernov, the leader of the SRs, became Minister of Agriculture with a mandate to address peasant grievances; and Kerensky took over from Guchkov as Minister of War and Deputy Prime Minister.

The new coalition was not, at first, unpopular. The inclusion of the socialist ministers was welcomed by many workers and peasants. A protocol issued by a general meeting of workers of the Okulovsky Paper Factory and local peasants of Krestetsk Uzed in Novgorod Province on 21st May declaimed the workers and peasants,

> having listened to the reports of their delegates from the Petrograd Soviet of Workers' and Soldiers' Deputies on the issues of the moment, have issued the following resolution: Recognising the tremendous tasks lying before the ministers who are fighting for our freedom, Kerensky, Skobelev, Tseretelli, Chernov and Peshekonov, and comparing them with the difficulties advanced by anarchist elements at the present difficult time, they fervently welcome the coalition ministry that has been formed.

The protocol concluded with support for the "Democratic Russian Republic".[17]

The SRs held a special conference to consider its position

on joining the Provisional Government. Chernov told delegates that the removal of Miliukov and Guchkov fundamentally altered the political tempo of the government and the entry of socialists into its ranks would "strengthen and reinforce Russia's role as a basis for a 'third force', making its voice heard amidst the clash of international imperialisms". He finished:

> And finally, it is essential that the revolutionary army and navy are not in the hands of people from the old world, but of representatives of the socialist vanguard of the movement. These battle posts—labour, food supply, agriculture, and the army—should be occupied by people from the workers' socialist democracy.[18]

The conference strongly endorsed Chernov's position with few questioning what, aside from occupying them, socialist ministers intended to do with these battle posts.

Not all were as enthusiastic. Martov, still in exile, cabled to his Menshevik colleagues that he strongly disapproved of them joining the Provisional Government until it withdrew Russia from the war and agreed extensive land redistribution. He warned that until the government adopted the policies of the Soviet it would remain discredited and the Mensheviks would suffer politically from their inclusion within it. They already were. Notwithstanding SR support for the new ministry and dismissal of "anarchist elements" who criticised it, by late May the Soviets of Petrograd's engineering districts—Vyborg, Vasilievsky Island and Kolomna—had Bolshevik majorities. When Martov arrived in Petrograd he had a hard task to drag his party back to Marxist internationalism and a consistent socialism.

Vero Broido's definitive work on the fate of the Mensheviks under the Bolshevik regime concludes that at this time, in comparison to Menshevik leaders Tseretelli and Cheikedze, "the small group of anti-war Mensheviks led by Martov were more aware of the people's mood, but they had very little influence in the party". This meant a protracted internal struggle for the soul of the party during the critical summer months. This eventually resulted in "a significant shift to the left, which expressed itself in Martov's leadership".[19] But from May to October the Left Mensheviks led by Martov found themselves in open disagreement with their party leaders who sat on the Soviet Executive or held ministerial office in the Provisional Government.

The fate of the Mensheviks provides an example and a warning to reformist socialist parties who enter into coalition governments. The experience of the German and Irish green parties, both of whom have been junior partners in coalition governments in the last two decades, is instructive. The German Green Party (*Die Grünen*), influenced by 1960s radicals like Petra Kelly and Joschka Fischer, stood by its "Four Pillars": Social Justice, Ecology, Non-Violence and Grassroots Democracy. In 1982, in response to the party's move to the left and its support for LGBT rights, legalisation of drugs and direct action protest, more conservative ecologists left the party. In 1990, the Greens merged with the Alliance 90 (*Bündnis 90*) party of heterogeneous civil-rights activists, as a result of which they reached 8% of the vote and secured 49 seats. In 1998 they entered a "Red-Green" coalition government with the German SDP, with Fischer as Vice-Chancellor and Foreign Minister.

The results were mixed. On the one hand they were required to support German involvement in the NATO intervention in Kosovo in 1999 and support the invasion of Afghanistan in 2002, leading to some members resigning. On the other, they used their leverage with the SDP to achieve the phasing out and eventual termination of the country's nuclear power plants and cessation of civil nuclear power by 2020. Partly as a result of this, their positive environmental and social policies, and the tolerant manner in which they had dealt with internal dissent to their support of the coalition, the Greens secured 55 seats in the 2002 elections and again entered a Green-SDP coalition, the overall record of which (including opposition to the invasion of Iraq) was sufficiently positive that the Green vote in the following European elections significantly increased.

By contrast, the record of the Irish Green Party (*Comhaontas Glas*) in government was disastrous. After the General Election of 2007 the Greens formed a coalition government with the centre-right Fianna Fáil, despite securing almost none of the pre-conditions they established to do so. Unlike the German party, the Irish Greens compromised on virtually every key principle they had professed before 2007: opposition to a natural gas pipeline through Kilcommon in County Mayo, rerouting the M3 motorway away from the historic town of Tara, and refusal to be complicit in the CIA's use of Shannon Airport for rendition flights. The ultimate symbol of their capitulation was Green Energy Minister Eamon Ryan's approval of Shell

UK's Corib Gas Project to extract offshore natural gas. When the 2008 financial crash hit Ireland (whose economy rested on a bubble of credit and property speculation) the Greens mounted no defence of Irish public services or Irish workers. In the 2011 elections they reaped the whirlwind. Their vote collapsed to less than 2% and they lost all their seats in the national assembly. The Irish Green Party is now electorally irrelevant, its role as a radical voice to the left of Fine Gael taken by a resurgent, increasingly anti-capitalist Sinn Féin.

The fate of the Irish Greens is a more bathetic version of that which befell the Russian Mensheviks in 1917. They had been proactive in setting up the Petrograd Soviet but after entering the Government they faltered. Their social base, unlike the Bolsheviks', was not attuned to the revolutionary *milieu*. In E.H. Carr's analysis "the Mensheviks found their adherents amongst the most highly skilled and organised workers, the printers, the railwaymen and the steelworkers in the modern industrial centres of the south", whereas the Bolsheviks' more simplistic political message appealed to "the relatively unskilled labour of the mass industries – the old fashioned heavy industry of the Petersburg region and the textile factories of Petersburg and Moscow".[20] Bolshevik workers were of more recent peasant origin than were Mensheviks, who tended to be second- or third-generation working class and wedded to trade union discipline. Consciously or not, Mensheviks tended to accept the Provisional Government and underestimate the immense challenges it faced.

One of those challenges was the status of the territories within the Russian Empire. After February, was it still an

Empire at all? In March, the newly formed Rada (Central Council) of Ukraine in Kiev issued a statement of support for the Provisional Government which also called for the immediate convocation of a Constituent Assembly. It made clear that it expected the Assembly, when it met, to ratify the decrees of the Rada, which were likely to be those of an independent state. The Estonian national assembly did likewise. These demands reflected suspicion amongst the former national territories that the electoral base of the Constituent Assembly would provide it a built-in majority of Russians over any separate group of non-Russians. With minor variations the non-Russian territories wanted, as a minimum, internal autonomy within a federal structure. The Poles wanted outright independence. With Poland part-occupied by the German army, the Provisional Government had little choice but to support its call for independent statehood.

Finland and Ukraine pushed for the same. In June, the All-Russian Congress of Soviets called for the Provisional Government to negotiate a treaty of independence with Finland. The congress intended this to be done after the war but the Finnish parliament, in which socialists held 103 seats out of 200, interpreted it differently. On 23rd June it issued a unilateral declaration of independence. The Provisional Government, supported by the Soviet, threatened military invasion if the declaration was not withdrawn. This provided the Bolsheviks, who had many activists in the Baltic Fleet, part of which was permanently docked in the Finnish capital Helsinki, a further opportunity to undermine the Provisional Government. At the same time the Ukrainian Rada put a series of demands to the Provisional Government on devolved powers and cultural autonomy which the government rejected. This provoked the Rada into declaring a "First Universal" – a declaration calling for convocation of a parliament under the Ukrainian nationalist leader Vinnichenko.

The Provisional Government was thus faced with simultaneous declarations of independence from two strategically important regions at a time when it was trying to launch a major new offensive against the Germans. Panicked, it agreed to broadly recognise Ukrainian autonomy. Before any more could be done Lvov's coalition collapsed and was replaced by a "socialist" coalition under Kerensky. Its political colouration made no difference. Nationalists in all territories saw this government, in the words of a resolution passed by the Ukrainian Rada in August, as "imbued with the imperialist tendencies of the Russian bourgeoisie".

The Bolsheviks, who ostensibly supported the right of nations to self-determination, were left untouched by this. Yet Lenin carefully qualified that policy. He made clear that "the proletariat assesses any national demand, any national separation, from the angle of the workers' class struggle".[21] In theory this presented no difficulties, for he genuinely detested "Great-Russian chauvinism" and supported regional autonomy including complete freedom of language and culture. Lenin had taken a lead within the social-democratic movement in identifying revolutionary nationalism as an important component of anti-imperialism. His support for the Easter Rising of 1916, despite its nationalist-Catholic elements, showed a keener insight than many internationalists. But he always placed this in the context of the greater needs of a wider socialist revolution. He stated plainly that "Marxists are opposed to federation and decentralisation, for the simple reason that capitalism requires for its development the largest and most centralised possible states".[22]

This was not the view of Russian, Polish, Latvian or Ukrainian peasants. The peasants of 1917, once fully engaged and politically active, displayed a similar level of organised self-activity as the Zapatista rebellion in Mexico 85 years later. After the fall of the Tsar's government, peasant radicals took over the *Volost* agrarian committees set up by the Provisional Government to maintain order in the absence of the police and army. They then used them as vehicles to approve peasant seizures of landed estates. After February some landowners, anticipating the seizures, parceled up their holdings into smaller allotments to avoid expropriation. Some sold these to foreign owners or untraceable cartels. Others left their estates to grow fallow and then sold them to the more affluent *Kulaks*, i.e. richer peasants who bought up and combined small holdings and then employed poorer peasants to work them.

The *Kulaks* were a diffuse class, or subset of a class, whose social status was and remains a matter of enormous controversy. Some were simply peasants who made a profit from their smallholding and rose above their peers in the village. A few became large farmers and merchants, ceasing in the process to be peasants in any meaningful sense. It was these "rich Kulaks" who saw an opportunity in the decline of the landed gentry. As Trotsky put it in his *History*, "Kulak speculation and landlord trickery threatened to leave nothing of the public land by the time the Constituent

Assembly was convoked".[23]

The elemental desires of Russian peasants, who now seemed so close to achieving the vision of personal land ownership that had always animated them, were expressed by the "peasant poet" Pyotr Oreshin in his poem "A Flame of Gold Ablaze", printed in the SR newspaper *Delo Naroda* in May 1917[24]:

> A flame of gold ablaze
> The night-time sky lit bright
> Did we not for ages toil like slaves
> Bent before the Tsar's brute might?
>
> No freedom to us was given
> and land they would not yield
> like clockwork we were driven
> to a shameful blackened field

Oreshin, a self-educated itinerant worker-peasant and neo-populist, was inclined to the SRs but knew in his bones that the peasants would support anyone who promised them the land they craved. He would continue to advocate for peasant culture and peasant aspirations until his execution in 1938 in the Great Terror.

Peasant Soviets and temporary land communes now sprung up throughout the country, culminating in the First All-Russian Peasant Assembly on 4th-25th May, whose Executive was dominated by the SRs. Although supportive of land redistribution, SR leaders found themselves in a similar dilemma to the Mensheviks. With Chernov and Kerensky serving as ministers in Lvov's second coalition government, the SR party was obliged to support the government's slower approach to rural reform, i.e. to await the convocation of the Constituent Assembly (elections to which the SRs were likely to win) and then legislate for a new national settlement on land ownership. But the peasants were not waiting. Therefore, the SR-led Assembly sanctioned actions already underway, such as the Kazan Assembly's unilateral announcement that it authorised the transfer of all land in its region to local peasant committees.

Other regional assemblies followed suit. They expected SR support, but the party's leaders in government were not entirely free agents. Agriculture Minister Chernov drafted a governmental decree forbidding land sales, but the Trudovik Minister of Justice Pereverzev issued instructions to local authorities that land sales should not be prevented. Bolshevik policy on land redistribution was equally incoherent, and would remain so, but in the months before October, Lenin attempted to edge it towards endorsement of peasant land seizures. In theory, as good socialists, the Bolsheviks only supported *Volosts* who wished to pool their land into collective farms but Lenin—keen to attract peasant support for a revolutionary dictatorship of the proletariat and peasantry—produced a policy of support for land seizures as long as they were "organised".

John L.H. Keep's essential work on mass mobilization during 1917-18 concluded, "this ambiguous document gave activists *carte blanche* to commit every kind of excess, while deluding party leaders (Lenin included) as to the ease to which the agrarian movement could be directed into ideologically acceptable channels".[25] While this was useful in stoking a further stage of the revolution, in the long run it presented enormous obstacles to the centralised state socialism Lenin ultimately wished to introduce. When Lenin addressed the Assembly he was not as well received as SR leaders who had spoken for the peasants since 1901. But the Menshevik historian Sukhanov sensed that some poorer peasant delegates sympathised when he declared "If you wait until the law is written, and do not yourself develop revolutionary energy, you will get neither law nor land".[26]

The land seizures were the rural equivalent of the factory occupations convulsing Russian industry. In the same manner that the *Volosts* took unilateral action to redistribute large landed estates, the Factory Committees did not wait for authorisation by the Provisional Government or from the socialist parties. With the exception of the anarchists and some more imaginative socialists, the Russian left, while offering rhetorical support to the Factory Committees, regarded them with suspicion. On 23rd April Lenin wrote:

> Such measures as the nationalisation of the land and of the banks and syndicates of capitalists, or at least the immediate establishment of the control of the Soviets of Workers' Deputies over them (measures which do not in any way imply the 'introduction of socialism') must be absolutely insisted on and whenever possible introduced by revolutionary means.

However he made clear he saw this as a "prelude to nationalization".[27] Under fierce attack for his call in the April Theses to expand the revolution from a liberal–democratic phase to a socialist one, few noticed that his emphasis on state-led socialisation was more akin to an extreme version of Russian Fabianism than the decentralised workers' control advocated by the Factory Committees.

Like the "Recovered Factories" of Argentina in 2001-03, the Russian Factory Committees of 1917 arose from the failure of capitalist owners to discharge their responsibilities. In 2001 the neoliberal Argentinean economy collapsed, resulting in massive debt, fiscal austerity, cuts to public services and mass privatisation. With half the country driven below the poverty line the Argentine working class took to the streets, setting up roadblocks to commandeer food and fuel deliveries. On December 19th-20th, 2001 a popular insurrection brought down the government of President de la Rua and prevented the imposition of an IMF Structural Adjustment Programme.

From here grew the *Fabricas Recuperados* – the Recovered Factories – which saw about 200 Argentine companies occupied and run by their workforce as workers' cooperatives. Not all were factories – the most prominent examples being the Hotel Bauen in Buenos Aires and the transport company Transportes del Oeste. Initially, most worker takeovers were simply to ensure that owners could not liquidate assets before filing for bankruptcy to avoid paying back salaries and redundancy, but over time they grew from a tactic to safeguard jobs into a system of self-management.

The "taken" factories were not utopian havens. They had little capital. The technology left to them was usually second-rate. Their relationship with the public sector was unclear. Many occupied factories, such as Brukman and

Zanon, asked for nationalisation under workers' control, a formulation the government rejected on the same grounds that the post-October Bolshevik government would reject it, i.e. lack of central government control.

The occupied factories worked with their customers to generate capital by customers providing supplies to the factory, which then paid for the industrial processing. In return they produced cheaper products. Whilst not ideal, this allowed the cooperatives to survive. As they did so they began to create new work environments, bolstered by egalitarian income systems. Marina Kabat's study of the taken factories found "Not long ago, these workers occupied an isolated place in production, and had no chance to transmit their opinions, not even about their own specific jobs. Now they collectively decide about all aspects of production".[28]

Similar experiments in workers' self-management occurred, and are still occurring, in Venezuela as part of its "Bolivarian Revolution". After an employers' lock-out in 2002 – part of an illegal US-supported attempt to remove President Hugo Chavez – workers took over factories to keep them running. This led the government to legislate for "co-management" and to fund and support workers' cooperatives. The programme was more than an ad hoc response to crisis. It was an integral part of Chavez's programme to create a "communal state" and a "social economy" composed of self-governing institutions such as social enterprises, communal councils, and eventually communal cities. As Gregory Wilpert records in the most comprehensive study of the Chavez government's policies, "The role of the social economy and of endogenous development thus came to occupy centre-stage in the construction of an alternative to capitalism".[29]

Also known as the "Solidaristic Economy", the social economy promoted workers' self-management in a wide variety of cooperatives, micro-enterprises or publicly controlled factories, under a supportive economic architecture established by the government. In 2004 the foundations for a fundamentally different kind of economy began to be laid with the creation of the Ministry for Popular Economy. The ministry provided training, credit and logistical support to help this sector grow, so that by 2005 there were over 100,000 cooperative enterprises in Venezuela, industrial co-management and worker-managed factories, including Venezuela's main electricity company, and specially created Social Production Enterprises that re-invest profits back into the community. Social "missions" funded by the government from its oil revenue sought to eradicate poverty, illiteracy and ill health amongst the poor of the urban *barrios*. Mission About Face assisted the unemployed to start co-operatives and integrate them into the government's wider economic programme.

As a result, by 2007 around 8,000 people had been trained in building the Solidaristic Economy and 10,000 new cooperatives had been founded. In the same year, the government extended the economic programme to the building of 200 "Socialist Production Companies" (ESPs), staffed by and accountable to local democratic bodies. Their ultimate aim is to create non-market systems for the exchange of commodities. Although now subject to sustained right-wing attack, the ESPs and other elements of the Solidaristic Economy are an imaginative attempt to do more than simply talk about socialist transition whilst leaving it to the magical transformation of a future day, and instead to legislate and enable it to happen.

Argentinean and Venezuelan socialists drew lessons from Russia in 1917. On 2nd April, at an Exploratory Conference of Factory Committees of Petrograd War Industries, the delegates issued a proclamation, which read:

From the Factory Committee should emanate all instructions concerning internal factory organisation (i.e. instructions concerning such matters as hours of work, hiring and firing, holidays, etc.). The whole administrative personnel (management at all levels and technicians) is taken with the consent of the Factory Committee which has to notify the workers of its decisions at mass meetings of the whole factory or through shop committees.

From 30th May to 5th June, at the First Conference of Petrograd Factory Committees, different concepts of workers' control were debated. The conference represented 367 committees and 337,464 workers, about 80% of the workers of Petrograd. The final resolution of the conference, supported by 336 out of 421 delegates, proclaimed that Factory Committees were "fighting organisations, elected on the basis of the widest democracy and with a collective leadership". It called for "the organisation of thorough control by labour over production and distribution" and for "a proletarian majority in all institutions having executive power". The conference also called for a universal labour law, the creation of a workers' militia, an immediate end to the war and the transfer of all political power to the Soviets.[30]

Skobelev, the Menshevik Minister of Labour, who attended and addressed the conference, repeated the standard social-democratic view. He told delegates,

> Upon the individual class, especially the working class, lies the responsibility of helping the state in its organisational work [...] The Committees would best serve the workers' cause by becoming subordinate units in a state-wide network of trade unions.

Skobelev at least made clear where he differed from the Factory Committees. Lenin hid his differences behind militant rhetoric. Ostensibly supporting workers' control, he told the conference, "The majority of workers should enter all responsible institutions and the administration should render an account of its actions to the most authoritative workers' organisations". Nobody stopped to ask what kind of "administration" would exist separately from the Factory Committees, or if "the most authoritative workers' organisations" might be appendages of a political party with a monopoly of power.

The First Conference created a Central Council of Factory Committees for Petrograd. This consisted of nineteen Bolsheviks, two Mensheviks, two SRs, one anarcho-syndicalist and one Inter-Districter (a group of radical socialists who stood between the Bolsheviks and Mensheviks). The heavy preponderance of Bolsheviks indicates that since February they had successfully reoriented their approach to the Factory Committees so that workers now perceived them as the most inclined to support their aspirations (although in Siranni's estimation the Bolsheviks remained "ideologically inconsistent" about workers' control).

The Central Council's role was to enable fuel, machinery, raw materials and access to markets for the factories, ensure that workers had the financial and technical assistance required to fulfill their plans, and liaise with peasant committees outside Petrograd. It was the Council that channeled aid from the robust Putilov and Treugolnik Factory Committees to keep the endangered Brenner plant open, whilst both Soviet and government sat by. By June, similar Councils covered at least 25 cities and districts. Plans were afoot to set up an All-Russia Central Council of Factory Committees, which would coordinate national production within a federated democratic structure.

Perhaps the most politicised and energised group of workers were those of the Kronstadt naval base on Kotlin Island in the Gulf of Finland. During the revolutionary events of 1905 and February 1917, Kronstadt's Anchor Square, large enough to hold 25,000 people, functioned as an assembly point and debating chamber for the sailors. It was the base for what Manuel Castells calls "a free community in a symbolic place", something which ultimately becomes "a political space, a space for sovereign assemblies to meet and to recover their rights of representation, which have been captured in political institutions predominately tailored for the convenience of the dominant interests and values".[31] The Kronstadt Soviet's general meetings, held nearly every day between February and October 1917, were less like the Central Committee of the Bolshevik Party and much more like the General Assemblies of the polyglot anti-capitalist activists of Occupy Wall Street, so much so that Anchor Square and its vibrant democratic debating forum became known as a "free university" for the untutored worker-peasants of the Baltic Fleet.

The Kronstadt Soviet's political demands between February and October were not simply party slogans, and certainly not Bolshevik ones. Although it desired a "decisive rupture" with capitalism and a transfer of power to revolutionary workers and peasants, it also wanted a "democratic republic" and a broad socialist government. Reflecting the sailors' demands, independent socialists like Trotsky echoed the call for a radical socialist government. What that government might be or what exact form it might take was unclear. Although there was much debate on the Russian left about a future socialist government, no one in any faction or party advocated one-party rule.

Menshevik policy at the time was that the working class should establish a radical democracy with a freely elected Constituent Assembly, but not proceed beyond that or seek direct control of the production process. The Mensheviks' under-estimation and disregard of the Factory Committees deeply damaged their relationship with militant workers. In contrast, the Bolsheviks *appeared* to support workers' control. There were good reasons for Factory Committee militants to back the Bolsheviks in the escalating political crises that led to October. They could not foresee the future. Nonetheless, it was a massive mistake.

CHAPTER SEVEN

All Power to the Soviets

By the early summer of 1917, Lenin's new policies and slogans—"Peace, Bread and Land" and "All Power to the Soviets!"—began to attract the support of workers and soldiers who wanted economic justice and an immediate end to the war. Had the Provisional Government offered these things, they would have supported it. If it did not, they would support those who did offer them. These realignments came to a head in June at the 1st All-Russian Congress of Workers and Soldiers Deputies, a three-week-long gathering in Petrograd of elected delegates from Soviets across the country.

In the absence of a Constituent Assembly (whose delay in convocation was one of the main complaints of the radical left, including the Bolsheviks) the Congress was the first mass-based national democratic forum to convene since the overthrow of the Tsar. 820 delegates, representing Soviets of over 25,000 people, had a vote; 265 delegates, representing Soviets of between 10,000–25,000 people, had a right to speak but no vote. Delegates represented 305 local Soviets plus a wide variety of popular bodies, such as soldiers' organisations at the front, and some peasant bodies not attached to rural Soviets. Its electoral procedures were erratic but it was nevertheless a rough gauge of popular feeling in June 1917, mid-way between the February and October revolutions.

About 80% of delegates were from the broad democratic left, i.e. the Mensheviks, SRs and Trudoviks, with a substantial "left opposition" (mostly Bolsheviks and Left Mensheviks) sent from working-class heartlands such as the Putilov works and the Nevsky district. Although many had no specific party membership, being simply an active part of the great social upheaval, of 777 delegates who provided party affiliations 285 were SRs, 248 Mensheviks and 105 Bolsheviks.[1] The delegates elected a new 250-member Soviet Central Executive Committee, the overwhelming majority of whom were SRs and Mensheviks. In reality, though, the All-Russian Central Executive tended to be dominated and led by the Petrograd Executive. It had the fame and the glory and it sat in the capital. It was also much more inclined to the Bolsheviks than Soviets in provincial towns and cities.

At this stage the focus of debate was not the overthrow of the Provisional Government but how to shift it to the left. The foremost concern was the war. Kerensky, as Minister of War, had committed the Russian army to a new offensive against the Germans. Bedazzled by his own oratory, Kerensky had taken to touring the front in Napoleonic mode, exhorting the soldiers to one more glorious offensive to save the revolution. At the Soviet Congress Trotsky pointed out that whereas the army would not fight for outdated imperialist war aims, it might do so for more revolutionary ones. "What is the crux of the matter?" he asked the Congress:

> It is this. No such purpose that would rally the army exists
> now. Every thinking soldier asks himself: for every five drops
> of blood which I am going to shed today, will not one drop
> only be shed in the interest of the Russian Revolution, and four
> in the interests of the French Stock Exchange and of English
> Imperialism?[2]

Responding for the government, Tseretelli told the delegates, "In taking upon itself the fight for universal peace, the Russian Revolution has also to take over the war, begun by other governments". He tried to differentiate the war aims of the Provisional Government from those of its predecessorw but in doing so he could only assert, as if he himself were not a part of the government, "it must say clearly and emphatically that it has broken with the old imperialist policy, and must propose to the Allies that the first question in order of importance is to re-examine on a new basis all agreements made until now". Addressing the issue of making a separate peace, he told the congress, "The worst thing that could happen to us would be a separate peace. It would be ruinous for the Russian Revolution, ruinous for international democracy".

Tseretelli said such a peace would impel Russia to transfer allegiance from France and England to Germany, and it would thus end up fighting for German Imperialism. After promising that "the land question" would be settled by the Constituent Assembly in due course, Tseretelli finished by surveying the immense challenges faced by the Provisional

Government. He declared, "At the present moment there is not a single political party which would say 'Hand the power over to us, resign, and we will take your place'".[3] From the floor of the Congress Lenin interrupted that there was such a party – the Bolsheviks. Most delegates simply laughed at the presumption.

But the wind was changing. Support for the Bolsheviks grew as they opened their ranks, decentralised their operations and adapted their slogans and policies to attract peasant-soldiers as well as working-class militants. This began a process of what Trotsky called the "de-Bolshevisation" of Lenin's party. In January 1917 the Bolshevik Party had about 23,600 members. Such was the momentum of revolutionary change unleashed by February that by the time of the Bolshevik conference in April it had nearly 80,000. By August it would have somewhere between 200,000 and 240,000 (estimates vary), with 41,000 members in Petrograd alone and 50,000 in the Moscow region.[4]

The rapid increase in membership reflected what Marcel Liebman called a "metamorphosis" of the Bolshevik Party, so much so that the party that carried out the successful October Revolution and had a genuine claim – for a brief time at least – to speak for most of the Russian proletariat, had very little in common with the centralised party of professional revolutionaries created by Lenin in 1903. Liebman's conclusion is that in 1917 the party "opened itself to the life-giving breeze of democracy", and as result of its transformation it was "dubious, even false, to identify without qualification the party of the revolution, the party that 'made' the October Revolution, with the party that prepared the way for it under the Tsarist regime".[5]

This was a new Bolshevik Party with a new constituency. It was the vital factor that anti-Bolshevik socialists failed to appreciate. Even Martov, more attuned to the shift in popular feeling since the fall of the Tsar, confined himself to working inside the Menshevik Party and the trade unions. As his sympathetic biographer Israel Getzler concedes:

> Whilst Martov and the Menshevik-internationalists were busy arguing with fellow intellectuals, trying to convert a party whose mass support was dwindling away at frightening speed, the Bolshevik leaders and activists by-passed the intellectuals, to the point of dropping even their Marxist jargon, in an all-out effort to pander to the primitive needs, class instincts and hatreds of the masses and to win them over to their side.[6]

That effort was increasingly successful, aided by a growing network of factory and army committees, rural and urban Soviets, and newly formed "Red Guard" civil militias.

Martov now watched appalled as old comrades like Tseretelli and Dan supported the government's deportation from Russia of the Swiss socialist Robert Grimm, with whom Martov had organised the Zimmerwald Conference. Grimm had continued his efforts for peace by forwarding a German peace offer to the new Russian government. The government refused to entertain it and deported Grimm as a "German agent". Kerensky then launched the offensive with an appeal to Russian forces to strike at the Germans on the Southwestern Front. For the first time the Central Executive of the Soviets came out in support of continuation of the war. In a blistering speech, Martov told the Soviet, "In this offensive we discern clearly the face of world imperialism and therefore refuse to lend support to it. We re-iterate our old slogan—'Down with the War; Long Live the International!'"[7]

When the new commander of the Russian army, General Brusilov, assumed command he spoke to many rank-and-file soldiers and asked them what they wanted. Almost without exception they replied "Land and Freedom". As Orlando Figes records, "It was more a case of tired and angry soldiers picking up the slogans of the Bolshevik press and using them to legitimise their own growing resistance to the war" than a specific desire for socialist revolution.[8] As the time approached for the resumption of hostilities many troops refused to advance to the front. After a two-day bombardment beginning on 16th June, Russian troops advanced for two or three days over shattered German lines but as soon as the Germans rallied the advance collapsed. Many soldiers simply fled and set up camps behind the lines, living as bandits. Tens of thousands of lives and millions of square miles of Russian territory were lost in days.

On 3rd July Lvov resigned as Prime Minister. The Kadets were now veering to the right and staking all on defence of the landowners. They accused the Menshevik and SR ministers in the Cabinet of serving the interests of militant workers, and citied Agriculture Minister Chernov's attempts to facilitate land redistribution as an overt attack on the landed nobility. Lvov considered Chernov's policy "nothing less than a Bolshevik programme of organised confiscation". Had it not derived from a Provisional Government still wedded to the war, it would have received more acknowledgment from the socialist left (and socialist historians) than it has. For Lvov it was the final straw. "I have reached the end of the road", he told his secretary, "and so, I am afraid, has my sort of liberalism".[9] He was replaced by Kerensky. In theory the SRs now controlled the government, yet its political complexion still leaned towards the Kadets and the SR Prime Minister was an ambitious, opportunistic newcomer to their ranks.

The military command now ordered up regiments that had remained in the capital, such as the Bolshevik-dominated 1st Machine Gun Regiment and 176th Reserve Regiment. The 1st Machine Gun Regiment was well armed and its barracks in the Vyborg district provided easy access to workers at Putilov and sailors at Kronstadt. On 3rd July, as Lvov tendered his resignation in despair, it refused to mobilise for the front. It joined with workers in Vyborg to demand the Petrograd Soviet remove the government and assume power itself. Many felt at the time that the Bolsheviks were orchestrating this activity, but the "July Days" appear to have caught the Bolsheviks by surprise. Lenin had gone to Finland for a brief recuperation from fatigue. Trotsky was inside the Soviet at the Tauride Palace and did not know about the demonstration (although at that point he was not yet technically a Bolshevik). By the next day the mass demonstration had grown to nearly 50,000 angry soldiers, sailors and workers. The existence of the Provisional Government now hung by a thread.

The Bolshevik Central Committee was torn about how far to take the demonstrations. After much debate it decided, still without Lenin, to back what looked like a final uprising against the government, especially once it was confirmed that the Kronstadt sailors had left their base and set out for the city. But when other reports arrived of fighting taking place throughout the city and of a vigorous fight back by pro-government forces, it backtracked and tried to call the demonstration off. *Pravda*, given no clear line, appeared with a blank front page. Confused and disappointed, the demonstrators marched to Bolshevik HQ at the Kheshinskaya Mansion, to which Lenin hurriedly returned.

This was the moment when Lenin could have assumed command of a huge revolutionary force and directed it to his ends. For once he was not issuing commands to others through letters and pamphlets. He was physically present and in the line of fire. If he ordered the arrest of the Provisional Government or the Soviet Executive and it failed to come off, he would be arrested and shot. It was a defining moment, "one of the few in his long career when he was faced with the task of leading a revolutionary crowd that was standing before him".[10] But after a few mumbled words about the eventual victory of Soviet power, the man who wrote in loving detail in letters to party cadres about physical attacks on policemen and the need for attacking banks left the balcony, leaving it to Lunarcharsky to take charge. Lunacharsky, a "moderate" Bolshevik, literary critic and essayist, told the crowd to march to the Tauride Palace and demand the Soviet assume power. He then put himself at the front of the procession.

Twenty thousand armed sailors and workers arrived at the Tauride, led by the Kronstadt Bolshevik leader Raskolnikov. They demanded that the leaders of the Soviet come out and justify their actions, specifically their support for a Provisional Government that was willing to send them to die in a war they had thought was over. Chernov came out to address them, perhaps expecting that as the SR Minister who had defended the rights of rural Soviets to seize landed estates he might be well received. He was wrong. He was surrounded by angry sailors, one of whom yelled in his face, "Take power you son-of-a-bitch, when its given to you!"

After a few minutes in which he tried to justify the Soviet's actions he was brusquely manhandled into a car and put under armed arrest. The mood turned ugly and for a while it looked as if Chernov might be summarily executed. Only a physically brave intervention by Trotsky, diving into the middle of the Kronstadt sailors and assuring them that this was not the time and place for such activity, secured his release. Trotsky escorted Chernov back inside and the mood of the crowd began to calm down.

The only guidance Raskolnikov received from Bolshevik HQ was to proceed as he thought fit, which placed the entire responsibility of the future of the revolution on the shoulders of a young Bolshevik naval ensign. Taking his cue from Trotsky's actions Raskolnikov dispersed the sailors with vague promises of future action. The "July Days" then dribbled out as different waves of Bolshevik supporters—the Putilov workers and the 176th Reserve Regiment—arrived at different times and failed to take decisive action. The Putilov workers actually stormed inside the Tauride only to be told to leave, which they did. And the 176th Regiment, arriving last and unsure what to do, was ordered by Menshevik leader Theodore Dan to guard the building, which it did.

The picture in the rest of the country was equally chaotic. In Moscow the Bolsheviks discussed launching an insurrection but after a few street rallies called it off. In cities where local Soviets were already under the control of the Bolsheviks, such as Ivanovo-Voznesensk, they teetered on the brink of decisive action but once news came of the collapse in Petrograd they retreated. In Riga and Ekaterinburg local Soviets adopted resolutions calling for a purely Soviet-led government but refrained from further action until sure it had succeeded in Petrograd. These quiverings of possible insurrection subsided once the surge in Petrograd fell back. With the immediate threat passed, the Provisional Government, now with the open support of Soviet leaders Tseretelli and Dan, moved to arrest leading Bolsheviks whom they believed had planned to overthrow the government and the Soviet Executive. On 6th July armed troops loyal to the Provisional Government surrounded the Khesinskaya Mansion and moved in, arresting many Bolshevik leaders and clearing the building. Lenin and Zinoviev had already fled to Finland.

The moderate socialists in the Soviet Executive had now made clear that they had no desire to "take power". As they saw it they already *had* power through their working alliance with the Menshevik and SR Ministers in Kerensky's government. The leading dissenter from this line within the Menshevik Party was Martov. Faced with the Soviet Executive supporting the continuation of an imperialist war and throwing Bolsheviks in the Peter and Paul Fortress, he put aside his reluctance for socialists to assume governmental power.

It was now clear that the Russian bourgeoisie had no wish to carry out a radical revolution. Martov therefore called for a new, exclusively socialist government based on the Soviets. At a Menshevik congress he demanded such a government begin immediate peace negotiations while renouncing annexations and democratising the army; prepare for a Constituent Assembly to begin agrarian reform "on the basis of the confiscation and handing over to the people of all land belonging to Crown, monasteries, and landowners"; introduce financial reforms and progressive taxation on property; and implement a "planned redistribution of productive forces" by way of nationalisation of the pillars of the economy.

This was a clear departure from the policy of socialist abstention from power in the "bourgeois revolution". For the first time it offered a programme that could be agreed by Menshevik-Internationalists, the SRs and most Bolsheviks. Tsereteli responded to it head on, replying, "Should we, the Soviet majority, take power into our hands, would not then all of you, from Martov to Lenin, demand of us actions which, in our opinion, would lead to a separate war, and would you not want to foist upon us your slogan 'no offensive but an armistice'? But such policies are unacceptable to us".[11] Martov, disgusted, refused to support the arrest warrant issued for Lenin. He grew increasingly alienated from Tsereteli and Dan, and in August sent fraternal greetings to the Bolshevik Party's 6th Congress. Once again, as in August 1914 and at Zimmerwald, Lenin and Martov inched closer to an alliance. But it was not to be.

Instead, the alliance cemented during the summer months was between Lenin and Trotsky. In the months leading up to October 1917, the two men discovered they shared a common vision. Almost unnoticed in the RSDLP's fratricidal strife of 1905-14, Trotsky and the Marxist theorist Alexander Parvus had produced an ingenious theory that would perfectly compliment Lenin's April Theses, a theory that was a radical departure from the entire theoretical paradigm of Russian Social Democracy. What came to be known as the theory of Permanent Revolution arose from Trotsky's experience in the 1905 Revolution, after which he concluded that the relatively small Russian working class must take the leading role in whatever revolutionary process grew out of the collapse of the autocracy. From this he and Parvus created a justification for socialist revolution in economically and socially backward countries that turned Marxism on its head.

The core of Marx's and Engels' conception of socialist revolution was that it would be carried out by a "mature" proletariat. Because of its position within the capitalist system – exploited yet indispensable – the working class would inevitably shake off the fetters of that system and take command of it for the common good. This flattered socialists in Germany, France and America, but it offered little to Marxists in Russia who were compelled to accept a secondary role in the forthcoming world revolution. Yet Russia, not America, had experienced revolution in 1905. In *Results and Prospects* (1907), Trotsky fleshed out a new theory of how anti-capitalist revolution might arise. Impatient with the caution of official Social Democracy, he wrote:

In spite of the fact that the productive forces of the United States are ten times as great as those of Russia, nevertheless the political role of the Russian Proletariat, its influence on the

politics of its own country and the possibility of its influencing
the politics of the world in the future, are incomparably greater
than those of the proletariat of the United States.[12]

Subsequent events proved him right.

When first published, the theory of Permanent
Revolution was derided by the great seers of European
Social Democracy, including Lenin. Yet in 1917, without
overt acknowledgement, he would in all essentials adopt it.
For what was the April Theses if not a programmatic version
of Permanent Revolution? Certainly Trotsky saw it as such
and upon his return to Russia he struggled to find reasons
not to join the Bolsheviks, finally doing so in July 1917 after
the July Days demonstrated to him that only Lenin saw
the need to expand beyond the Provisional Government
to the Dictatorship of the Proletariat. In return Lenin, as
he had in 1905, "again detached himself from the clear and
simple notion of the two revolutions, bourgeois and socialist,
profoundly distinct from one another, with only the former
a matter for the present moment".[13]

With Trotsky joining the Bolsheviks, Lenin secured as one
of his principal lieutenants a Marxist agitator of incomparable
intellectual and organisational gifts, a tornado of revolutionary
energy who eclipsed veteran Bolsheviks like Zinoviev and
Kamenev. Both of these would gladly have formed alliances
with Left Mensheviks like Martov in the broad-based socialist
government the latter was now calling for. Trotsky, until
recently a Menshevik Internationalist and close collaborator
of Martov, would never have done this. As he later put it
in his history of 1917, "The relation of class forces is not a

mathematical quantity permitting *a priori* computations. When the old regime is thrown out of equilibrium, a new correlation of forces can be established only as a result of a trial by battle. That is revolution".[14]

For Lenin the trial by battle had arrived. But what was it for? Whilst in hiding in Finland during August and September he wrote what remained his only attempt to describe the kind of socialist society he envisaged *after* the revolution. The result, *The State and Revolution*, is his most utopian and problematic work. In the words of a conservative yet astute biographer, "no work could be more un-representative of its author's political philosophy and general frame of mind than this one by Lenin".[15] This has not prevented Leninist theorists devoting much effort to analysing *The State and Revolution* to discover what it implies for Lenin's conception of socialism before October 1917, even though the state socialism the Bolsheviks constructed after October 1917 was its polar opposite. In reality, *The State and Revolution* has as much relation to Leninist practice as Ayn Rand's heroic vision of individualistic free enterprise has to the corporate state capitalism of Reagan and Bush.

The basic argument of *The State and Revolution* is that a socialist society cannot be reached via gradualist parliamentary methods, such as those practiced by the German SPD or British Labour Party. Lenin leant heavily on citations from Marx and Engels in which they argued the bourgeois capitalist state was a simple instrument of class rule and as such could not be "taken over" by those hostile to that rule and used for other purposes. It had to be "smashed" and another form of state built upon its ruins. It would, like the 1871 Paris Commune, be directly linked to the working masses. It would be based on regular election and recall, endlessly replenished by popular participation and not formed of a permanent class of civil servants and "experts" who were themselves an adjunct of the ruling class.

In *Anti-Duhring* (1877), Engels suggested that once the conditions for socialist production were achieved there would be less and less need for the existence of any kind of state machine. In his words:

> The first act in which the state really comes forward as the representative of the whole of society—the taking possession of the means of production in the name of society—is at the same time its last independent act as a state. The interference of the state power in social relations becomes superfluous in one sphere after another, and then dies away of itself. The government of persons is replaced by the administration of things and the direction of the processes of production. The state is not "abolished", it *withers away*.[16]

The "withering away of the state" was a beguiling vision, although Engels was vague about the transition period. Lenin condemned any notion that the "withering away" might be a cumulative process, "a vague notion of a slow, even gradual change, of absence of leaps and storms, of absence of revolution". This reflected the revolutionary voluntarism of his *Philosophical Notebooks* and underpinned his conclusion that "the suppression of the bourgeois state by the proletarian state is impossible without a violent revolution".[17] Even in 1917 this argument was simplistic. The mid-19th-century state with which Marx and Engels were familiar was a much smaller and less complex entity than it would later become, and fulfilled far fewer functions (primarily revenue collection and military action). The modern state, although used in a variety of ways to safeguard ruling-class interests, is not simply and solely, as Lenin put it, "a product and manifestation of the irreconcilability of class contradictions".

For Lenin, the state "consists of special bodies of armed men having prisons, etc., at their command". But whilst this was a major aspect of what the state was, it was not *all* it was. Lenin's world-view had been shaped by a one-dimensional experience of government and a curious lack of engagement with the politics of Western Europe. Although clearly "bourgeois", the states of Western Europe were expanding and diversifying to include a range of civic and social obligations not integral to ruling-class interests, such as a basic form of primary and higher education, health and old-age insurance, conservation and environmental legislation, expanded suffrage, and some employment protections. The British 1906 Trade Disputes Act, which protected trade unions from losses incurred as a result of industrial action, was one such example.

These obligations and social services were not conceded out of kindness. Fierce social and industrial struggles had compelled bourgeois states to begin regulation of elements of capitalist society hitherto untouched. Marxists like Lenin considered these concessions bribes to buy off a "labour aristocracy". Bribes or not the effect was the same—a lessening of the distance between the state and ordinary people and an expectation that they could influence and occasionally direct it. "Smashing" it so that something unknown and untested could replace it, something that would itself wither away in due course, seemed a dangerous fantasy.

Lenin's faith in the ability of ordinary workers, regardless of their education or skills, to immediately take over every aspect of a technologically advanced capitalist economy was, as E.H. Carr wrote, "utopian to the point of naivety".[18] Lenin argued that, "given the economic prerequisites"–which he saw as universal literacy and the "training and disciplining of millions of workers by the huge, complex, socialised apparatus of the postal service, railways, big factories, large scale commerce, banking, etc."–then it should be "quite possible, after the overthrow of the capitalists and the bureaucrats, to proceed immediately, overnight, to replace them in the control of production in the work of keeping account of labour and products, by the armed workers, by the universally armed workers".[19] In later years, as Chair of Sovnarcom (the Soviet government), he would ignore the vision of *The State and Revolution* and insist on the need for well-paid bourgeois specialists to make the economy run efficiently.

Lenin put so much effort into preparing for revolution that he neglected to plan for its aftermath. Of the great theorists of the Second International only Bebel had sketched what a post-revolution society might look like. Of the reformists only the British Fabians and the Swedish Social Democrats had done serious policy planning, which in Sweden led in the 1930s to the introduction of extensive jobs and housing programmes, maternity benefits, index-linked pensions and paid holidays. These were underpinned by the radical economic policies of Knut Wicksell's Stockholm School, early

Keynesians who advocated investment and reflation to attack unemployment and rebuild the economy. In comparison, British Labour leaders like Ramsay MacDonald believed that socialism would arise organically from "the well-defined processes which the living social organisation allows".

MacDonald's *Socialism: Critical and Constructive* (1921), written three years before he became the first Labour Prime Minister, was an eloquent critique of capitalist inefficiency and irrationality. Although he criticised both Marxism and syndicalism, he concluded that "Labour and capital cannot be reconciled within the capitalist system". But his proposals to supersede capitalism were undefined. "Society itself", he wrote, "is steadily stepping in and is gaining authority over itself by controlling the material powers and organisation of Capitalism".[20] Not surprisingly, when confronted in 1931 by an economic crisis stoked by powerful elements of that society (the City and New York banks, who offered rescue loans on the condition of massive cuts to social spending), MacDonald and his allies wilted like dead flowers.

Although motivated by an entirely different vision of socialism, Lenin's unpreparedness for power was of the same order as MacDonald's. While far too many of today's left exhibit the same unpreparedness and lack of interest in the specifics of a post-capitalist economy, some have taken up the challenge and proposed models for a non-capitalist world. One of the most interesting is Michael Albert's model of Participatory Economics, or "Parecon". Parecon is a vision of a decentralised, non-market economic system based on the common ownership of the means of production, in which participatory decision-making at all levels allocates resources in different enterprises and organisations to achieve communally determined ends.

The basic model constructed by Albert has three defining characteristics: participatory decision-making, or self-management, of all aspects of social and economic life; "Balanced Job Complexes" designed to produce an equitable division of labour, so that all individuals enjoy a broadly equal level of empowerment within the work environment; and compensation for effort and sacrifice, i.e. more compensation for unpleasant and demanding work as against work that is less so (although with many exemptions for disability, carers, etc. who would be remunerated according to need). The requirement to perform socially useful work would, in a Parecon, occur in the context of a society providing free healthcare, education, training etc., and the freedom to choose between jobs in democratically structured workplaces.

Albert's work on Parecon was original enough to win the 2004 award from the International Scientific Committee of the prestigious Pio Manzu Centre. In his statement accompanying the award, Pio Manzu's President, Mikhail Gorbachev, said that Parecon "constitutes the most powerful and fully articulated challenge to the current models of socio-economic thought, and Albert's outstanding merit is that he has indicated a major new highway in economic organisation as a feasible proposition". But whilst Parecon suggests the kinds of economic governance possible in a post-capitalist world, it is not without serious flaws. Its refusal to countenance *any* role for the market is problematic. It is hard to see how its plan for deciding exactly how many goods need to be produced in any forthcoming year – down to numbers of shoes and socks — would not become a cumbersome bureaucratic exercise, no matter how participatory or how sophisticated its computer modeling.

Parecon's great virtue is in *offering* a model, even if it is too prescriptive, and identifying the pernicious effect of what Albert calls the "coordinator class" — i.e. workers (senior managers, highly educated specialists, etc.) who enjoy empowering roles and conditions and enforce their will on workers with disempowered roles. In Albert's view, this coordinator class has the potential, in particular circumstances, to become a new ruling elite, much like the elite that emerged after the October 1917 Revolution under the direction of the Bolshevik Party. For Albert, "Marxism's economic goals amounted to advocating a coordinator mode of production that elevated administrators, intellectual workers and planners to ruling status".[21] For this reason he insisted on the need for Balanced Job Complexes in any democratically controlled economy.

The values of Parecon have been better expressed by others, notably Murray Bookchin's advocacy of confederated municipal democracy as a means to achieve his vision of Social Ecology. Bookchin's work, criminally overlooked in his day, has had a direct influence in the Western Kurdistan region of liberated Syria known as Rojava. Here the Kurds fight an unregarded battle to establish what Derek Wall called "a practical example of an anti-capitalist, ecological and feminist alternative".[22]

After reading Bookchin's works in prison, the Kurdish leader Abdullah Ocalan moved away from Marxism-Leninism, and persuaded his forces to do likewise. The Rojava autonomous region was built from the bottom up by the Kurds themselves, and aims at community self-management, gender equality and ecological sustainability. The governing Supreme Council is made up of representatives of the Democratic Union Party and the Kurdish National Council, whose political ideology is a mixture of communalism and social ecology. The Council oversees external and military affairs while the Community Defence Force (YPG) defends the region from both the Syrian Army and ISIS. The YPG is a non-sexist armed militia force made up of male and female volunteers, and includes a special unit made up of women only who deal with issues of rape and domestic violence.

The governance programme for Rojava rests on elected Neighborhood Assemblies that include Christians, Muslims and Yazidis. Although private property is protected by law, the ultimate aim is to replace capitalism with a form of democratic confederalism. Its economic model is a smaller version of the Chavez/Maduro Venezuelan government's plans for a "Solidaristic Economy", operating to values of solidarity and sustainability, and delivered by social enterprises, cooperatives, communes and collectives. In Rojava about three quarters of all property is held in community ownership and a third of the region's economic production is carried out by the direct management of workers' councils. The price of basic goods such as food and medical supplies are set by sub-committees of the Neighborhood Assemblies.

Like Parecon, but less all-encompassing, the committees plan public production of staples such as wheat that underpin the broader economy. The society being established in Rojava has far more in common with the ideas of the post-October

1917 "Council Communists" than with the top-down, centralised system introduced by the Bolsheviks. Western capitalist powers that are happy to oppose ISIS with bombs ignore an already existing democratic, secular, libertarian socialist state in the north of Syria that is a genuine alternative to both Islamic fundamentalism and Baath Party fascism.

The European radical left—although its policies have not yet been realised in practice in the same manner as in Rojava, the Zaptatista liberated zones or Venezuela's Solidaristic Economy—is beginning to explore bridgeheads to a post-capitalist society. As well as analysing the abject failure of the neoliberal economic model in Britain, Jeremy Corbyn's Director of Policy Andrew Fisher, in *The Failed Experiment* (2014), offered concrete proposals for a different kind of economy. These ranged from public ownership of a new type (focused more on housing, renewable energy and transport infrastructure than outdated industries with a high carbon footprint); a Land Value Tax; publicly owned banks leading a systematic attack on tax evasion and tax havens; effective capital controls including a Financial Transaction Tax; a legal right for workers to buy out firms and, with government assistance and generous terms, to establish workers' cooperatives; a basic Citizens Income to alter the relation of workers to work; and the use of new technology to reduce the working week without loss of pay or benefits.[23]

None of this kind of thinking occurred within the Bolshevik Party in the pre-revolution years. Not one leading Bolshevik, not even Bukharin who was more open to heterodox ideas, wrote about workers' control or self-management of the economy in a post-revolution society. Nor did they have feasible plans to nationalise and run banks and utilities. Despite the complete absence of a practical programme for democratic government, alternative institutions and participatory planning—i.e. for the actual implementation of a socialist economic model—Lenin pushed on. At difficult and uncertain moments he was fond of quoting Napoleon's maxim, "*On s'engage et puis, on voit*" ("First engage in battle, then see"). The Bolsheviks were about to engage in battle. Then they would see.

CHAPTER EIGHT
October 1917

In July 1917, Kerensky replaced the honest soldier Brusilov as head of the Russian army with the vainglorious and insubordinate General Kornilov. Kornilov, in close touch with Octobrists and Monarchists who wished to overthrow the Provisional Government, saw himself as the "man on a white horse" who would, like Napoleon, rescue his homeland from the chaos of revolution. Behind the General stood the "Society for the Economic Recovery of Russia" run by the great industrialist A.I. Putilov and composed of representatives of large banks and insurance companies. It included Guchkov, Minister of War in Lvov's first coalition; N.N. Kutler, President of the Urals Mining Company; and representatives of the Russian-Asiatic and Azov-Don Banks.

At first, helped by a secret subscription of four million rubles, the Society tried to influence and direct political events covertly but, in the summary of Marc Ferro, it soon became clear that "There would have to be a military dictatorship. Kornilov was the obvious choice". Kornilov himself was tutored in his duties by his political advisor V.S

Zavoysko, a member of both the Cabinet and the Society, and a Director of the Russian-Asiatic Bank. The Society worked in close alliance with ultra-right groups such as the sinister Republican Centre with its motto "Order, Discipline, Victory".[1]

In August, Kerensky invited Kornilov to address a "State Conference" in Petrograd of delegates from all political parties, employers' federations and trade unions (the Bolsheviks boycotted it and there was general strike in the city that day in protest). This raised his political prestige and encouraged those on the right who wished to see a military dictatorship with Kornilov as its puppet ruler. Kerensky walked straight into this conspiracy when he issued orders to Kornilov that capital punishment in the army, abolished in February, be reinstated, and that troops loyal to the government be dispatched to Petrograd. Kornilov misunderstood what was being requested (messages between Kerensky and Kornilov relayed by a third party appear to have been garbled) and the General responded by "accepting" what he thought was an offer to become the temporary dictator of Russia, with Kerensky standing down to serve in an Octobrist-Kadet cabinet. When Kerensky heard this he panicked and ordered Kornilov to resign and return immediately to the capital.

At this point Kornilov, urged on by the Society and reactionaries at Army HQ, began to plan a military coup. After informing his soldiers that the Bolsheviks were attempting an insurrection he ordered the Savage Division to advance on the capital and to depose the Soviet. No sooner was this known than the Soviet formed a "Committee of Struggle against Counter-Revolution", composed of three representatives each from the Mensheviks, Bolsheviks and SRs. Similar committees sprung up throughout the northern region of European Russia. The most active elements were the Bolsheviks, whose Red Guards were armed, organised and ready to defend the capital. The Kronstadt sailors again crossed the Gulf of Finland to Petrograd, this time at the request of the Soviet that they defend it from attack.

With the defence secure the Committee of Struggle sent out agitators to talk to soldiers closing in on the city. In the meantime, the militant All-Russian Union of Railwaymen blocked railway tracks and sent carriages with Kornilov's troops off in different directions. This gave time for Red Guards to reach the foot soldiers and to explain that they had been lied to and there was no Bolshevik coup. The Savage Division disintegrated, some refusing to advance and some simply deserting. When Kornilov realised that his power play had failed he resigned from his post and was arrested. Not one shot had been fired.

Militant workers, mostly Bolshevik, had saved Kerensky's government, and he had little choice but to quietly release the jailed Bolshevik leaders. In the wake of the failed military coup a wave of reprisals against the officer corps swept the army and navy, with officers in many cities arrested. According to the Bolshevik militant Podvoysky:

As a result of the Kornilov revolt the propaganda of the military organisation and pro-Bolshevik soldiers, which had been temporarily quelled after the July reaction, now spread with renewed energy among the troops and found a most receptive audience in the nervously exhausted mass of soldiers who refused to wait, who would not consider anything or listen to anyone.[2]

At Kronstadt three generals and a colonel, arrested on the orders of the Soviet Executive, were dragged to the bridge of one of the ships, thrown off, and gunned down in the water. In all eleven officers were murdered at the naval base. At the height of the drama one of the Kronstadt sailors asked Trotsky if now was not the time to press on and depose Kerensky. He replied, "No, not yet. Use Kerensky as a gun-rest to shoot Kornilov. Afterward we will settle with Kerensky".[3]

In one stroke the Kornilov "coup" reversed the fortunes of the Bolsheviks and fatally weakened the Provisional Government and its supporters in the Soviet Executive. Suspecting (rightly) that Kerensky had originally intended to use Kornilov against the Soviet, a plan which then backfired, socialist ministers such as Skobelev, Tseretelli and Chernov had no choice but to resign from the government. They were replaced by lesser figures in their parties. This was fatal. In refusing to distance themselves completely from Kerensky, the Mensheviks and SRs lost all credibility with most of the workers in the cities. In the words of Trotsky, the attempted coup "created an abrupt shift in the situation in our favour", although even before the Kornilov affair the Bolsheviks had already won majorities in the Soviets of Kronstadt, Ekaterinburg, Tsaritsyn, Samara and Ivanovo-Voznesensk.

On 31st August the Petrograd Soviet for the first time passed a Bolshevik resolution, by 279 votes to 115. The resolution demanded a government be formed from "the revolutionary proletariat and peasantry", and that this be accompanied by immediate peace negotiations, workers' control of industry and the complete confiscation of the remaining large landed estates. A few days later, on 5th September, the entire Menshevik–SR Executive resigned. The newly elected Executive had a Bolshevik majority with Trotsky as Chair. A resolution from workers at the Petrograd Admiralty yards summed up the new atmosphere. It explicitly condemned the coalition government as "a government of bourgeois–landlord dictatorship" with a policy of "ruinous compromise with the propertied classes".[4] The effect on the Bolshevik Party was electric. Membership of its Petrograd branch alone jumped from 16,000 in April to 43,000 in October. Many of the new recruits were disillusioned Mensheviks and SRs.

Kerensky knew that his government, never having been elected, lacked legitimacy. In the absence of a properly elected Constituent Assembly, elections to which the government had postponed to November because of the immense logistical difficulties involved, he proposed a "Democratic Conference" of all left parties, cooperative bodies and Zemstvos to appoint a Provisional Council or "Pre-Parliament". The Pre-Parliament would, in theory, command wide-spread support on the left, thus stabilising the government until the elections to the Constituent Assembly. Lenin sensed the danger of this plan and urged that the Bolsheviks boycott the conference. Other Bolsheviks, primarily Lenin's senior lieutenant Lev Kamenev, disagreed. Kamenev wished for the Bolsheviks to attend the Democratic Conference and then to act as a radical left opposition in the Pre-Parliament in alliance with Martov and the Left Mensheviks. Lenin, still in hiding in the Finnish capital Helsinki, sent fierce letters to the Bolshevik Central Committee urging an immediate insurrection against a weakened Provisional Government.

Dogged by Lenin's accusations that those who wished to work with the Democratic Conference were "unprincipled", the Central Committee gave Trotsky permission to attend the conference as long as he did so solely to denounce Kerensky and announce that the Bolsheviks would have nothing to do with the Pre-Parliament. Lenin and Trotsky quickly divined that (as Trotsky later put it), "the struggle for our participation in the Pre-Parliament was the struggle for the 'Europeanization' of the working class movement, for directing it as quickly as possible into the channel of a democratic struggle for power, i.e. into the channel of social democracy".[5] The Democratic Conference went ahead but it did not have the effect Kerensky had hoped for.

By the end of September, the government was on its last legs. More landed estates were being seized by the peasants. The supply of food to the cities began to break down. Militarily the Germans threatened Petrograd itself, with the German navy roaming freely in the Gulf of Finland, while conservatives like former Duma President Rodzianko admitted they would "rejoice" if the German army took Petrograd and "restored order".

The Pre-Parliament was the last spasm of constitutional politics in 1917. With its failure the Bolsheviks moved towards an armed insurrection against the Provisional Government, the first and most important step of which was the creation by the Petrograd Soviet Executive on 9th October of a

"Military Revolutionary Committee" (MRC). The MRC was formed ostensibly to coordinate the defence of the city against German attack, but in reality it would be the organisational centre of the October Insurrection. The key to its success was that it did this in the name of the Soviet, not the Bolshevik Party.

The responsibilities of the MRC, granted by the Soviet, were to establish how many troops were needed to defend Petrograd and ensure manpower and munitions were available; to coordinate the efforts of the Baltic Fleet, the Finnish garrison, and the Northern Front; to formulate a plan of defence of the capital; and to keep order in the city. To carry out these tasks it formed separate sub-committees dealing with defence, supplies, liaison, information and a workers' militia. The MRC consisted of three Bolsheviks and two "Left SRs", with Trotsky as Chairman. He later acknowledged that the Left SRs were there merely to disguise that the MRC answered to the Bolshevik Party and not the Soviet Executive. He told them little of its real plans.[6]

Under cover of a legitimately established defence force answerable to the Soviet, Trotsky was in fact creating the machinery of insurrection. Within a few days he announced that the military units of the Petrograd garrison now answered to the MRC, not the Army General Staff. The MRC then sent its own Commissars into the regiments to establish its authority. With this action the October Insurrection had in effect already succeeded. All the MRC now had to do was order the troops to take the main strategic points of the city and arrest the ministers of the Provisional Government. The decision to do so rested with the Bolshevik Central Committee.

The Bolshevik Party, at this juncture, was very far from a united bloc. There were factions and differences of opinion at all levels. Now they threatened to tear the party asunder. Since the fall of Kornilov, the resignation of the major socialist ministers and the forming of Kerensky's last, feeble coalition government, Lenin had been frantically calling for an insurrection. In a letter to the Central Committee written on 12th September he wrote, "The Bolsheviks, having obtained a majority in the Soviets of Workers' and Soldiers' Deputies of both capitals, can and *must* take state power into their own hands". He warned that the Democratic Conference "represents not a majority of the revolutionary people but only the compromising upper strata of the petty bourgeoisie".[7] He also warned against election returns that indicated otherwise, for "elections prove nothing"–except, of course, elections to the Petrograd and Moscow Soviets.

The Central Committee met without Lenin and Trotsky present. Senior members such as Kamenev, Zinoviev and Nogin argued against an immediate insurrection. In the end, the Committee adopted a wait-and-see approach. The decision would have been no different had Trotsky been present for at this point he thought Lenin was being too impatient. He did not think counter-revolution was imminent and he preferred to prepare an uprising to coincide with the forthcoming Second National Congress of Soviets. Deutscher summarised his thinking:

> He reasoned that as the Bolsheviks had conducted their entire agitation under the slogan 'All Power to the Soviets', they

should stage the rising in such a manner that it should appear to everyone as the direct conclusion of this agitation. The rising should therefore be timed to coincide with, or slightly precede, the Congress of the Soviets, into whose hands the insurgents should then lay the power seized.

Lenin was not keen to lay power in anyone's hands but the Bolsheviks. In a further letter of 8th October he went further than he intended. "It is clear that all power should pass to the Soviets", he began, but added:

It should be equally indisputable for every Bolshevik that proletarian revolutionary power (or Bolshevik power, which is now one and the same thing) is assured of the utmost sympathy and unreserved support of the working and exploited people all over the world in general, and in the belligerent countries in particular, and among the Russian peasants especially.

This was a revealing statement. Firstly, that Lenin considered that Soviet power and Bolshevik power were "one and the same thing" (as they very shortly would be). Secondly, the belief that the mass of European workers felt "unreserved support" for the Bolsheviks, when at that point the vast majority of them had never heard of them. Thirdly, the belief that this support extended to the bulk of Russian peasants, who in the main still supported the SRs.

Two days earlier, in the letter subsequently published as *Advice of an Onlooker*, Lenin had laid out in stark terms to Petrograd Bolsheviks the tactics he expected of them. Unlike his hesitation when personally placed in front of a revolutionary crowd, his pen was fearless.

> Our three main forces—the fleet, the workers and the army
> units—must be so combined as to occupy without fail and to
> hold at any cost: a) the telephone exchange; b) the telegraph
> office; c) the railway stations; d) and above all, the bridges.

Further urging that the Red Guards and Kronstadt sailors
"encircle and cut off Petrograd", he concluded that, "The
success of both the Russian and world revolution depends on
two or three days fighting".[8] He then travelled in disguise to
Petrograd to attend a meeting of the Central Committee held
on 10th October in an apartment at 32 Karpovka Street, called
to decide if the Bolsheviks, acting through the MRC, would
launch an armed overthrow of the Provisional Government.

The meeting lasted from 10pm until 6am. Only twelve
of the Central Committee of twenty-one could attend due
to other duties. Trotsky later recorded that "the debate was
stormy, disorderly, chaotic". Without providing details, he
reported that the discussion expanded beyond simply arguing
whether to launch an insurrection. The CC also discussed
what form of socialism would follow a successful insurrection,
asking of the Soviets "were they necessary? What for? Could
they be dispensed with?"[9]

Since July, when the Petrograd Soviet had refused to
assume power on its own even when confronted by armed
demonstrators insisting it do so, the Bolsheviks had quietly
dropped the slogan "All Power to the Soviets". Now, with
Bolshevik majorities in many Soviets including Petrograd and
Moscow, they saw the Soviets primarily as useful vehicles to

legitimise a seizure of state power. At the end of the night Lenin wrote a resolution on a piece of paper which read "The party calls for the organisation of an armed insurrection", and put it to the vote. The vote was ten for, two against, the two being Lenin's long-standing senior lieutenants Gregory Zinoviev and Lev Kamenev. It was not the only decision of historic consequence. At the close of the meeting a new body, a "Political Bureau" (soon shortened to Politburo) was elected, consisting of Lenin, Stalin, Trotsky, Zinoviev, Kamenev, Bubnov and Sokolnikov.

This was not the end of the matter. The bloc of senior Bolsheviks who opposed an insurrection were respected and influential. Many of them had not been able to be present on 10th October. As well as Kamenev and Zinoviev it included CC members Rykov, Nogin and Miliutin, the ex-Inter-Districter Lunacharsky, the highly regarded Marxist scholar David Riazanov and those, like ex-Left Menshevik leader Yury Larin, who had recently joined the Bolsheviks. In the summary of Alexander Rabinowitch, this informal grouping saw a transfer of power to the Soviets as "a vehicle for building a strong alliance of left socialist parties and factions which would form a caretaker, exclusively socialist coalition government to begin peace negotiations and prepare for fundamental social reform by a Constituent Assembly".[10]

It was under the influence of these "moderates" that the Bolshevik Central Committee had, in July, begun to organise a conference of all left bodies (Bolsheviks, Left Mensheviks, Left SRs and trade unions) to pave the way for merger and unification, and to form a coherent alternative to the Provisional Government. This project was sidelined by the July Days but the impetus behind it fed through to the publicly declared policies of the Bolsheviks in August and September.

In this crucial period, just prior to the October insurrection, the Bolshevik Party did *not* call for a one-party Proletarian Dictatorship. On the contrary, it stood for an extension of local, grassroots democracy and, on the national level, immediate convocation of the Constituent Assembly, the elections to which Bolshevik Regional Committees were instructed to fully engage in. Their core policies, which had made them so popular, were clear: workers' control of industry, redistribution of land to the peasants and an immediate end to the war. Zinoviev and Kamenev felt that armed insurrection, decided upon by a handful of people on the Bolshevik Central Committee and carried out by the Petrograd Soviet's MRC without any mandate from that Soviet to do so, was not the best or most democratic way to achieve these goals.

They took their objections to a further meeting of the CC on 16th October, this time attended by leading local Bolshevik activists from the Petrograd Committee, the Military Organisation of the Bolshevik Party and the Petrograd Soviet. The debate was even more fractious. The leader of the Military Organisation, Krylenko, reported that a majority of the Organisation did not support an armed uprising and even those that did wished for the initiative to come from the Soviet, not the party. Sokolonikov shifted his position but stressed that any uprising must occur after the Second Congress of Soviets, not before. Others, like Miliutin, were not keen on an uprising no matter what the timing.

But with Lenin forcefully arguing for an insurrection as soon as possible, the meeting agreed that the initial decision to plan an armed insurrection would proceed, although the final "go" for the uprising would be at the discretion of both the party (i.e. the CC) and the Soviet (i.e. the MRC, not the actual Soviet).

At this point, Zinoviev and Kamenev broke ranks and sent a letter entitled "On the Current Situation" to key party organisations. In it they laid out the case against an armed insurrection. "We are deeply convinced", they wrote, "that to call at present for an armed uprising means to stake on one card not only the fate of our party but also the fate of the Russian and international revolution". Proposing instead that the Bolsheviks throw themselves into the elections for the Constituent Assembly, in which they anticipated securing about a third of the seats, they suggested that "The Constituent Assembly will be able to find support for its revolutionary work only in the Soviets. The Constituent Assembly plus the Soviets – that is the combined type of state institution towards which we are going".

Zinoviev and Kamenev challenged Lenin's assertion that the mass of the people supported the Bolsheviks. "In Russia a majority of the workers", the letter explained, "and a substantial part of the soldiers are with us. But all the rest is dubious. We are all convinced, for instance, that if elections to the Constituent Assembly were to take place now, a majority of peasants would vote for the SRs. What is this, an accident?" This was to prove a far more accurate assessment than that of Lenin or Trotsky. Yet it missed the key point, later explained by Trotsky, which was that "the peasants might have strong revolutionary interests and an intense urge to realise them, but cannot have an independent political position".[11] At the time neither Trotsky nor Lenin explained to the vast majority of Russia's people that they were not sociologically important enough to be allowed a political position independent of that assigned to them by the Bolsheviks.

Zinoviev and Kamenev stressed a further weakness in plans for insurrection—a total lack of planning for the aftermath. "If amongst the great masses of the poor of the capital there were a militant sentiment burning to go into the streets", they wrote,

> it might have served as guarantee that an uprising initiated by them would draw in the biggest organisations (railroad unions, unions of postal and telegraph unions, etc.) where the influence of our party is weak. But since there is no such sentiment even in the factories and barracks, it would be a self-deception to build any plans on it.

As events post-October were to demonstrate—when trade unions and Factory Committees opposed the Bolsheviks' plans for one-party government and a top-down re-organisation of industry—it *was* a self-deception.

Kamenev and Zinoviev had allies in the Menshevik and SR parties who desired socialist reform but feared the Leninists were simply unrealistic. The influential SR journalist Pitirim Sorokin, in one of his popular "Notes of a Sociologist" newspaper columns, put his finger on the similarity of Lenin and Trotsky's belief in Russia setting off a worldwide revolution to the right's idealistic "Slavophilism", i.e. the concept that apparently backward Slav nations would provide fresh, uncorrupted cultural leadership to degenerate Western Europeans. "Bolshevism is surely that same Slavophilism inside out", wrote Sorokin in September. "Just like the Slavophiles, we have come to believe that we are indeed the saviours of humanity". But, as Sorokin pointed out, "The west has not reached the stage of majority socialist government, while we are already demanding a proletarian dictatorship".[12]

Sorokin's blunt assertion that the Bolsheviks were running before they could walk would have been approved of by Zinoviev and Kamenev. They would have preferred to work within the kind of Bolshevik-Menshevik-SR alliance that was briefly on offer before the July Days. Although later compelled to repudiate and recant their letter, it accurately foresaw the disastrous results of independent Bolshevik action if sundered from the wider left and eventually from the Soviets themselves. Of the Bolshevik dissenters a particularly astute socialist biographer of Trotsky later concluded, "It is hard to believe that the fate of Russia would have been worse had the party followed the line of Zinoviev, Kamenev, Nogin and the other moderates".[13]

Trotsky had already successfully sent MRC commissars into the Petrograd garrison to assume command from the General Staff. On 23rd October, as a further test of his power as Chair of the MRC, he ordered 5,000 extra rifles for the civilian Red Guards. The rifles were delivered, but the plans of the MRC had not gone unnoticed. In the Soviet he was openly challenged about rumours of a planned insurrection and whether the order for the rifles was part of those plans. Trotsky, a master of linguistic evasion, replied, "I declare on behalf of the Soviet—we have not decided on any armed action". That was true. The Soviet had not. The Bolshevik Party had.

With the Second Congress of Soviets postponed to 26th October, Trotsky and the MRC began to position their forces for an armed insurrection the day before. The Menshevik historian Sukhanov caught a flavor of Trotsky's activity during these crucial days. "Trotsky, breaking off from his work in the Smolny Institute, flew from the Obukhov factory to the Pipe factory, from the Putilov works to the Baltic works, from the Manege to the garrisons, and it seemed as if he talked simultaneously at all these places. Every Petrograd worker and solider personally knew and heard him".[14] Even the Provisional Government, often paralysed, had to respond to what was clearly preparation for an attempt at its overthrow. On 23rd October it sent in troops to close *Pravda*. This provided Trotsky the pretext he needed.

When Kerensky started to deploy troops loyal to the Provisional Government around the city to forestall rebellion, Trotsky launched the insurrection. On the evening of 24th October he issued "Order Number One" to the MRC and its forces. This read:

The Petrograd Soviet is in imminent danger. Last night the counter-revolutionary conspirators tried to call the Junkers and the shock battalions into Petrograd. You are hereby ordered to prepare your regiment for action. Await further orders. All procrastination and hesitation will be regarded as treason to the revolution.[15]

Trotsky later admitted the forces at his disposal amounted to no more than "a few thousand Red Guards, two or three thousand sailors, and a score of infantry companies".[16] He controlled these forces from the Smolny Institute, an ex-convent now turned into the bustling centre of the MRC's work. The total number of those who took part in the insurrection was at the most about 20,000, including sailors on the battleship *Aurora* and the Red Guards.

Starting at 2am on 25th October, they quickly took over the railway stations, the banks, the telegraph offices, the power stations and the bridges. They met no resistance. The Tauride Palace itself, home of the Soviet and only a few minutes away from the Smolny Institute, was swiftly taken. By the morning it was done. Only the Winter Palace, seat of the Provisional Government, did not fall as planned. Lenin, who had returned from Finland and slipped quietly into the Smolny, was frantic for news that the Winter Palace had fallen and the Ministers of the Provisional Government arrested. Only then could he legitimately claim that one government had been replaced with another.

The Soviet made one last attempt on the morning of 25th October to speak for itself. The day before, on the cusp of the insurrection, the Pre-Parliament, at which Mensheviks, Bundists and SRs still laboured to try to bring the government round to more radical policies, had heard from Kerensky that he had "incontrovertible proof" that the Bolsheviks were about to launch an insurrection. Kerensky then left for military headquarters to call for Cossack reinforcements.

After his departure, the Menshevik leader Theodore Dan, who under Martov's relentless pressure was detaching himself from Kerensky and beginning to move the Menshevik party further left, put a new resolution to the Pre-Parliament. Whilst it condemned the Bolsheviks for unilateral actions and for ignoring the wishes of the Soviet, it said clearly that the only way to defuse a Bolshevik insurrection was to instigate "decisive measures in the struggle for peace, an immediate transfer of landed estates into the hands of the peasants, and the speediest possible convocation of the Constituent Assembly".

Dan blamed both the Bolsheviks and the Provisional Government for the chaos that would follow an insurrection. He suggested the best means to prevent subversion of the democratic revolution from both left and right was to establish a broad-based Committee of Public Defence. The resolution was passed 122 votes to 102, upon which Dan and SR leader Avram Gots took it to Kerensky and demanded its terms be implemented. Kerensky then argued with Dan and Gots about who was to blame for the imminent collapse of the government. Dan wanted the terms of the resolution, which might placate discontented workers and peasants, immediately posted around the city, but Kerensky was lost in fantasies of crushing the Bolsheviks. This last attempt by Mensheviks and SRs to head off the collapse of the government by dragging it sharply to the left was far too little, far too late.

By the morning of 25th October, the insurrection in Petrograd was virtually over. The Soviet woke up to a transformed capital. At 3pm on the same day,

Trotsky announced to the Soviet:

> In the name of the Military Revolutionary Committee I declare
> that the Provisional Government has ceased to exist. Individual
> Ministers are under arrest, the others will be arrested in the next
> few days or hours. The revolutionary garrison has dispersed
> the Pre-Parliament.

Trotsky claimed that the overthrow of the Provisional
Government had so far proceeded without bloodshed.
He went on to announce:

> At the present time the Soviets of Workers', Soldiers' and
> Peasants' deputies faces the historically unprecedented
> experiment of the creation of a regime which will have no
> other interest but the needs of the workers, peasants and soldiers.
> The state must be an instrument of the masses in the struggle
> of their liberation from all bondage.

After Trotsky had spoken, Lenin told the packed Soviet:

> The oppressed masses themselves will form a government. The
> old state apparatus will be destroyed root and branch, and a
> new administrative apparatus will be created in the form of
> the Soviet organisations. Now begins a new era in the history
> of Russia, and this third Russian Revolution must finally lead
> to the victory of socialism.[17]

But as Sukhanov, who was watching from the back row,
put it in his invaluable history, "to construct (not merely a

Soviet) but a 'Proletarian Socialist state' in a vast economically shattered peasant country, meant taking on oneself tasks known to be utopian".[18]

No such considerations were allowed to spoil the moment. No Mensheviks were given the podium. The Soviet, in a fit of enthusiasm, passed a motion which read:

> The Soviet expresses its confidence that a Soviet government will firmly advance towards socialism, the only salvation of the country. The Soviet is convinced that the proletariat of Western Europe will help lead the cause of socialism to total victory.

When Trotsky suggested that commissars be sent throughout the country to inform the people what had happened in Petrograd, someone shouted from the floor, "You're anticipating the will of the Congress!" Trotsky shot back, "The will of the Congress has been anticipated by the tremendous fact of the insurrection of the Petrograd workers and soldiers, which has taken place tonight".[19]

The night was not over. Trotsky had assigned MRC Secretary Vladimir Antonov-Ovseenko to lead the force to take the Winter Palace and arrest the Ministers. They had formidable assistance in the form of the cruiser *Aurora*, manned by Bolshevik sailors at anchor in the Neva River. The only forces left guarding the Winter Palace were ceremonial sentries, military cadets and a woman's "shock battalion". Kerensky had issued orders for Cossack regiments stationed outside Petrograd to enter the city to defend the government, but the Cossacks questioned his authority and decided to wait. Those few forces that did embark for Petrograd were once again obstructed and delayed by the All-Russian Union of Railwaymen.

When Antonov-Ovseenko's forces reached the Winter Palace on dawn of 25th October, they encircled it and issued instructions to those within to surrender. They did not know that Kerensky was already on his way out of the capital. The Ministers who remained within ignored the demand to surrender and the small forces at their disposal set up barricades. The insurgents spent the day engaged in brief, desultory skirmishes with the defenders. Although up to 10,000 Bolshevik supporters milled around Palace Square throughout the day, by the evening they had dwindled to a few hundred men. Inside the Palace, the women's shock-battalion and some cadets decided to leave. No one stopped them. Much of the city did not even notice anything was occurring. In the evening Nevsky Prospect bustled with crowds as usual and the theatres, restaurants and shops remained open. Taxis and streetcars ran across the city. Reports from district police chiefs on 25th–26th October all agreed it was a quiet night.[20]

At 10pm the insurgents brought up armoured cars and issued an ultimatum that unless the Palace surrendered the *Aurora* would open fire. The Ministers decided that they would bluff it out and hope that reinforcements arrived soon. The *Aurora* fired blank shots across the Palace as a last warning, and there was gunfire between the Palace and besiegers. The *Aurora* then fired a 6-inch shell into the Palace which blew some walls in. At this point some of the Red Guards and sailors rushed into the Palace, but they met resistance and were disarmed. Over the next few hours further troops infiltrated the Palace and gradually, with desultory fighting, it passed into the hands of the insurgents. Antonov-Ovseenko marched into the cabinet room where the Ministers had been confined since the previous night and proclaimed, "I inform all of you, members of the Provisional Government, that you are under arrest. I am Antonov-Ovseenko of the Military Revolutionary Committee".

Only then did the insurgents realise that Kerensky had escaped. Frustrated, the Red Guards yelled at the Ministers and threatened violence. Antonov-Ovseenko called them to order. "I'll permit no violence!" he commanded. "Calm yourselves. Maintain order. Power is now in your hands". The Ministers were taken to the Peter and Paul Fortress but not before one of them, P.N. Maliantovich, who later left an invaluable account of 25th-26th October in the Winter Palace, found Antonov-Ovseenko in the cabinet room writing a protocol establishing the removal of the Provisional Government. Once, before the war, the Menshevik Maliantovich had hidden the Bolshevik Antonov-Ovseenko from the Okhrana in his attic. Antonov-Ovseenko, suitably embarrassed at the turn of events, treated him courteously. After reading the proclamation aloud to Maliantovich, Antonov-Ovseenko paused and seemed to ponder the enormity of what the Bolsheviks had just done. "Yes", he said, "it will be an interesting social experiment".[21]

Sukhanov later wrote that those who stormed the Winter Palace and packed the Petrograd Soviet were not as fiercely ideological as those they followed. In his view, "their socialism was hunger and an unendurable longing for rest. Not bad material for an experiment, but—those experiments would be risky".[22] Exactly how risky was demonstrated when the Red Guards clearing out the Winter Palace the next day came across "one of the largest wine cellars ever known"[23] and decided it was only fit that the victors enjoy the spoils. The order that Antonov-Ovseenko insisted upon broke down completely and the Winter Palace was thoroughly vandalised. The disorder spread to the streets of the capital, with shops and liquor stores broken into, their contents liberated, and attacks on any who looked well-dressed and affluent.

The new government had to station units on street corners to fire over the heads of drunken mobs. Police cells were jammed to capacity and it took weeks for the violent celebrations to burn out. Fuel was added to the fire by looting of the 570 government liquor depots in the capital, holding spirits confiscated under the wartime ban on distilling and selling alcohol. It was not only Petrograd that was convulsed by drunken riots. On 1st-2nd December, Odessa and Samara suffered the same when large mobs stormed government liquor holds. In Odessa they were dispersed with machine-gun fire. In Samara the Red Guard sided with the rioters and let them smash and loot shops in the city. Order in the capital was finally restored in early December when martial law was imposed and all the confiscated liquor hoards were poured into the City's canals.[24]

The Petrograd insurrection of 25th October, for all its historical consequences, was a localised event coordinated and carried out by a relatively small group of men with no mandate to do so. The vast majority of the Russian population did not take part in it or even know about it. The 2nd Soviet Congress, which would "legitimise" the coup after the fact, had a very limited representative function. Elections to its plenary were haphazard and irregular. It had minimal representation for peasants, who constituted the bulk of Russia's population and who still mostly supported the SRs. There was almost no representation for women, urban or rural. Lastly—not that this mattered to anybody outside a tiny number of Marxist theorists—the insurrection flew in the face of classical Marxist theory about a transfer of political power based on the leading role of a mature working class who were a majority of the population. From that perspective it was hardly a revolution at all. It was an insurrection that would very shortly herald a counter-revolution.

CHAPTER NINE

Sovnarcom

Moscow's Bolsheviks, unlike those of Petrograd, were always more inclined to work with other socialists. It was not until 25th October that they formed a Military Revolutionary Committee, which consisted of four Bolsheviks, two Mensheviks and an independent. On the 26th they reluctantly followed Trotsky's instructions to launch an insurrection. Street fighting raged across the city, particularly outside the walls of the Kremlin, which the insurgents failed to take. The key northern industrial city of Ivanovo–Voznesensk was taken speedily, as were other towns in the industrial northwest of the country, but middle and lower Volga cities like Samara hung in the balance and in the south, especially in Ukraine, the situation was confused and chaotic. Industrial Kharkov went over to the Bolsheviks quickly but the Ukrainian capital Kiev looked to the Ukrainian Rada for leadership.

The outcome of the Second Congress of Soviets held in the Smolny Institute on 25th and 26th October was therefore crucial. The Bolsheviks hoped the congress would endorse the insurrection on the grounds that their party clearly had popular support in working-class areas of Petrograd and Moscow, and the removal of a deeply discredited government by force was the result of a popular insurrection. On the other hand, it was obvious to many delegates that Lenin and the Bolsheviks were confronting them with a *fait accompli* backed by armed Red Guards. In theory the Bolshevik insurrection had been undertaken to create a government elected by and accountable to the National Congress of Soviets, but what if the congress did not approve the action, or demanded that the new government be a broad socialist coalition, as many delegates wished?

When the Second Congress opened at 10.40pm on the evening of 25th October the storming of the Winter Palace was still taking place, and during the debates delegates could hear the cruiser *Aurora* fire its guns. Not that the congress needed added drama. Most of the key players of Petrograd's radical left were all assembled in one packed hall. They had been meeting in side rooms throughout the day, waiting for the siege of the Winter Palace to conclude and arguing amongst themselves. The Mensheviks were torn between trying to convert the congress to the idea of a broad socialist government which would now obviously have to include the Bolsheviks, or walking out of the congress in protest at the events of the last 24 hours (many of the arrested Ministers, such as Maliantovich, were Mensheviks). Martov and Sukhanov, leaders of the Left Mensheviks, argued strongly that leaving the Soviet now would isolate their party from the most active workers.

The delegates packed out the great hall of the Smolny, filling it with noise and tobacco smoke. As so often

Trotsky best captures the texture of events:

> The officers' chevrons, the eye-glasses and neckties of intellectuals to be seen at the first congress had almost completely disappeared. A grey colour prevailed, in costumes and in faces. All had worn out their clothes during the war. Many of the city workers had provided themselves with soldiers' coats. The trench delegates were by no means a pretty picture: long unshaven, in old worn trenchcoats, with heavy *papahki* (fur hats) on their disheveled hair, often with cotton sticking out through a hole, with coarse weather-beaten faces, heavy cracked hands, fingers yellowed with tobacco, buttons torn off, belts hanging loose, and long unoiled boots wrinkled and rusty. The plebian nation had for the first time sent up an honest representation made in its own image and not retouched.[1]

There were roughly 650 delegates jammed into the hall, of which nearly 400 were Bolshevik. This reflected support for the Bolsheviks in local Soviets, although Rabinowitch records it also reflected a disproportionately large number of delegates from the northern industrial region (heavily Bolshevik) and a smaller number than was warranted from the Volga and southern regions (heavily SR). The Mensheviks, damaged by their participation in the Provisional Government, had about 90 delegates. The SRs had about 150, although it was difficult to judge which of those were "Left SRs" and which "Right SRs" (under the pressure of events and the demands of the Provisional Government, the SR party was in the process of splitting into right and left tendencies). A couple of hundred more delegates drifted in during the course of the congress in the next two days, mainly pro-Bolshevik Latvian soldiers. As Trotsky admits, "The registration was carried on intermittently, documents have been lost, information about party affiliations was incomplete".[2] Yet the delegates, whoever they were, were about to decide Russia's future.

Kamenev was appointed Chair of the Congress. He immediately announced that its main business was: a) the formation of a new government, b) ending the war, and c) convocation of the Constituent Assembly. Martov spoke first. "The question of power is beginning to be decided by conspiratorial methods", he told the delegates.

> All the revolutionary parties have been placed before a *fait accompli*. A civil war threatens us with an explosion of counter revolution. A peaceful solution of the crisis can be obtained by creating a government which will be recognised by the whole democracy.

The resolution was widely applauded, prompting Sukhanov to note that "a very great many Bolsheviks, not having assimilated the spirit of the teaching of Lenin and Trotsky, would have been happy to take exactly this path".[3]

Many of the delegates, including many Bolsheviks, had taken at face value Trotsky's declaration that the MRC was simply an expression of the will of the Soviet and its actions were intended to defend the Soviet by creating a government answerable to it. Martov's resolution, which encapsulated this position, was therefore strongly supported by Bolsheviks, Mensheviks, the independent socialists around Gorky's paper *Novaya Zhizn*, and the Left SRs. With this base of support

Trotsky had to backtrack. He sent Lunacharsky to the podium to declare that the Bolsheviks agreed with the resolution. It was voted upon and passed unanimously.

Then history turned. Martov had backed the Bolsheviks into a corner. They had little choice but to accede to his resolution and agree to a socialist coalition government. The non-Bolshevik socialists had won as much as they could possibly expect to win at that moment. They then, for reasons that remain unclear but were probably a mixture of confusion, tiredness and misunderstanding, threw it all away.

Without consulting Martov, the Right Menshevik Khinchuk declared on behalf of the Mensheviks that the policy of the Congress should be to negotiate an agreement with the now defunct Provisional Government. He told the Congress that they would under no circumstances enter a government with the Bolsheviks, and therefore "divest ourselves for all responsibility for what is happening, and leave the Congress, and ask the other fractions to meet to discuss the present situation". The Congress greeted this with surprise and anger, despite which Geldeman for the srs and Ehrlich for the Bund declared they were also leaving. Most delegates of these parties departed the hall amidst jeers, curses and cries of "Traitors!" and "Kornivalites!" and "Counter-revolutionaries!"

By this action, the Mensheviks, Bundists and Right srs fatally discredited themselves in the eyes of the most active representatives of the working class. They also left Martov alone on the platform to face Trotsky. Trotsky was not known for his mercy and he did not display any now. "What has taken place", he said with cruel logic and withering scorn,

> is an insurrection, not a conspiracy. An insurrection of the
> popular masses needs no justification [...] our insurrection
> has conquered, and now you propose to us: renounce your
> victory, make a compromise. With whom? I ask: with whom
> ought we to make a compromise? With that pitiful handful who
> just went out? Haven't we seen them through and through?
> There is no longer anybody in Russia who is for them [...]
> A compromise is supposed to be made between two equal sides.
> Here no compromise is possible. To those who have gone out,
> and to all who have made like proposals, we must say: you are
> pitiful, isolated individuals. You are bankrupt. Your role is played
> out. Go where you belong—to the rubbish heap of history!

The hall applauded wildly, seemingly blind to the fact
that Trotsky had not only buried those who had just left
the Congress but had also repudiated—through his dismissal
of "all who made like proposals"—the resolution that the
Congress had passed unanimously in favour of a government
of all the Soviet parties. Between the Bolsheviks who rejected
this approach and the Mensheviks/Right SRs/Bundists who
had just walked away, there was now little left of it save a
few moderate Bolsheviks and Left Mensheviks like Martov,
who stood insulted and humiliated on the platform. In a
fit of anger, he shouted, "Then we'll leave!" and began to
walk towards the exit. Before he could reach it a young
Bolshevik worker, Ivan Akulov, stopped him. "And we
amongst ourselves", Akulov said bitterly, "had thought Martov
at least will remain with us". Martov was taken aback, torn

between his disgust with the Bolsheviks and his desire to stand with the Russian working class no matter what. "One day you will understand the crime in which you are taking part", he said quietly, and left Smolny.[4]

The Mensheviks wavered between broad right and left factions. The Jewish Bund was for the moment more cohesive (although a breakaway group called Poalei Zion, advocating a mixture of socialism and Zionism, began to attract support amongst Jewish workers after the Balfour Declaration of British support for a Jewish homeland in Palestine). An emergency session of the Bund's Central Committee held in Minsk a few weeks later declared the Bolsheviks must assume full responsibility for

> the insurrection and civil war that was begun by them against the will of the majority of the revolutionary democratic parties during the two weeks before elections to the Constituent Assembly, where the problems of re-organising the structures of power could have been achieved in concert with all of the revolutionary democratic forces.

The cc's resolution warned that by isolating themselves from the broad democratic forces that had made the February Revolution, the Bolsheviks would inevitably have to sustain themselves in power by "means that would suppress democratic freedoms and condone unchecked terror, which is always a characteristic of government by a minority".[5]

The resolution was a statement of principle. Although it formally rejected the October Insurrection, the Bund leader and Left Menshevik Raphael Abramovich counseled against taking up arms against the Bolsheviks as he felt that to do so when they were under attack from Kerensky's forces would be counter-productive, and would drive workers into their arms. Other Bundists such as Mark Liber were more viscerally hostile to the Bolsheviks and began to plan physical resistance (Liber was so out of step with Menshevik and Bund policy that he lost his leadership positions within both groups, eclipsed by those like Abramovich, Martov and Dan who sought an accommodation with moderate Bolsheviks). The Eighth Congress of the Bund, its last on Russian soil, was held in December 1917, with 100 representatives of the party covering 357 local branches and 40,000 members. The congress overwhelmingly opposed what they called the methods of Blanquism — *coup d'état* led by a minority — and demanded that the Constituent Assembly be properly elected and become the prime legislative body of the democratic republic.

The SRs, literally split into Left and Right, took less nuanced positions. The Left SRs, led by the legendary freedom fighter Maria Spiridonova, were dazzled by the audacity of the Bolshevik insurrection and inclined to support it. The majority of SRs were not. They regarded the insurrection as an illegitimate power play that had removed a government in which SR ministers played a key role, and had pre-empted imminent elections to the Constituent Assembly. Victor Chernov, having made every effort to make the Provisional Government work and to deliver redistribution of landed estates to the peasants, prepared for the Constituent Assembly elections. Other SR leaders such as Avram Gots, who had not been uncritical of Kerensky and the Provisional Government, favoured armed resistance to Sovnarcom. Gots helped set up the "Committee of Salvation of the Homeland and the Revolution", which attempted to mobilise a popular militia to resist the Bolshevik government.

Despite opposition from the Mensheviks, the SRs and the Bund, the Bolsheviks had avoided their nightmare scenario – that the Second Congress would vote against the insurrection and demand a broad-based socialist government (although it had actually supported that proposal, only to have its movers self-sabotage it). Delegates from the All-Russian Union of Railwaymen had demanded that any new government be a socialist coalition, but they were voted down. Many present seemed for a moment to ignore the world beyond the walls of the Second Congress. It did not ignore them.

The army outside Petrograd was not as infiltrated by Bolsheviks as the garrison in the capital. Kerensky still claimed to be the head of the legitimate government, and he ordered General Krasnov to attack Petrograd. The first military engagement of the Bolshevik Revolution took place on 27th October at Gatchina. In heavy fighting MRC units were pushed back, but over the next few days Bolshevik agitators moved through Krasnov's men and encouraged them to desert. When Krasnov's depleted forces then pushed on to Polkovo, just outside Petrograd, they were defeated by MRC troops. This bought time for the Bolsheviks to establish their new government and issue vitally important Decrees on land redistribution, peace and workers' control.

The new government already had a structure. The first sitting of the Second Congress closed at 5am on 26th

October to enable exhausted delegates to rest. Its second session opened that evening. It was in this session, now without delegates who had supported the Right SRs and the Mensheviks, that crucial decisions were taken about the organisation of the government. Its most important and historic decision was to authorise the creation of a "Council of People's Commissars", to be known as Sovnarcom.

At this stage of the revolution, with the Bolshevik Party still seeking Soviet legitimacy for its assumption of power, it was Sovnarcom, not the Bolshevik Central Committee or its Politburo, that sat at the apex of government. Lenin was Chair of the Council. Leading Bolsheviks took specific departmental responsibilities such as Interior (Rykov), Agriculture (Miliutin), Labour (Shliapnikov), Commerce and Industry (Nogin), Education (Lunacharsky), Foreign Affairs (Trotsky), Justice (Lomov), Social Welfare (Kollontai) and Nationalities (Stalin). The departments followed those of the Tsarist and Provisional Governments almost exactly. There had been no "smashing of the existing state machine", nor was this ever proposed. The Decree establishing Sovnarcom declared:

For the administration of the country up to the convening of the Constituent Assembly, a temporary Worker and Peasant government is to be formed, which will be named the Council of People's Commissars. Charge of particular branches of state life are entrusted to Commissions, the composition of which should ensure the carrying into life of the programme proclaimed by the Congress in close unity with the mass organizations of working men and women, sailors, soldiers, peasants and office workers. Governmental power belongs to the collegiums of chairmen of these commissions, i.e. the Council of People's Commissars. Control over the activity of the of the People's Commissars and the right of replacing them belongs to the All-Russian Congress of Soviets of Workers', Peasants' and Soldiers' Deputies and its Central Executive Committee.[6]

T.H. Rigby's definitive study of Sovnarcom's administrative machine from 1917-22 found that there was no internal debate or discussion in the Bolshevik Party about how exactly this structure would work, or how accountable the People's Commissars would be to the Soviets and the Soviet Congress. In reality no People's Commissar was ever replaced by the Congress of Soviets or its Executive.

Sovnarcom's first proclamations were progressive and emancipatory. The Decree on Peace called on "all belligerent peoples and their governments to start immediately negotiations for a just and democratic peace". It explained that "by such a peace the government means an immediate peace without annexations and without indemnities". Thus far the Decree did not go further than the Left Mensheviks and SRs, even those like Dan and Chernov who had supported the Provisional Government. But it went on, "the government announces its determination immediately to sign terms of peace to stop this war on the terms indicated, which are equally just for all nationalities without exceptions". This was a new departure and signaled the Bolsheviks' willingness, driven by recognition that the Russian people would not carry on the war, to sign a peace deal without the quid-pro-quo of detailed peace negotiations. As a sign of the new era it added that it intended to publish all the secret accords and treaties agreed by previous Russian governments, as well as the "immediate annulment" of any terms in the treaties that secured advantages for Russian landowners and "the retention, or extension, of the annexations made by Great Russia".

The Decree on Land, drafted by Lenin personally, was issued on the same day. Its first proclamation read:

> Private ownership of land shall be abolished forever; land shall not be sold, purchased, leased, mortgaged or otherwise alienated. All land, whether state, crown, monastery, church, factory, entailed, private, public, peasant, etc., shall be confiscated without compensation and become the property of the whole people.

After reserving "high level scientific farms" for use as "model farms", it said:

> The right to use the land shall be accorded to all citizens of the Russian state (without distinction of sex) desiring to cultivate it by their own labour, with the help of their families or in partnership, but only as long as they are able to cultivate it. The employment of hired labour is not permitted.

The Land Decree shamelessly stole the agrarian programme of the SRs, which the Provisional Government had been attempting to implement in gradual stages, and offered it wholesale to the peasants. In the excitement few of them noticed that the Decree did not actually confer personal land ownership. It spoke of social ownership to be run by local authorities. For most peasants this meant the Zemstvos having general oversight, with peasants owning and disposing as they wished of their parcels of land. Few peasants paid heed to Lenin's qualification that the provisions of the Decree were to be implemented immediately "as far as possible", but "in regard to certain of its parts with such necessary gradualness as the county peasant Soviets shall determine". Lenin anticipated that peasant Soviets not under the control of the Bolsheviks soon would be, and they would then set the pace and the scale of peasant landownership. It was not clear what would happen if rural Soviets stayed under the control of the SRs.

Further decrees had to await the result of fighting outside Petrograd and in Moscow. It was not until 2nd November that Sovnarcom issued a decree on the Rights of the Peoples of Russia, which granted equality and sovereignty to all peoples of the Empire, their right to self-determination up to secession and formation of independent states, and full civil and cultural freedoms for ethnic groups.

On 14th November Sovnarcom published the Decree on Workers' Control, one of the most misunderstood and contentious of the many declarations of the new regime. It began:

> In order to provide planned regulation of the national economy, workers' control over the manufacture, purchase, sale and storage of produce and of raw materials, and over the financial activity of enterprises is introduced in all industrial, commercial, banking, agricultural, cooperative, and other enterprises which employ

hired labour or give work to be done at home.

The Decree defined workers' control as "exercised by all the workers of the given enterprise through their elected bodies, such as factory committees, shop stewards councils etc.".[7]

In *Can the Bolsheviks Retain State Power?* (published on 1st October), Lenin had made clear he regarded "workers' control" as dependent on the nature of the government conferring it. "When we say workers' control", he wrote,

> always associating that slogan with the dictatorship of the proletariat, and always putting it after the latter, we thereby make plain what state we have in mind. If it is a proletarian state we are referring to, then workers' control can become a national, all-embracing, omni-present, extremely precise and extremely scrupulous *accounting* of the production and distribution of goods.

This was a vision very different from the popular, plant-level self-management of the Factory Committees, rooted in democratic decision-making in the workplace. It had nothing in common with the workers' control of industry seen in Italy in 1922 or Spain in 1936. It was an accountant's vision of socialism. As Maurice Brinton pointed out, "Nowhere in Lenin's writings is workers' control ever equated with fundamental decision-making (i.e. with the *initiation* of decisions) relating to production".[8]

Lenin buried his ideas on the limitations of workers' control in the sub-sections of the Decree, which made clear that any decisions by Factory Committees could be "annulled by trade unions and congresses", and that elected delegates from enterprises "of importance to the State" were "answerable to the State for the maintenance of the strictest order and discipline and the protection of property". As "enterprises of importance to the State" were defined as those engaged in defence work or producing articles necessary for the existence of the population, this meant that virtually every enterprise, under workers' control or not, was now answerable to the state. And the state was run by Sovnarcom.

The conflict of interest was demonstrated almost immediately. On 28th November the Moscow Printers Union took strike action after Sovnarcom closed the liberal newspaper *Russkoe Slovo* and the new owner, the Moscow Soviet, ordered the printers to go home. The printers struck in protest, whereupon the union leadership persuaded the Soviet to employ the printers to print the Soviet's newspaper. However, the Soviet failed to pay the workers, who went on strike again. The Soviet's reaction to this was to order Red Guards to occupy the print shop and dismiss the 1,500 printers, who were labeled "counter-revolutionary" for taking part in a "political strike". In the next round of internal union elections in early 1918, the printers turned heavily against the Bolsheviks and elected Mensheviks to head the union.[9]

These were early rumblings. Those with a vested interest in the decrees (e.g. peasants who had seized land, workers on Factory Committees, and nationalists declaring independence from the Empire) took them literally, as the law or framework of law of the future socialist society. They were not told at the time what Lenin admitted to the Eighth Congress of the party in March 1919. "Let us assume that Decrees contain much that is useless", he said, "much that in practice cannot be put into effect; but they contain much material for practical action, and the purpose of a decree is to teach practical steps to the hundreds, thousands and millions of people who heed the voice of the Soviet Government".

In some instances, such as the abolition of the judiciary and the existing marriage and divorce laws, instituting civil marriage and the separation of church and state, the effects were real and immediate. In other areas the illusion of massive, revolutionary change was fostered more by the removal of existing codes and laws than by their replacement. Shortly after October the new government simply abolished the entire Criminal Code of the Russian Empire, which automatically de-criminalised many actions and lifestyles that had been illegal before, such as homosexuality. But this was not the same as approving them.

Despite later claims that the Bolsheviks had a principled support for same-sex relationships there is no evidence to support this. In contrast to the German SPD, which had long opposed Imperial Germany's anti-gay Paragraph 175 law and whose most "reformist" leader Eduard Bernstein publicly defended Oscar Wilde in the pages of *Neue Zeit*, they had no policy on the matter at all. There were no "out" gay men or lesbians amongst the Bolshevik leadership, although given the social mores of the time that would have been unusual. Even Alexandra Kollontai did not mention the subject in her seminal 1921 essay "Sexual Relations and the Class Struggle". As with workers' control and national self-determination, when Lenin proclaimed on 25th October "We shall now proceed to build, on the space cleared of historical rubbish, the airy, towering edifice of socialist society", he and his party underestimated the amount of historical rubbish they themselves brought with them.

A Decree of 2nd November abolished the five legal "estates" of citizenship granted under Tsarism and created one single legal category of citizen. But as Bolshevik doctrine decreed that equality of citizenship could only occur in a classless society, this was meaningless. Post-October Russia was not a classless society. According to its new government it was passing through a period in which class power—defined as the power of the working class expressed through the Soviets—was to be used to eradicate the hitherto dominant class, i.e. the bourgeoisie. The constitution of the Russian Socialist Federation of Soviet Republics (RSFSR), adopted in late 1918, specifically stated: "In the general interest of the working class the RSFSR deprives individuals or separate groups of any privileges which may be used by them to the detriment of the socialist revolution".[10] The constitution was clear that "the franchise ceases to be a right and is transformed into a social function of the electors". As a result, whole categories of people—i.e. private-sector businessmen, those who employed others, those who lived on unearned income, monks and priests—were excluded.

One could argue that this simply reversed centuries of similar exclusion during which an indifferent ruling class denied working people any say in their destiny. The Bolsheviks did argue this and asserted that "Soviet democracy" was superior to the formal yet politically cosmetic democracy of bourgeois societies (most of which still excluded whole categories of working men and nearly all women). Other socialists like Martov pointed out that the flipside of oppression was still oppression and that granting Sovnarcom the power to remove civic and legal rights from "individuals and separate groups" of whom it disapproved was a recipe for state tyranny and self-perpetuating one-party rule.

For all their careful and progressive verbiage, the new constitution, Code of Law and Revolutionary Tribunals were essentially fronts for state power wielded by violent men. Lenin, seldom a hypocrite, was honest enough to admit this. "The revolutionary dictatorship of the proletariat", he wrote in 1918, "is power unrestricted by any law". In 1920 he was confident enough to elaborate and explain that "the scientific concept of dictatorship means nothing else but this—power without limits, resting directly upon force, restrained by no law, absolutely unrestricted by rules".[11] This was both naïve and dangerous. Not only was the concept not remotely "scientific", but its essence—power without limits, unrestricted by rules—was the perfect seedbed for Stalinism.

On 29th October the All-Russian Executive Committee of the Union of Railwaymen, known as the Vikzhel, offered to host talks to create what Rabinowitch described as "an all-inclusive, homogeneous socialist government from the Bolsheviks on the extreme left to the popular socialists on the right".[12] Vikzhel threatened to call a national strike unless the Bolsheviks and the Mensheviks/SRs/Trudoviks halted what it called a "fratricidal war". The majority of the Bolshevik Central Committee were keen to participate in these talks. With Lenin and Trotsky busy elsewhere the CC unanimously declared that it wished to broaden the composition of Sovnarcom to include *all* Soviet parties, and that Sovnarcom itself be answerable to the Central Executive of the All-Russia Soviet Congress. On that basis talks began immediately with the other socialist parties.

A wave of resolutions from factories and army units welcomed the Vikzhel initiative. Bolshevik sailors on the destroyer *Oleg* broadcast via ship's radio their relief at the "glad tidings" of negotiations between "all socialist parties who are trying to form a bloc".[13] A resolution passed by a large majority at the Baltic Shipbuilding and Machine Works in Petrograd on 2nd November declared:

> Seeing the full horror of civil war, we decisively and insistently demand the immediate cessation of this bloody nightmare and the creation of a unified socialist authority based on understanding and mutual concessions by all the socialist parties, from the comrade Bolsheviks to the popular socialists.

It demanded that such a coalition government should carry out four urgent tasks: 1) approval of the Decree on Land, 2) immediate proposal for a democratic peace to all warring countries, 3) control over production and distribution, and 4) the convocation of the Constituent Assembly as scheduled.[14]

The wishes of these workers were clear enough, but the very fact that talks were occurring, and at the behest of the militant trade union that had seen off Kornilov, gave hope to the Mensheviks and Right SRs who had walked out of the Second Congress that the Bolsheviks could not retain power. They therefore proposed a set of unrealistic demands: that a coalition be formed that excluded "the parties of privilege" (the Octobrists and Kadets) *and* the Bolsheviks, that the decisions of the Second Congress be declared null and void, and that attempts be made to negotiate a truce with Kerensky.

The hardline position of the Mensheviks and Trudoviks stemmed from their bruising experience at the Second Congress and the closure of their newspapers. Even Martov, desperate to reach an agreement between moderate Bolsheviks, Mensheviks and SRs, felt compelled to say clearly to the Bolshevik delegation that the Mensheviks could not agree with the latest Decree issued by the People's Commissar for Justice. "We will not accept a decree which includes shootings and military revolutionary courts, i.e. executions without a trial", he said. This condemnation of political terror was distributed as an official Vikzhel telegram to Petrograd workers.[15]

Kamenev, leading the Bolshevik negotiating team, replied that any socialist coalition government that excluded them would not have majority working-class support. This was true for the moment although Riazanov, chairman of the Petrograd Trade Union Council, sensed that despite temporary support for Bolshevik actions on 25th October many workers supported the Vikzhel initiative. He therefore tried to accommodate the Mensheviks. At the same time he voiced his fears that disarmament of MRC units—currently fighting Krasnov's troops outside Petrograd—would lead to a slaughter of workers by the regular army. He did not need to push this further as the MRC's defeat of Krasnov at Polkovo altered the mood of the Menshevik and SR leaderships. They were also coming under heavy pressure from their own factory branches demanding they shelve differences with the Bolsheviks and form a coalition. The next Menshevik proposal on 31st October therefore agreed to a coalition with the Bolsheviks although it insisted this not include Lenin or Trotsky.

The Bolshevik representatives did not object to the exclusion of Lenin and Trotsky, and the talks soon produced a draft "agreement". Its terms were plain – that a socialist coalition be formed with Victor Chernov, the long-standing SR leader, as Prime Minister; that although Lenin and Trotsky were to be excluded from the government the Bolshevik Party would have four senior ministerial portfolios (Labour, Commerce & Industry, Education and Foreign Affairs); and that the government be accountable to a new body, the Provisional People's Council, with representatives from the Petrograd and Moscow City Dumas, the Trade Union Council, and the first (pre-26th October) Soviet Executive.

With the prospect of a solid agreement on the left and the avoidance of inevitable civil war and famine, the Bolshevik negotiators provisionally agreed these terms, with one reservation. Kamenev insisted that the *current* Soviet Executive, elected on 26th October at the Second Congress, should be represented on the People's Council as it had the better mandate. Although this element of the agreement was left undecided, Vikzhel officials publicly announced that a final agreement was imminent. The bulletin of the Petrograd Soviet, *Rabochii I soldat*, controlled by the Bolsheviks, wrote in its editorial of 1st November that "agreement among all factions at the talks has been reached based on the principle that the government shall be composed of all socialist parties in the Soviet".[16]

This was premature. The Bolshevik Central Committee had not signed off on the agreement. On 1st November the CC met and an angry Lenin said he considered that Vikzhel was "on the side of the Kaledins and the Kornilovs". Riazanov flatly disagreed. He argued that

> Even in Petrograd, power is not in our hands but in the hands of the Soviet, and this has to be faced. If we abandon this course we will be utterly and hopelessly alone. We will be faced with the fact that we tricked the masses, having promised them a Soviet government.[17]

Viktor Nogin, chairman of the Moscow Soviet, predicted any attempt to go it alone would result in civil war and the dissolution of the Soviets. Anton Slutski, representing the hardline Petrograd Committee, insisted that "the question of the Soviets" had been decided and that the Bolsheviks should not consider "broadened Soviets of any kind". Lenin demanded that the Bolsheviks immediately withdraw from the negotiations. Despite this, the CC voted 10-4 to carry on with the talks, but with new conditions.

Lenin reacted as he always did when a democratic decision went against him. He immediately rejected it. Earlier in the day, at a stormy meeting of the Petrograd District Committee, he told those who argued for acceptance of the Vikzhel proposals, "If you get the majority, take power in the Central Executive Committee and carry on. But we will go the sailors". By this he seemed to threaten that if the Bolshevik CC accepted the proposal and worked with the Soviet Executive, installed at the Second Congress *after* 25th October to create a socialist coalition government, he would ignore that decision and ask the Kronstadt sailors to overthrow the Soviet as well. But the Kronstadt sailors had supported the October Insurrection because it was an uprising *in support* of Soviet power. The policy of the Kronstadt Soviet was for a Soviet-based government of all the socialist parties, i.e. the kind of government suggested by Vikzhel and Martov. If Lenin had "gone to the sailors" and asked for their support for an exclusively Bolshevik government, he would have failed.

He never had to take that risk because he ensured the CC added pre-conditions to any final agreement which were sure to be unacceptable to the Mensheviks and SRs. On 1st November, the Soviet Central Executive debated the Vikzhel proposals. The Vikzhel spokesman Krushinsky began by asserting, "It is absolutely vital for all the socialist parties to agree on forming a homogeneous socialist administration". Boris Kamkov, a Left SR, said that his party stood for a "homogenous revolutionary democratic government". With counter-revolutionaries at the gates of Petrograd, "the socialist parties should set aside partisan calculation and close ranks to form a single progressive front". The Left SRs held to their view that "the Soviets are the pivot around which revolutionary democracy can unite".

The Bolshevik delegate Mikhail Volodarsky responded that they could not conclude an agreement "at any price". He outlined the Bolshevik position in a resolution that demanded 1) the Decrees on peace, land and workers' control must be accepted before any coalition government be formed; 2) there must be a "merciless struggle" against counter-revolution;

3) recognition of the Second All-Russian Congress of Soviets as the sole source of authority; 4) any new government to be responsible to the CEC; 5) no organisation to be represented in the CEC not present in the Soviets; and 6) the CEC be expanded to include Soviets not currently represented. The Menshevik-Internationalists and Polish Socialists claimed the Bolshevik resolution was a "bolt from the blue" which prevented reaching agreement. In the heat of the debate nobody remarked that the Bolshevik resolution contradicted itself – that it demanded the Second Congress be the "sole authority" and that the government answer to the CEC while at the same time laying down conditions to the CEC to which it had to agree.[18]

Within the Bolshevik Party, where the real decisions were being made, Lenin called upon the activists of the Petrograd Committee to exert pressure on "the Muscovites" Rykov and Nogin, who stood for a socialist coalition. A stream of resolutions and messages then began to arrive from Petrograd Bolsheviks demanding no concessions be made in the negotiations. Faced with this onslaught, some CC moderates backtracked and agreed that Kamenev had exceeded his remit. The CC decided that whilst the Bolshevik team would return to the talks it would do so only to issue an ultimatum to the other participants.

At the CEC session of 2nd November, the Left SR Boris Malkin fiercely condemned the Bolshevik position. He told the CEC,

the tactics adopted by the Bolshevik Party now in power are leading irrevocably to a schism among the toiling masses; that the dictatorship of a single political group, which it has in effect established, will with inevitable logic bring about severe repression, not only of members of the propertied classes, but also of the masses; that such a policy has already been put into practice by the Council of People's Commissars and other executive bodies, in regard to the press as well as various individuals and organizations; that this policy is inexorably leading to the ruin of the revolution.

He ended with a warning that the Bolsheviks' intransigent position on reaching an agreement "is plunging the country into the abyss of civil war".[19]

After hearing out Malkin's attack, Kamenev repeated the Bolshevik resolution of the previous day. He told the CEC that a socialist coalition government, of whatever complexion, must implement the Decrees on land, peace, workers' control and nationalities passed at the Second Congress of Soviets; that it must be beholden not to a new People's Council but to the current Soviet Executive; and both Lenin and Trotsky must have positions in the new government. Despite Malkin's assault on the Bolsheviks, other Left SRs were tempted to back the Bolshevik majority on the CEC, especially as the Bolshevik position quite clearly stated that Sovnarcom was answerable to the CEC. Proshyan of the Left SRs undercut Malkin completely by suggesting that the Left SRs could support the Bolsheviks as long as a Left SR got to head the Ministry of Agriculture. The majority on the CEC shifted away from its initial rejection of the Bolshevikposition to acceptance.

The CEC was for the moment convinced, but when Riazanov put the Bolshevik CC's new terms to the other

Vikzhel negotiators on 3rd November, they came as an unpleasant shock. The Left SRs/Left Mensheviks wanted to accept them but the majority did not. They regarded Sovnarcom's Decrees – and Sovnarcom itself – as arising from a violent act that had no legitimacy. Whilst this was technically true, it was woefully out of touch with reality. Martov knew the Bolsheviks had to be accommodated if any coalition would work, but the majority of the Mensheviks, the Right SRs and the Bundists – sharing the widespread belief that the Bolsheviks could not retain power for more than a few weeks – rejected the conditions. They blamed the Bolsheviks and the Bolshevik-led CEC for altering the terms of the initial agreement. The talks were not abandoned, but in all essentials they had ceased. The Bolshevik "moderates" – Kamenev, Zinoviev, Rykov, Nogin and Miliutin, though not Lunacharsky – resigned from the CC in protest.

The collapse of the only attempt to form a broad socialist coalition after the October Insurrection, and the general impression amongst the militant working class that it resulted from the refusal of the non-Bolshevik socialists to compromise and not from Lenin's adamant rejection of the idea, gave to Bolsheviks still fighting in other cities added self-confidence and energy. By 3rd November Bolshevik forces had secured Moscow and the sinews of a new regime were beginning to take shape. Its initial Decrees were popular. Sovnarcom, as the face of the new regime, could have exploited that popularity and used it to build a popular socialist consensus amongst the majority of Russian people. Its opponents were in total disarray and commanded little support. Despite resistance to its rule from the remnants of Kerensky's forces and armed rebellion in the Don Region, there was no need to restrict civil rights and freedom of the press. Yet within days of 25th October the new regime had already closed most of Russia's newspapers.

On 29th October, Sovnarcom issued a Decree restricting freedom of the press. The clampdown began immediately. The legendary SR leader Catherine Breshkovsky's *Volia Naroda* was shut down, with the editor and founder of the SR party Andrey Argunov imprisoned in the Peter and Paul Fortress. So too was the social-democratic *Yednistvo*, edited by the "Father of Russian Marxism" George Plekhanov. The printing presses of *Russkaya Volia*, edited by the novelist and playwright Leonard Andreyev (supportive of the February Revolution but critical of the Bolsheviks) were immediately confiscated. Although the official SR journal *Dyelo Narodo* was banned, militant soldiers sympathetic to the SRs guarded its premises and for a while it was produced illegally.

Even the Left Menshevik newspaper *Rabochaya Gazeta*, inclined to support the Bolshevik regime and implacably hostile to counter-revolution, was closed down because it did not slavishly reproduce the Bolshevik line at all times. In February 1918 at the Fourth Congress of Soviets, Lenin confronted socialist delegates who complained that their newspapers had been closed down. "Of course, unfortunately not all of them!" he responded from the top table. "Soon all of them will be closed".[20] Between October 1917 and July 1918 Sovnarcom closed down over 300 newspapers and periodicals.[21]

Between February and October 1917, the Bolshevik Party,

as Trotsky admitted, had "de-Bolshevised" itself in order to respond to mass movements and popular feeling and to attract a wider membership. That phase was over. Already, on 3rd November, Lenin put a resolution to the Central Committee titled "Ultimatum from the majority of the Central Committee to the minority" that demanded that those who wished to pursue talks with other socialist parties desist or be expelled from the party. Lenin insisted on the removal of the dissenters not just from their CC positions but all other posts. Thus Kamenev was replaced as Chair of the Soviet Executive by the uber-loyal functionary Yacob Sverdlov, who was also head of the CC's informal Secretariat.

On 4th November the Bolshevik moderate Yuri Larin put a resolution to the Soviet Executive that newspapers should remain free of censorship and repression unless they incited armed rebellion against Sovnarcom. The resolution was supported by many socialists including Bolshevik moderates and Left SRs. Larin told the CEC, "The measures taken against press freedom could be justified during the actual course of the struggle, but not now. The press should be free so long as it does not incite subversion and insurrection. Censorship of every kind must be completely eliminated". Larin's resolution demanded that Lenin's press Decree be revoked and that "no acts of political repression may be carried out except by authorisation of a special tribunal chosen by the CEC".

Malkin again attacked the Bolsheviks. He demanded the CEC "examine the question of the powers of the Council of People's Commissars, which is issuing one decree after another without any sanction by the CEC". When the Bolshevik CEC Secretary Avenesov replied that it was ridiculous for the

Soviet to "stand up for antiquated notions about liberty of the press", the Left SR Kamkov interjected,

> Either we recognise freedom in words, or else we are behaving hypocritically [...] No one has yet called for the overthrow of the existing regime, yet press freedom is being infringed without due cause. We are morally obliged to rescind these repressive measures, which bring shame on the Russian Revolution.

Lenin and Trotsky themselves led the opposition to Larin's resolution. "You say that we demanded freedom of the press for *Pravda*", Trotsky told delegates who criticised the Bolsheviks for a *volte face* on freedom of the press. "But then we were in a situation where we demanded the Minimum Programme. Now we demand the Maximum Programme. When the state power was in the hands of the bourgeoisie we stood for legal freedom of the press". Lenin added, "We stated earlier that if we took power we would close down bourgeois newspapers. To allow them to exist is to cease to be socialists".[22] Larin's resolution lost by 31 votes to 22. The Bolshevik resolution supporting restrictions on the press passed by 34 votes to 24.

After the resolution was passed the Left SR Prosyhan made a declaration on behalf of the Left SR party:

> The resolution on the press passed by the majority of the CEC is a clear and unambiguous expression of support for a system of political terror and for unleashing civil war. The SR fraction, while remaining in the CEC [...] has no desire to bear any responsibility for this system of terror, ruinous for the revolution,

and therefore withdraws all representatives from the Military Revolutionary Committee, the staff, and all responsible posts.

With Proshyan's words ringing in the air, People's Commissar for Trade and Industry Nogin asked to be given the floor to read an urgent statement on behalf of a group of four of Sovnarcom's People's Commissars: himself, Commissar for Internal Affairs Rykov, Commissar for Agriculture Miliutin and Commissar for Supply Teodorovich.

He read out:

> We take the stand that it is vital to form a socialist government from all parties represented in the Soviets. Only such a government can seal the heroic struggle of the working class and revolutionary army in the October–November days. We consider that a purely Bolshevik government has no choice but to maintain itself by political terror. This is the course on which Sovnarcom is embarked. We cannot follow this course, which will lead to the proletarian mass organizations becoming estranged from those who direct our political affairs, to the establishment of an irresponsible government, and to the annihilation of the revolution and the country.

The four People's Commissars therefore resigned from Sovnarcom. Their statement was officially "adhered to" by Riazanov and other leading Bolsheviks. People's Commissar for Labour Alexander Shliapnikov added that while he agreed with the statement he felt it was "impermissible to lay down my responsibilities".[23] Kamenev also resigned as

Chair of the CEC.

It was a crucial moment. If Kamenev, Rykov and the Bolshevik "moderates" had won out, the October Insurrection might have delivered power to the Soviets instead of to the Bolshevik Party. As it was, Sovnarcom took power and never relinquished it. Central to that power was a Decree titled "Concerning the Procedure for the Ratification and Promulgation of Laws", which gave Sovnarcom the right to act in a legislative capacity. The unilateral assumption of both executive *and* legislative power sidelined the CEC and the Soviets and reversed the entire rationale of the October Insurrection. When Lenin and Trotsky were summoned by the CEC and asked to explain, Lenin simply said he rejected "bourgeois formalism". Trotsky, developing this theme, claimed that Sovnarcom could issue legislation because Sovnarcom and the masses were linked by "a vital and direct bond", although he did not explain how the vital and direct bond actually functioned.[24]

Public division between the Soviet and Sovnarcom called the entire basis of the Bolshevik insurrection into question. Two things came to Lenin's rescue. Firstly, the new regime was mobilising large numbers of volunteers to fight Krasnov's forces. People had died for it. This gave it enormous credibility. Secondly, Lenin's opponents played their cards badly. His critics within the Bolshevik Party resigned from key positions just when they could have used them to hold him to account. The Left SRs had just broken with the main SRs and as yet had no real organisation or structure. When they formed their own party they needed Bolshevik support to survive. Despite their protests about Sovnarcom they were tempted to join it in junior positions. This both defused their criticisms and enabled Lenin to claim that Sovnarcom was, after all, a socialist coalition government.

The Mensheviks were not tempted. Between February and October 1917 they appeared to lose their political bearings. Some of this was due to Martov's absence until May 1917 and the dominance of the forceful but conservative Tseretelli. At their best they had stood for political liberty, civil rights and a controlled expansion of public ownership–although the Provisional Government's endorsement of the *Volosts'* seizure of landed estates and attempt to provide communal oversight of the redistributed land came from Chernov and the SRs. At their worst they slipped into support for imperialist war aims and a centralised capitalist economy, if with added trade union engagement.

After the October Insurrection and Martov's renewed command of the party, the Mensheviks rediscovered their radical spirit. Even before October leading Mensheviks like Theodore Dan were attacking Kerensky from the left. At the Extraordinary Congress of the Menshevik party held on 4th December, Dan and Tseretelli acknowledged their mistakes when in office and Dan supported Martov for leader. The Congress elected a new Menshevik Central Committee in which Left Mensheviks predominated. Martov now took the mantle of undisputed Menshevik leader.

Martov understood why the urban working class had switched from Menshevism, so powerful in February, to Bolshevism, but he also sensed that this support was for Soviet power and not for one-party dictatorship. He broadly supported Sovnarcom's early Decrees although he tried, through the Vikzhel negotiations, to establish Sovnarcom as a *Soviet* government, accountable to the Soviet Executive and Congress. At the Extraordinary Congress, Martov proposed a programme for the Mensheviks that repeated his line at the Vikzhel talks, i.e. for a socialist coalition government answerable to a Central Council consisting of representatives of the Soviets, the trade unions, and urban and rural local government. Whilst the Mensheviks refused to enter a government that did not implement a democratic programme they refused to support the violent overthrow of the Bolshevik government. It was this programme that they intended to put before the Soviets in the early months of 1918.

CHAPTER TEN

No Power to the Soviets

By January 1918, with most of their opponents' newspapers suppressed, the Bolsheviks had secured a massive majority on the Soviet CEC, which reduced it to a rubber stamp for Sovnarcom's policies. If democratic mechanisms had existed to alter the balance of forces on the Executive—i.e. free and fair elections in which other parties could attain a majority and thus, in theory, create a new Sovnarcom—that need not have been a permanent problem. But these mechanisms were being phased out. The first "purge" of Bolshevik dissenters in early November and the subsequent wide use of governmental decrees demonstrated that Sovnarcom was not about to share power.

In the immediate aftermath of 25th October, the State Bank and Treasury refused to recognise Sovnarcom. Civil servants in all ministries went on strike to protest the imposition of a government whose mandate they did not accept. The People's Commissar for Finance, Menzhinsky, was reduced to arriving at the State Bank with armed soldiers and demanding the transfer of ten million rubles to the government. Even when Sovnarcom established control of the Bank it had very little idea how to run it. Contrary to *The State and Revolution*, it turned out that ordinary workers and peasants could not take over the existing organs of the state and run them without some level of training and specialist knowledge. Nor could they "smash" them without a viable alternative to put in their place. It took Sovnarcom several weeks to break this resistance. The leaders of the civil-service strike were arrested and imprisoned. Junior civil servants were promoted to follow Sovnarcom's orders and the banks began to print money as instructed. The immediate threat of a complete stoppage of government services had been averted.

The hopes of those who opposed the Bolsheviks now hinged on the outcome of the national elections being held for a Constituent Assembly. These elections had been long prepared by the Provisional Government (one of the Bolshevik's most vocal complaints against it was that it had taken so long to hold them) and they were held on a regional "Party List" basis. Voting took place on 12th-14th November in less than ideal circumstances—sporadic fighting was still taking place throughout the Empire and many of the parties participating in the elections could not communicate with the electorate because of press censorship. Nonetheless, the creaking Russian state-machine did its best to deliver a meaningful election.[1] The overall result, in Sheila Fitzpatrick's view, was "the best barometer we have of national popular opinion at the time the Bolsheviks took power".[2]

Using Oliver H. Radkey's definitive reconstruction of the returns, the elections gave the SRs 15,848,004 votes; the Bolsheviks 9,844,637; the Mensheviks 1,364,826; the

Trudoviks 322,078; the Kadets (made illegal shortly after the elections) 1,986,601; and the Cossack party 663,112. The Landowner Party secured only 171,245 votes, with a variety of rightist/Orthodox Christian parties getting even less. Added to this were the nationalist branches of the larger parties, which complicated the overall result but did not detract from the general victory of the SRs, mainly because it was nationalist SRs who came top of the regional lists. In Ukraine, the Ukrainian SR Party secured 1,286,157 votes over the Ukrainian Social Democrats (which stood as one party, not split into Bolsheviks and Mensheviks), who secured only 95,117. The "Ukrainian Socialist bloc" (whose socialism was a fusion of SR land redistribution with added nationalism) secured more than either of these. The Muslim nationalist and socialist parties attracted about half a million votes each in those areas where they stood, although they would have obtained more had they not been banned from standing in the central Asian regions where Muslims predominated.

The urban electorates of Petrograd and Moscow returned Bolshevik majorities. In Petrograd the result was Bolsheviks 424,027; Kadets 246,506; SR 152,231; and Menshevik 29,167. In Moscow it was similar—Bolsheviks 366,148; Kadets 263,859; SRs 62,260; and Mensheviks 21,597. These results emphasised the huge polarisation in the cities between the middle class and the working class, and the marginalising of non-Bolshevik socialists. The Kadets only secured this level of support in the great metropolises of Petrograd and Moscow whilst the SRs, relatively weak here, were in a majority nearly everywhere else. In terms of how the 707 deputies of the Assembly would be divided, the result translated into 370 SRs (with about 40 of these Left SR), 175 Bolsheviks, 17 Kadets, 16 Mensheviks, and 99 others.[3]

This was a crushing blow to the Bolsheviks, who had "entered with zeal, and sometimes with real enthusiasm, into the election campaign, in which the party militants had shown tremendous activity".[4] They had not expected to lose, and as soon as the results were in they sought to discredit them. The Bolsheviks claimed the overall result did not convey the actuality of post-October Russia as there was a Left SR "party" which was not counted as such. Yet even if it had been recorded as a separate Left SR vote, this would not have increased the Bolshevik vote.[5] At the same time they claimed that only those who voted Bolshevik cast meaningful votes anyway, because a vote for Bolshevism derived from advanced class consciousness whilst a vote against them was evidence of lack of class consciousness (except for the Kadets, who *did* have class consciousness, but of the wrong type). Other votes, whether nationalist, Orthodox, Muslim, Cossack, Jewish socialist, Finnish socialist, Ukrainian socialist etc., were disregarded as backward or misguided.

These were desperate arguments. The result was obvious for all to see. The mainstream SRs – representing a form of popular Narodnik socialism allied to Soviet democracy, a true reflection of the Russian revolutionary tradition of the last fifty years – had won. As Radkey put it, "Three weeks after the October Revolution the Bolsheviks had signally failed to secure popular sanction for their seizure of power and had mustered only one fourth of the electorate behind their banner".[6]

As soon as Lenin received the results he postponed

convocation of the Assembly until 18th January, 1918. This gave the government more time to harass, arrest and imprison elected delegates (the Kadet party was made illegal soon after, making its attendance almost impossible). On 13th December, *Pravda* published Lenin's "Theses on the Constituent Assembly", which put the two main grounds of Bolshevik dismissal of the legitimacy of the Assembly. These were 1) that "a republic of Soviets is a higher form of democracy than the usual bourgeois republic with a Constituent Assembly"[7]; and 2) the elections returns did not, as Cliff later put it, "correspond to the actual will of the people", as since October "...the masses had moved further to the left, a change not reflected in the Assembly".[8]

Lenin did not explain how he had more accurately divined the will of the people than a national general election which took place three weeks *after* 25th October and whose results came in only a month before he wrote. Nor did Sovnarcom offer to re-run the election to produce a more accurate result. Lenin simply asserted that if the Constituent Assembly did not recognise Soviet power and the decrees passed by Sovnarcom since 25th October then "the crisis in connection with the Constituent Assembly can be settled only in a revolutionary way, by Soviet power adopting the most energetic, speedy, firm and determined revolutionary measures".

Lenin's initial idea was to declare the Assembly illegal before it could even meet, but the Left SRs would not agree to this. Instead the government targeted many of those elected. After it was announced that convocation of the Assembly would be delayed there was a 100,000 strong demonstration in Petrograd in its support. The march was mostly supported by middle-class Kadets, moderate socialists and mainstream SRs. The fact that the march was part-organised by the Kadet Central Committee, at the same time as prominent Kadets like Miliukov were working with the "Volunteer Army" of the Don Region to overthrow the Bolshevik government, gave Sovnarcom a valid reason to move against the entire Kadet party and in doing so discredit all agitation in favour of the Assembly.

In mid-December several prominent SR leaders, including Chairman of the All-Russian Soviet of Peasant Deputies Nicolai Avkenstyev and the popular satirist Sorokin, were arrested because of anti-Sovnarcom statements. In spite of this, the SRs and Mensheviks prepared for convocation of the Assembly and drew up policy statements for a new government. As they did so Sovnarcom called up its most reliable military units – the sailors of the Baltic Fleet and the crack Lettish Sharpshooters. As 18th January approached the government declared that it had learnt that the "forces of Kerensky and Kaledin" were planning an attack "on Soviet power" that very day, and therefore the city was declared to be in a state of siege and under martial law. Its citizens were forbidden to take part in any marches or rallies.[9]

Despite this, on 5th January 50,000 people marched to the Mars Field to rally in support of the Assembly. Although there were some delegations from Petrograd factories, the marchers were mostly white-collar employees, middle-class professionals and students. When the march approached the Tauride Palace it was suddenly fired upon from the rooftops. Some marchers were killed outright. Others were injured when Bolshevik contingents attacked them and tore down their banners. Gorky's newspaper *Novaya Zhizn* reported the next day that there were at least fifteen dead and dozens wounded.[10] "For almost a hundred years", wrote Gorky in the newspaper on 9th January,

> the finest Russians have lived by the idea of the Constituent Assembly. In the struggle for this idea, thousands of the intelligentsia and tens of thousands of workers and peasants have perished in prisons, in exile, and at hard labour [...] And now the People's Commissars have given orders to shoot the democracy that demonstrated in honour of this idea.[11]

Fifty-five years later, with no threat hanging over him, Marcel Liebman wrote in his widely praised study of Leninism that the Bolsheviks had "briskly dispersed" a pro–Assembly demonstration, but otherwise did not elaborate.[12]

The Constituent Assembly opened at 4pm in the old State Duma chamber of the Tauride in an atmosphere of barely suppressed violence. The SR leader Victor Chernov was elected the Assembly's President. He tried in vain to make a speech over catcalls from the galleries. The old revolutionary declared that the two main goals of the Assembly were to transfer land ownership to the peasants and to achieve a democratic peace (though it would not sign a separate peace with Germany). Chernov said that the Assembly was willing to submit all its decrees to popular referendum and to work with the Soviets.

Before any further business could be taken, Sverdlov marched to the podium and introduced the "Declaration of the Rights of Working and Exploited People", which approved all the Decrees already passed by Sovnarcom. He demanded it be immediately voted upon. The Assembly might have accepted the Declaration had it not contained an additional clause clearly designed to provoke its rejection – agreement that the Assembly's only role was to formulate general principles and that it had no power to legislate. The Assembly therefore rejected the Declaration by 247 votes to 146. After this the Bolshevik delegation withdrew, followed shortly after by the Left SRS.[13]

Chernov then moved a "Draft Basic Law on Land" prepared by the SR party. The Draft abolished all property rights in land within the Russian Empire; nationalised "all land, mineral wealth, forests and waters currently held by individuals, groups or institutions as property or under another law of estate" without compensation; and placed the right to dispose of it in the hands of central and local government. Chernov had just finished reading the Draft when a Bolshevik sailor stood up at the podium and said, "I have been instructed to inform you that everyone present should vacate the hall as the guard is tired" (it was by now 4am). Chernov asked, "What instruction? From whom?", to which the sailor replied, "I am the head of the Tauride Palace Guard and I have instructions from Commissar Dybenko". Chernov told the head of the Guard, "All members of the Constituent Assembly are also very tired, but tiredness must not interrupt the proclamation of the land law for which all Russia has been waiting".[14]

This led to more abusive shouting from soldiers in the galleries. Chernov said he did not recognise the instruction and he pressed on with business. At 4.40am, in order to avoid violence, he declared the session closed, to be resumed at 5pm the same day. The delegates left the Tauride. When they returned that afternoon they found the entrance barred by troops and two field guns. Newspapers which printed a true record of what had occurred inside the Assembly were removed from newsstands by armed soldiers, ripped up or burnt. Later that day Sovnarcom passed a decree abolishing the Constituent Assembly.

Three days later, on 9th January, crowds manned a ten-mile-long route for the funerals of those killed in the pro-Assembly demonstration of 5th January, including a banner carried by workers from the Semiennkov factory which proclaimed, "Eternal memory to the victims of the violence of the Smolny autocrats!". After the demonstration, Menshevik trade union activists were greeted warmly at the factory. Thousands of workers congregated at the Obukhov Works and at other factories throughout the Nevsky district to protest the closing of the Assembly. Even the Vyborg district evinced rumblings of discontent at the shutdown of the Assembly, a sign that the pro-Bolshevik atmosphere of October was already beginning to shift.[15] The primary reason the dissolution was achieved so easily was that the peasants, having apparently secured land redistribution through the Land Decree, were no longer concerned about events in Petrograd. Without its mass base the SR party was powerless.

The Constituent Assembly, like the Kronstandt rebellion of 1921, has been consistently misrepresented by Leninist propagandists. It had been elected under universal suffrage and a free, fair and secret national ballot. The result of the election had produced a populist, agrarian-inclined socialist majority in tune with the long-held desires of most of Russia's people. The Assembly convened despite the use of repression and violence on the part of a defeated governmental party unwilling to give up power. It selected a veteran anti-Tsarist radical socialist to be its president and it opened with all delegates singing "The Internationale". Its last act was to pass land reform legislation nationalising landed estates without compensation and redistributing them to peasant communities. It is likely that had it survived it would have reached a better working accord with the Soviets than did the Bolshevik government, under which the Soviets as functioning democratic bodies soon died out. If it was "counter-revolutionary", it was no more so than the state power that killed it.

The majority of workers and peasants cared far more about ending the war than they did about the fate of the Assembly. Sovnarcom, well aware of this, had sent Trotsky, the Commissar for Foreign Affairs, to negotiate with the Germans at the Polish city of Brest-Litovsk. Immediately after 25th October Sovnarcom agreed a temporary armistice with Germany, but although Russian forces were rapidly demobilising the German army in the east remained intact. After its insistence that Russia engage in proper negotiation about a peace treaty—in which it expected Russia to surrender a large amount of territory or it would cross the armistice line and march straight to Petrograd and Moscow—Trotsky arrived at Brest-Litovsk on 1st December with a remit to drag out the process as long as possible in the hope that, before long, a proletarian revolution would begin in Germany that would make such diplomacy superfluous.

This was extremely optimistic. Although the war was nowhere near as popular in Germany as it had been, Rosa Luxemburg's Spartacist League, formed after the SPD's betrayal of internationalism in 1914, had only about 2,000 members and little connection to the organised labour movement. As the war dragged on there were sparks of anti-war activity and in April 1917 200,000 workers across Germany went on strike to protest a cut in war rations. But there was a long distance between such protests and the overthrow of Germany's military-state machine by a revolutionary party with mass working-class support. In May 1916, Liebknecht was arrested for leading an anti-war protest in Berlin, shortly after followed by Luxemburg and Mehring. Faced with mounting repression within the SPD against members who voiced anti-war sentiments, and an announcement by German trade union leaders that the unions would remain loyal to the government during war-time, the Spartacists and the "centrists" Haase, Bernstein and Kautsky met in January 1917 to consider a way forward.

The outcome was the formation in April 1917 of the Independent Social Democratic Party (USPD), which took about 100,000 of the SPD's 240,000 members with it when it split away. Born from the war, it was a volatile fusion of anti-war centrists and radical socialists, counting Kautsky, Bernstein, Haase, Hilferding, Mehring, Luxemburg and Liebknecht amongst its key figures. Its manifesto, written by Kautsky, attacked "government socialists" and trade union leaders for having moved to the right and betrayed German workers. The manifesto demanded an immediate amnesty for political prisoners, freedom of the press and freedom of assembly, the eight-hour day, and universal suffrage for men and women to all elective bodies. It welcomed Russia's February Revolution and noted that while the Russian proletariat had established a democratic republic the SPD continued to accept the monarchy.

This was the most important development on the German political scene during the war. The Spartacists knew it—they worked within the USPD as it represented the most radical elements of the German working class. The Bolsheviks, however, condemned the USPD as much as the SPD and pinned their hopes on the Spartacists alone. This totally misinterpreted German politics. The SPD was still the main workers' party. Although there was little chance of a revolutionary overthrow of the German state, this did not preclude the capture of the state by the SPD or USPD in the event of Germany's defeat in the war and the formation of a democratic republic. This was as far as most German workers wished to go, leaving the Bolsheviks, as Kamenev and Zinoviev had predicted prior to October 1917, isolated.

Lenin was beginning to sense this. By early 1918 he was urging acceptance of whatever annexationist peace was available rather than take what he called a "blind gamble" on imminent European revolution. Trotsky, at Brest-Litovsk, took a position of "neither war nor peace", i.e. Russia should simply withdraw from the war without signing a peace treaty with Germany. The nominally independent states of Ukraine and Poland were keen to sign a deal with Germany and thus secure some form of statehood, but Trotsky ignored them and concentrated on specifically Russian concerns. If revolution broke out in Germany, this would all be irrelevant anyway.

The Bolshevik "Left Communists" around Bukharin and Kollontai regarded a treaty with Imperial Germany as a retreat from the Bolshevik commitment to extend the revolution westward. They wanted a "revolutionary war" led by volunteer Bolshevik cadres who would suborn the German army just as they had Kornilov and Krasnov. Lenin considered this a suicidal strategy. Millions of peasant soldiers had deserted, returning home to secure the land promised them by the Land Decree. Reports from factories and urban Soviets were clear that workers did not want to resume the war, revolutionary or otherwise. When Trotsky declared at Brest-Litovsk that although Russia would not sign a peace treaty with Germany it was "leaving the war" and no longer considered itself a belligerent, the result was that the German army immediately marched into Ukraine and northern Russia, meeting absolutely no resistance.

Had it continued its advance, Petrograd would have fallen within days. After titanic arguments within Sovnarcom and the Bolshevik cc, Lenin rammed through his policy of signing any deal on the table as long as it stopped hostilities with Germany. So the Treaty of Brest-Litovsk was signed, with acceptance of all the German conditions. It was a Carthaginian peace, requiring Russian to cede to Germany all of its Baltic territories, Poland, Finland, Ukraine and part of Belorussia. This totaled 1,267,000 square miles of territory and 55 million people (amounting to a third of the old Russian Empire and 34% of its population). It also meant the new Russian government giving up a third of its agriculture, 73% of its iron production and 75% of its coalmines.

The terms of the treaty were accepted at a special Congress of the Bolshevik Party (now renamed the Russian Communist Party, or RCP) in March 1918. The Left SRs, who like the Right SRs represented a mainly peasant constituency, many of whom lived in the territories ceded to Germany, resigned from the government in protest. The Bolsheviks were now utterly alone. With the possibility of rescue by other European revolutions receding, they tightened their grip on the new Russian state machine, which meant tightening their grip on the new society itself.

By October 1917 there were about 900 local Soviets throughout the country controlling virtually every aspect of social life from housing to hospitals, plus more than 2,000 elected Factory Committees. Lenin's Draft Decree on Workers' Control had declared that workers' control was to be carried out "by all workers and employees in a given enterprise, either directly if the enterprise is small enough to permit it, or through delegates to be immediately elected at mass meetings". But after its publication Sovnarcom clarified that all existing Factory Committees would be subject to an "All-Russian Council of Workers' Control" (ARCWC). The ARCWC was to be made up of representatives from the Soviets and trade unions, bodies likely to be dominated by Bolsheviks, and for the time being it was the employers, not the Committees, who controlled production. In view of these provisions Brinton concluded, "The Decree on Workers' Control proved, in practice, not to be worth the paper it was written on".[16]

When the Decree went to the Soviet Executive for

ratification the Bolshevik trade union official Lozovsky said it was vital that "workers in various enterprises don't run away with the idea that the factories belong to them".[17] The amended Decree, which gave ultimate authority to the ARCWC, was passed by the Executive and signed by Sovnarcom the next day. People's Commissar Miliutin (who had now rejoined Sovnarcom) admitted that "legislation on Workers' Control which should logically have fitted into the framework of an economic plan had had to precede legislation on the plan itself". This had happened because "life overtook us" and it became necessary to "unite into one solid state apparatus the workers' control which was being operated on the spot". By December 1917 the number of independent Factory Committees had mushroomed to 2,100, including 68% of firms with over 200 employees. Although most of these wished for state support, and in some cases nationalisation, they did so as a means to access goods, resources, funds and specialist expertise to help them achieve their goals, not for the imposition of new management.

The problems facing the Factory Committees arose not just from social collapse but what Sirianni called "concerted sabotage by Russian capital".[18] Russian employers were, of course, hostile to the new regime. But their special hatred was reserved for the Factory Committees, who fundamentally challenged their managerial prerogatives. In response to the 14th November Decree on Workers' Control, mine owners in the Urals and Donetz basin threatened to close mines. The Petrograd Manufacturers Association threatened to do the same to all major plants in the capital, especially those who followed the instructions of the Central Council of

Factory Committees. Some employers withheld wages as economic punishment of workers who challenged them for control of the production process. The employers' actions raised again whether workers' control should now become workers' self-management.

The Factory Committees were accused by both employers and Bolsheviks of not seeing the bigger picture and of disregarding the urgent need for coordinated national production. But, as David Mandel demonstrated in his study of the movement, "this argument was to a large degree disingenuous, since committee conferences consistently emphasised that workers' control could be effective only within a framework of national economic regulation".[19] To help achieve this they planned an All-Russian Congress of Factory Committees that would create a federated structure within which regional and local committees could operate. Had this proceeded it would have been a clear threat to the hegemony of the Bolshevik Party. In response, Bolshevik trade union officials quickly mobilised to block any call for a national congress. Without a congress it was almost impossible for the Committees to create a national, federated structure of workers' control built upon local networks.

Meanwhile the core structures of the new state began to solidify. Within six weeks of 25th October, Sovnarcom had created a secret police, the Cheka. Its remit to uncover and suppress "counter-revolutionary activities" was sufficiently wide that it would quickly begin to harass and arrest not just disaffected members of the bourgeoisie but any on the labour-socialist left who failed to support Sovnarcom. As early as 9th November, two weeks after an insurrection whose ostensible goal was to transfer all power to the Soviets, Sovnarcom unilaterally dissolved the Soviet in the Commissariat of Posts and Telegraphs. On 28th November it did the same to the Soviet in the Admiralty. On the economic front a Decree of 5th December set up a Supreme Economic Council (known as Vesenka) which was to "direct to a uniform end" the activities of all the other economic bodies in the state.

Given the breakdown of the Russian economy at the time, the creation of such a body was, in itself, a sensible and practical move. It was not Vesenka's existence but its powers and personnel that were problematic. Although it contained a few representatives from the ARCWC, it was mainly a body of appointed managers and "experts". Within weeks it had absorbed the ARCWC. Lenin was candid about this, admitting "we passed from workers' control to the creation of the Supreme Council of National Economy".[20] William G. Rosenberg's study of labour relations in post-October Petrograd finds that although workers wanted state support for their plant-level initiatives they did not wish to lose control over their own destiny, which they had secured by occupation of the factories and creation of Factory Committees. "Yet almost without exception", Rosenberg records, "spokesmen for the various chief committees and commissions set up within the Council of People's Commissars condemned the independence and autonomy of factory and railroad committees, and assailed workers for lack of discipline".[21]

In December, the Central Council of Petrograd Factory Committees published a "Practical Manual for the Implementation of Workers' Control of Industry", which explained how workers' control could be expanded into workers' self-management. Amongst its suggestions were plans to convert war production to social production, including Factory Committees coordinating amongst themselves to ensure an adequate supply of fuel and other materials. It suggested Regional Federations of Factory Committees reporting to an All-Russian Federation. The Manual stated its ambition that "workers' control of industry, as part of workers' control of the totality of economic life, must not be seen in the narrow sense of a reform of institutions but in the widest possible sense: that of moving into fields previously dominated by others. Control should merge into management".[22]

In sharp contrast, the ARCWC's "General Instructions on Workers' Control in Conformity with the Decree of November 14th", known as the "Counter-Manual", laid out which functions fell to Factory Committees and which to owner-managers. Its General Instructions stated that the role of the Committees was confined to carrying out directives issued by central government agencies "specifically entrusted with the regulation of economic activities on a national scale". The Counter-Manual stressed that Committees should not concern themselves with financial management of enterprises, nor occupy any more factories. It made explicit that "the right to issue orders related to the management, running and functioning of enterprises remains in the hands of the owner".[23]

As early as March 1918 Sovnarcom unilaterally ended workers' control of the railways. It granted "dictatorial powers" to the Commissariat of Ways and Communications and made it explicit that "administrative technical executives" in every region and locality were answerable to the People's Commissar only. These were "the embodiment of the whole of the dictatorial power of the proletariat in the given railways centre". In response, the Left Communist Nikolai Ossinski wrote in *Kommunist*:

> We stand for the construction of the proletarian society by the class creativity of the workers themselves, not by ukases from the captains of industry [...] Socialism and socialist organisation must be set up by the proletariat itself, or they will not be set up at all; something else will be set up: state capitalism.[24]

An inevitable offshoot of the restriction of industrial democracy was the death of the most independent, rampantly democratic bodies of all: the Soviets. Alexander Rabinowitch's granular study of Petrograd's First City District Soviet found that "the breakdown of democratic practices and the bureaucratisation of political affairs began almost at once after October, and certainly well before the explosion of what is usually considered the civil war crisis in May and June 1918".[25] But the picture was complex. Working-class socialists struggled, in the most challenging conditions, to transform society from the bottom up. Rabinowitch concedes that in spite of the erosion of democratic practices the system of local government introduced by the District Soviet was—at least until 1919—a genuine revolutionary dictatorship of the proletariat, run and staffed by people of working-class origin committed to meaningful revolutionary change.

The Petrograd First City District Soviet covered 25% of

the land area of Petrograd and was responsible for over half a million people. After October it entirely replaced local Dumas and municipal boards. It had its own departments for housing and resettlement; social welfare including pensions, care of orphans and food kitchens; culture and education; and a legal section to determine exactly how Sovnarcom's decrees would be implemented.[26] And yet the more governmental responsibility city and regional Soviets took on, the more their democratic freedom was curtailed. Sovnarcom was not about to let the Mensheviks or SRs run a large part of Petrograd, nor any other large city.

This was made brutally clear between March and June 1918, in "a unique period of multi-party elections to the Soviets".[27] A Sovnarcom decree of 5th January declared, "The entire country must be covered with a network of new Soviets", and explained that all Soviets were now invested with the powers of former local and regional government. At the Seventh Party Congress in March 1918 Lenin stressed that the Soviets were the basis of a new form of state. He told the Congress:

> Soviet power is a new type of state without a bureaucracy, without police, without a regular army, a democracy that brings to the fore the vanguard of the working people, gives them legislative and executive authority, makes them responsible for military defence, and creates machinery that can re-educate the masses.[28]

Lenin's vision, at least initially, was one of genuine social emancipation, of the raising up of the downtrodden through organs of self-rule. That vision died on the vine. The Soviets had real powers but Lenin never claimed they would always reflect the will of the majority of workers who could participate in them. If Soviets exercised their powers by voting for non-Bolshevik majorities or questioning the direction of Sovnarcom's policies, that power was swiftly removed. The hostile reaction to the closing of the Constituent Assembly and the Brest-Litovsk treaty made the government back off on overt repression for a short while. This led to an explosion of democracy amongst the only bodies left in the state that could express it, and a direct challenge to the government.

In the Central Industrial Region during this period the Menshevik party won elections to every city Soviet in which elections were allowed. With the propertied classes denied the vote, this attests to a major increase in its working-class and peasant base of support in a very short time. The consequences of this support were demonstrated in the provincial town of Kaluga, where the Mensheviks demanded Bolshevik commissars provide an account of their expenditure of Soviet funds. In response, all the Menshevik deputies of the Kaluga Soviet were arrested as they sat in the Palace of Labour. Such was the local outrage that they had to be released the next day. After this their support increased again until on 8th June, when all Mensheviks and SRs were expelled permanently from the Kaluga Soviet.[29] All across the region the Bolsheviks lost town and city Soviets to the Mensheviks and SRs. In Kostroma, Tver, Ryazan, Tula, Yaroslavl and other towns the results were the same. The Bolsheviks now had a choice—accept the outcome of the votes of an exclusively worker-peasant constituency or reject them and rely on state violence to cling to power. Violence was chosen.

In Kostroma, the Bolsheviks had a majority in the Soviet until March 1918. The Kostroma Mensheviks demanded a relaxation of state control over bread prices and removal of the ban on workers travelling out of town to purchase food. The result was that on 23rd May the Mensheviks and SRs gained a majority on the local Soviet. After an internal debate in which some Bolsheviks argued they must respect the people's wishes and give up their seats on the Executive, a majority refused to do so. Instead, Kostroma's Bolsheviks issued a bulletin which said they had "taken power without relying on the majority in the Soviet". It finished, "Since the events of May 23rd we have stopped talking to the Mensheviks and SRs as comrades and we have started talking to them with the language of power".[30] The "language of power" consisted of bringing in armed Cheka units to raid the offices of the local Menshevik newspaper and arrest Kostroma's leading Mensheviks.

In the industrial city of Tula, dominated by two large armaments factories of 40,000 workers, the Mensheviks were so strong that it took until December 1917 for the Bolsheviks to establish control of the city. Even then the Mensheviks held a majority in the Soviet. A special conference of workers discussed issues ranging from unemployment to wages to how to manage the problems arising from Brest-Litovsk. The conference drew up a series of demands, including the re-establishment of a democratic republic, the recall of the Constituent Assembly, measures against unemployment, and organisation of the country to defend against German aggression. This level of independence could not be allowed, and the Bolsheviks quickly shut down the Menshevik paper *Narodnyi Golos*, raided and smashed up the Menshevik local party's HQ and a worker's social club, and made further arrests.[31]

In Yaraslavl suppression was even more violent. Since October 1917 the Bolsheviks had held a majority in the city's Soviet, but they refused to allow new elections. After the Mensheviks kept pressing for elections, the Commander of the Yaraslavl Red Guards publically announced, "Those who are spreading Menshevik counter-revolutionary literature will be shot on the spot". The intimidation failed, and new elections were called on 9th April, in which the Mensheviks secured 47 seats to the Bolsheviks' 38 and the SRs' 13. Following the result, the Bolshevik chair of the Soviet Executive declared the election null and void and the Soviet itself illegal. The reaction of Yaraslavl workers was immediate – a conference was called to defend the Soviet and some workers took strike action in protest at its closure. After these strikers were all dismissed the protest spread to other factories and plants, shops, streetcars, printing shops and the railways. Following this, new elections were held in which the Mensheviks secured four times as many votes as the Bolsheviks. This was the final straw for the Bolsheviks, who closed down the Soviet and declared martial law.

The same pattern was followed in Kovrov, where marches by striking workers demanding new elections were fired upon by Red Guards. And in Roslavl, where in May 1918 after elections returned a Menshevik majority, the Menshevik deputies were refused admittance to the Soviet by armed Red Guards. After a strike by railway workers in protest, the

Red Guards attacked a strikers' rally, then arrested and shot several strike leaders.[32] In Rostov-on-Don, a broad-based Bolshevik-led MRC had seized power in the city after 25th October and fought off General Kaledin's military forces. When Red Guards entered the city in February 1918 and tried to take over, they managed to alienate not just Rostov's citizens but also the MRC, who had believed that the purpose of the revolution was to transfer "all power to the Soviets". After Red Guards attempted to shut down the Soviet, the Bolshevik MRC joined forces with Mensheviks and SRs to fight them off. After months of civil strife in the city, the Mensheviks won Soviet elections in April 1918 on a platform of returning to democratic local government, whereupon the Red Guards disbanded the Soviet entirely and declared the Mensheviks and SRs counter-revolutionaries.[33]

The final epitaph for the Soviets was delivered in Tambov, when after election to the city Soviet the Mensheviks and SRs held three-quarters of the seats and attempted to form a new Executive. As they sat in session armed Red Guards burst in and demanded they disperse. When asked what mandate they had to do so the commander pulled out his pistol and exclaimed, "This is my mandate!" The next day it attempted to convene again, only to be met by a proclamation from the Red Guards that read, "The Soviet is disbanded forever! The time has come to establish not the power of the Soviets but the dictatorship of the revolutionary parties".[34]

The workers of Yaraslavl, Kostroma, Tambov, Komrov, Tula, Tver, Rostov-on-Don and many other towns and cities now knew how much the Bolsheviks valued their "self-activity". As a result, many workers began to draw parallels between the dispersal of the Constituent Assembly and the similar dispersal of local Soviets that returned non-Bolshevik majorities. The Mensheviks secured these majorities not just in the Central Industrial Region but across the Black Earth Region (south of Moscow) and the Upper Volga and Urals Region. In the Lower Volga, Kuban and Don Regions the picture was more complex, with constantly shifting power struggles between Bolsheviks, Mensheviks, SRs, Cossacks, anarchist bands and incipient "White" armies (i.e. real counter-revolutionaries, whom the Mensheviks, unlike some of the more protean and undisciplined SRs, refused on principle to work with no matter what the ostensible aim).

Examining the record of Soviet elections in the first half of 1918, one of the most authoritative historians of early Soviet Russia concludes that by June 1918 the Mensheviks could justly claim that "large numbers of the industrial working class were now behind them, and that but for systematic dispersal and packing of the Soviets, and the mass arrests at workers' meetings and congresses, their party could eventually have won power by its policy of constitutional opposition".[35] This may have been true had constitutional opposition been allowed. But the chance to express genuine dissent that existed in the first half of 1918 – when newspapers such as the Mensheviks' *Vperod* and Maxim Gorky's *Novaya Zhihn* were allowed to publish, and Mensheviks and SRs could sit on the Soviet CEC – was soon extinguished.

Martov, as a member of the CEC, attempted to use that platform to voice criticisms at its packed and rowdy sessions in the Hotel Metropole, until 14th June, 1918 when all Mensheviks and SRs were expelled from the Executive, reducing it to a one-party bloc. At the same time *Vperod* and *Novyi luch*, the last remnants of the Menshevik press, were closed down. It was not a coincidence that the Mensheviks were denied these platforms on the eve of both the Fifth All-Russian Congress of Soviets, at which they were expected to return a majority, and a planned general strike in Petrograd to protest government policies on the economy and the Soviets.

Petrograd was suffering terrible food shortages, made worse by the loss of Ukraine, which produced more than half of Russia's grain. The mass demobilisation of the army had swamped towns and cities. This resulted in an unemployment rate of nearly 50% in the capital. Added to this was growing unhappiness with the administration of local and district Soviets, many of whose personnel were amateurs drawn from the Bolshevik Party with little idea how to run the municipal services required by a large metropolis. It did not help the Bolsheviks' popularity that they chose this moment, March 1918, to transfer the central government to Moscow as German troops advanced on Petrograd. This conveyed the impression to Petrograd workers that they were being abandoned. They were thus receptive to the idea of the Extraordinary Assembly of Delegates from Petrograd Factories and Plants (EAD).

The EAD was an idea that emerged initially from Petrograd Mensheviks, although it was kept a non-party affair. The intention was to build "a new, representative movement from below, shedding formal party affiliations".[36] It had its first plenary meeting on 13th March, 1918, including delegates from fifteen metalworking plants, such as the Obukhov, Trebochnyi and Aleksandrovsk, whose workers had protested against the dissolution of the Constituent Assembly. On 3rd April a second plenary was held that explicitly attacked the government for "assaulting the workers' movement with Tsarist methods". On 7th April the Menshevik Central Committee endorsed the EAD initiative and it began to attract support in the working–class Nevsky district, as well as in outlying towns.

Rabinowitch records that the majority of delegates to the EAD "represented a significant portion of Petrograd's most important factories and plants".[37] Their political demands were not counter-revolutionary, on the contrary they wished to revitilise and renew the revolutionary spirit of February 1917 in which so many of them had taken part, specifically by reconvening the Constituent Assembly, a central demand of the Russian revolutionary left prior to October 1917. They also demanded an end to political persecution and reintroduction of press and civil liberties gained in February 1917 but lost after October 1917. In April an EAD delegation visited Moscow and was well received by Moscow workers.

Food shortages continued. When women in the Petrograd suburb of Kolpino protested outside the local Soviet about lack of food they were fired on by Red Guards. This led to riots and strikes. When the EAD returned to Moscow in June their reception was even stronger, with delegates from towns whose Soviets had been shut down, such as Tula and Briansk, sent to Moscow to offer support. At a session of 1st June the EAD issued an appeal to Petrograd workers "to prepare the working masses for a political strike against the present regime, which in the name of the working class shoots it, throws it into prison, strangles freedom of speech, of the press, of the unions, the right to strike and workers' representation".[38] It set 2nd July as the date for the General Strike.

This was a clear challenge to Sovnarcom and the Bolshevik Party, who used elections to the Petrograd Soviet to reassert control and crush the EAD. The official result gave the Bolsheviks a 3:1 majority in the Soviet, although many analysts of the election, such as Rabinowitch and Rosenberg, consider the result to be questionable due to intimidation of Mensheviks and SRs, severe press restrictions and dubious electoral practices. Significantly, it was the largest industrial plants such as the Putilov and the Obukhov, the best organised and most difficult to manipulate, that returned Menshevik majorities. After this the Petrograd Soviet passed a resolution condemning the EAD as counter-revolutionary. All factories were informed that if they took part in the strike they would be immediately shut down. EAD premises were raided and its leaders arrested.[39]

On 28th June, a few days before the planned general strike, Sovnarcom passed the Decree on General Nationalisation. This nationalised all enterprises owned by joint-stock companies and partnerships with capital over one million rubles. The Decree opened with the statement: "To declare the following industrial and commercial enterprises situated in the territory of the Soviet Republic, with all their capital and properties in whatever form, the property of the Russian Socialist Federative Soviet Republic". It covered the mining, textiles, metallurgical, electrical, timber, rubber, tobacco, glass and ceramics, leather and shoemaking, cement and pottery industries, along with lesser industries such as paper production with basic capital not less than 300,000 rubles, plus any remaining private local utilities and railways. Oversight and organisation fell to Vesenka. The Decree mandated that, "From the moment of the issue of this Decree, the Board members, Directors and other executives of nationalised enterprises are accountable to the Soviet Republic for their safety and normal operation".[40]

Promulgation of the Decree gave the government a plausible answer to the criticisms of the EAD and Factory Committees that it had backtracked on the promises of October and left the old bosses in charge, but it also laid the ground for Lenin's own form of state-controlled public ownership. After the Decree it was indisputable that there *had* been a revolutionary change in property relations. To the end of his life Trotsky would defend the Soviet Union as a "deformed workers' state" on the grounds that this fundamental transfer had occurred and not been reversed. Sadly, it manifested itself not in democratic workers' control but in top-heavy state direction often imposed by one-man management. The one man worked for the state but many workers saw little difference from the old private management hierarchies.

The Decree on Nationalisation was accompanied by decisive action to repel the general strike. Machine gun regiments were stationed at railway junctions, EAD meetings were dispersed by force and its leading activists arrested. Printing plants suspected of EAD sympathies were closed. The head offices of any trade union that supported the EAD were raided and their staff arrested. Armed patrols with authority to prevent strikes were deployed around the city.

The strike collapsed before it had started and the EAD threat had been dissolved. The EAD Bureau issued a hasty statement that concluded bitterly, "no government in the Russia of the Romanovs had ever taken such extreme measures to thwart a strike as the Soviet government had".

One of the key reasons the Bolsheviks ultimately prevailed over their opponents was that the Mensheviks' own version of state-directed democratic socialism, whilst it valued the independence of the unions and the Soviets, had little in common with the anarcho-syndicalism of the Factory Committees. Although the Factory Committees would have found a role within a democratically administered socialist system easier than within a Bolshevik one, many advocates of workers' control distrusted the Mensheviks as much as the Bolsheviks. Thus the two great poles of working-class resistance to Bolshevik authoritarianism – the Menshevik activists of the EAD and the militant Factory Committees – did not act in synergy. Yet despite the lack of coordinated political objectives the upsurge of working-class activity in the EAD and the campaigns to defend the right of the Soviets to elect Menshevik majorities were the true heir and continuation of pre-October proletarian radicalism.

The discontent against Sovnarcom had not been confined solely to the Mensheviks. On 20th April, 1918 the Petrograd District Committee of the Bolshevik Party published the first issue of *Kommunist*, a journal of Left Communism edited by Bukharin and Radek which took a stand against the "labour discipline" that Sovnarcom sought to impose. Warning of "bureaucratic centralization, the rule of the commissars, the loss of independence for local Soviets and the rejection of the state-commune administered from below", Radek wrote:

> If the Russian Revolution were overthrown by violence on the part of bourgeois counter-revolution, it would rise again like a phoenix; if however it lost its socialist character and thereby disappointed the working masses, the blow would have ten times more terrible consequences for the future of the Russian and international revolution.[41]

A coordinated storm of abuse from Lenin loyalists ensured that *Kommunist* had to transfer its operations to Moscow. Even there it could only produce three more issues before it was forced to shut down permanently.

Lenin's own vision of socialism was set out with brutal clarity in his most important post-October statement, published in *Izvestia* on 28th April as "The Immediate Tasks of the Soviet Government". It was a complete rejection of Left Communism. Lenin stressed the primary task of the working class was to learn how to administer a large modern economy efficiently, whilst also dealing with the crippling problems left over from the war: mass unemployment, industrial collapse, food shortages and famine. For Lenin, socialism was primarily a task of "accounting and control". He explained:

> The centre of gravity of our struggle against the bourgeoisie is shifting to the organisation of such accounting and control. Only with this as our starting point will it be possible to determine the immediate tasks of economic and financial policy in the sphere of nationlisation of the banks, monopolisation of foreign trade,

the state control of money circulation [...] and the introduction
of compulsory labour service.

The key problem was indiscipline and lack of order. "It
is now particularly clear to us", he wrote, "how correct is
the Marxist thesis that anarchism and anarcho-syndicalism
are bourgeois trends, how irreconcilably opposed they are
to socialism, proletarian dictatorship and communism". On
top of this, he wrote, "The Russian is a bad worker compared
with people in advanced countries", and so the productivity
of labour was low. The solution was "unity of will". Lenin
considered that

the technical, economic and historical necessity of this is
obvious, and all those who have thought about socialism have
always regarded it as one of the conditions of socialism. But how
can strict unity of will be ensured? By thousands subordinating
their will to the will of one.

Lenin lamented that Sovnarcom was "late in introducing
compulsory labour service". He was adamant that workers
demonstrate "obedience, and unquestioning obedience at that,
during work to the one-man decisions of Soviet Directors,
of the dictators elected or appointed by Soviet institutions,
vested with dictatorial powers". Outside the factories, in
the Soviets, the need was the same. For Lenin, "The fight
against the bureaucratic distortion of the Soviet form of
organisation is assured by the firmness of the connection
between the Soviets and the people, meaning by this the

working and exploited people".[42]

By the time Lenin wrote this there was hardly any connection left. The Soviets were hollow shells, administrative bodies drained of democratic life-blood. In 1920 Trotsky felt confident enough to reveal his real opinion of the Soviets. "The dictatorship of the Soviets became possible only by means of the dictatorship of the party", he wrote.

> It is thanks to the clarity of its theoretical vision and its strong revolutionary organisation that the party has afforded to the Soviets the possibility of becoming transformed from shapeless parliaments of labour into the apparatus of the supremacy of labour.[43]

The Soviets' original form was now dismissed by the ultimate Bolshevik intellectual as undisciplined talking shops that required the orders of a one-party dictatorship to give them focus and direction. As a direct result of this policy, and not because of the terrible pressures of a civil war that had not yet begun, by June 1918 the Soviets were effectively dead.

CHAPTER ELEVEN
Surveillance State

On 7th December, 1917, six weeks after the Bolshevik insurrection, Sovnarcom created the All-Russian Extraordinary Commission for the Struggle Against Counter-Revolution and Sabotage, popularly known by its Russian initials – Cheka. The Cheka was answerable only to the Council of People's Commissars, not to the Soviet Executive. In his biography of Lenin, Tony Cliff emphasised how small the Cheka was to begin with and that the few death sentences it passed "were on common criminals" (he then barely mentioned it again except for a few pages on the civil war). In reality, by the end of 1917 the Cheka were releasing common criminals from Petrograd jails in order to make room for political prisoners.

It is true that immediately after 25th October the Bolsheviks released many of those who had fought against the Insurrection and, at Martov's request, the Menshevik and SR Ministers who had been arrested. There was an element of genuine idealism in this, although the main reason was the urgent need to assuage the Soviet Congress and the Left SRs. It was also why the post of People's Commissar for Justice was given to the Left SR Isaac Steinberg when his party joined Sovnarcom. Steinberg would attempt, unsuccessfully, to control and regulate the Cheka.

Cheka officers, under their feared chief Felix Dzerzhinsky, had wide discretionary powers to enter premises and arrest any they suspected of "counter-revolutionary" activity. With the Kadet Party declared illegal in November 1917 and all who supported the convoking of the Constituent Assembly smeared as counter-revolutionary, this was in effect anybody beyond the ranks of the Bolshevik Party. Very quickly the Cheka began to arrest and execute political opponents. The nature of the Cheka's work, its untrammeled powers, its special ethos and identity (down to the leather overcoats Dzerzhinsky secured for his men as protection from the typhus virus which bred easily in woolen clothes) attracted a certain type of man, one who found satisfaction in investigation, surveillance, intimidation and coercion. Dzerzhinsky's deputies Unschlicht, Peters and Katsis reflected the force they commanded: a mix of puritanical political activists, secret policemen and bullying sadists. The "Special Purpose Units" led by Unschlict grew in time to a paramilitary force of 300,000 men authorised to detain and execute as they pleased.

Western commentators and historians who condemn the Cheka invariably ignore the activities of their own state's political police. At the same time as Russia was convulsed by revolutionary upheaval the US Congress passed the 1917 Espionage Act and 1918 Sedition Act. The Espionage Act removed the right of free speech against the war. The US Postal Service immediately stopped delivery of the Socialist

Party's magazine, *The American Socialist*, followed shortly after by almost every other radical publication. Socialist Party offices were raided and ransacked and the Chicago office was occupied for three days by federal agents. The socialist Kate O'Hara was sentenced to five years in prison for the crime of making a speech in which she said, "the women of the United States are nothing more nor less than brood sows, to raise children to get into the army and be made into fertilizer".[1] The US's leading socialist and Presidential candidate Eugene Debs was sentenced to ten years (later commuted to three). The Espionage Act's clauses against undermining the military or the security services are still in use today and were deployed against Chelsea Manning and Edward Snowden.

The Sedition Act outlawed "disloyal, profane, scurrilous, or abusive language" about the United States government, its flag and its armed forces. The Industrial Workers of the World (IWW), whose organizers had always been viciously persecuted by state police, was outlawed for "criminal syndicalism". Its leader Big Bill Haywood escaped and fled to Russia. In November 1919 the US Attorney General, Mitchell Palmer, ordered Justice Department agents to raid the offices of socialist organisations in twelve cities. New York State declared the Socialist Party illegal. On 2nd January, 1920 raids against socialist and communist organisations were launched in a further 33 cities.[2] Over 5,000 people were arrested in their offices and homes – 400 in New York, 500 in New Jersey, 700 in Detroit. In Boston hundreds of socialists were shackled together and paraded through the streets. In 1920 thousands of political "undesirables" were deported, following the 249 immigrants of Russian birth (including Emma Goldman and Alexander Berkman) already deported to Russia in December 1919. The ensuing "Red Scare" was the Invisible Worm of 20th-century American history. It engendered the FBI, the CIA and the American Security State.

From here the atrocities multiplied. The CIA's Phoenix programme kidnapped, tortured and murdered 20,000 Vietnamese civilians in the late 1960s suspected of supporting the Viet Cong. At home the FBI's COINTELPRO (Counter-Intelligence Programme) against domestic "subversives" such as the Black Panthers, the American Indian Movement, Black Civil Rights groups, the New Left, and feminist and anti-Vietnam War activists aimed to "expose, disrupt, misdirect, discredit, neutralize or otherwise eliminate" leading political dissidents. It targeted individuals such as Martin Luther King, of whom FBI Deputy Director William Sullivan wrote in 1963, "In the light of King's powerful demagogic speech […] we must mark him now, if we have not done so before, as the most dangerous Negro in this nation from the standpoint of communism, the Negro, and national security".[3] Sullivan later admitted that COINTELPRO's activities were illegal. Carrying on this tradition, on 17th September, 2001 President George W. Bush ordered the CIA to "hunt, capture, imprison and interrogate" suspected terrorists anywhere in the world. In his history of the CIA, Tim Weiner concluded, "It was the foundation for a system of secret prisons where CIA officers and contractors used techniques that included torture […] This was not the role of a civilian intelligence service in a democratic society".[4]

The Phoenix Programme, COINTELPRO and the persecution

of Julian Assange and Edward Snowden demonstrate how far the security organs of Western capitalist states will go to crush major threats to ruling elites. If today they resort less to these methods it is because genuine threats have receded. When they do arise – as with WikiLeaks or the election of a socialist government in a strategically important country like Venezuela – the full panoply of state surveillance, fabrication, repression and subversion is quickly brought to bear.[5]

The record of the CIA and MI6 in organising and supporting coups against democratic left governments that threaten American and British geo-strategic and business interests is too long to summarise here, running from Mexico, the Philippines and Cuba early in the 20th century to Iran in 1953, Guatemala in 1954, Brazil in 1964, Greece in 1967, Chile in 1973, Nicaragua throughout the 1980s, Venezuela under Chavez and Honduras in 2010; not to mention active complicity in murderous, sometimes genocidal policies in Malaya, Indonesia, Vietnam, South Africa, East Timor, El Salvador, Iraq and Palestine. It is a record that in total number of victims easily matches that of the Cheka/NKVD/KGB across the same time period.

The Cheka was a secret police with powers similar to those of the CIA or FBI but under far less scrutiny and restraint. As Isaac Deutscher acknowledged, when considering the activities of the Cheka (by then the GPU) in 1923, long after they had turned their attention to breaking strikes and arresting trade unionists, "the attitude of the Bolsheviks to the GPU had nothing in it of that haughty distaste with which the good bourgeois democrat normally views any political police".[6] Some haughty distaste might have been in order. Although many Bolsheviks believed that the Cheka was the "sword of the revolution", it was in all essentials their Okhrana. It demonstrated how far they had departed from the generous, libertarian tradition of the Russian revolutionary left.

The survivors of that left saw this intimately. In a private letter to Axelrod (who was living abroad) of 1st December, 1917, Martov analysed the current state and likely future of Bolshevik rule. "Even though the mass of workers are behind Lenin", Martov recorded, "his regime is becoming more and more a regime based on terror". Martov had a clear sense of where this was heading:

> The regime of terror, the trampling of civil liberties, and the outrages against the Constituent Assembly in the name of class dictatorship are nipping in the bud the seeds of democratic education that the people had acquired during the eight months between February and October, and preparing fertile soil for any kind of Bonapartism.

Martov rejected the idea that the Mensheviks should join a bloc of those opposed to Lenin. But he stressed:

> we now have to concentrate all our efforts on denouncing and exposing Leninist policy in the hope that the best elements among the workers following him will understand whence they have been led, and will form a nucleus capable of directing the course of the dictatorship along a different path.

He concluded with a rueful acknowledgement to Axelrod

that "only now can we clearly see the Jacobin nature of Leninism that you revealed in your 1903 article in no. 65 of *Iskra*".[7]

Bolshevism's Jacobin nature found its greatest expression in the Cheka and those who worked for it. Its head, Dzerzhinsky, a minor Polish nobleman who turned to Bolshevism as a replacement for Catholicism, was "a man not excessively endowed with intellect but of personal probity and great loyalty to Lenin".[8] From the creation of the Cheka he knew it had no relation whatsoever to a police force bound by laws or the requirements of evidence tested in open court. It was a paramilitary force in a war against any who opposed the Bolsheviks. "We need to send to that front", he said at the Sovnarcom meeting that authorised its creation, "determined, hard, dedicated comrades ready to do anything in defence of the Revolution. Do not think I seek forms of revolutionary justice. We are not now in need of justice. It is war now. Face to face – a fight to the finish. Life or death!"[9]

By January 1918 Dzerzhinsky's original investigatory Commission of eight men had ballooned to a staff of 120. By the end of the year Cheka HQ, run from a converted office block in Moscow's Lubyanka Square, had nearly 5,000 staff, although these were greatly supplemented by local Chekas that operated in every major city and town with *carte blanche* to arrest, detain and execute. There *were* counter-revolutionaries, before and after October. The ring of industrialists who had manipulated Kornilov were the first, and the White Armies the most savage. Given the chance they would have imposed a military dictatorship whose bloodlust would have matched that of the vengeful French bourgeoisie who massacred 30,000 Parisian workers after the fall of the Paris Commune. Some kind of security force was needed to prevent this. If the Cheka had operated within a framework of civil and criminal law it might have conducted legitimate operations, but there was no such framework.

Bolsheviks with a more civilised conscience than Lenin feared where it would lead. Trotsky's great friend Adolph Joffe had the job of representing the new regime abroad and knew the damage being done to its reputation by the Cheka's activities. In July 1918 he asked for it to be abolished, but was ignored. At the same time the pro-Bolshevik lawyer A.D. Zhadanov wrote to Lenin's secretary Bonch-Bruevich complaining about "the absence of control, the right to decide cases, the absence of defence, publicity or the right of appeal, the use of provocation", and concluding, "the activity of the Cheka will inevitably be the strongest element discrediting Soviet power".[10]

Lenin had no time for such concerns. The Dictatorship of the Proletariat scorned the independence of the law as a hypocritical bourgeois concept used to disguise class rule. But Lenin saw only the corruption of the concept and not its use as a bulwark against despotism. Even in Tsarist Russia there had been space for radical lawyers to save revolutionaries from exile and execution. That could only happen because underneath naked state power there was a concept of independent law that could, in certain circumstances and with enough publicity and countervailing power, defy the political agenda of the ruling class. Without this possibility there existed a power vacuum filled by untouchable policemen and bureaucrats. Lenin, whose final days were filled with rage at the massive unaccountable bureaucracy that dominated the USSR, never once considered that without at least a theoretically independent judiciary and legislature, based on universal rights, there would only be bureaucracy.

Although the Cheka initially focused its attentions on the Kadets and any who might plausibly be engaged in physical resistance to the regime, it soon expanded its attention to socialists like the Mensheviks and SRs, most of whom were not. In April 1918 it moved to crush the anarchists. After Lenin returned to Russia and published the April Theses, most Russian anarchists sensed common ground with Bolshevism, assuming that it was what it appeared to be—a departure from classical Marxism, a radical anti-statist philosophy that sought to replace the structures of centralised government with local Soviet democracy and workers' control. But immediately after the Bolshevik insurrection, which they supported, the anarchists began to issue warnings.

On 3rd November the anarchist newspaper *Golos Truda* wrote:

> We summon the workers of the world to self-organisation and self-determination [...] We call on them to reject any new master. We call on them to create their own non-party labour organisations, freely united in the cities, villages, districts and provinces. We call on them to help each other create a cooperative union of free cities and free villages.

The editorial concluded, "The disputes among the Bolsheviks themselves and popular opposition to a government of 'people's commissars' show better than anything else that the seizure of power and the social revolution are diametrically opposed".[11]

Two weeks later the anarchist writer N.I. Pavlov wrote in *Golos Truda* that 25th October had not been a vindication of the Bolshevik Party. "What is taking place now is not a rising of the Bolsheviks but a rising of all the laboring masses", Pavlov claimed. "The Bolsheviks are not so very numerous, and it is not really their affair. A large percentage of the rebels are absolutely non-party workers, peasants and soldiers". Pavlov asserted:

> Neither the Chernovs nor the Lenins, by their decrees, laws, edicts, and authority, can help starving Russia. The only way out [...] is for the peasants themselves, in an organised manner, to take all the land and grain and by their common effort begin to construct a new agricultural economy; and for the factory workers, without relying on any 'control over production' [...] to take all production in their own hands.

Whilst he rejected the Constituent Assembly as an outdated bourgeois parliament, he finished with, "Long live the Soviets in local regions, reorganised on new, truly revolutionary, working class and non-party lines!"[12]

For the next six months the anarchists continued to agitate against the Bolsheviks. They bitterly denounced the Treaty of Brest-Litovsk as an intolerable compromise with German imperialism. To the anarchists, the multiple blows of the Treaty, the nationalisation of the land and suppression of the Factory Committees, added to the concentration of power in governmental bodies like Sovnarcom, Vesenka and the Cheka, had created what they labeled a "Commissarocracy". When the Fourth All-Russian Soviet Congress met in March 1918 to decide on ratification of the Treaty, all fourteen anarchist delegates voted against. Some even began to make noises about partisan resistance to the Bolsheviks.

On 12th April armed Cheka detachments surrounded twenty-six anarchist centres in Moscow and demanded they surrender. When they refused the Cheka stormed the premises, killing forty and arresting over five hundred. After this many anarchists relocated to Ukraine to join Nestor Makhno's Revolutionary Insurrectionary Army of Ukraine, which over the next three years fought the White and Red army alike to preserve the freedom of the independent peasant communes set up there.

Makhno's army and the region over which it presided were a functioning alternative to the regime being established by Sovnarcom. While the Bolshevik government dismantled free Soviets and independent Factory Committees in the areas under its controls, the "Black Army" protected and promoted Soviets and self-managed peasant communes within the "Free Territory" (roughly the southeastern quarter of present-day Ukraine). The Free Territory emerged from the Ukrainian People's Republic, which declared itself a sovereign independent state in January 1918. The Republic lasted two months before most of Ukraine was ceded to Germany by the Treaty of Brest-Litovsk.

In April 1918 an autocratic anti-socialist regime headed by the "Hetman" Pavlo Skoropadsky grabbed power in alliance with the German army. In response to the occupation the young anarchist Nestor Makhno formed the Black Army, whose total size would fluctuate between 20,000 and 110,000 men. Its heartland was the Gulyai-Polye region of south-east Ukraine. Makhno's partisans covered great distances over the Ukranian steppes between the River Dnieper and the Sea of Azof, expropriating landed estates, liberating towns, freeing prisoners and redistributing wealth.

Makhno was born into a poor peasant family in Ukraine and became an anarchist at the age of sixteen during the 1905 Revolution. Arrested in 1908 for "terroristic" acts, he was sentenced to life with hard labour. While in prison he educated himself in mathematics, political economy and Russian history. He shared a cell with the older anarchist Peter Arshinov (who would later be his political adviser and produce the definitive *History of the Makhnovist Movement*), who broadened his knowledge of the intellectual history of anarchism and the works of Bakunin and Kropotkin.

Released from prison after the February 1917 Revolution, Makhno returned to Gulyai-Polye. He founded a farm workers' union and a Peasants Soviet so that peasants could run their own affairs free of the government and the landed gentry. He also became President of the Union of Metal and Carpentry Workers, the Peasants Union and finally of the Workers and Peasants Soviet of Gulyai-Polye. After October 1917, as President of the local Soviet, he brought all these forces together to create autonomous, self-managed peasant communes across southern Ukraine. In Richard Stites's estimation, he "emerged directly from the people, and was perhaps the closest thing the Russian Revolution produced to a peasant leader with a utopian vision that seemed to fit the culture of his people".[13]

Around his "capital" of Gulyai-Polye, a town of about 30,000 people, Makhno established dozens of libertarian communes in which the land was held in common. The German occupation army put a temporary stop to this. After a brief but unsatisfactory visit to Moscow to seek Bolshevik aid he returned to Ukraine and formed the Revolutionary Insurrectionary Army to fight the Germans, the Whites and Skoropadsky. The communes started up again, each one allocated land and livestock by elected Regional Congresses of peasants. At the end of the war the Germans withdrew and Skoropadsky fell. For the first six months of 1919, as the Red Army fought the White Army of General Denikin and Kiev changed hands several times, Makhno and his supporters were left alone to construct an anarcho-communist society in southern Ukraine that came to be known as *Makhnovshchina*. The first step towards that society was the election by Regional Congresses of a Military Revolutionary Council of Peasants, Workers and Insurgents to carry out the decisions of the Congresses.

Makhno has been presented by his detractors as a "Primitive Rebel", a free-wheeling brigand in the tradition of the Russian steppes. But as Paul Avrich makes clear, he was "motivated by a specific anarchist ideology".[14] One of his first acts upon liberating a town from the Whites or local bourgeois authorities was to post proclamations that stated the citizens were now free to run their affairs in any way they saw fit. In reality there were exceptions, for although free speech, free assembly and a free press were proclaimed and abided by (strikingly different from the areas controlled by Sovnarcom), the army forbade institutions that tried to impose a separate political authority. As a result it dissolved the Bolsheviks' Revolutionary Committees which claimed for themselves a governing authority with no popular mandate. The most complete summary of Makhno's political philosophy is contained in the "Declaration of the Revolutionary Insurgent Army of the Ukraine (Makhnovist)", issued 7th January, 1920 as the Red Army closed in on the Free Territory with the intent of shutting it down.

The Declaration begins by declaring that the Army was "called into existence as a protest against the oppression of the workers and peasants by the bourgeois-landlord authority on the one hand and the Bolshevik-Communist dictatorship on the other". It claimed one goal—"The battle for total liberation of the working people of the Ukraine from the oppression of various authorities and the creation of a TRUE SOVIET SOCIALIST ORDER". Beyond that, "All decrees of the Denikin authority are abolished. Those decrees of the Communist authority which conflict with the interests of the peasants and workers are also repealed". It made clear that "the lands of the service gentry, of the monasteries, of the princes and other enemies of the toiling masses, with all their livestock and goods, are passed on to the use of those peasants who support themselves solely through their labour".

The Declaration proclaimed that

factories, workshops, mines and other tools and means of production become the property of the working class as a whole, which will run all enterprises themselves, through their trade unions, getting production under way and striving to tie together all industry in the country in a single, unitary organisation.

These aims echoed the rhetorical goals of the Bolsheviks, with the crucial difference that they were underpinned by a federated, democratic "government" that allowed them to develop at their own pace, rather than a centralised dictatorship that imposed economic policy regardless of what workers wanted. The Declaration also supported free worker-peasant Soviets, proscription of the Cheka, abolition of any state militia or police and the "inalienable right" of free expression in newspapers, political parties and trade unions.[15]

In January 1919 the Red Army, under Commander Dybenko, attacked and took Kiev from the nationalist government of Petliura. For a brief time, the Makhnovists and the Bolsheviks worked together. In March 1919 Makhno and Dybenko concluded a pact for joint military action and Makhno's forces held down a major portion of Denikin's White Army. But Bolshevik policy in Ukraine was to replace local democratic bodies with Revolutionary Committees (i.e. Bolshevik Party cells) and disperse any Soviet that did not elect Bolshevik majorities. In contrast, the Makhnovists allowed free elections to Soviets and all other bodies (the Makhnovist Revolutionary Military Soviet elected at the Congress of Olexandrivske in late 1919 had a variety of socialists, including three Bolsheviks and six Mensheviks).[16] Attempts by the Bolsheviks to implant Poor Peasant Committees in southern Ukraine, backed up by Cheka units, were met with armed resistance by Ukrainian peasants who supported Makhno.

In response the Bolsheviks began to insinuate that the Makhnovists were Kulaks and counter-revolutionaries. In April 1919, in response to the calling of the Third Regional Congress of Peasants, Workers, and Insurgents, Dybenko issued a telegram:

Novoalekseevka, No 283, 10th April 2.45pm. Forward to Comrade Makhno, General Staff of the Alexandrovsk Division. Copy to Volnovakha, Mariupol, to transmit to Comrade Makhno, Copy to the Gulyai-Polya Soviet:

Any Congress called in the name of the Revolutionary Military General Staff, which is now dissolved by my order, shall be considered manifestly counter-revolutionary, and its organisers will expose themselves to the severest repressive measures, to the extent of their being declared outlaws. I order that steps be taken immediately so that such measures may not be necessary. (Signed): Dybenko

Makhno ignored the order and the Congress went ahead, with delegates from 72 districts, representing more than two million people, discussing how they wanted to run their society. Later, the response of the Makhnovist Revolutionary Military Council to the Bolsheviks attempt to ban it was simply to re-affirm basic democratic principles. It stated that it "holds itself above the pressure and influence of all parties and only recognises the people who elected it. Its duty is to accomplish what the people have instructed it to do, and to create no obstacles to any left socialist party in the propagation of ideas".[17]

The anarchists of the big Russian cities had far fewer options than Makhno's forces. The very thing they had fought for – autonomous, local self-management of economy and society – was perverted by authoritarian socialists to produce repressive state organs. Factory Committees were absorbed into big trade unions who were in turn controlled by Vesenka. The Soviets became mini one-party statelets. People's Militias enforcing revolutionary justice degenerated into vehicles of revenge used not just against the bourgeoisie and war speculators but against all dissidents, including those whom the Bolsheviks considered "petty bourgeois anarcho-syndicalists".

During 1917 Imperial Russia's judicial system had collapsed – hardly surprising when in February the police had resorted to indiscriminate shooting of civilian crowds. With the police and courts virtually extinct, justice was increasingly meted out by violent mobs. Thieves, or suspected thieves, were sometimes beaten to death or strung up by enraged crowds, even in the middle of Petrograd and Moscow. The People's Courts and Revolutionary Tribunals introduced by the Bolshevik government after October 1917 simply institutionalised this. People's Courts had twelve elected judges, but they were not required to have legal training or qualifications. As the old regime's Criminal Code had been abolished, the proceedings of the Courts had no set legal procedures and were, in Figes's description, "formalised mob trials".[18] The Revolutionary Tribunals set up specifically to assist the Cheka in crushing counter-revolution and "crimes against the state" were equally random.

The most famous and emblematic policy of the Bolshevik government was the expropriation and redistribution of the wealth and property of the Russian bourgeoisie and aristocracy to workers and poor peasants. As a principle this policy commanded wide-spread support across the Russian left. The Mensheviks and SRs had always stood for social justice and wealth redistribution – the Mensheviks through progressive social and labour legislation and trade union power, the SRs through the nationalisation of the land and its reallocation to peasant *Volosts* and to individual peasant owners. It was not the objective of expropriation and redistribution that was at issue, but the means and speed.

Instead of a planned programme of progressive taxation, redistribution of wealth, regulation of banks and socialisation of industry, the Bolsheviks from late 1917 stoked and unleashed what even Lenin's friend Maxim Gorky called "a mass pogrom". In December 1917 Lenin wrote an article that encouraged all villages and towns to develop their own methods of "cleansing the Russian land of all vermin, of scoundrel fleas, the bedbug rich and so on". He ruminated that "in one place they will put in prison a dozen rich men, a dozen scoundrels, half a dozen workers who shirk on the job", whilst in others these types will be put to cleaning toilets or, sometimes, simply shot. "The more variety the better", he concluded, "for only practice can devise the best methods of struggle".[19]

The Bolshevik policy on confiscation of bourgeois property was a visceral response to the long-standing injustice of vast comfort and riches for a few resting atop grinding poverty and oppression for the many, but it did so in such an unplanned and irresponsible manner that it achieved little except emotional satisfaction for those enforcing it. The Bolsheviks called such confiscations "looting the looters", which was more accurate than intended. In theory it was a necessary part of the transition to a more socially just society. In reality, given the circumstances of long-suppressed, exhausted, hungry and embittered worker-peasants trying to survive in conditions of economic collapse, it became mass looting of homes, country estates, shops, churches and museums, which some Soviets tried to prevent or control but which was basically unstoppable.

The emotional impetus behind it was summed up by a Bolshevik decree in Ekaterinslav which instructed workers to take from the local bourgeoisie "the millions taken from the masses, and cunningly turned into silken undergarments, furs, carpets, gold, furniture, paintings, china. We have to take it and give it to the proletariat and then force the bourgeoisie to work for their rations for the Soviet regime". The affluent bourgeoisie of Petrograd, Moscow and other cities may have been turfed out of their mansions or forced to share them with the displaced and homeless poor, and this may have achieved a measure of rough justice, but it did little in itself to reorganise the economy or heat the (now collective) residences.

The sanction given to the proletariat to enter bourgeois and municipal property and take what they felt they needed to survive, allied to continuous government propaganda that all middle-class Kadets were counter-revolutionaries attempting to reverse the freedoms gained since February

1917, led inevitably to assault and murder. In mid-November 1917 the homes of prominent Kadets were ransacked by the Cheka. On 28th November the Kadet Party as a whole was outlawed, and many of its leaders were arrested and imprisoned. In December Sofia Panina, a member of the Kadet Central Committee and a well-known liberal reformer who had been Minister for Education in the Provisional Government, was brought before a Revolutionary Tribunal on spurious charges. On 7th January, 1918 two ex-Kadet Ministers, Andrei Shingarev and Fyodor Kokoshkin, active in the 1905 Revolution and elected as deputies to the Constituent Assembly just before the Kadets were outlawed, were brutally murdered in their hospital beds by vengeful Baltic sailors. The murders were not ordered by the Cheka, but the local Red Guard had stood by and let them happen. While not directly state-sanctioned, the murders flowed from state policy towards the Kadets and the entire structure of revolutionary justice.

That structure was enhanced by a Sovnarcom Decree of 21st February, 1918 titled: "The Socialist Fatherland is in Danger!" The Decree was issued as the German army crossed into Russia and approached Petrograd, before the Bolsheviks hurriedly signed the Treaty of Brest-Litovsk. It exhorted, "All Soviets and revolutionary organizations are ordered to defend every position to the last drop of blood", and laid out a series of urgent measures, including a scorched-earth policy on railway tracks and food and grain stocks. It demanded that Petrograd, Kiev and towns and villages along the new frontline mobilise and dig trenches, adding that "these battalions are to include all able-bodied members of the bourgeois class, men and women, under the supervision of Red Guards; those who resist are to be shot". It concluded that "enemy agents, profiteers, marauders, hooligans, counter-revolutionary agitators and German spies are to be shot on the spot".[20] It laid out no procedures for proof of guilt before people were shot on the spot, nor what constituted "counter-revolutionary agitation". Even E.H. Carr conceded that from the promulgation of the Decree the Cheka carried out executions "without any regular or public judicial process".[21]

It had been doing so almost from its inception, restrained initially only by its limited resources. Isaac Steinberg, the Left SR People's Commissar for Justice to whom the Cheka was theoretically answerable, knew exactly in what direction it was travelling. Upon his appointment he tried to subordinate the Cheka to the courts and to due process of law, but with little success. Although he headed the Commissariat of Justice he was not consulted on the "The Socialist Fatherland is in Danger!" and its sanction to shoot entire categories of people such as hooligans, profiteers and counter-revolutionaries without a trial. When it was published Steinberg took the matter directly to Lenin. "Why do we bother with a Commissariat of Justice at all?" he asked him. "Why not call it frankly the Commissariat of Social Extermination and be done with it?" Lenin seemed excited by the idea. "Well put", he said, "that's exactly what it should be called! But of course we can't say that".[22]

In a report to the Soviet Executive of 17th February, 1919, Dzerzhinsky prepared the ground for the systematic use of political prisoners as slave labour. He told the Executive:

> Even today the labour of those under arrest is far from being
> utilized in public works, and so I recommend that we retain
> these concentration camps for the exploitation of labour
> of persons under arrest: gentlemen who live without any
> occupation and those incapable of doing work without some
> compulsion [...] In this way we will create schools of labour.

Following his recommendation, the Soviet Executive passed
a resolution with a clear instruction: "The All-Russian
Extraordinary Commission (Cheka) is empowered to
confine to concentration camps, under the guidance of
precise instructions concerning the rules of imprisonment
in a concentration camp approved by the All-Russian Central
Executive Committee".

A further CEC decree of 12th May, 1919 ordered every
provincial capital city to set up a concentration camp to hold
300 or more inmates for forced labour.[23] By the end of 1919,
21 official labour camps had been set up in Soviet Russia.
By the end of 1920 there were 84 camps in 43 provinces,
including the first "camp of special significance", i.e. the first
one to use slave labour as part of national economic policy,
on Solovetsky Island in the White Sea.

Lenin and Trotsky were set free by the civil war. The
opportunity it gave them to use political terror against all
who did not support their government was openly welcomed.
Lenin expanded his case for political terror in *The Proletarian
Revolution and the Renegade Kautsky*, written in 1918 in
response to Karl Kautsky's *The Dictatorship of the Proletariat*

(also 1918), a sustained attack on the Bolshevik concept of the Dictatorship of the Proletariat from the perspective of democratic Marxism. The works are strikingly different. Kautsky's is balanced and reasonable, methodically building a persuasive case, dry in tone but occasionally breaking into forceful criticism of what he saw as Lenin's perversion of Marxism. Lenin's response is an unrelenting screed of hostile sarcasm in which a crude, simplistic argument is presented in the mocking tone of a frustrated adolescent. Despite repeatedly labeling Kautsky an "imbecile", Lenin's intellectual inferiority complex towards the older man is palpable.

Kautsky denied that the Dictatorship of the Proletariat had to be based on one-party rule or denial of democratic rights to others. For Kautsky it was essential that socialism be achieved through democratic methods or it would cease to be socialism. "Thus democracy and socialism do not differ in the sense that one is a means and one is an end", he wrote.

> Both are means to the same end [...] For us, socialism is unthinkable without democracy. By modern socialism we mean not only a social organisation of production but also a democratic organisation of society [...] There is no socialism without democracy.[24]

From this perspective, Bolshevism was "not an insufficiently mature socialism, but a non-socialism."[25] He predicted that if the small Russian working class attempted to lead the transition to socialism it would be compelled to do so through a minority dictatorship using methods of extreme bureaucratic and police control. Given that this is exactly what came about it is difficult to understand the airy confidence with which Lenin's defenders routinely dismiss Kautsky's critique.

Kautsky went further and questioned whether the working class was actually governing in Russia, and the validity of Bolshevik claims to represent it. Immediately after October 1917, Lenin had claimed that as a result of the Bolshevik Revolution "the transfer of government power from one Soviet party to another is guaranteed without any revolution, simply by a decision of the Soviets, simply by new elections of deputies to the Soviets".[26] After the multiple closures of Soviets that dared to elect deputies from other parties this was clearly not a sustainable argument. By mid-1918 Lenin had changed the terms of the argument by asserting that the Bolshevik Party was the *only* party that could represent the working masses, no matter what the working masses themselves thought. Thus there could no longer be a "transfer of power from one Soviet party to another".

Faced with the complete reversal of the Bolsheviks' main justification for the October Revolution, Kautsky bluntly responded that they now governed "by virtue of the superiority of a centralised organisation over the unorganised popular masses and by virtue of the superiority of its armed forces". This had come about because the Bolsheviks had replaced the Constituent Assembly, a representative body elected on an equal, direct and secret universal suffrage with an assembly – the Soviet Congress and local Soviets – based on "unequal, indirect, public, and limited suffrage, elected by privileged categories of workers, soldiers and peasants". Kautsky predicted that this partial democracy run by one political party would inevitably mutate into a despotism, and would concentrate power so much that the revolution "necessarily leads to a Cromwell or a Napoleon".[27]

Lenin could not contain his anger that a prominent European socialist, with great influence on the left in Germany and elsewhere, should criticise the Bolshevik regime in this manner. He had nothing but contempt for "this windbag" and for the "irrelevant twaddle" with which he sought to "befog and confuse the issue, for he poses it in the manner of liberals, speaks of democracy in general and not of *bourgeois* democracy". Lenin considered that Kautsky substituted "eclecticism and sophistry for dialectics", and thus no longer correctly interpreted Marxism. His own interpretation was that "the revolutionary dictatorship of the proletariat is rule won and maintained by the use of violence by the proletariat against the bourgeoisie, rule that is unrestricted by any laws".[28]

There was a far more attractive variant of the Dictatorship of the Proletariat – the "Commune State" – that inspired idealistic and libertarian communists both at home and abroad, most prominently Makhno, who had actually created one in southern Ukraine. In 1918 Lenin wrote that the Soviet state would represent

a higher form of democratic state, a state which in some respects, as Engels said, ceases to be a state, is no more a state in the proper sense of the word. This is a state of the type of the Paris Commune, which replaces an army and police force set apart from the people with an armed people.

In a 1917 article, "On Dual Power", he predicted that in the new Soviet state "the officialdom, the bureaucracy, are either replaced with the direct power of the people [...] becoming not only elected deputies but ones that can be removed at the first popular demand".[29]

Although this bore no relation at all to the state introduced by the Bolshevik government post-October, it flowed from Marx's description of the Paris Commune in *The Civil War in France* (1871). In this important work Marx examined the legacy of the Commune and hailed its democratic structures and policies as a benchmark for future socialist revolution. He lauded its commitment to the election of state officials whose appointments were revocable at any time by popular referenda. But he made clear that "nothing could be more foreign to the spirit of the Commune than to supersede universal suffrage by hierarchic investiture".[30]

In 1920 Kautsky replied to Lenin's contention that democracy *per se* had no special status outside of social conditions and was, in Western bourgeois countries, a con trick, a fetter on working-class emancipation. Kautsky conceded that Marxists did not accept that "the mere existence of democracy was sufficient for the liberation of the working class". Of the Leninists he wrote,

> They are telling us something we have known for half a century. Except our conclusion was simply that mere democracy is *insufficient,* not that it was *detestable.* This insufficiency is clear today wherever the proletariat is not ideologically independent.[31]

He condemned the replacement of the democratic freedoms

won by the February Revolution with a "proletarian aristocracy", which was simply another social elite. In Salvadori's view Kautsky's attitude derived not only from democratic Marxism but also from an "ethical-cultural tradition with its roots in liberal humanism". The rejection of that tradition for a morality of class-based *realpolitik* had been a disaster for the Russian socialist movement – with far worse to come.

CHAPTER TWELVE
Civil War

The "social extermination" of Lenin's fantasies was unleashed in all its fury by the Russian Civil War, which flared up into full-scale military conflict in June 1918. It had been simmering for many months, during which Trotsky, the new People's Commissar for Military Affairs, began to create the Red Army from the remnants of the shattered Imperial Army. From the moment he took charge in March 1918, Trotsky dispensed with democratic procedures. The election of officers by men was immediately abolished. "The elective basis", he wrote, "is politically pointless and technically inexpedient and has been set aside by Decree".[1]

The death penalty for disobedient soldiers, abolished in February 1917, was restored, as was the requirement to salute officers, all distinctions of rank, and separate living quarters for officers and men. Trotsky actively sought the cooperation of trained military specialists from the old Tsarist army, and guaranteed them status and respect within the new army. As Isaac Deutscher admitted, Trotsky "seemed to be burning all that he had worshipped and worshipping all that he had burned".[2]

In the first few months of 1918 Trotsky burned it all. As well as sweeping aside soldiers' democracy and re-instating ex-Tsarist officers (if on a short leash), he abolished all partisan detachments and Red Guards in favour of a centralised military with formal Divisions and Regiments. Left Communists complained that he was destroying the liberties the soldiers had recently won. Mensheviks warned of a new Napoleon. But Trotsky's reasoning mirrored Lenin's abandonment of the utopian vision of *The State and Revolution*. Without a disciplined and efficient army the Bolshevik Revolution would succumb to its military enemies. To ensure the ex-Tsarist officers confined themselves solely to military affairs, Trotsky assigned political commissars to shadow all officers from company commanders to Commander-in-Chief. The commander was responsible for training, strategic decisions and tactical deployment. The commissar was responsible for the loyalty of the commander, plus the political morale of the troops. Orders had to be signed by both. When disagreements arose, Trotsky intervened.

In May 1918 the Czech Legion, a contingent of the Czech Army stranded in Russia after the disintegration of the Eastern Front, was allowed to travel via the Trans-Siberian Railroad to the Pacific coast to take ship for France. On the way they received garbled instructions from Trotsky to disarm. Fearing betrayal by the Bolshevik government, the Legion ignored the instruction, took over the trains and headed back into European Russia. Their plan was to liaise with a new anti-Bolshevik rival national government called the Committee for the Constituent Assembly (Komuch) based in the Volga region to the east of Moscow. Komuch was created by Right SR Constituent Assembly deputies in June 1918. These SRs, who represented the core of the old SR party in a way that the Left SRs did not, felt that after the national elections to the Constituent Assembly, in which they had emerged as the majority party, they were now the legitimate government of Russia.

They were not alone in thinking so and they quickly attracted a People's Army around them. With the Czech Legion's help Komuch took the key strategic city of Samara on the Volga river and from there the entire Volga region. Simbirsk and Kazan fell to Komuch forces in July and August. On 8th August the workers of the munitions factory of Izhevsk mutinied against the local Soviet and declared for Komuch. It was a critical moment. If anti-Bolshevik forces in the south and east linked up, Sovnarcom would probably fall. Trotsky, furious that Red Army detachments in the Volga region had fled when faced with the Czech Legion, issued a clear instruction to his commanders—"If any detachment retreats without orders, the first to be shot will be the commissar, the next the commander. Cowards, scoundrels and traitors will not escape the bullet".[3]

At this stage neither the Czech Legion nor Komuch were "White" organisations in the strict sense. Having been denied any means of political expression, Komuch sought to physically replace the Bolshevik government and recall the Constituent Assembly. But its policies, as Orlando Figes has characterised them, were "dressed stiffly in the liberal pretence of political neutrality"[4] and thus had an air of unreality. It ostensibly championed the democratic revolution of February 1917 and some of its policies, such as the eight-hour day, freedom of the press and trade unions. It also sought to replace rural Soviets with elected Zemstvos, while postponing real social reforms until after the convoking of the Assembly.

Komuch, like Sovnarcom, stripped the Factory Committees of their powers, yet instead of nationalisation they simply returned factories and banks to their previous owners. Its biggest mistake was the failure to fully endorse land redistribution. Lenin's Land Decree was still in force and extremely popular. While Komuch upheld the Constituent Assembly's land reform law passed on the only day of its existence, it weakened it by allowing previous owners to take back fields sown before the land seizures. As a result, it lost the support of Volga peasants without convincing the middle classes of Samara and Kazan that it would protect their interests. The fate of Komuch demonstrated there was no longer space for political neutrality.

The situation was different in the southern Don and Kuban regions, where power had been taken much earlier by White Generals Krasnov and Alekseev. Their first acts were to declare null and void all laws of Sovnarcom *and* the Provisional Government, i.e. to totally suppress the remnants of democracy left over from the democratic republic and the Soviet system in favour of the Tsarist *ancien regime*. Because the Bolsheviks refused to concede any freedom to socialist opponents like the Mensheviks and SRs — even when, as with the majority of the Menshevik Party, they refused to side with liberals or rightists engaged in armed struggle against Sovnarcom — they alienated many working-class and peasant supporters and ensured that in some regions the Whites appeared to be the only option for those who opposed Bolshevik rule.

The result was total social polarisation. It was not only Kadets like Miliukov and Struve who sided with the Whites. So too did some Right SRs and a smaller number of right-wing Mensheviks like Potresov, although he was expelled from the Menshevik Party for doing so. Menshevik Internationalists like Martov, as well as most anarchists, Bundists and Left SRs, supported the Bolsheviks against White forces whose political agenda, while it sometimes professed allegiance to the Constituent Assembly to ensure the continued support of the Kadets, was more often a toxic mixture of monarchism and anti-Semitism. The Whites' pretend concern for democracy vanished entirely in September 1918 when the Red Army retook Samara and Simbirsk. Komuch retreated east of the Ural Mountains to the city of Omsk and there began to disintegrate. Finally, the reactionary White Army leader Admiral Kolchak abolished Komuch outright and became "Supreme Ruler" of the entire province of western Siberia.

Upon establishment of his regime Kolchak ordered a mass pogrom of SRs and anyone to the left of his own ultra-monarchism. His men were famous for mass killings of prisoners. On 9th May, 1918 some of Kolchak's troops took the village of Alexansdrovich-Gai, after which they shot 700 villagers and buried 2,000 Red Army prisoners alive. If a peasant *Volost* resisted him its village was razed to the ground and all inhabitants killed. Any criticism or insult of the Supreme Ruler was forbidden on pain of hard labour.

Omsk became a mini-police state with sr deputies hunted down, arrested and executed. sr leaders such as Gots, who had considered armed resistance to Sovnarcom and the Red Army, suspended their anti-Bolshevik operations. The real face of the White counter-revolution had emerged and for a while it united the left.

The Russian Civil War was a brutal conflict made uglier by class and ethnic cleansing, famine and social collapse, and was further complicated by foreign intervention. At no point were the relatively small forces of foreign powers militarily decisive. When the British landed 600 troops at Archangel in April 1918 it was to protect the British stockpiles kept there and prevent the Germans, who had recently landed a division in Finland, from taking the strategically important port of Murmansk. The plan was to re-establish an Eastern Front against the Germans rather than overthrow the Bolsheviks, although in 1918–19 a British Navy Squadron roamed the Gulf of Finland, occasionally firing on Soviet ships.

The British also requested that the US send troops to the Northern and Siberian Fronts. The US sent 5,000 troops to Archangel and 8,000 to Vladivostok. After the Armistice in December 1918 the French occupied the port of Odessa and linked up with Denikin's White forces, but then withdrew five months later. The Japanese landed 70,000 troops, but these stayed in eastern Siberia. Other expeditionary forces, such as the 2,500 Italians, 2,300 Chinese or 150 Australians, were miniscule. Estimates of a total 150,000 foreign troops on Russian soil conflate the 70,000 Japanese and 50,000 Czechs, throw in forces like the French who barely fired a shot before leaving, and adduce a coordinated invasion to crush Bolshevism.

On some battle fronts foreign forces prevented White defeats, but they did not make serious efforts to go beyond that. The one exception was the White attack on Petrograd in October 1919, which the British Navy supported from a distance as part of "Operation Red Trek", its intervention in the Baltic to secure Estonia and Latvia. Aside from that, the major effect of the allied interventions was to provide an enormous propaganda gift to the Bolsheviks. The occupation of Russian territory by soldiers of countries that had recently been allies of Tsarist Russia, to directly or indirectly fight a government perceived as an authentic representative of the Russian working class, confirmed for many workers that this was a naked class war. As a result, something like a mutiny occurred in Archangel. The men of the 13th Battalion of the Yorkshire Light Infantry did not wish to be there, and they set up a Soviet to make their displeasure known. With cold class allegiance the British Commander Lord Ironside prepared to order White Russian forces to fire on British troops.

The Civil War was terrible enough without foreign intervention at its margins. Between 1918 and 1920 over seven million Russians died of famine and epidemic alone, more than were killed in the actual fighting. Offshoots of the Civil War, such as the Polish–Soviet War of 1920, the suppression of the peasant "Green" rebellions in 1920-21 and the Bolshevik invasion of the Menshevik Republic of Georgia, would extend beyond the Civil War itself, but by 1920 the key struggle, that of Red versus White, was over. Although outnumbered and surrounded, the final victory of the embattled Bolshevik regime rested on three factors. Firstly, Sovnarcom fought with shorter internal lines of supply and communication than the Whites. Secondly, although White Armies advanced on Bolshevik territory from all sides – Yudenich from Estonia, Kolchak from Siberia and Denikin from Ukraine – they seldom concerted their efforts. Thirdly, the Bolsheviks, despite ruthless use of coercion against peasants who resisted confiscations of food, could still generate an authentic feeling amongst many peasants and even socialist opponents like Martov, that ultimately they represented the revolution against the old society, whilst the Whites wanted to return to autocracy.

It is impossible to weigh the scales of Red Terror and White Terror. Both went far beyond any accepted level of military necessity to a deliberate targeting of non-combatant civilians of all ages. Both flowed from the fundamental politics of Red and White, which were at heart eliminationist. Both used and exploited political acts as an excuse to unleash terror programmes they had long nurtured. For the Whites, the banning of the Kadets and the Constituent Assembly provided justification for their counter-revolutionary assault on the Bolsheviks, although once the struggle began they dropped the demand that it be reconvened and preferred straight-up military dictatorship. For the Bolsheviks, the actions of the Left SRs' in July 1918 gave them a perfect pretext to tighten the screws of state terror.

The Left SRs had become a real threat to Sovnarcom. Unlike the mainstream SRs, they had joined the government and held some senior posts, even in the Cheka. They had mass support amongst the peasantry. They led the growing discontent with Brest-Litovsk. For a while it appeared they might form a working alliance with the Left Communists. Left SR leaders hoped that the Fifth All-Russian Congress of Soviets, due to meet on 4th July and at which they expected a majority of delegates, would constrain Sovnarcom and revoke Brest-Litovsk. Yet the Bolsheviks easily dominated the Congress. Alexander Rabinowitch found "substantial evidence that the huge Bolshevik majority in the congress was fabricated". That majority was used ruthlessly. Trotsky asked for and received authority to shoot "on the spot" anyone who resisted the German occupation forces in Ukraine. Lenin suggested that if the Left SRs could not agree to the Congress's decisions they should leave, but they should remember that "Socialists who abandon us at such a critical time [...] are enemies of the people".[5]

With their backs against the wall Left SR leaders took a fatal decision. On 6th July, acting on the orders of their Central Committee, the Left SR Cheka officers Blumkin and Andreev assassinated the German Ambassador Count Mirbach in Moscow in the hope that this would re-ignite war with Germany and destroy Brest-Litovsk. Left SR detachments in Yaroslavl, where they dominated the local Cheka apparatus, launched a hastily prepared insurrection against the Bolshevik regime. They seem to have pre-empted what the Left SR CC actually desired, which was not to replace Sovnarcom but to shake it up and change its policy. Lenin had to send Red Army units to fight them precisely when they were needed to battle the Czech Legion in the south. At the same time the Germans threatened to invade and occupy Moscow in revenge for Mirbach. The only way to prevent this was for the Bolsheviks to demonstrate to the Germans that they were still fully in control by crushing those behind Mirbach's assassination.

Although there was fierce fighting between Bolsheviks and Left SRs in Moscow and Yaroslavl, the outcome was never in doubt. The entire Left SR Party Congress, meeting at the time in ignorance of what its own CC had ordered, was arrested. Left SRs in Petrograd, who knew nothing of the CC's decision to kill Mirbach and were stunned to hear of it, were nevertheless arrested and shut out of the Petrograd Soviet. Only Left SRs who repudiated their own CC could stand for re-election. In effect this meant hardly anybody. With the Mensheviks already banned from standing, the Soviets now officially became one-party organs. On 30th August, when Lenin himself was shot and nearly killed by Fanny Kaplan, a mentally unbalanced Left SR acting on her own, the Cheka ran wild. The SRs, Left and Right, were rounded up *en masse*. The political party that undoubtedly represented the majority of Russia's people was now outlawed.

The Red Terror is not a fiction dreamt up by anti-Bolshevik propagandists. It was acknowledged, even celebrated, by Bolsheviks from Lenin and Trotsky to Bukharin and Victor Serge. Gordon Legget, in the authoritative *The Cheka: Lenin's Political Police*, conservatively estimates that the extra-judicial, non-military executions carried out by the Cheka during the Civil War numbered approximately 140,000, although Figes considers that the total was "certainly several hundred thousand, if one includes all those in its camps and prisons as well as those who were executed or killed by the Cheka's troops in the suppression of strikes and revolts".[6]

The full-scale terror began immediately after Lenin's attempted assassination, of which the Bolshevik newspaper *Krasnaya Gazeta* wrote, "Each drop of Lenin's blood must be paid for by the bourgeoisie and the Whites in hundreds of deaths. The interests of the revolution demand the physical extermination of the bourgeoisie. They have no pity. It is time for us to be pitiless". 800 "counter-revolutionaries" already in custody in Petrograd were then summarily shot without trial and dumped in mass graves. It is impossible to determine if these were real counter-revolutionaries or were merely arrested because they had been members of the Kadets or SRs, or simply hostages of some kind.

For the Bolsheviks the distinction did not matter. In November 1918 the Cheka leader Latsis wrote to the local Cheka in Kazan,

> Do not ask for incriminating evidence that the prisoner opposed the Soviet either by arms or by word. Your first duty is to ask him what class he belongs to, what were his origin, education and occupation. These questions should decide the fate of the prisoner. This is the meaning and essence of Red Terror.[7]

Lenin himself called for the death penalty for a wide range of people including speculators, prostitutes, undisciplined or incompetent workers, as well as the "ruthless extermination of the Kulaks".

Lenin had set the direction of policy before he was shot by Fanny Kaplan. On 9th August he issued an order in his capacity as Chairman of Sovnarcom which read, "It is necessary to organise an extra guard of well-chosen, trustworthy men. They must carry out a ruthless mass terror against the Kulaks, priests, and White Guards. All suspicious persons must be detained in a concentration camp outside the city". On 11th August he followed this up with a cable to the Soviet of Nizhini Novgorod demanding it confiscate all surpluses of bread as well as suppressing rebellion in the area. "To accomplish this take from every area (do not take, but select by name) hostages from amongst the Kulak, the rich and oppressors of their neighbours, and charge them with the duty of gathering, delivering, and turning over to the authorities all surplus bread in the district", the cable read. It concluded, "The hostages answer with their lives for the speedy and thorough execution of their task".[8]

On the same day, in response to reports of a Kulak uprising against the government in the Penza district, Lenin wrote a letter to "Comrades Kuraev, Bosh, Minkin, and other Penza Communists", in which he demanded the rebellion be "mercilessly suppressed" and then went on to list exactly how he wanted this done. "1. Hang (hang without fail, *so the people see*) no fewer than one hundred known Kulaks, rich men, bloodsuckers. 2. Publish their names. 3. Take from them all the grain. 4. Designate hostages – as per yesterday's telegram". He finished, "Do it such a way that for hundreds of versts around the people will see, tremble, know, shout: they are strangling and will strangle to death the bloodsucker Kulaks". In case they had not fully understood he added a p.s. – "Find some *truly hard* men".[9]

After Lenin had advised the Penza communists on public hanging by truly hard men he took his thoughts to

Sovnarcom. On 3rd September, 1918 he wrote to Sovnarcom Secretary N. Krestinsky that he wished to form a special five-man commission. He explained this was because "It is necessary secretly – and *urgently* – to prepare the terror. On Tuesday we will decide whether it will be through Sovnarcom or otherwise".[10]

Two days later Trotsky, as People's Commissar for War, published a declaration stating:

> The working class of Soviet Russia [...] for every drop of proletarian blood it will shed torrents of blood of those who go against the revolution, against the Soviets and proletarian leaders. For every proletarian life it will seek to destroy the scions of bourgeois families and white guardists. From now on the working class declares to its enemies that every single act of white terror will be answered with a ruthless, proletarian mass terror.

People's Commissar for Internal Affairs Petrovsky issued a decree titled "An order about hostages", which mandated taking hostages "from bourgeois and officer ranks". He added, "The slightest show of resistance or the slightest move made by white guardist circles should be met unreservedly by mass executions".[11] All over territory controlled by Sovnarcom Chekists carried out mass executions of people arrested on random sweeps of "bourgeois" areas or simply on hearsay.

The Red Terror was a stain on Russian socialism and Russian socialists knew it. The legendary anarchist Peter Kropotkin wrote in 1919, "To throw the country into a red terror, even more so to arrest hostages in order to protect the lives of its leaders, is not worthy of a socialist party and disgraceful for its leaders". It was not only Mensheviks and anarchists who condemned the terror. Many Bolsheviks and Bolshevik sympathisers were disgusted with what they saw as a great perversion of the socialist ideal. The Bolshevik engineer and social entrepreneur Leonard Krassin, who had supported Lenin since 1903 and in 1920 would become People's Commissar of Foreign Trade, wrote to his wife in late 1918 that after the attempted assassination of Lenin

> about 600 to 700 persons were shot in Moscow and Petrograd, none-tenths of them having been arrested quite at random or merely on suspicion of belonging to the right wing of the Socialist Revolutionaries. In the provinces this developed in to a series of revolting incidents, such as arrests and mass executions.[12]

The Italian communist Angelica Balabanov protested personally to Lenin about Cheka executions she had witnessed in Ukraine, to no avail.

Before she was murdered in 1919 by right-wing thugs, Rosa Luxemburg became a fierce if subtle critic of Lenin's regime. In her essay "The Russian Revolution" (1918), she made clear that she supported a socialist revolution based on the leading role of the Soviets. Nor did she disguise her admiration for the Bolshevik Party which, unlike others, had *dared*, had given a lead to an international proletariat that had then "betrayed" them. Of the pre-October period she wrote, "The party of Lenin was thus the only one in Russia which grasped the true interest of the revolution in that first period".

But her doubts about the Bolsheviks were contained even in her praise. On the issue of democracy Luxemburg eviscerated Lenin and Trotsky, pointing out that Trotsky's critique of what he called "the cumbersome mechanism of democratic institutions" led logically to the suppression of *all* democratic institutions in which the mass of people were represented. Finally, she criticised the Bolsheviks' denial of press and political freedom in words that, had they been written in Russia, would have seen her arrested. "Freedom only for the supporters of the government, only for the members of one party—however numerous they may be—is no freedom at all", she wrote. "Freedom is always and exclusively freedom for the one who thinks differently".[13] Luxemburg never saw the full development of the Red Terror, but had she lived it is certain she would have condemned it.

The White Terror was equally as savage. After a desultory attempt to present a democratic political face to the world through alliances with Kadets such as Milukov and Struve, to whom they rarely listened, the Whites quickly reverted to type—a mix of Imperial military, dispossessed landowners, sons of the aristocracy and the provincial mercantile bourgeoisie, holding together armies made up of Cossacks, peasants and nationalists. Led by ex-Imperial officers such as Krasnov, Kolchak, Yudenich and Denikin, they had no specific political programme except a vague return to the *status quo ante* before October 1917. For some this meant a bourgeois constitutional regime, for others a restoration of monarchy and the old order in the countryside. They had a fierce loathing for those they held responsible for the revolution and the dispossession of their families' property and wealth, i.e. any and all leftists and intellectuals, most especially the Jews, who for them epitomised the urban cosmopolitanism of the intelligentsia. As the White armies advanced and retook cities held by Red Guards and run by Soviets they took their revenge.

The *Manchester Guardian*'s correspondent reported the fate of those taken prisoner by the Whites. "When questioned on the subject", he reported, "the White officers always said 'Oh, we kill all of them that are Communists'. Jews and Commissars stood no chance, of course".[14] Often just being working-class was enough. Krasnov's Volunteer Army in the Don is estimated to have killed 45,000 civilians during its occupation of the province. When White forces retook Finland from the Red Army in October 1918, over 30,000 workers were summarily executed in a few days in a paroxysm of pure class rage, and some estimate that the eventual death toll was nearly 100,000. Across the waters of the Gulf of Finland, in besieged Petrograd, the message was heard loud and clear.

In June 1919 White forces were nearing Petrograd. Victor Serge, a man of fine literary and political sensitivities who later stood bravely against Stalin, wrote in his diary,

It is kill or be killed. I know very well that if the Whites enter the city all those who are dear to me can expect no mercy. Everyone knows this as well as I do. The air is permeated with a vague smell of blood, creating among us a state of mind in which terror cannot fail to grow.[15]

White Terror also targeted the Jews, especially in Ukraine. Denikin's army, loaded with Cossack officers, was viciously anti-Semitic, convinced—as were many Russians of all political persuasions—that the Bolshevik Party was led primarily by Jews (Trotsky was always called "Bronstein" by the White press and he was blamed personally for the murder of the Tsar and the persecution of the Orthodox Church).

When the Whites entered Kiev in October 1919 they carried out a mass pogrom of its Jewish citizens. "We reacted to the Yids just as the Bolsheviks reacted to the *burzhoois*", admitted the right-wing anti-Semite V.V. Shulgin. "They shouted 'Death to the Burzhoois!' And we shouted 'Death to the Yids!'"[16] White and Cossack forces often demanded vast payments from Jewish shopkeepers or small merchants in the belief they were rich, taking family members as hostages. When the demands could not be met the hostages were killed (the Bolsheviks did much the same, but in their case because the Jewish middle class was deemed "bourgeois" and hence counter-revolutionary). As the White armies began to fall back from Red counter-attack in 1919-20, they unleashed orgies of violence against the Jewish populations of towns they passed through. In one Ukrainian town, Fastov, Denikin's men murdered over 1,500 Jews, mostly old men, women and children. Estimates of the total number of Jewish deaths in the Russian Civil War are as high as 150,000, the vast majority killed by the Whites.

The Red and White Terrors were not military operations. They were the targeting of entire social groups to achieve wider political aims or simply to satisfy sectarian bigotry. Of the Red Terror Tony Cliff wrote, "The revolutionary terror, like its predecessor in France during *its* great revolution, was a reaction to foreign invasion and the immensity of the threat to the revolution".[17] This is untrue. The White Terror was a slaughter that, as far as can be determined, easily matched that of the Cheka, but the use of revolutionary terror by the Bolsheviks did not follow the outbreak of the war and was not simply a reaction to it. It *intensified* in reaction to the clear intentions of the Whites to exterminate the Bolshevik regime and its supporters, but it *began* in 1917 with the creation of the Cheka and escalated in early 1918 when the Soviets began to elect non-Bolshevik majorities.

The inability of Leninists to openly recognise or condemn political terror was a road to hell, trod even by principled and humane Bolsheviks like Anatoly Lunacharsky, Alexandra Kollontai and Nikolai Bukharin. Unlike Lenin, they did not wallow in macho postures of being "merciless" and "hard", but they supplied intellectual justification to the economic coercion that was an integral part of the Terror and which came to be known as "War Communism". Initially this arose from the urgent need to feed the cities, most especially Moscow and Petrograd. Although the industrial regions of northern Russia remained in Bolshevik hands, they had less and less fuel and food. The cities of northern and central Russia had always depended on the Don Basin for coal, the Urals for iron and Baku for oil. All these were now inaccessible.

After the government moved to Moscow for greater safety, Petrograd began to resemble a ghost town in which the shops were boarded up, the factories barely functioned and weeds grew between the cracks of the pavements. Vera

Broido, a child at the time, recalls that the city "bore a drained, hushed look".[18] Lights were turned on for only a few hours a day. There was no heat. Refuse was uncollected. Sewers and pipes cracked and broke, spreading cholera and typhus. With peasant food production disrupted by the Civil War and the rail network virtually destroyed, food deliveries to the cities almost came to a halt. In 1919 the "Petrocommune" cafeterias fed over 600,000 desperate people, but it was thin gruel in every sense of the word. Horses, cats and dogs disappeared from the cities of the north, all fed into what became known as "civil war sausage".[19] A mass exodus began, with both bourgeoisie and workers seeking whatever sanctuary could be found in the countryside. By 1919 Petrograd's population was a quarter of what it had been in 1914.

In these circumstances the Bolshevik government had only two options – concede complete defeat and withdraw, or move to mass forcible requisition of the grain and food supplies they needed from the countryside. This had started almost from the day they took power. On 27th October, 1917 a "supply detachment" of 500 Kronstadt sailors was sent outside the city to secure food. Within a month the number of workers involved in these detachments had risen to 7,000.[20] Early in the new year Sovnarcom created a Supreme Supply Council. In April 1918 the People's Commissar for Supply instructed local committees to record transit and distribution of food every ten days and take initial steps to intervene if they suspected hoarding of supplies.

On 9th May, 1918, as the first pangs of famine in the cities began to bite, Sovnarcom issued a "Decree to confer on the People's Commissariat of Supply extraordinary powers for the struggle with the rural bourgeoisie which conceals grain stocks and speculates in them". The decree's purpose was to "recognise the necessity of continuing a merciless fight against the bread speculators and bagmen and of compelling every possessor of surplus grain to declare within a week from the promulgation of this resolution in the *Volost* that he is ready to hand over all in excess of what he needs". It made clear that anyone not abiding by the Decree would be "handed over to the Revolutionary Court to be sentenced to prison for a term of not less than ten years". The supply detachments had authority "To use armed force in cases of resistance to the requisition of grain and other food products".[21]

On 18th May Sverdlov candidly announced to the Soviet Central Executive Committee the aim of the policy. Claiming that "revolutionary Soviet authority" was strong in the cities, he admitted it was less so in the villages. "For that reason we must seriously confront the question of the differentiation of the village, the question of creating in the village two contrasting and hostile forces", he said.

> Only if we succeed in splitting the village into two irreconcilably hostile camps, if we are able to enflame there the civil war that occurred not so long ago in the cities […] only then will we be in a position to say that we will do in relation to the village that we were able to do for the city.[22]

By this policy Sovnarcom aimed to *create* social divisions in the village in order to build up its power base there and loosen that of the SRs.

But the Russian village did not conform to Bolshevik

ideology. There were hardly any "rich peasants" left. If they were genuinely rich, they became merchants in the towns. There was some differentiation, i.e. peasants who owned more fields than others, but often within the same family or kinship network. Lenin was driven by the *idée fixe* he had held of the penetration of capitalism into the Russian rural economy since he wrote *The Development of Capitalism in Russia* in 1899, a work loaded with specific statistics to prove a thesis he knew in advance was true. Had he looked instead at the data of the 1917 agrarian census (published by the Soviet government itself in 1929), he would have found that only about 2% of rural households, excluding the landed estates, employed hired labour, and that was mostly one hired hand rather than servants or a workforce.[23]

Once the state grain monopoly was announced, Sovnarcom sent out armed supply detachments to villages and towns to expropriate "hoarded" grain and food supplies. Lenin wanted a "reliable workers' army" from Petrograd to launch "a disciplined military campaign against the village bourgeoisie and the bribe takers". But the campaign was neither military nor disciplined. The detachments had no guidance on what kind of peasant constituted a "Kulak" or "rich peasant". Urban workers sent to the villages made snap decisions on who was a Kulak or a counter-revolutionary and executed them on the spot. To make things worse the detachments were not provided with food for themselves, so the first thing they did upon arriving in peasant villages was confiscate food for their own use. This made enemies of *all* peasants. John Keep summarised the effect of the supply detachments as a policy that "ranged

Russia's countryside against the towns in a struggle without precedent in modern times".[24]

To counteract this, Sovnarcom set up "Poor Peasants Committees", supposed to transform the semi-bourgeois revolution in the countryside into a properly proletarian one. But there was no proletariat in the countryside, and forming Poor Peasants Committees did not magically create one. Nearly all peasants wished to cultivate their own land. Many supported the Bolshevik Party which passed the Land Decree, whilst simultaneously opposing the Communist Party which sent the requisitioning squads, not aware they were the same entity. Some fought back and pitched battles broke out. The intention of creating a rural proletariat and extending the revolution was still-born, and even Lenin had to admit that reality had defeated him. On 2nd December, 1918 Sovnarcom disbanded the Poor Peasants Committees because, in Lenin's words, the poor peasants "have become middle peasants".[25]

On 8th October, 1918 Sovnarcom nationalised all domestic trade and commercial enterprises, closing the remaining shops in the cities and using their goods to barter with the peasants for grain. This had little effect. Battered by the supply detachments and the Cheka, many villages began to produce only as much as they needed, thus leaving nothing for the detachments to take back to the cities. In turn the cities starved. Although Lenin and Trotsky remained truculent at all times, other Bolsheviks began to voice criticisms of the direction of policy.

One such Bolshevik was Alexei Rykov, who had stood with Zinoviev and Kamenev in opposing the Bolshevik insurrection and arguing for a socialist coalition government, precisely to avoid the alienation of the peasantry and the slide into civil war. He was now Chairman of Vesenka and Vice-Chair of Sovnarcom. In late 1918 at a meeting of the Council for Labour and Defence, Rykov responded to a report of the supply problems with biting sarcasm. "We are able, thank God, by dint of our revolutionary pathos, to get our workers and peasants accustomed to working even without bread", he said dryly. "But unfortunately we could not get our horses to do it. You may declare the horses to be counter-revolutionary, but you cannot ignore the fact and you must give them oats". Then, gesturing at Dzerzhinsky, he demonstrated what many Bolsheviks must have secretly felt about the Cheka and its methods. "Even Felix Edmundovich can do little about it", he said. "Let him try to shoot a few dozen horses".[26]

Later, after the New Economic Policy (NEP) was introduced in 1921, Lenin would seek to portray War Communism as a regrettable necessity that had sadly led to the alienation of the peasantry from the regime. But as Victor Serge recalled in his memoirs, War Communism was accepted at the time as the permanent, intentional policy of the government and only accrued its title retrospectively. "At the time it was called simply 'Communism'", he wrote of the period 1918-21, "and anyone who, like myself, went so far as to consider it purely temporary was looked upon with disdain".[27] In 1919 Lenin said explicitly that "the organisation of the communist activity of the proletariat, and the entire policy of the Communists, have now acquired a final, lasting form".[28] This was not a policy reluctantly pursued or forced upon the Bolsheviks against their will. It was Lenin's preferred policy, the essence of his socialism.

In the end it was only massive industrial and agrarian resistance that led to the abandonment of War Communism. As late as early 1920 Lenin heartily endorsed Bukharin's *The Economics of the Transition Period* (1920), the supreme theoretical expression of War Communism as the means to create a new society. After 1921 Bukharin, an intelligent and sensitive man who was not personally attracted to violent coercion in the same way that Lenin, Trotsky and Dzerzhinsky were, would become the most eloquent and effective proponent of the NEP's "mixed economy" and the relative liberalisation of social and cultural life. For three years from 1925 he was effectively co-leader of the USSR with Stalin, until the latter's volte-face on the NEP and mass collectivisation of the peasantry. But in 1918-20 he was still attracted to the radical vision of War Communism, which he saw not as a tactical necessity but a specific economic programme to effect the transition between capitalism and communism.

Bukharin offered a Marxist analysis of the "disequilibrium" which arose from the transition to communism. In his view the transition was not sustained by deep-seated organic economic processes and their reflection in institutional and legal forms, such as had characterised the relatively slow transition from feudalism to capitalism, but by the collective desire of the working class engaged in political action. "While the process of the creation of capitalism was spontaneous", he wrote, "the process of building communism is to a large decree a conscious, i.e. organised process".[29] This was not only true in the specific circumstances (if one believed that what was being built was communism), but it also justified the voluntarism of the Bolsheviks in jump-starting and force-feeding the historical process.

In a chapter titled "Extra-Economic Coercion in the Transition Period", Bukharin explicitly endorsed terror as a method of economic reconstruction. "Proletarian coercion in all its forms", he wrote, "beginning with shooting and ending with labour conscription, is a method of creating communist mankind out of the human materials of the transition period".[30] This was an astonishingly naïve conclusion based on the premise that the dictatorship of the proletariat, i.e. rule by Sovnarcom, could not exploit the working class because it was a regime in which the working class was itself in control. It entirely ignored the messy reality of who really controlled the levers of power and coercion, and the lack of input the masses had to Soviets now dominated by one political party. Bukharin also linked coercion to the need to bring the peasantry into the production process, juxtaposing the "organised tendencies of the proletariat and the commodity-anarchical tendencies of the peasantry".

Reviewing the book, Lenin made many annotations in the margins, which are a guide to his own thinking. He peppered his copy with violent dismissals (e.g. "rubbish!") of any references to modern sociological concepts or any concepts beyond those of Marx and Engels, even though he himself ruefully admitted Marx and Engels had said nothing about organising a socialist society *after* the revolution. But he adored the chapter which explained and justified the most extreme form of state coercion. "Now this chapter is superb!" he wrote, and heavily underlined. Stephen F. Cohen, Bukharin's usually sympathetic biographer, tartly summarised the implications: "Left unclear was whether the extreme measures used to forge a new equilibrium would continue to be the norm after equilibrium was established".[31]

That War Communism could attract a civilised man like Bukharin explains much about how the Red Terror took hold in Russia. Clothed in rationalisations about the survival of the revolution, the Terror was Bolshevism's id unleashed. But Bolshevism was fuelled as much by a passion for working-class freedom and social justice as by revenge, command and control. With the revolution and the concept of Soviet democracy on the defensive, with its forces pulled back to defend Petrograd and Moscow from the advancing White Army, whose savagery easily matched that of the Cheka, nearly all variants of socialists, from Menshevik Internationalists to Council Communists to anarcho-syndicalists, rallied to the proletarian revolution and to the Bolshevik government.

Although many anarchists refused to work with the Bolsheviks, preferring instead partisan anti-government activity or supporting Makhno in Ukraine, some made different choices. The former anarchist and IWW organiser Bill Shatov returned to his native Russia in 1917 with the American socialist John Reed, author of *Ten Days that Shook the World*. Although he never repudiated his anarchist convictions or joined the Communist Party, he helped the Bolsheviks defend their regime and directed a division of the 10th Red Army outside the city. Inside the city his anarcho-syndicalist friend Victor Serge, freezing and almost starving, worked on Bolshevik propaganda material. Serge's wife served in a Red Guard field ambulance.

The Anarchist Federation of Petrograd, a band of partisans under the Russian anarchist Kolokushkin, decided, "not without reservations and not without friction",[32] to stand with the Bolsheviks against White counter-revolution. By great irony they ended up taking up armed defence of the printing works of *Pravda*, a paper which routinely attacked them. Many Petrograd Mensheviks, although politically alienated from the Bolsheviks by the events of 1917 and 1918, volunteered to defend the city from the Whites.

In August 1918 the Menshevik Central Committee under Martov's direction spelt out its position on the Civil War and foreign intervention. "Notwithstanding the terrors of the Bolshevik regime", the CC resolution stated,

> the socialist working class of Russia rejects any intervention
> by capitalist governments for the purpose of delivering it from
> the bloody Bolshevik dictatorship, and relies solely on its own
> strength, the strength of the democratic masses, and the support
> of the international proletariat for the removal of this regime .[33]

In July 1918, when the Left SRs launched their anti–Bolshevik rebellion, the Menshevik Central Committee issued instructions that under no circumstances were Mensheviks to join or support it. Their task was to organise workers into "an independent third force" whose goal was the "reconstruction of the democratic organs of local self-government" and the "cessation of bloodshed and reprisals".[34]

When the Menshevik leader Ivan Maisky travelled to Samara to work with Komuch, he was instantly expelled from the party's Central Committee. This gained the Mensheviks very little. In the next few months the government stepped up its persecution of the party and its press. Even Martov was arrested, although Lenin had him quickly released. Under this pressure the Mensheviks almost split, with those like ex-Bundist leader Mark Liber wishing to ally with Komuch and the SRs to fight the government, and Martov holding that whatever the provocation this would be to turn against the working class. Faced with these defections, Martov laid down a new, firmer position that dispensed with illusions about a "third force" and asserted socialist unity in the face of White counter-revolution.

In October 1918 the Menshevik CC announced that it accepted the October Revolution had been "historically necessary". It no longer sought convocation of the Constituent Assembly, although it did not compromise its position on civil liberties. It still demanded "the abolition of the extraordinary organs of police repression and of the Extraordinary Tribunals, and the cessation of all political and economic terror". It rejected any policy that "strove to turn the class dictatorship of the proletariat into a rule over state and society on the basis of the political disenfranchisement of all nonproletrian strata of the population, *a fortiori* the dictatorship of one section of the proletariat".[35] However it accepted that it would now campaign solely within the Soviets and the Soviet Executive.

On 30th November, in response to Martov's new policy and needing every atom of support it could secure, Sovnarcom tentatively re-legalised the Menshevik Party and allowed its deputies back into the Soviets. The Menshevik

Party would only ever be semi-tolerated. After it began to notch up serious majorities within the Soviets in 1919 it would again be subject to censorship and persecution, but for a brief period, with White counter-revolutionaries almost at the gates of Petrograd and Moscow, the RSDLP stood together one last time.

The siege conditions and sacrifices in Petrograd and Moscow created intense camaraderie and solidarity. The Kronstadt naval base was struggling to hold out. On 2nd June Serge reported to his diary, "The White army is gathering outside Petrograd". A few days later he wrote, "Hunger is permanently established in at least 300,000 homes. Anxiety is everywhere [...] Queues of fifty to a hundred people stand outside the bakeries where the commune distributes to everybody the bread it has available". Most Petrograd workers bought bread illegally on the black market. Many foraged in the dangerous country outside the city instead of going to work. Yet despite the appalling privation and fear of what the White armies would do if they took the city, Serge found that many of its defenders still held musical concerts and listened to opera and poetry recitals. For him the inspiring example of the armed communists, especially the youngest fighters, meant "We shall not be destroyed! This soul of the revolutionary city contains too much beauty; this flesh and blood of the city contains too much energy!"[36]

For all its heroism and self-sacrifice, the bloody defence of Petrograd inevitably produced more coercion and terror. In response to the defection of some former Tsarist officers from the Red Army to the Whites, on 12th June *Izvestia* published on its front page a decree from Trotsky and Zinoviev stating,

"You are instructed to establish the family situation of all former officers who have been integrated into the command structure of the Red Army and to inform them that the consequences of any treachery will fall on their families". On 24th June Order No 960 instructed every citizen to carry a "labour certificate" issued at their place of work. Militias and House Committees went from residence to residence enforcing the order. Orders to restrict movement, to check all motor cars, and to register any weapons (on pain of immediate execution) followed. These were all justified by the urgent need to secure the defence of Petrograd against Whites both outside and inside the city. Serge, a truly libertarian socialist, wrote, "Crush this incipient reaction at whatever cost, because if they were to triumph even for a moment it would be a calamity for the whole of humanity".[37]

On 17th October Yudenich's forces were only twenty-five miles from the city. On 19th October they were nine miles away. "It seemed quite plainly to be our death agony", wrote Serge years later.[38] Bill Shatov took a few thousand men out to meet Yudenich's force of 15,000, not expecting to return. With the city about to fall, the Politburo sent Trotsky to oversee the defence. Upon arrival he found Zinoviev, the boss of the Petrograd Branch of the RCP, stretched out on a sofa in utter despair, his officials defeatist. "As usual in such situations I turned to my trainforce, men who could be depended on under any circumstances", Trotsky wrote in his autobiography, referring to the militarised train that took him from front to front in the Civil War:

They checked up, put on pressure, established connections,

removed those who were unfit, and filled in the gaps. From the official apparatus, which had become completely demoralised, I descended two or three floors to the district organisations of the party, the mills, the factories, and the barracks.[39]

Trotsky's arrival turned the tide. As even his political enemy Lashevich later admitted, "Trotsky's orders, clear and precise, sparing nobody and exacting from everybody the utmost exertion and accurate execution of combat orders, at once showed there was a firm, directing hand".[40] Trotsky addressed an emergency session of the Petrograd Soviet and urged one last, supreme effort. Serge was present and later recorded, "The decision to fight to the death was taken enthusiastically, and the whole amphitheatre raised a song of immense power".[41]

Roads, squares and bridges were barricaded, barbed wire was put up, trenches were dug on the southern approaches. At one crucial moment, when Red Army units had fallen back to Alexandrovka on the outskirts of the city, Trotsky himself mounted a horse and rode up and down under fire, turning them around and inspiring them to hold firm. On 21st October, on the Pulkovo Heights over Petrograd, the reinforced Red Army made its final stand against Yudenich's advancing forces and defeated them. Yudenich fell back to Estonia. Shortly after, in November, Admiral Kolchak's forces were ejected from Omsk, their Siberian capital. The threat from the Whites was over.

The heroic last-ditch defence of Petrograd in October 1919 — and the eventual defeat of all the White armies and their foreign allies by the more cohesive force of the Red Army — was the Soviet Union's "creation myth", as much as was the storming of the Winter Palace. It inspired and mobilised not only convinced Bolsheviks but all in the city who fought for democracy and social liberation against the reactionary forces of Old Russia, of autocracy, militarism, privilege and anti-Semitism. The tragedy for those Mensheviks, libertarians and anarchists who rallied to the Bolsheviks in their hour of need was that Lenin's regime did not deserve this support and self-sacrifice. It certainly did not repay it.

CHAPTER THIRTEEN

Sex-Pol

Whilst the physical survival of the Soviet regime was decided on the battlefields of the Civil War, other battles, less dramatic but equally important, were being fought. In a regime whose declared mission was to create a fundamentally new society, two of the most important sites of this struggle were the People's Commissariat of Education (known as Nakompros), and the People's Commissariat of Social Welfare.

Under the People's Commissar for Education, Anatoly Lunacharsky, Nakompros was one of the few Commissariats that did not simply rename an old Tsarist Ministry and carry on. It encompassed the old Ministry of Public Education but also integrated the functions of the Palace Ministry, which controlled the Academy of Arts, the imperial theatres and the royal palaces. Lunacharsky encountered the same obstruction from Tsarist civil servants as did other People's Commissars. He eventually occupied the Ministry on 18th November, where he and his assistants were greeted warmly by technical staff. He issued an appeal for the officials to report for duty on 27th November but nobody came. It was then discovered that officials had taken with them 93,000 rubles from the teachers' pension fund and refused to return it.[1]

As it dealt with areas regarded by a strongly patriarchal culture as of secondary importance—education, culture—many male Bolshevik Party members did not wish to work in Nakompros. Consequently, Lunacharsky's key lieutenants were often women, the wives of Lenin, Trotsky, Kamenev, Zinoviev, Dzerzhinsky and others. It was also, like all Commissariats, pitifully underfunded, despite the need to maintain all of Soviet Russia's schools, teacher-training institutes, universities, scientific work, theatres, cinemas, opera houses, libraries, historical archives, literacy and youth work, public memorials and extra-mural work for public occasions. Sovnarcom was keen that the philosophy, great texts and heroes of the socialist movement be celebrated in the new public culture, but rarely provided the money to do this. The result was to fall back on the work of the "Proletarian Culture" (Proletkult) organisation.

Nakompros's most immediate priority was the preservation of the treasures left to it from the fallen Empire. Two days after the October Insurrection, *Izvestia* published an appeal stating that the new regime had inherited "enormous cultural riches, buildings of rare beauty, museums full of rare and marvelous objects, things that enlighten and inspire, and libraries containing vast intellectual treasures. All this now belongs to the people".[2] With the help of Gorky and the ex-World of Art director Alexander Benois, Lunacharsky organised special commissions to protect endangered monuments and national treasures. Although many mansions and privately owned museums were taken into public ownership their contents were, mostly, protected, and were in time thrown open to the public. Even amidst the worst conditions of the Civil War, in besieged, freezing and starving Petrograd, Victor Serge recorded that the city

> never, even its most tragic days, lost the concern for art; it never neglected rhythms, fine gestures, beautiful voices full of pathos, dream-like settings, poems, anthems played on the organ, the sobbing notes of violins [...] the Red City is suffering and fighting so that one day leisure and art shall be the property of all.[3]

By 1920 Sovnarcom's Section for Museums and Preservation of Monuments had registered over 550 old mansions, previously the occasional homes of a wealthy aristocratic elite, as new museums, as well as over a thousand new collections of hitherto private art collections. These were carefully preserved and made available to workers and peasants who had never before had the opportunity to see and experience great art. The private market in art was abolished. Even the Bolsheviks' sternest critics concede they safeguarded Russia's artistic treasures to the extent they were able. By the device of transforming private mansions into museums they met the twin aims of expropriating the riches of the ruling class with providing more access to art and culture for the masses.

It was one of the revolution's most democratic and libertarian innovations. As Stites says, "By placing crowns, thrones and imperial regalia in a People's Museum the regime depoliticised them, neutralised their former symbolic power, and offered them as a gift to the masses".[4] Yet although the Bolsheviks' initial programme to liberate cultural private property for the benefit of all was bold and successful, their long-term policy was ultimately self-defeating. The regime preserved the culture of the past, even venerated it, but it did not value or sustain the institutions, freedom of expression and social pluralism that had created it in the first place, and might create more in the future.

Lunacharsky's most challenging task was to build a socialist education system, and to a great extent he succeeded. An entirely new governance system was introduced whereby schools would henceforth be administered by workers' cooperatives of all staff, not just the teachers, and representatives of pupils above 12 years of age, plus one representative from Nakompros. In some instances, teachers would be elected. Lunacharsky, the "moderate" Bolshevik who had wished to form a socialist coalition government after October 1917, proved much more comfortable with the elective principle than did Trotsky.

The general policy was outlined in a June 1918 "Statement on the Organisation of Education in the Russian Republic", which established an "Educational Soviet" to run the national education system under the broad oversight of Nakompros. The Soviet was to consist of elected representatives from all bodies represented in the Central Soviet as well as representatives of teachers, pupils and educational experts. But even then Nakompros ensured that local schools had a significant amount of autonomy, consistent with the broad thrust of educational policy.

The introduction of democracy within the school system

was not welcomed by educational traditionalists. The Teachers Union, the VUS, took strike action between November 1917 and March 1918 in protest against the changes ordered by Nakompros. Lunacharsky did not wish to break the strike and arrest it leaders, as had been done with the civil-service strike in the immediate aftermath of October, and he set out to convince younger teachers to work with, not against, Nakompros. He had some success as more left-wing teachers set up the Union of Teacher-Internationalists and began to work with the government. Nakompros also allowed private schools to continue in existence, although they could no longer charge for their services. It thereby incurred the wrath of, on the one side, Bolshevik zealots who demanded direct involvement by Nakompros, and on the other, conservatives appalled by the erosion of teachers' previously absolute authority and the removal of religious education from the curriculum.

From its earliest days Nakompros drew inspiration not only from Marxism but also from the liberal approach to child-centred education pioneered by John Dewey in America and Bertrand Russell in Britain. This resulted in a new curriculum that emphasised activity over lectures, more pupil participation and more democratic, informal relations between pupils and teachers. The Soviet regime's educational philosophy was explained in a document written by Lunacharsky and published in October 1918. The "Declaration on the United Labour School" outlined the aim of having a school system that functioned as a "single, unbroken staircase" from kindergarten to university. It explained that "All children must enter the same type of school and begin their education alike, and all have the right to rise up the ladder to its highest rungs". It recommended what it called an "encyclopedia of culture", including staples such as history, maths, geography, aesthetics, biology, physics, chemistry and modern languages, although these were to be taught as part of a "sociology of labour". It was a polytechnical vision of education to be delivered in a non-hierarchical manner.

In May 1918 the Commissariat abolished single-sex schools and began to combine academic and technical courses. In October 1918 it abolished the examination system and homework, replacing them with continuous assessment of coursework. Tests of memory and learning by rote were done away with, inaugurating programmes that developed critical ability and learning tailored to individual pupils. Schools were also instructed to provide hot breakfasts for all children, although in conditions of Civil War in which schools and teachers were starved (sometimes literally) of resources this was more aspiration than reality. There were also tensions between teachers at the sharp end and those they considered unqualified to instruct them in the Educational Soviet, tensions smoothed over by Nakompros. But for all these difficulties Marcel Liebman was entirely right to characterise the Bolsheviks' educational reforms as heralding "a profound and serious liberation of the human spirit".[5]

Beyond that, the Bolshevik regime launched a full-scale crusade against mass illiteracy, with all illiterate citizens between age 8 and 50 mandated to attend literacy classes. Libraries were ordered to stay open seven days a week. A Sovnarcom Decree of November 1918 mobilised literate citizens as "readers" to teach the illiterate to read communist newspapers. From its first days the Bolshevik government had ordered cheap, mass-produced copies of the classics be easily available to workers and peasants. Given the many and immediate threats to its existence in the first few years of its life, this was a policy that expressed the best of Bolshevism.

It prefigured and indirectly inspired the highly successful "Mission Robinson" literacy and primary education programme of the Venezuelan government, which between 2003 and 2012 taught 1.75 million poor Venezuelans to read and write.[6] Mission Robinson enrolled over 247,000 Venezuelan citizens into the programme, supported by 33,000 volunteer teachers or "facilitators". As an offshoot of Mission Robinson, in May 2009 the Venezuelan Ministry of Culture distributed free books, children's stories, magazines, movies and documentaries, and hosted public theatrical and musical presentations in the central plazas of major cities across the country. The Mission was directly based on Cuba's massive "Yes I Can" literacy project, which had achieved unprecedented success in raising literacy rates in Cuba, and which itself drew on Nakompros' literacy programme for historical inspiration.

Education was vitally important to building a new society in Soviet Russia, but the biggest challenge facing the new regime, if it were to honestly claim that it was inaugurating a real social revolution, was to radically transform the lives and freedoms of Russian women. In comparison to the social situation of most women in Western European countries in 1917 – no bed of roses – that of Russian women was incredibly hard. Peasant women, especially, felt the full force of Russia's semi-feudal social relations. They had no legal rights, could not participate in the work of the Mir or the Zemstvo, spent much of their time pregnant, and had to fulfill all of the housekeeping and child-rearing duties as well as work in the fields. A village would celebrate the birth of baby boy, but not a girl. That girl would spend her entire life under the control of her male relatives and husband, the only exception being widows who were allowed to run their strip of land (though the pressure within the village to sell or re-marry was intense).

The only escape was to the cities of the Russian Empire, either as a seasonal labourer or a permanent resident. Between 1887 and 1914 the number of women employed in industrial factory work jumped from 192,000 to 723,000. The total increased markedly in 1904-06, as women replaced male workers mobilised for the Russo-Japanese war. It was only then that employers and socialists began to notice the female proletariat – employers because they found women workers cheaper and easier to manage, and socialists because, in spite of this, clusters of women workers were beginning to organise and exhibit a basic class consciousness.

Nothing demonstrated this process better than the strike at the Laferme Cigarette Factory on Vasilevsky Island, St Petersburg, in November 1895, in which between 800 and 1,500 women workers went on strike to protest a cut in wages and the abusive behavior of male managers. The response from the owners was to call the police, who surrounded the strikers and hosed them down with water. Martov, sent from the St Petersburg Combat Union to assist the strike, overheard the St Petersburg police chief tell female strikers that they should make up the wage cut by "picking up extra money on the street".[7] Thirty strike leaders were banished from the city but, faced with a mass strike, some of their demands, such as withdrawal of a fee for hanging up their coats, were conceded.

The majority of women workers in the cities were employed as domestic servants. As compliant peasant women with little to no experience of urban life, they were usually treated badly, sometimes given no more than a corner to sleep in. Many of them suffered sexual abuse and exploitation. The patriarch of the house would often take advantage of the new maid and then sack her if she became pregnant. In factories, the owner or supervisor saw it as his right to pick which of the young women workers he wanted. Male relatives regarded the informal arrangement as a means to make extra money for the family.[8] The result was a tide of unwanted and illegitimate children, many of whom were simply killed in infancy as their mothers were forced into prostitution. The grim end-point was the notorious "Angel Factories"—gangs of baby-farmers who delivered baskets of malnourished or dead babies to the official shelters so as to collect the two-ruble fee for each one.

The record of Russian political parties on women's emancipation was mixed. After the creation of the Duma in 1905 suggestions were made to extend the suffrage to women. Conservatives simply scorned the idea. The leaders of the Kadet Party felt it was premature, although some of its female members, drawn from the liberal intelligentsia of the capital, challenged this. This led to the creation of Russia's first female suffragist organisation, the Union of

Women's Equality, which for a brief period attracted a large number of bourgeois women.

The SRs and Trudoviks looked both ways. As socialists they supported women's emancipation, and the 1904 SR Programme included a demand for "universal suffrage without distinction of sex". But the "Peasant Unions" from which the SRs drew support wanted this demand removed. In 1906, radicalised by the 1905 Revolution and the peasant seizures of landed estates, an alliance of urban-based SRs and peasant women pushed the All-Russian Peasant Union to the left. It officially affiliated to the SRs, which declared its support for full gender equality. The Marxists, on the other hand, had long supported equal rights for women as an integral part of their political programme, but seldom challenged deep-seated sexist attitudes within their own ranks. The leaders of both factions of the RSDLP were almost exclusively male.

Yet women were beginning to carve out small freedoms for themselves. At the turn of the century only 12% of women in the villages could read and write, but in the cities nearly 50% of women were literate. This inevitably led to greater interest and involvement in life outside the family. Whilst most female workers, especially those recently arrived from the villages, played no role at all in political parties or trade unions, a minority of the more independent-minded broke that tradition. The Laferme strike was the first sign, as a result of which the social democrats started to recruit women workers. At first all they had to guide them was August Bebel's *Woman and Socialism* (1879), the only major Marxist work to directly address the issue of women's oppression in capitalist society. 1900 saw the publication of the first serious treatment of the condition of working–class and peasant women in Russia, *The Woman Worker*, written by Lenin's wife Nadezhda Krupskaya. It laid bare the conditions of female labour, the lot of the female peasant, systemic sexual exploitation in village and town, and the scandal of mass illegitimacy and prostitution.

The Woman Worker was widely read amongst female socialists. But despite the RSDLP's progressive rhetoric, it consistently underestimated the extent to which exploited female workers might lead the way in mass strikes and protests. The textile industry, for example, was a centre of women's trade unionism. Female textile workers led resistance during the war and took to the streets to protest about high food prices and low wages, thereby igniting the February 1917 Revolution. Having helped remove the biggest patriarch of all, the Tsar, they had no desire to go back in their box. The Bolsheviks were keenly aware that after October women workers looked to them to remove the legal shackles that bound them.

The primary responsibility for addressing these issues devolved to the Commissariat for Social Welfare and its People's Commissar, Alexandra Kollontai. In *The Social Basis of the Woman Question* (1908), Kollontai had attempted a Marxist analysis of the family, marriage, sexual relations and childcare. The book arose from her struggles with Russian bourgeois feminists and the need, as she saw it, to draw women away from supporting a programme that suggested women of all classes had common aims and interests. Although Kollontai did not rule out tactical cooperation with feminists on specific campaigns, she was clear that Marxists must "reject the existence of a special woman question separate from the general social question of our day […] The feminists seek equality in the framework of the existing class society; in no way do they attack the basis of this society". In later years she would defend radical, emancipatory notions about sex and personal relationships, but in 1908 she stuck to the more conventional Marxist position that before "free relationships" and "free love" could become common practice, "it is above all necessary that a fundamental reform of all social relationships between people take place".[9]

The October Revolution placed this fundamental reform on the agenda. On 16th December, 1917 Sovnarcom issued the Decree on Divorce, which stated a number of new legal precepts, the first of which was, "Marriage is dissolved at the request of both spouses or either of them", the request to be addressed to the local court. Once the judge had ascertained whether the request was genuine he would "issue a certificate thereof". If the husband and wife had children, the judge would also decide which of them would have care of them, the division of the financial upkeep of the children, and whether the husband was obliged to pay childcare maintenance to his divorced wife.[10] The Divorce Decree was a truly collaborative document, written by the Menshevik lawyer A.G. Goikhbarg, overseen by the Bolshevik Kollontai and promulgated under the SR People's Commissar for Justice Steinberg. It was "an accurate reflection of the Russian left on matrimonial matters".[11]

The government followed this later in 1918 with a Family Code, which simplified the proceedings further and abolished any legal distinction between children born in or out of wedlock. Kollontai was under no illusions about the new laws. "It is not essentially any more progressive than those existing in other progressive democracies", she wrote in 1926, when the Code was revised again to allow for "registered divorce", a procedure instigated by the couple without a judge's approval. "On the divorce question we are on a level with North America, whereas on the question of illegitimate children we have not even progressed as far as the Norwegians".[12]

Nevertheless, the reform of the marriage law was the first shot in a historically unprecedented attempt to reform and improve the legal and social status of Russian women. Initially this arose from the Commissariat for Social Welfare. The Commissariat was responsible for provision of services to pensioners, orphans, the homeless, and wounded and disabled war veterans, although as Imperial Russia disintegrated it had been overwhelmed by the scale of its work and had virtually ceased to function (in late 1917 there were about 350,000 homeless children on the streets, falling into crime and prey to sexual abuse – by 1921 there were seven million).

When Kollontai arrived at the Commissariat a few days after 25th October she was denied entrance. When she finally forced her way in with a group of sympathetic junior staff she found chaos – the senior officials had destroyed much of the paperwork before leaving. With no administrative staff and no money, she was besieged by thousands of petitioners begging for assistance for starving children, homeless orphans, the disabled and destitute. While Kollontai struggled to secure funding so that the Commissariat of Social Welfare could fulfill at least some of its responsibilities, she began to organise an ambitious All-Russian Conference of Working Women and Peasant Women to determine the policies that women themselves desired. Even before it met she set up a special section of her Commissariat to implement policies of benefit to women and children, such as sixteen weeks paid maternity leave, free crèches and nurseries, and a new system of orphanages and foster homes. Unfortunately, there was no money to pay for them, and the Commissariat's role was reduced to that of dispenser of advice, plastered with posters about contraception and breast-feeding.

The Conference, though, revealed a great desire for the services the Commissariat was offering. Kollontai estimated it would attract 80 delegates. In the event over 500 delegates representing 80,000 women attended and discussed issues such as equal pay, maternity leave, abortion, civil marriage and housework. Most of the decisions could not be actioned in conditions of social collapse and civil war, and complaints that policies of direct benefit to working women were being left unimplemented began to flood from women members of the Bolshevik (then Communist) Party. In response, in September 1919 Sovnarcom created a special Women's Department, the Zhenotdel, headed by Inessa Armand, to give greater focus to its work on women and the family. It is unclear why Kollontai was not put in charge. Probably her explicit agitation on sexual and gender issues made the Central Committee distrust her more than the reliable party loyalist Armand.

After Armand died of cholera in 1920, Sovnacrom had little choice but to put Kollontai in charge. With its own journal, *Communist Woman*, and a network of regional

organisers assigned to local Soviets, the Zhenotdel set out
to enforce equality policies that to this point existed on paper
only. It ensured that all teams of Factory Inspectors included
a Zhenotdel representative, whose job it was to ensure
that equality legislation – on maternity leave, protection
for pregnant women on overtime and long hours, and
hygiene rules – was being followed. Although exaggerated
by a hostile, deeply sexist White press and by conservative
peasants, the popular image of the Zhenotdel – an earnest
young female Bolshevik from the city wearing its distinctive
red headscarf – had a basis in reality. Often she would arrive
in a village or town and demand to know how equality
legislation was being carried out. She would then arrange
for the care of homeless children, set up nurseries and ensure
that abused women were protected. Sometimes she would
lecture peasant women on hygiene and contraception. These
lectures were not always welcome.

The most controversial elements of Zhenotdel's work
centred on its policies for the family and child-rearing.
Kollontai, Armand and other leading Zhenotdel officials
such as Krupskaya believed that for women to be truly
emancipated from patriarchal social relations they had to
be relieved of domestic and child-rearing duties, which
should be provided by public institutions. As a result they
organised communal nurseries, kitchens and laundries where
children could be looked after and cleaning done while
parents were at work.

The programmes had a positive aim, but they over-
estimated the extent to which Russian women were ready
to discard the social and family roles they had grown up with

and to which many clung in the middle of a chaotic and frightening world. Barbara Evans Clements' investigation of working-class and peasant women in 1917-23 found that whilst thousands of women joined the Zhenotdel programmes, "millions more did not, still intent on private concerns that they saw as unrelated to, or unalleviated by, Bolshevik promises".[13] Many peasant women, in particular, were frightened that the new government wished to take babies away from their mothers and to provide men (on whom they were dependent for protection and status) an excuse for sexual license and abandonment of their wives.

Kollontai and Armand's efforts to free Russian women from social and domestic servitude ultimately foundered on the rock of sexism. Kollontai, especially, laid herself open to attack by her forthright challenge to patriarchal sexual attitudes with which many Bolshevik men felt comfortable (Lenin, although he endorsed Zhendotel's social reforms such as the provision of communal kitchens and laundries, was for his entire life looked after by his mother, sister and wife, with no domestic concern allowed to bother him). Kollontai was far ahead of most of the Bolshevik Party in rejecting conventional marriage and championing free sexual partnerships based on love and respect. She attracted fierce criticism not just for the policies she advocated and the legislation on divorce, abortion and marriage, but for her forays into imaginative fiction and her speculative rhapsodies on the perfect sexual union. In particular, her much misunderstood and misquoted concept of "winged eros" incensed the puritans of the left.

In "Make Way for Winged Eros: A Letter to Working

Youth" (1923), Kollontai laid out two contrasting concepts of sexual relations: one based on instant gratification and one on what was called "sex-love". The concept of "winged eros" was not a charter for mindless hedonism. On the contrary it advocated an ideal fusion of the sexual, emotional and intellectual. It was also a union of two people who were not simply self-obsessed but who understood the greater needs of the new communist society and worked to better it. It was the opposite of "wingless eros", which was simple sexual self-indulgence. "The unadorned sexual drive is easily aroused but it is soon spent", Kollontai wrote.

> Thus 'wingless eros' consumes less inner strength than 'winged eros', whose love is woven of delicate strands of every kind of emotion. Wingless eros does not make one suffer from sleepless nights, does not sap one's will, and does not entangle the rational workings of the mind.[14]

Kollontai's great sin was believing that winged eros—the emotional-erotic union she idealised—need not occur in a conventional marriage or a permanent relationship. There could be wingless eros inside marriage (e.g. the stereotype of the loveless bourgeois union with the husband taking prostitutes on the side) and winged eros outside of it. Worse, although she did not say so explicitly, the concept of "multi-faceted love" implied that as long as sex-love was honest and experienced by good communists with a social conscience, it could fluctuate across genders and from partnership to partnership.

In response to the new divorce laws, especially after the

introduction of "registered divorce" in 1926, working-class couples in the cities divorced and remarried in great numbers and frequency. The decriminalisation of the old Criminal Code had also produced, at least in Petrograd and Moscow, a space for gays and lesbians to come out. Some Bolsheviks, such as Kollontai and Zetkin, even occasionally discussed the subject. "Proletarian ideology", wrote Kollontai, "cannot accept exclusiveness and 'all-embracing love'. The proletariat is not filled with horror and moral indignation at the many forms and facets of 'winged eros'". If only indirectly, it was a shocking challenge to patriarchal authority and hetero-normativity.

Kollontai put the sexual morality taught by the old church and its feudal offshoots, including the folderol of "courtly love", under a harsh spotlight. She wrote witheringly,

> The knight who would not be parted from the emblem of the lady of his heart, who composed poetry in her honour and risked his life to win her smile would rape a girl of the urban classes without a second thought, or order his steward to bring a beautiful peasant for his pleasure.[15]

In the new capitalist order it was necessary that capital be concentrated in bourgeois marriages to make inheritance easier, and that the working class, although without capital, perpetuate itself as a labour force. The most efficient machine to do this was the family. Love in families existed, of course, but it was not *required*, and in any case that was where it was meant to stay. A socialist revolution would free it. Kollontai's 1923 essay, and her earlier *Theses on Communist Morality in the Sphere of Marital Relations* (1921), fell victim not only to their own heterodox daring but to the decline of Kollontai's star within the Bolshevik Party after 1921 following her support for the Workers' Opposition. In all respects, she was out of time.

Despite historic legislative victories (the vote, equal pay, abortion) and the provision of contraceptives allowing women to control the reproductive cycle, the challenges facing modern feminism are surprisingly little altered from the 1920s. The same core problems remain, especially the massively unequal division of domestic labour and childcare and its effect on professional and career status. The glass ceiling is unbroken, with most large public and private organisations exhibiting a pyramid structure for female employees – wide at the base, narrowing to a tip of almost none at the top. The media and fashion industries, the acme of professional middle-class careers, are arguably more sexist and misogynist than working-class occupations like bus driver or street cleaner. Fashion and lifestyle magazines impose a ridiculous "ideal" of emaciation on the psychology of their readers and the bodies of their models. Women working full-time earn 15% less than men, increasing to 18% for older women. Two-thirds of low-paid workers are women. In the UK the gender pay gap, for the first time in decades, is now widening, not diminishing.

This rests on systemic social inequality and the disinclination of mainstream political parties to seriously address it. Women perform 66% of the world's work, produce 50% of the food, earn 10% of the income and own 1% of the property. And then there is the final and defining characteristic of all sexism past and present: male violence against women. 89% of domestic-violence victims in the UK are women, and two women a week are killed by a male partner or former partner. In the UK approximately 100,000 women are raped each year, yet just 6% of reported rapes end in a conviction.[16]

The first wave of feminism in the early decades of the 20th century secured basic legal and property rights. The second wave, developed from the 1960s to the 1980s, focused on deeper structures of social, cultural and sexual oppression. In seminal works such as *The Dialectic of Sex* (1970), *Gyn/Ecology* (1979) and *Pornography* (1981), American feminists Shulamith Firestone, Mary Daly and Andrea Dworkin challenged the sexist psychology, imagery, language and cultural norms that ensured women, regardless of their nominal legal rights, remained what Simone de Beauvoir labeled the "Other", i.e secondary and external to the default option of social reality—the white, straight, middle-class male. They sought not simply new laws but a new consciousness, a liberation from objectification and male oppression in all its forms.

The achievements of second-wave feminism—recognition of widespread domestic violence, rape and child abuse; new legal protections, including the provision by local authorities of shelters for abused wives and children; sexual equality and harassment policies in the workplace; feminist history and womens' studies programmes—were real, essential and historic. But they fell victim to their success, with some prominent feminists lost in fantasy projects for a new language for women (Daly) and a female-only independent homeland (Dworkin) that meant absolutely nothing to most working women. Thus distracted, the partial advances made by women in the 1970s and 1980s were vulnerable to a sexist "backlash", which duly arrived on the back of Thatcher and Reagan's neoliberal counter-revolution. Lad Culture followed like a wolf at its heels.

After a period of internal debate, the modern feminist response is increasingly "intersectional". Intersectionality as a theory arose in the 1960s in response to mainstream feminism's assertion that gender is the prime factor determining a person's experience in society. Black women, in particular, challenged this, and denied that they and affluent white women shared the same oppression. This gave a boost to socialist feminism. In the 1970s and 1980s the socialist movement was enriched by an infusion of feminist thinking on consensus decision-making and non-hierarchical organising. By the 1990s feminism was exploring the idea that it was impossible to challenge social, cultural and sexual oppression in separate categories. For example, it was one-sided to focus on gender oppression of working-class black women without also focusing on their racial and class status.

The feminist sociologist Patricia Hill Collins, who first defined the concept of intersectionality, identified a "matrix of domination", or an inter-locking system of power constructs and their baleful effects, that was intended as an *extension* of orthodox Marxist theory. It was a reaction against an identity politics that put those resisting a particular form of oppression, i.e. homophobia, in an organisational and political ghetto where only that form of oppression was challenged. Yet critics of intersectionality continue to miss the point. In 2013 Eve Mitchell pulled feminist analysis back to the Marxist concept of waged work which produces value for the capitalist, and unwaged work, i.e. domestic and carer work, which does not. The gendered division of labour thus produced is, in this argument, the basis of women's oppression and should be the primary focus of political challenge. The only factor that matters in defining anti-capitalist activity is not one's cultural identity, but the status of one's "labour-power".[17]

There may be economic logic here but it is the politics of a pie chart. It implies that any "identity" felt under capitalism, not simply of occupation but of sexuality, gender and race, is transient and artificial. Mitchell's conclusion that "we will struggle for a society that does not limit us as 'bus drivers', 'women', or 'queers', but a society that allows everyone to freely use their multi-sided life activity in whatever ways they want" is a noble vision for a hypothetical utopia, but it places individuals alive right now, in all their complexity and subjectivity, into one big category (or two: proletariat and bourgeoisie). But while one's labour—its rewards and status, or lack of them—may determine one's position in society, it need not determine one's *identity*.

Ironically, many on the left who dismiss identity politics out of hand often exhibit a form of working-class identity politics which privileges the older, white, male proletariat (or its patronising stereotype) over more diverse forms of working-class identity, i.e. younger, female, BAME and LGBT. The outcome of the UK Referendum on the EU, and the 2016 US Presidential election, boosted and legitimised reactionary social attitudes in those countries, not solely anti-immigrant xenophobia but an entire corpus of racism, sexism and homophobia. It is a reactionary wave that some on the left have indulged, echoing the far-right's condemnation of "liberal elites" and their cosmopolitan values. This can only end in disaster. If the left does not uphold and defend liberal cultural values, it is paving the way for the right's victory. Not least because, as the socialist writer Owen Jones had to remind those who secretly yearn for the traditional working class *circa* 1957, "The emancipation of the working class means the whole working class: men and women, white and black, straight and LGBT"[18].

The alternative is to whitewash patriarchal attitudes within "the class". One of the most culturally working-class and undemocratic trade unions in the UK, the GMB, notoriously advised its women members on Birmingham City Council in 2007 not to challenge unequal pay as that might negatively impact the higher pay of its male members (the women ignored the advice, took the legal route and secured a record pay-out and historic victory). There are always excuses for these attitudes. "We will never free ourselves of machismo within the movement", wrote Mitchell, "without abolishing gender itself, and therefore alienated labour itself". Unfortunately, it may take some time to abolish gender and alienated labour, leaving the problem of machismo within the movement unaddressed.

Today's feminism has recovered from the backlash of the last two decades. Groups and websites like Everyday Sexism and UK Feminista have left old debates behind to engage with specific examples of misogyny and discrimination. Social media means that sexist and misogynist attitudes in politics, the media, advertising, sport and business can be immediately challenged, although its dark side – the freedom given to viciously sexist men to spew rape threats and other insults at any independent-minded woman – more than balances that. Anti-austerity campaigns like Sisters Uncut emphasise that austerity economics and social welfare cuts hit low-paid, single-parent women hardest. They also call-out middle-class corporate feminism.

Dawn Foster's *Lean Out* (2016) is a blistering response to Facebook CEO Sheryl Sandberg's advice book for under-promoted female professionals. As Foster puts it, "Sandburg's corporate feminism doesn't extend to calling for collective rights such as state maternity pay, or a stronger welfare net, or even encouraging women to unionise".[19] New feminist writers such as Foster, Jessica Valenti and Nina Power encapsulate a revived, culturally savvy and politically radical feminism. Trade unions and left parties will have to keep up with them or risk irrelevance to younger feminists looking for action and justice now. Sadly, the appalling response of the leadership of the British Socialist Workers Party (SWP) to allegations of rape against one of their own demonstrated that the Leninist left has a very long way to go.

By the standards of his time Lenin himself was not especially misogynist. He had supported his wife in the work required to research and write *The Woman Worker* and after the revolution he endorsed the broad thrust of Kollontai's legislation. In a speech delivered to the Fourth Moscow City Conference of Non-Party Working Women in September 1919, Lenin began by asserting that while Western democracies had aspirations to make men and women equal, none had done so, "because wherever there is capitalism, wherever there is private property in land and factories, wherever the power of capital is preserved, the men retain their privileges". But, he claimed, the Soviet Union had "left nothing of the old unjust laws that were intolerable for working people [...] In the sphere of legislation we have done everything required of us to put women in a position of equality and we have every right to be proud of it".[20]

He was right. Sovnarcom's decrees on equality were exemplary, especially at a time of massive social upheaval. But practical legislation on education and childcare, whilst progressive, was not the same thing as a fundamental transformation of sexual relations and attitudes. As a rule, Lenin distrusted any kind of sexual liberty or experimentation, seeing it as an impermissible distraction from revolutionary activity. In 1920 Clara Zetkin, a founding member of the German Communist Party and a friend and supporter of Kollontai, discussed with him the Soviet state's policies on sex and marriage, specifically what was widely regarded as the excessive sexual license it provided to the young to engage in pre-marital sex and to explore different varieties of sexual experience. "I was told that questions of sex and marriage are the main subjects dealt with in the reading and discussion evenings of women comrades", Lenin admonished Zetkin. "What a waste!"

Dismissing Freudian theory as "the modern fashion", Lenin said that "these flourishing sexual theories which are mainly hypothetical, and often quite arbitrary, arise from the personal need to justify personal abnormality or hypertrophy in sexual life before bourgeois morality, and to entreat its patience". He considered this "a hobby of the intellectuals" and that "There is no place for it in the Party, in the class conscious, fighting proletariat".[21] This kind of attitude became more prevalent after 1921 and Kollontai's political eclipse. It was led by the puritanical theoreticians of the Young Communist journal *Komsomol*, most especially the Marxist psychologist Aron Zalkind, founder of the Marxist Society of Psychoneurologists. He decried any hint of "free love" as bourgeois and reactionary and insisted that dedicated communists should sublimate their sexual energies in work for the revolution.

Zalkind led a sexual counter-revolution. He savaged Kollontai for even discussing issues of sex and love. "The collective, the purely revolutionary, is obscured when 'love' is too much in the ascendant", he wrote. His philosophy of "revolutionary sublimation" was expressed in "Zalkind's Twelve Commandments". Amongst other sublimations he recommended no sexual experience before marriage at age 20 or 25, and no sex outside marriage at all. He explained that "purely physical sexual desire is impermissible from the revolutionary-proletarian viewpoint". "Even in marriage", he admonished, "the sex act should not be enjoyed too frequently and never with perversions". For women the natural state was monogamy—anything else was clearly nymphomania.

Although Kollontai was condemned for bringing decadent bourgeois notions into the revolution, it was Lenin who demonstrated the controlling, repressive tendency of orthodox psychoanalysis. In analysing and describing, without moral judgment, the role of repressed sexual impulses in personal neuroses, Freud had instigated one of the major intellectual revolutions of Western history. Yet he had also channeled his discoveries into systems of categorisation and control. Freud's prescription that the sex drive, though it should be sympathetically understood in order that the individual may better function in society, must in many vital respects be sublimated if civilisation was to thrive, fitted neatly the preference of Marxists like Lenin and Zalkind. Freud's view in *The Future of an Illusion* that because "the masses are lazy and unintelligent" it was therefore "as impossible to do without control of the mass by a minority as it is to dispense with coercion in the work of civilization" was in complete accord with Lenin's post-October programme laid out in the "Immediate Tasks".

Zalkind was one side of a coin. The other was epitomised in the work of Freud's idiosyncratic disciple Wilhelm Reich. After the First World War Freud became more pessimistic about humanity. He suggested mankind had a "Death Instinct", Thanatos, that was in constant battle with the sex and life instinct, Eros. In *Civilisation and Its Discontents* (1929) he argued that humanity not only did but *must* repress its unconscious urges, must choose the "Reality Principle" over the "Pleasure Principle". Reich considered this a backward step and a fundamental departure from early Freudianism. He did not believe that the Death Instinct was innate in human beings but rather a symptom of a dysfunctional society.

Reich's experience of working in the Free Psychoanalytic Clinic of Vienna in the 1920s brought him into contact with traumatised Viennese workers. As a result, he saw how social factors such as poverty, poor housing, education, etc. reinforced sexual neuroses. Reich stayed true to Freud's core concept of the libido and of repressed sexuality as the cause of neuroses, but he considered that repression centred specifically on the sexual act and the orgasm. In *The Function of the Orgasm* (1926) he hypothesised that the orgasm was "biological energy" that, if not properly released and experienced, produced harmful psychological effects.

In his greatest work, *The Mass Psychology of Fascism* (1934), Reich produced a psychoanalytical theory of fascism which identified sexual repression as one of the drivers of political authoritarianism. He did not overlook the social causes of fascism. "That a fascist movement exists at all", he wrote, "is undoubtedly the social expression of nationalistic imperialism. However, that this fascist movement could become a mass movement, indeed could seize power [...] is to be ascribed to the full backing it received from the middle-class".[22] For Reich the mass appeal of fascism drew on deep impulses of sexual repression and power worship inculcated by the patriarchal family and other forms of authority. "Sexual repression aids political reaction", Reich explained, "not only through a process which makes the mass individual passive and unpolitical, but also by creating in his structure an interest in actively supporting the authoritarian order".[23]

Of the lower-middle-class fascist and his upper-middle-class leader plagued by emotional and social insecurities, Reich found, "In one case it is compensated by the brutalisation of sexuality, in the other by rigid character traits. The compulsion to control one's sexuality, to maintain sexual repression, leads to the development of pathologic, emotionally tinged notions of honour and duty, bravery and self-control".[24] For orthodox communists, this raised uncomfortable parallels. By 1934 sexual sublimation and the "leader principle" characterised the Soviet Union as much as Nazi Germany.

From 1927 Reich spent ten years trying to reconcile Marxist and psychoanalytical theory. In 1929 he founded the Socialist Society for Sexual Advice and Sexual Research. After an unsatisfying trip to the Soviet Union he moved to Berlin where, he felt, he would have more freedom to develop his own ideas. In the five years in which he was an active member of the German Communist Party (KPD) – 1929 to 1934 – he produced some of his most radical and provocative work. In 1930 he formed the German Association for Proletarian Sexual Politics and opened a number of sex clinics in Berlin with the aim of helping German workers deal with sexual repression and neuroses. This work, which was carried out under the auspices of the KPD, became known as the Sex-Political or "Sex-Pol" programme.

Reich conceded that while psychoanalysis could not replace a sociological analysis of capitalism it could be of use as an "auxiliary" of sociology. By this route he identified, in similar fashion to Antonio Gramsci, the means by which capitalist values became "anchored in the psychical structures" of the working class. "The fact, however, that large strata of the oppressed class accept or even support exploitation in one form or another", he wrote, "must be interpreted directly in terms of psychology and only indirectly in terms of sociology".[25]

This was deeply original thinking (Gramsci's concept of capitalist cultural "hegemony", although written in the 1930s, was mostly unknown until the publication of his *Prison Notebooks* in the 1960s). In "What is Class Consciousness?",

Reich said plainly what German Marxists could not bear to hear — that the Nazis were better at appealing to emotional instincts than the communists, that they has mastered the art of "politics as fetish", that their reactionary policy for German women was in tune with the patriarchal attitudes of many German men. The only way to combat this was to create a "joining of the consciousness of the revolutionary avant-garde with the consciousness of the average citizen". And one of the most effective ways to achieve this was to address their most personal and intimate concerns. In his most controversial essay, "Politicising the Sexual Problem of Youth", which KPD functionaries tried to prevent being published, he discussed issues of sexual ignorance, sexually transmitted diseases, "perversions", sexual technique and contraception in a fresh and non-judgmental manner.

Reich described plainly what Kollontai, as a woman in a culturally conservative country, was obliged to paint as "winged eros". He actively encouraged the free expression of sexuality and celebration of the orgasm. He concluded:

> In capitalist society today there can be no sexual liberation of youth, no healthy, satisfying sex life; if you want to be rid of your sexual troubles, fight for socialism. Only through socialism can you achieve sexual *joie de vivre*. Pay no attention to the opinions of people who don't know anything about sex. Socialism will put an end to the power of people who gaze up towards heaven as they speak of love while they crush and destroy the sexuality of youth.[26]

Although popular with KPD youth, the essay went too

far. In February 1933 Reich was expelled from the KPD (incredibly, this took place between Hitler's appointment as Chancellor in January and the Nazi crushing of the left in March, when one might have thought KPD leaders had better things to do). A year later, with fitting symmetry, he was also expelled from the International Psychoanalytical Association. His subsequent career in America was a tragic waste.

Reich's expulsion epitomised the sexual counter-revolution. In March 1934 the Soviet Union re-criminalised homosexuality. In June 1935 an editorial in *Pravda* informed its readers that "only a good family man can be a good Soviet citizen". In 1936 abortion was once more made illegal. Stalin himself wrote in the Soviet trade union journal *Trud* (Labour),

> abortion, which destroys life, is inadmissible in any country. Soviet woman has the same rights as Soviet man, but that does not absolve her from the great and honourable duty imposed on her by nature: she is to be a mother. She is to bear life.[27]

It would be unfair to ascribe this reactionary sexual legislation to Lenin, who died in 1924, but it flowed easily enough from his criticisms of Kollontai's positions on love, sex and marriage, which were tolerated by the Bolsheviks for only a few years before the state's need for traditional family and gender discipline reasserted itself. Stalin took Bolshevik scepticism about her work to its logical conclusion, by reversing it.

CHAPTER FOURTEEN
Proletkult

In the two decades before the outbreak of war in 1914, Imperial
Russia experienced an explosion of artistic modernism
entirely at odds with its conservative social structure. That this
was confined mostly to the intellectual class of St Petersburg
and Moscow does not diminish its significance any more
than that of the revolution in French art and poetry of the
late 19th century that emerged mainly from the Montmartre
and Pigalle areas of Paris. In similar fashion, Russian art broke
free from the constraints of bourgeois culture to experiment
with representation, form and language. No sooner was the
latest work of the French Post-Impressionists and Fauvists
displayed in St Petersburg and Moscow art galleries than the
"World of Art" movement which championed them was
superseded by the more radical experiments of Symbolism
and Futurism. Like early Renaissance thinkers trapped inside
Catholic Europe, the Symbolists, Cubists and Futurists of
Nicholas II's Russia were seeds of modernity germinating
inside an archaic monolith about to collapse. Not surprisingly
they yearned for an end to the autocracy and had great

emotional sympathy for the political left.

Major figures in Russian and European culture emerged in the years before the war: Blok, Gumielov and Mandelstam in poetry; Bely and Andreyev in the novel; Kandinsky, Larionov, Malevich and Tatlin in art. The entire school of 20th-century abstract art had its genesis in the early works of Vasilly Kandinsky such as *Light Picture* and *Black Lines* (both 1913). His written exegesis *Concerning the Spiritual in Art* (1910), along with Bely's essays on Symbolism published the same year, eloquently summarised the goals of abstract art and symbolist prose. Larionov developed the Fauvist style into a new Russian primitivism whilst Malevich and Tatlin, the premier Russian artists of the first two decades of the 20th century, fused Abstract Expressionism with Futurism to create "Suprematism", the precursor of schematic modern art.

Malevich came from working-class stock in Kiev. He arrived in Moscow in 1905 where he distributed revolutionary literature during the December uprising. After its suppression he returned to art, moving rapidly from the simplistic Cezanne-like tableau of *Peasants in Church* (1910) to his Cubo-Futurist masterwork *The Knife-Grinder* (1912). During the war he produced several challenging new masterpieces, including *Suprematist Composition* (1916), *Dynamic Suprematism* (1916) and *Sensation of a Mystical Wave Coming from the Earth* (1917), which utilised geometric forms and quasi-architectural diagrams to imprint order on the whiteness of the canvas, much as the Provisional Government and Sovnarcom would attempt to bring order out of the breakdown of the Tsarist Empire.

The new wave of Russian writers, poets and artists rejected

the elitism of the World of Art. Kustnesov's *The Blue Fountain* (1905), with its impressionistic use of blue, grey and white, set a benchmark for a separate Russian school, the Blue Rose Group, that rivaled French art in vibrant brushwork and yet retained a semi-mystical occultism all its own. By contrast Russian Futurism drew from the Italian artist Marinetti, who visited Moscow in 1909 and whose "Manifesto of Futurism" was translated into Russian that same year. The Futurist Manifesto was a landmark in Western art but its politics were the wet dreams of fascism. "We intend to glorify aggressive action, a restive wakefulness, life at the double, the slap and the punching fist", declaimed Marinetti:

> We wish to glorify war – the sole cleanser of the world – militarism, patriotism, the destructive act of the libertarian, beautiful ideas worth dying for, and scorn for women. We wish to destroy museums, libraries, academies of any sort, and fight against moralism, feminism, and every kind of materialistic, self-serving cowardice.[1]

In Camilla Gray's opinion, "as with Impressionism and Cubism, the interpretation of Futurism in Russia owes little more than a superficial calligraphy to the Western counterpart",[2] and Russian Futurism preferred socialism to fascism. For Trotsky it was "the revolt of Bohemia [...] the semi-pauparised left-wing of the intelligentsia against the closed and caste-like aesthetics of the bourgeois intelligentsia".[3]

In the chaos of war and revolution, traditional divisions between artists and writers began to melt away. Many Russian

Futurist writers and poets took their cues from or started their careers in arts and design, which led to experiments in prose and verse. In turn, some of the Futurist poets, most notably Mayakovsky, took their cultural dissidence into politics and became fervent supporters of the Bolsheviks. Even non-socialist writers gravitated to the revolution. The great symbolist Andrei Bely supported the February and October revolutions. In 1918 he wrote *Christ Is Risen*, a novel in verse that celebrated the revolution as a great upsurge of primal energy. In the 1920s he worked willingly for Soviet cultural organisations whilst trying to retain some space for his experiments in form and style. Others, like the future winner of the Noble Prize for Literature Ivan Bunin, disliked socially committed literature and emigrated from Soviet Russia in 1920.

Futurist poets like Mayakovsky responded not just to the revolution's rejection of bourgeois culture, but to the idealism and utopianism inherent in Bolshevik ideology. The Russian revolutionary tradition had always had a strong utopian strain. "Land and Freedom" was never just a policy for agriculture. It meant exactly what it said. The SRs were the original inheritors of this desire. Their troubled involvement with the Provisional Government was a testament to how difficult it was to reconcile the organisation of a socialist society with the peasant wish to be left alone to till the soil in complete freedom. Even Lenin, in *The State and Revolution*, indulged himself in utopian dreams of communal living, free labour and the death of the state. After achieving power his dreams instantly mutated into a dark negative of *The State and Revolution* – centralised state capitalism, mass electrification and Taylorism in industrial production.

In the pre-war years his political enemy Alexander Bogdanov had taken Bolshevik dreaming about the post-revolutionary society to its logical extreme in two SF novels about a future communist utopia on Mars, *Red Star* (1908) and *Engineer Menni* (1913). In Bogdanov's utopia there was no state coercion, all class division and exploitation was abolished, and there was total equality of the sexes. The novels were not without complexity, as Bogdanov's hero, a socialist who travels to Mars for a better life, discovers that the communist society is facing problems of overpopulation and environmental decay, and longer life has led to the creation of "Suicide Clinics". The novels were reprinted in Russia after 1917 and were hugely popular with literate working-class militants looking for a concrete vision of the future. Yet as Richard Stites's provocative work on cultural experimentation during the Russian Revolution makes clear, "When such a counter-culture did appear in the form of workers' control, anarchism, syndicalism, and various intra-party oppositionists, it was repudiated by the Bolshevik leadership".[4]

The Bolsheviks, in their view, *had* created state organs that allowed the working class to participate in direct economic and social reconstruction. The most genuinely libertarian and experimental of those organs was Lunacharsky's Nakompros. Before the war, Lunacharsky had headed a school for RSDLP workers on Capri with Bogdanov and Gorky. The kind of education offered by these independent-minded Marxists was not dissimilar to that of the Mensheviks, in that it was designed to produce working-class leaders who could think for themselves rather than parrot the orders of a Central Committee. The Marxism of this dissident fringe of the Bolshevik Party presaged by a hundred years the "autonomism" of Hardt and Negri, the "Marx and Engels of the Internet Age".[5]

Autonomism arose from the Italian radical left of the 1960s. It rejected Leninism, political parties and trade unions for a belief that the "autonomous" working class could affect political change without the hierarchical structures of the unions and the Italian Communist Party. At the core of autonomist philosophy is a broader conception of the working class than that of the traditional industrial proletariat. The Marxist economist Harry Cleaver summarised this new working class as

> a loose tribe of highly mobile drop-outs, part-time workers, part-time students, participants in the underground economy, creators of temporary and ever-changing autonomous zones of social life that force a fragmentation of and crisis in the mass worker organisations of the social factory.[6]

Although its analysis of capitalism as an exploitative system is not markedly different from Marx's, autonomism is, in the words of Derek Wall, "a form of 'subjective' rather than 'objective' Marxism".[7]

Subjective Marxism calls attention to the creation of a global economy based on highly sophisticated communications technology, and the labour on which this economy intimately relies. This Hardt and Negri call "affected labour", i.e. labour based on knowledge, networks, sharing and "the creation of social life itself, in which the political, the economic and the cultural increasingly overlap and invest in one another".[8] The priority for socialists, therefore, is to create from this affected labour a self-conscious Multitude that fights capitalist hegemony on numerous fronts, through the creation of a variety of living alternatives such as squatting, protest camps, workers' cooperatives, flashmobs, wildcat strikes, etc. Hardt and Negri's belief that "in the passage to the informational economy, the assembly line has been replaced by the network as the organisational model of production"[9] reflects the rise of the "networked individual" as a more connected and effective anti-capitalist protestor than the rule-bound trade unionist.

The autonomist project to forge an effective anti-capitalist counter-culture is not dissimilar from the desire of dissident Bolsheviks like Bogdanov to create the conditions in which a re-educated, liberated working class is able to identify its own interests. That desire found expression in the Proletarian Cultural and Educational Organisations, or Proletkult. Proletkult was part of the Left Communist trend within the party. After October it took on organisational form as a loose federation of bodies sponsored by Nakompros. Lunacharsky himself had thrown open the gates to the cultural iconoclasm practiced by Proletkult. His first declaration as People's Commissar for Enlightenment proclaimed:

The people themselves, consciously or unconsciously, must evolve their own culture [...] The independent action of workers', soldiers' and peasants' cultural-educational organizations must achieve full autonomy, both in relation to the central government and the municipal centres.

When he said this he had been People's Commissar for only three days. By April 1918 he was expressing "doubt that Proletkult is a real manifestation of spontaneous proletarian activity".[10]

Proletkult was in basic conflict with Lunacharsky's vision of a pluralistic, progressive socialism. In 1917 it had emerged as an organised grouping that advocated a cultural version of Lenin's *The State and Revolution*. Its core belief was that the "real", class-conscious working class, concentrated in capitalism's factory complexes, alone possessed and demonstrated the collective culture of the future. It may not have yet expressed that culture in the traditional manner—novels, poetry, plays, symphonies, etc.—but that was because capitalism's social structure had denied it the chance to do so. Now that the bourgeoisie had been driven from power a genuine Proletarian Culture would emerge like a phoenix from the ashes. The precondition for this was the immediate expunging of the old culture.

In the first half of 1918 Proletkult received a budget of 9.2 million rubles, about a third of the total Nakompros budget for Adult Education. As the social historian Lynn Mally observed, "Although the Proletkult was autonomous it still expected Nakompros to foot the bills".[11] Nakompros provided Proletkult with a large building on Nevsky Prospect as an HQ and the Prospect itself was renamed Proletkult St. By 1920 Proletkult had nearly 85,000 members running a network of 300 multi-media "studios". These studios scorned bourgeois cultural categories (and bourgeois art in general) and aimed to produce experimental Proletarian Art across a range of visual, literary and dramatic fields. Mayakovsky, a fervent supporter of Proletkult, believed that art should be displayed "not in dead museum-temples, but everywhere – on the streets, in trams, in factories, in workshops, and in workers' apartments".[12]

In some towns over-enthusiastic Proletkultists wanted to burn all the books in the libraries, confident that they would soon be replaced by those of proletarian writers. Proletkult, as a body, was difficult to fit into the structure of the Soviet state, and in many respects it did not want to fit. It attracted many of the dissident and unmalleable elements of the revolutionary left and offered them a semi-official organisation to work within. Inside Nakompros, one of Lunacharsky's senior advisors, Lenin's wife Krupskaya, constantly pressed her boss to bring Proletkult to heel.

Lunacharsky walked a tight-rope between conflicting tendencies within Bolshevism – that of Lenin and the "political" revolutionaries who saw the new Soviet state as defined by its economic and political system; and that of Left Communists who wished to advance the revolution into all spheres of social life. Lunacharsky took fire from both sides – from Lenin, who thought Nakompros too tolerant of experiments in Futurist poetry and design, and spending money on projects of no interest to workers and peasants; and from adherents of Proletkult who wanted a "cultural October", for continuing to value and protect the legacy of pre-October art and culture. Because he went to some effort to protect the monuments, art and, to a certain extent, the artists and writers of "bourgeois culture", Lunacharsky was attacked by Proletkult as a closet reactionary. In view of the fact that Nakompros generously funded and protected Proletkult and its studios Marcel Liebman is, again, entirely justified in finding that "the avant-gardist zeal of many of these artists was equaled only by their ingratitude".[13]

Partly as a result of this attitude, Proletkult's modern reputation is a byword for cultural vandalism by the ignorant and talentless. Yet Richard Stites's groundbreaking and sympathetic work on utopian sub-cultures and experimental lifestyles in the revolutionary era uncovered "a genuinely novel experiment designed to arm and teach an entire class in quick time to construct wholly new culture in a still very much illiterate society, and to do so with minimum guidance from the past".[14] Just as Lenin had advocated smashing the old state machine and building a new one from the ground up, Proletkult sought to uncover and nurture an entirely new working-class aesthetic. Despite its limitations, it achieved some remarkable innovations in style and form which still influence popular art and marketing today. Its weakness was not that it focused on the emblems of industrial modernity—the city, the machine, the teletype, the car and the factory—but that it disallowed virtually anything else.

What was intended as a positive programme to provide working-class men and women with opportunity to express themselves authentically in art and culture could slide into an anti-intellectual nihilism. At the first Proletkult conference, just before October 1917, a passionate advocate declared there was nothing worthy of retention in the old bourgeois culture "except for natural science and technical skills". Many Proletkultists consciously rejected the "greats" of

Russian literature such as Pushkin, whom Lenin revered. When Nakompros instigated a prize for "Best Proletarian Poet" an angry Proletkult worker wrote, "We who were born in the thunder of plants and factories, in the mines and pits and behind the plow, we do not recognise 'Kings' or 'Best Poets'". [15]

In *Literature and Revolution* (1923), Trotsky offered lucid comment on the revolutionary art that had emerged from October. "The call of the Futurists to break with the past", he wrote, "to do away with Pushkin, to liquidate tradition, etc., has a meaning as far as it is addressed to the old literary caste". But the call was meaningless once addressed to the relatively uneducated working class. "The working class does not have to, and cannot, break with literary tradition, because it is not in the grip of such a tradition. The working class does not know the old literature, it still has to master Pushkin, to absorb him, and so overcome him". [16] Lunacharsky agreed. Nakompros subsidised Proletkult, but it also protected the museums and libraries of the old world. It helped the Marxist theatre producer Meyerhold stage his innovative productions but it also allowed and valued Chekhov and Shakespeare, who were far more popular amongst the "advanced" workers.

With the exception of family and sexual policy, there was no field that unsettled the Bolshevik Revolution more than art and culture. Lunacharsky instituted a remarkably liberal regime. Whilst he gave Proletkult enough space to experiment he also channeled resources to the Futurist and Suprematist schools of art around Tatlin and Malevich. These were not allies of Proletkult, often competing for the same audience. Although Mayakovsky had been one of the most eminent pre-war Futurist poets, after October he immersed himself in Proletkult and the "Rosta Windows" (from Russian Telegraph Agency – Rosta) school of propaganda art. These were large stenciled sheets that told multi-frame sequential stories of the Civil War and revolution, a politicised version of the American tabloids' "Funny Pages", themselves the precursor of the comic and the graphic novel.

Sheila Fitzpatrick observed that the Bolsheviks shared with the liberal intelligentsia an instinctive dismissal of working-class popular culture, frequently condemned as "vulgar" or "backward" or, worst of all, "petty bourgeois". The last epitaph was "equally derogatory whether it came from the lips of a well-born liberal intellectual or those a militant proletarian Bolshevik".[17] Trotsky, in a series of essays collected together as *Problems of Everyday Life* (1924), offered advice to those attempting to guide the working class towards a higher, more cultivated existence, including the desirability of better personal hygiene, stopping smoking and not swearing. "The Russian worker, except the very top of the class", he opined, "usually lacks the most elementary habits and notions of culture (in regard to tidiness, instruction, punctuality, etc.)". The Russian masses were told some harsh truths:

> We are poor. We are wasteful. We are careless. We are sloppy. We are slovenly. These vices have deep roots in our slavish past and can be eradicated only gradually by persistent propaganda by deed, by example, and by illustration – and by means of careful control, vigilance and persistent exactitude.[18]

Some workers were attracted by this vision. Most were not.

How to appeal to a mass working-class audience has always been a central problem—perhaps *the* central problem—for the left. Even in the late 19th century, in the early days of the organised labour and socialist movement, the attraction and distraction of "bread and circuses"—the pub, the music hall, etc.—to under-educated masses was socialism's greatest obstacle. Technological development simply made it more so. By the middle of the 20th century, the intellectual left was paralysed by the seeming omnipotence of what Theodor Adorno and Max Horkhiemer, in *The Dialectic of Enlightenment* (1947), called the "culture industry".

Adorno and Horkhiemer were intimidated and mesmerised by the radio and the cinema, which they saw as all-powerful transmitters of mindless mass culture to a depoliticised working class. In their pessimism they did not notice or foresee that alternative messages and values still seeped through that culture. Indeed, they were often transmitted directly by it, such as the radical documentaries of the *Mass Observation* project in the 1930s, the socialist values of the *Daily Mirror* in the 1940s, or the self-education offered on late-night TV by the Open University in the 1960s and 1970s.

In the second decade of the 21st century the culture industry is, from one perspective, a grotesque and extreme version of that described by Adorno and Horkhiemer, a commercial machine in which amoral corporations produce slick soft-porn videos of Britney Spears telling young women that if they desire material riches—"You wanna a Bugatti? You wanna a Maserati?"—then "You better work,

Bitch", or businessmen like Simon Cowell pretend to be celebrities in order to exploit untutored musical talent under the cover of TV entertainment. But their control is slipping. Social media, portable IT and public funding have revolutionised both the product and the means of accessing it. To cite just three well-known examples, films like *Pride*, TV series like *The Wire*, and Russell Brand's *The Trews* on YouTube offer a very different world view to that of the conventional culture industry.

Great works of radical art are essential, but they achieve little in isolation. Shelley's *Masque of Anarchy*, Morris's *News from Nowhere*, Steinbeck's *The Grapes of Wrath*, Ken Loach's *Land and Freedom* and many others provide inspiration and solace, but capitalism takes the hit and moves on. The challenge is how to shape and transmit a radical and questioning culture to a mass audience and to make that a constant in their lives. The potential is there. Digital social media in all forms and on all platforms allows a continuous level of social collaboration and innovation that is inherently subversive of neoliberalism's individualist ethic. It has created vibrant mass anti-corporate/direct-action campaigns and sites of information such as Adbusters, Corporate Watch, WikiLeaks, the Global Justice Movement, Food Not Bombs and the Hunt Saboteurs Association.

These specific campaigns and networks may be new, but the general idea is not. The Left Book Club of the 1930s was a political-cultural network to exchange information and build mutual support for anti-capitalist activity, although by its nature it was confined to a literate minority. Since the 1960s anti-capitalists have been using and exploiting the PR and advertising techniques of commodified capitalism to undermine the system that produced them. The ultimate aim of "culture jamming", in all its forms, is to subvert the hold of the consumerist mindset on those who uncritically absorb it.

The idea derives from the Situationist International led by Guy Debord, who saw consumer capitalism as "the society of the spectacle", eternally geared to mindless buying and selling, which urgently needed a series of specially constructed "situations" to wake itself up. One way of doing that was to appropriate an existing media artifact, such as an iconic advert, and alter it to give it a subversive meaning. In the 1960s, Situationism was linked to the great upheavals of 1968 and so had inevitable political overtones. Today it achieves the same ends through more indirect campaigns and alternative lifestyle choices like Buy Nothing Day, Ethical Consumerism, Microgeneration, Autonomous Building and Anti-Oppressive Education initiatives.

These movements, laudable though they are, will have limited impact if they stay confined to bourgeois sub-cultures. They must replace, day in and day out, the news, the soap opera, the water-cooler TV drama, the communal multi-media event. They will not become a genuine threat to neoliberal cultural hegemony until they are what people read, enjoy, discuss and anticipate in their downtime, weekends and holidays. The leaders of the new Spanish anti-austerity party Podemos, who come from a generation radicalised by Hardt-Negri and autonomism, have realised this. As Podemos's general secretary Pablo Iglesias wrote, it is necessary to "generate discursively a popular identity that can be politicised along electoral lines".[19]

Flowing from the "Latin-americanisation" of Southern Europe after 2008, Iglesias and his collegues turned their popular television programmes *La Tuerka* (*The Screw*) and *Fort Apache* into lively message boards for anti-austerity. For them, the TV programmes "were the "parties" through which we would wage our political struggle on the most fundamental terrain of ideological production: television".[20] One terrain leads to another. To free workers, at all levels, from the culture industry's grip on what Reich called their "psychical structures", the left should broaden its communications strategies, funding and promoting a massive increase in open-source software, peer-to-peer production, multi-platform media co-operatives and the liberatory use of technology—not as one policy, but as the conduit for *all* its policies. Similarly, the ultimate goal of Proletkult—the creation of a new collective culture outside and beyond what had existed before—may have been crudely expressed and unaware of how much had been achieved by the culture it wished to replace, but it's impulse was sound. It defied the elitist intellectuals of academy and Vanguard Party and sought to give voice to the voiceless.

In 1920, as the Civil War drew to a close, Lenin turned his attention to Proletkult and did not like what he saw. At a time of mass working-class discontent with the regime, he was concerned that a significant part of the new state had a semi-autonomous status *and* claimed to speak for the proletariat. The political climate of the time, in which Left Communists and the Workers' Opposition were making criticisms of the state bureaucracy and the degeneration of the revolution, was not conducive to experiments in proletarian authenticity. In December 1920 *Pravda* published a letter, "On the Proletkults", ostensibly from the RCP Central Committee but written by Lenin. The letter condemned Proletkult as dominated by petty-bourgeois intellectuals who were foisting decadent and reactionary artistic schemes on the working class. It announced that Proletkult as an independent body was hereby abolished and its functions placed under Nakompros.

Most of Proletkult's experiments in painting, sculpture, theatre, verse and song had never impressed the actual proletariat. The great exception was the vast array of posters and slogans that emerged from the AgitProp department. These had real impact, perhaps because they utilised the tradition of Russian Orthodox religious art with which workers and peasants were familiar. AgitProp created what Victoria E. Bonnell called "a set of standardised images" based on clearly identifiable heroes (workers and peasants) and villains (speculators, aristocrats, etc.) laid out in simplistic tableau or sequential panels. These were held together by "an iconography with its own distinctive lexicon and syntax".[21] The use of traditional mythology to express revolutionary sentiments was best caught in Boris Zvorykin's *The Struggle of the Red Knight with the Dark Force* (1919), in which the "Red Knight", though astride a horse, fought with a hammer rather than a sword.

Given the high rate of illiteracy or semi-literacy and the lack of paper to print newspapers and books, the most effective way to communicate political messages was the propaganda poster. The power and range of Bolshevik posts was exemplified in the work of Alexander Apsit. His coloured lithograph *Year of the Proletarian Dictatorship October 1917-October 1918* captured the fusion of religious and socialist imagery characteristic of the early Bolshevik poster. The central image was framed by stern, noble workers standing either side of a large window. This opened on to a procession of people carrying red flags across a green field to a large factory feeding plumes of smoke into a sunny sky. Strewn at the workers' feet were emblems of imperial glory.

Apsit eschewed the more politicised AgitProp of the 1920s for simple historical and allegorical statements, an approach that eventually fell out of favour with Proletkult. His large, detailed lithograph *The Popular Movement in the Time of Troubles* (1918) vividly recreated an episode from a popular peasant rebellion of the 17th century and was highly influential in the Soviet school of historical-revolutionary art. His civil war propaganda posters *Day of the Wounded Red Army Man* (1919) and *To Horse, Proletarian!* (1920) illustrate how he used symbolism and allegory to stir emotions and drive home a political message. Although other, more ideological Proletkult poster artists such as Dmitri Moor regarded Apsit's work as "a conglomerate of cinema poster pseudo-dramatics, vulgar symbolism and the external elements of old-fashioned romanticism", they missed the point that this was precisely what made them so popular. Stephen White's outstanding study of the golden age of the Bolshevik poster considered Apsit's work "among the more notable achievements of poster art of any period".[22]

Apsit's work set the template for the worker-hero-blacksmith of numerous other Soviet posters (about 4,000, reproduced in their millions), usually dressed in a leather apron and wielding a hammer. This imagery carried through to the flags and banners used in mass processions and festivals, particularly those that marked the anniversary of October or other public holidays. After 1920, when artists such as Moor and Deny began to eclipse Apsit, the approach to Soviet posters would focus more on clear political messages tailored to specific crisis points and military campaigns, such as Moor's *Be the Guard* and the iconic *Have You Volunteered?*, the Soviet state's equivalent of Lord Kitchener and "Your Country Needs YOU".

It was vital that Bolshevik propaganda reach all areas controlled by Sovnarcom. To this end the government used "Agit-Trains", also known as "mobile posters" because the sides of the carriages were decorated with agitational pictures and slogans, to distribute not just posters but films and political literature. In August 1918 the first Agit-Train, called "The Mobile Military Front-Line Literary Train Named after V.I. Lenin", left Moscow to travel to Kazan and through the Volga regions then held by the Czech Legion. Other trains followed, equipped with their own library, printing presses, and small cinemas.

The trains were a success and they were added to by the *Red Star* agitational ship which plied the Volga and Kama rivers during 1919 (how it came by its name is not recorded, but is it fanciful to imagine it was after Bogdanov's utopian SF novel?). On one of its trips in summer 1919 it was accompanied by Krupskaya and Molotov. During the civil war the Bolsheviks' agitational trains and ships visited all the regions of Soviet Russia, spent 659 days in the field and made contact with 2.8 million citizens at 775 different locations.[23]

The only medium that outstripped the poster as a vivid and immediate means of conveying Bolshevik propaganda was film, most especially the bold cinematic experiments of Sergei Eisenstein, a pioneer of modernist film technique whose *Battleship Potemkin* (1925) and *October 1917* (1927) were a major influence on German Expressionist film and *Citizen Kane*. Trotsky early grasped the importance of cinema to the creation of a revolutionary culture. "The cinema is a great competitor not only of the tavern but also of the church", he wrote in his essay "Vodka, the Church and the Cinema" in 1923. "Here is an instrument which we must secure at all costs!"[24] The art of the revolutionary poster, the Rosta Windows, the agitational flyer and the political film thrived between 1917 and 1930. Artists like Apsit, Mayakovsky and Eisenstein did not need to be dragooned into producing propaganda because they believed in the dream and vision of the Soviet state. Their propaganda was art. But what of those artists who thought and felt differently?

In "Party Organisation and Party Literature" (1905) Lenin had foretold their fate. In this neglected essay, the germ of authoritarian control of culture is already present. Lenin considered that "All Social-Democratic literature must become Party literature. Every newspaper, journal, publishing house, etc., must immediately set about reorganising its work, leading up to a situation in which it will, in one form or another, be integrated into one party organisation or another". After asking "What is the principle of party literature?", he answered:

> It is not simply that, for the socialist proletariat, literature cannot be a means of enriching individuals or groups: it cannot, in fact, be an individual undertaking, independent of the common cause of the proletariat. Down with non-partisan writers! Down with literary supermen! Literature must become part of the common cause of the proletariat, a cog and a screw of one single great Social-Democratic mechanism set in motion by the politically conscious vanguard of the entire working class.[25]

This was intended only for party literature. But what if, after the revolution, a one-party system was established in which the party was inextricable from the state? It was a small step from Lenin's strictures on party literature to Sovnarcom's Commission for Newspaper Supervision, set up in 1922 to implement guidelines on what newspapers could and could not publish. At the same time, in the spirit of Lenin's condemnation of non-partisan writers and literary supermen, the Commission to Monitor the Private Book Market, chaired by the head of AgitProp A.S. Bubnov, established a system in which every article in every book published by non-party publishers was scrutinised and categorised to ensure it was not "subversive" or "counter-revolutionary". Many publishers were then rated as "Menshevik" or "Kadet". After that, their days were numbered.

Trotsky, although far more sensitive to modern art and literature than Lenin, still believed that the ultimate arbiter in cultural matters had to be the party. He allowed some latitude. "The methods of Marxism are not those of art", he explained in *Literature and Revolution*:

> The party leads the proletariat but not the processes of history. There are domains in which the party leads, directly and commandingly. There are domains in which it only cooperates. There are domains, finally, in which it only orientates itself. The domain of art is not one in which the party is called on to command.

Yet he asserted that only art the party considered supportive of the revolution could be tolerated. "Our policy in art, during a transitional period", he wrote,

> can and must be to assist the various groups or schools of art which have come over to the revolution to grasp correctly its historical meaning and to allow them complete freedom of self-determination in the field of art, once the categorical standard of being for or against the revolution has been placed before them.[26]

The experience of artists and intellectuals who never met the standard, or were judged insufficiently zealous in abiding by it, was very different from those that did. Especially vulnerable were those members of the Russian intelligentsia who rejected materialism, positivism and atheism, most prominently the idealist philosophers Nikolai Berdyaev and Semyon Frank, the theologian Sergei Bulgakov, and liberals such as Peter Struve. From 1905 Berdyaev had built an international reputation by fusing an idiosyncratic Christian socialism with philosophical idealism and a strong personal spirituality. After October 1917 Berdyaev, Frank, Struve and others formed the League of Russian Culture, a group of moderate liberals and conservatives who opposed the entire project of the Bolshevik Revolution.

After October Struve went into illegal opposition and then exile. Berdyaev returned to purely academic work. In 1918 he produced *The Philosophy of Inequality*, which discarded any vestige of ethical socialism for a pessimistic attack on all materialist and rationalist thought. He labeled the revolution a "great experiment" which "intensifies all the basic problems of social philosophy".[27] He wished to rejuvenate elitist individualism based on a Nietzschean "aristocracy of the spirit" and a rejection of mass culture. He claimed his philosophy was based on personal freedom, but it appeared to value the freedom of the exceptional individual more than that of ordinary people. Berdyaev could not publish his work in Soviet Russia, although he continued to hold his position at Moscow University until he was expelled from the country in 1922.

Lunacharsky maintained a relatively tolerant attitude towards the universities, even though many academics were either members of the Kadet Party or sympathetic to them. After October the Academy of Sciences, the Union of Engineers, the Teachers Unions and the Academics Union all passed resolutions condemning the insurrection and calling for a Constituent Assembly. Some faculties in cities near the front line of the Civil War, such as at Kazan and Perm Universities, defected *en masse* to the White forces (the entire faculty of Warsaw University, which had relocated to Rostov-on-Don, retreated with the White Army in 1920 to set itself up in Constantinople). Academics in cities like Petrograd and Moscow did not have these options. Despite the Civil War, non-Bolshevik academics such as the non-aligned Bogdanov, the Mensheviks Sukhanov and Gorev, and the anarchist Grossman-Roschin, were allowed to teach and lecture well into the 1920s.[28]

One reason for this was that Nakompros wanted to provide courses in Marxism to working-class students, and if it excluded liberal or Menshevik academics from doing so there would be hardly anyone left to teach them. During the Civil War, Nakompros tried to reorganise the old history, law and philology schools in to "Social Science Schools", in which academics graduating from a new Communist Academy would apply Marxist methodology to a wide range of social and cultural subjects. It was not until 1921 that Nakompros imposed a University Constitution on higher education, which gave the Commissariat the right to appoint the Rector and governing body. Even then it was selective in how it used its powers. It was well aware that most academics were covertly hostile to it, although there was a definite difference of approach between the arts and the sciences.

Despite the condemnation of the October Insurrection by the Academy of Sciences, most working scientists had stayed on the job. The Bolsheviks, as good materialists, also had a high opinion of the natural sciences. In 1919 when Nakompros proposed to abolish the Academy of Sciences, a plan that generated much anxiety amongst Russian scientists, Lenin called in Lunacharsky and told him "not to break any valuable china". The plan was quickly shelved. Sovnarcom wanted ideological control but it had no wish to alienate or lose "bourgeois specialists" in hard sciences such as biology, chemistry, engineering, maths and physics. The Soviet state granted these strata privileges which it never withdrew.

The arts and humanities were less protected. Alexander Blok, the great Russian symbolist poet of the pre-war years, initially welcomed the Revolution. He represented its elemental grandeur in two massive new poems, *The Twelve* and *The Scythians*. *The Twelve*, which depicted a dozen tired, blasphemous Red Guards marching through a snowstorm in Petrograd, finally encountering the symbolic figure of Jesus Christ, was hailed as a masterpiece by the new government and was widely reprinted. Trotsky, whose view of Blok's pre-war work was that it was "romantic, symbolic, mystical, formless and unreal" and would not outlive its author, considered that in *The Twelve* Blok had come half-way over to the Revolution. He therefore met the "categorical standard".

This meant nothing to Blok himself, who was appalled by the Red Terror and the Bolsheviks' hostility to any kind of philosophical idealism. After 1918 he ceased to write and during the Civil War was briefly arrested on spurious charges of anti-revolutionary activity. Trapped in Petrograd in a freezing flat without food, he developed inflammation of the heart and brain. Gorky's and Lunacharsky's pleas to the Politburo to allow him to go abroad for treatment were declined. He died in August 1921, following which Lunacharsky wrote in anger to the Politburo, "There will be no doubt and no refutation of the fact that we killed Russia's most talented poet".[29]

Trotsky was less concerned. In an appreciation written in 1923, he found that Blok "was not one of ours, though he reached towards us". The reason his creative drive dried up after 1918 was because he could not fully commit to a revolution he did not understand. Trotsky concluded:

> The march of history is not adapted to the psychic needs of a romanticist who is struck by the revolution. And to be able to maintain oneself on the temporary sandbanks, one has to have different training, a different faith in the Revolution, an understanding of its sequential rhythms, and not only an understanding of the chaotic music of its tides.[30]

The chaotic music struck many others, including the "Acemist" poet Nikolay Gumielov, who did not welcome the Revolution in the same way as Blok, Malevich and Tatlin. In 1920, without state approval, he formed the All Russia Union of Writers and openly derided the Bolsheviks and their cultural policies. Two weeks after Blok's death, Gumielov and 60 others were arrested as part of a "monarchist conspiracy" against the government (which in 1992 the Russian government admitted was "completely fabricated"). Gorky rushed to Moscow to see Lenin to secure his release. Although Lenin granted this, by the time Gorky got back to Petrograd the Cheka had taken all 61 defendants in the case, including Gumielov, out to the Kovalevsky Forest and shot them. There was no trial. When told he was too late, Gorky coughed up blood.

Russia's greatest 20th-century poet, Osip Mandelstam, lasted longer, but in the end his fate was crueler. Mandelstam had stayed aloof from politics, content to let the purity of his verse speak for him. His first collection of poems, *Stone*

(1913), had an immediate impact on his contemporaries. It established him as a poetic genius of the first rank who achieved a clarity and emotional precision unequalled in Russian poetry, driven by "a central, controlling simplicity of spirit".[31] Like Gumeilov, he rejected symbolism for verse that was rooted in an imagery of soil and earth and weather. Mandelstam's values were those of a personal, subjective humanism. Despite his lack of interest in Marxism or the Revolution, he managed to publish a further collection, *Tristia*, in 1923, mainly because he was under the informal protection of Bukharin, who greatly esteemed his poetry. In 1928 he published a last collection of poems and essays. After that he was under increasing suspicion from the state.

In 1934 Mandelstam read out one of his new poems (now known as "The Stalin Epigram") to a small gathering he thought he could trust. The poem was a biting view of Stalin's personal dictatorship. Mandelstam wrote that Stalin "toyed with the tributes of half-men" whilst he "forges decrees in a line of horseshoes"; a malevolent figure,

He rolls the executions on his tongue like berries.
He wishes he could hug them like big friends from home.

But someone present informed on him; he was arrested and tortured. Even though Bukharin was by that time in political purdah and under heavy suspicion, he intervened to ensure Mandelstam was not executed. Instead he was sentenced to internal exile in the Urals. In 1937 he was briefly allowed back to Moscow where he was lost, homeless and half insane. Arrested again for no specific reason he was sentenced to five years' hard labour in the Gulag. He was last seen alive at a transit camp near Vladivostok.

It was this experience – that of those who could not transform or mutilate their conscience or impulses to a standard set by a political party they did not support – that formed the basis of one of the two great fictional masterpieces to emerge from the post-Civil War years, Yevgeny Zemyatin's *We* (the other, although it took much longer to gestate, was Pasternak's *Doctor Zhivago*). Before the war, Zemyatin had been in trouble with the Tsarist state for left-wing sympathies. He spent much of the war in Newcastle, England, before returning to Russia upon hearing of the Revolution. Always individualistic, he was appalled at the direction of the Revolution, believing that writers should be "madmen, hermits, heretics, dreamers, rebels and skeptics", not "diligent and reliable officials".

We, written in 1920 and published abroad in 1924, is set a thousand years after the triumph of the One State during the rule of the Benefactor, in which humans are known only by numbers. It tells the story of D-503, an obedient functionary of the One State, who like all citizens lives in a glass house so he can be monitored, is piped to work by canned music from a Music Factory and is constantly watched by the Bureau of Guardians. His only friend, R-13, is a State Poet who recites his verses at state executions. D-503 is content to schedule impersonal sex with a woman called O-50 until he falls in love with the rebellious I-330, who involves him in the resistance to the One State. By the end D-503 has been brainwashed back into unquestioning submission to the Benefactor and I-330 has been imprisoned by the Guardians, but she tells her captors that they can never win because, like numbers, "revolutions are infinite".

We is an SF classic, the dystopian flipside of Bogdanov's *Red Star* and an enormous influence on Huxley's *Brave New World* and Orwell's *1984*. It was also the first novel to be officially banned in Soviet Russia by the newly established Main Directorate on Literary Affairs and Publishing (Glavlit), an organisation that perfectly reflected the mentality of Lenin's "Party Organisation and Party Literature".

On 22nd September, 1922 Dzerzhinsky met Lenin to discuss policy towards the intelligentsia. After the meeting he wrote a record for himself called "Directives from Vladimir Ilyich". The notes recorded:

> To continue steadily the exile of the anti-Soviet intelligentsia (and of the Mensheviks most of all) abroad. To draft lists and thoroughly check them. Seek out literature specialists and have them furnish reviews. Divide between them the entire literature. To draft lists of cooperative leaders inimical to us.[32]

Dzerzhinsky compiled lists of all intellectuals who might not support the government and divided them by categories: political commentators; economists; technicians and engineers; doctors; teachers; and literary critics. "Data must be gathered on all of them by our GPU departments", he wrote to his subordinates. One off-shoot of this policy was the quite literal brain-drain of the "Philosophy Steamer" on which, in September 1922, 160 prominent but "unreliable" academics, writers, and philosophers were deported from Russia on Lenin's express orders. In an article on the deportation in

Pravda, Trotsky wrote, "There aren't many takers to shake up the neo-religious liquid distilled before the war in the little apothecaries of Berdyaev and others".[33] He did not explain why, if this were so, they needed to be expelled from the country.

St Petersburg/Petrograd/Leningrad – the hub of the Russian intelligentsia's cultural vivacity between 1890 and 1917 and the living symbol of Russia's engagement with Europe's liberal, cosmopolitan culture – was gradually drained of its life-blood from 1917 to 1922. Much of this was due to economic collapse and the Civil War. But from 1918, when Sovnarcom transferred to socially conservative Moscow and settled behind the walls of the Kremlin, Russia's entire culture began to isolate itself from everything that distinguished St Petersburg from the enormous hinterland to its east, and the government began to resemble the paranoid, anti-intellectual Tsarist autarky it had replaced.

After 1922, in the era of the New Economic Policy (NEP), Soviet cultural life underwent a temporary revitalisation. But the undeniable energy of Soviet culture in the mid-1920s took place within, not against, the confines of Soviet art and Socialist Realism, i.e. in cinema, theatre and the general iconography of Constructivism, Futurism and Agit-Prop. Those artists who could not accommodate this did not flourish. The great innovations of early-20th-century Russian art – pre-Revolutionary Suprematism and post-revolutionary Constructivism – had an enormous impact on the culture of post-war Europe. Yet at the same time as the avant-garde of Berlin, London and New York began to develop the edifice of modern art, Soviet Russia shut down cultural experimentation. The cultural tolerance of the NEP years, provisional and limited as it was, was curtailed in 1929 when Bukharin was politically destroyed and Lunacharsky removed from Nakompros.

In 1934 Bukharin was allowed to address the inaugural Congress of Soviet Writers. Taking this rare opportunity, he warned against "the bureaucratisation of creative processes" and told delegates that socialism required a "powerful, rich and variegated art" driven by "humanism" and "diversity and quality".[34] Although his speech received rapturous applause, it had no wider impact. In the 1930s Soviet culture froze into a nightmare version of bourgeois philistinism—a retreat to the safety of the Classics, suspicion and dismissal of all modernity and innovation, and a filtering of every new novel, poem, film, play, symphony or opera through a dull and occasionally vicious bureaucratic machine. Sometimes the artistic impulse seeped through regardless (as in Yuri Pimenov's impressionistic *New Moscow*, which matched the best American paintings of urban life), but it was marred by the servitude under which it laboured. For all its grandiosity, Stalinist art was a chocolate-box cover on an ocean of dead peasants and political prisoners.

CHAPTER FIFTEEN

The Transitory Mood of the Workers' Democracy

From the first days of the Bolshevik Revolution, the justification for the system of governance it introduced was that it was a new form of state run by and for the working class. It was not and never intended to be a parliamentary republic, no matter how progressive that might be or the extent of its suffrage. It was the "Dictatorship of the Proletariat" in action and not to be judged in terms of qualitatively different regimes. But what, exactly, *was* the Dictatorship of the Proletariat? Did Sovnarcom's version measure up to the ideal? And even if it did, was that ideal defencible?

For Lenin and Trotsky, the concept of the Dictatorship of the Proletariat was central to Marx's thought, although Marx himself only used the phrase a few times in personal correspondence and never in any work intended for publication. In *The State and Revolution* Lenin quoted from Marx's *Critique of the Gotha Programme* on the post-revolutionary state. Published in 1891, eight years after Marx's death, the *Critique* was a work put together from a private letter about the first common programme of

German socialists in 1875. In it Marx said that whatever functions similar to the present-day state that will still exist in a communist society cannot be foreseen. His only reference to a Dictatorship of the Proletariat was in the context of "a period of revolutionary transformation", during which time "the state can be nothing but the revolutionary dictatorship of the proletariat".[1] Although Marx did not elaborate further, Lenin based an entire section of *The State and Revolution*, called "Presentation of the Question by Marx", on this brief reference.

By contrast, the first generation of major Marxist theorists—Bebel, Kautsky, Hilferding and Plekhanov—saw Marx's comment as simply a vivid metaphor for a society run by and for the majority of the population, i.e. the working class. So did their successors Martov and Luxemburg. Lenin and Trotsky imagined a different version, a disciplinarian regime based on the suppression and denial of democratic rights to those deemed non-proletarian. The Bolshevik concept of the Dictatorship of the Proletariat was that it embodied the will of the enfranchised working class through their revolutionary organs of governance, the Soviets. It existed to oversee and implement a forcible transfer of socio-economic power from the bourgeoisie to the proletariat, from the rich to the poor.

This was brutally simplistic and fundamentally anti-democratic. It withheld democratic and civil rights from huge numbers of people based on a crude categorisation of employment and income. Its central flaw was the assumption that the "real" and legitimate working class was epitomised by the Bolshevik militants of the Putilov Works or the

Kronstadt naval base, and that other workers such as the Menshevik trade unionists of the Printers Union or the SRs of the Moscow Metal Works had a false consciousness. The Bolsheviks were therefore stunned when many workers who had supported them during 1917 began to return to the Mensheviks and SRs during 1918 and 1919. Elections to the Soviets in these years produced clear Menshevik and SR majorities. In these circumstances the Bolsheviks could either abandon rule by one party or renege on the core principle of the Dictatorship of the Proletariat, i.e. that the will of the working class was expressed through the Soviets. They chose the latter.

Their attitude was perfectly encapsulated by Trotsky at the Tenth Party Congress in 1921, when confronted by the criticisms of the "Workers' Opposition" that the party no longer represented the working class. In response, Trotsky condemned the Opposition for "fetishising the principles of democracy". In doing so

> they seemed to place workers' voting rights above the party, as if the party did not have right to defend its dictatorship, even if that dictatorship were to collide for a time with the transitory mood of the workers' democracy.[2]

Trotsky had let the cat out of the bag. The Dictatorship of the Party, not the Proletariat, would always prevail over the "transitory mood" of the working class. Given the variety and fluidity of opinion within that class it could hardly be otherwise.

It became clear after 1917 that although he relentlessly

used the word "socialism", Lenin had no firm conception of what it was. His only consistent vision—the Dictatorship of the Proletariat—was negative and authoritarian, a concept of state power congenial to a man whose favourite adjectives were "ruthless", "merciless", "disciplined" etc., but who, unlike Trotsky in his better flights of fancy, could not conceive of a fundamentally more civilised society. Emma Goldman, after a traumatic few years in Soviet Russia, concluded that after October 1917 "the whole subsequent history of the Revolution is a kaleidoscope of Lenin's compromises and betrayals of his own slogans". This was only true if one took Lenin's slogans from the April Theses to October as the essence of Leninism. But those slogans were the necessities of the moment. Enthused by the onrush of revolution, Lenin appears to have toyed with genuine libertarian ideas for about six months. Once confronted with the challenges of real governmental power it was quickly apparent, as Goldman realised, that "the centralised political State was Lenin's deity".[3]

For all his fetish for organisation, Lenin had not bothered to prepare coherent economic policies for the post-revolution world. In 1916 Bukharin, who at least tried to think about such matters, recommended the economic policies of the Dutch Socialists to Lenin as a model to be followed. The Dutch programme included nationalisation of the banks, an eight-hour day, progressive taxation and a welfare state. Lenin dismissed the programme not because of specific disagreements, but because it was a waste of time to consider it before the revolution had arrived. "Since at present the socialist revolution in the designated sense has not begun", he wrote, "the programme of the Dutch is absurd".[4]

Lenin's vision was exclusively that of *political revolution*. It came easy to him to conceive of "smashing the state" and then letting workers build a new one, but in real terms this meant nothing. Society needed to continue to function in the days, weeks and months *after* revolution, and it could not do so simply through improvisation and terror. In 1921, after years of economic chaos partly rectified by the massive reversal of the NEP, Lenin candidly admitted:

> We expected – or perhaps it would be truer to see that we presumed without having given it adequate consideration – to be able to organise the state production and the state distribution of products on communist lines in a small peasant country directly as ordered by the proletarian state. Experience has proved that we were wrong.[5]

Lenin had an equally poor sense of the possible in foreign affairs. Emma Goldman records that when she met him in 1920 his first question to her was, "When can we expect the social revolution in America?"[6] It was true that post-war America was politically volatile. There was a General Strike in Seattle in 1919 in which 100,000 workers took action. For five days the city was run by a General Strike Committee. The experiment in city-wide direct democracy was only brought to a halt by an invasion of US marines. There were also race riots in several cities and mass strikes in the steel and textile industries. But national revolution was and remained a dim prospect, partly because the American left had fractured itself at precisely the wrong moment.

In the decade before the First World War, a mass-based American socialist movement had started to emerge. This found expression in the Socialist Party of America (SPA) led by Eugene V. Debs, and in the "One Big Union" of the Industrial Workers of the World (IWW), whose leader "Big Bill" Haywood sat on the SPA's Executive Committee. By 1912 the SPA had 150,000 members and over 1,000 public officials, including the socialist Mayor of Milwaukee and the first socialist elected to the US House of Representatives—Victor Berger—in 1910, to be followed by Meyer London in 1915. It had supporters in the wider labour movement (including the leaders of the mineworkers, brewery workers and ironworkers trade unions), immigrant communities, populist farmers organisations and the progressive middle class. In 1912 Debs, against the overwhelming hostility of American newspapers, received 6% of the vote in the Presidential election.

After 1912 the SPA went into a period of decline driven by poor leadership and failure to support fighting trade unions like the IWW. But since 1918 SPA membership had shot up to 100,000, although a great amount of this was foreign-born workers joining the SPA's foreign-language federations in a fit of enthusiasm for the Russian Revolution. The SPA's vote increased, especially in its urban heartlands, reaching 34% in Chicago and 35% in Cleveland. In 1919 four million American workers took part in strikes; as in Britain, mineworkers demanded the nationalistion of the mines. At the 1919 SPA congress Bolshevik supporters pressed for the party to affiliate to the Comintern. A massive split ensued, leading to the dubious expulsion of the SPA left wing and its own immediate split into the Communist Labour Party and the Communist Party of America. A divided left was easily dismantled by the "Red Scare" of 1919-20. Had the SPA maintained cohesion and built on Debs's tradition of popular native socialism, it might have matured into a mass party of the left. Instead by 1929 it had 6,000 members and had ceased to be a political force.

Goldman knew that the American Communist Party (as it became when the two factions merged) was a sectarian caricature of Bolshevism in a country where Bolshevism did not even apply. The chance of a social revolution in America, at least in the Bolshevik sense, was near zero. This did not mean there were no prospects for socialist and trade union advance, as the radical CIO unions demonstrated in the 1930s. But to have any chance of success they had to respect and reflect American culture and not tie themselves to a "foreign body" like the Comintern, whose strategies for revolutionary underground work were utterly irrelevant to America. This approach demanded a Menshevik attitude to trade union and working-class initiatives and a respect for democratic civil rights, things Lenin despised.

And yet the Bolshevik seizure of power had been predicated on Lenin's perception of the German working class and his belief that it would soon carry out its own revolution and come to the aid of its Russian comrades. Lenin's laxness in preparing an economic programme for post-revolutionary Russia was in great part because he assumed the Germans would do it for him. This was a gamble of enormous proportions. As even Isaac Deutscher admitted, "It was an extremely simple-minded notion that history could so precisely and so rapidly repeat itself in country after country".[7]

In 1917-18 the great dynasties of the pre-war epoch—Romanov, Hohenzollern and Hapsburg—all fell, and the political boundaries of the modern world shifted. Inevitably there was great social upheaval, but aside from a short-lived revolutionary government in Hungary in March-August 1919, which overreached itself and lost mass support, it did not produce socialist revolution. Germany, on the other hand, having been defeated in war, was far more volatile. After the Kiel Mutiny of November 1918 a Republic was declared and the Kaiser abdicated. The SPD took power under Chancellor Frederich Ebert, but it had to contend with militant forces on its left such as the Spartacist League, the USPD and the "Revolutionary Stewards" movement led by Richard Muller and Emil Barth. In November 1918 the Stewards formed Workers' and Soldiers' Councils, i.e. Soviets, across the country, and demanded they become an integral part of the new state. Ebert was forced to offer the radical USPD seats in his governmental coalition as well as work with the Executive of the Councils.

Although the Spartacists were a small minority within the German working-class movement, they and the Stewards brought 250,000 people on to the streets of Berlin on 16th December to demand "all power to the Workers' and Soldiers' Councils". As a result of Ebert's concession, SPD and USPD supporters won majorities in the First Congress of the Council of Workers and Soldiers, held in Berlin on 16th-21st December, 1918. Of 489 delegates, the SPD had 291, the USPD 90 and the Spartacists 10. The Congress debated what form of society the delegates wished to see. The SPD and USPD sought a parliamentary republic based on universal suffrage, while the Spartacists and most of the Stewards wanted a "Council Republic". Although the Congress referred the question to a future National Assembly the Spartacists and Stewards jumped the gun and began to take local and police powers to themselves.

This was a direct challenge to the new Republic for which the new German Communist Party (KPD) – formed on 1st January, 1919 out of the Spartacist League and the Stewards – was not remotely prepared. As even Donny Gluckstein's sympathetic work on European Workers' Councils between 1915 and 1920 admits, the enthusiastic young revolutionaries of the KPD "had never confronted the difficulties of winning workers to their ideas, or tried to lead them in the daily class struggle".[8] They totally underestimated the hold the SPD and the USPD had on the loyalties of most German workers.

From November 1918 to January 1919, Germany was governed by a "Council of People's Deputies", under the leadership of Ebert and Haase. Amongst other things, the Council appointed a "Socialisation Commission" headed by Kautsky and Hilferding to prepare proposals for the nationalisation of German industry. Although the Commission proposed socialisation of monopolistic sectors such as coal and iron and the involvement of German trade unions in setting wage rates and other conditions, the SPD had no intention of implementing these policies. Nevertheless it did implement an eight-hour work day and employment and labour reform, including protection from arbitrary dismissal, industrial works councils, agricultural labour reform, national health insurance, re-instatement of demobilised workers, regulated wage agreements and universal suffrage from age 20. Whatever the motivation for this raft of governmental decrees—and of course it was partly to offset the appeal of the radical socialists and the Workers' Councils—the result was that great numbers of German workers saw the Republic under the SPD as far more likely to deliver a better life for them and their families than those urging violent insurrection.

The situation escalated in early January when Ebert used military units against some of the Councils. In response, on 6th January, 1919 the most revolutionary elements of the Councils launched an insurrection against the SPD-USPD government. But this was no October. The German military had not disintegrated. The SPD-USPD had successfully replaced the imperial government and it had the support of the majority of the German working class. The Revolutionary Stewards movement was divided, with Muller and Barth opposed to an uprising. The Spartacists, strong in "Red Berlin", had little support elsewhere. Luxemburg and Liebknecht were reluctant to support an armed uprising against the government, but once it had started they felt they had no choice but to back it. At the same time Ebert and the thuggish Gustov Noske organised loyal military forces and mercenary Friekorps units to crush the revolt.

Between 9th and 12th January, 1919 over 200 people were killed in fierce fighting in Berlin. Luxemburg and Liebknecht, captured by Friekorps irregulars, were brutally murdered. The German Revolution was dead before it got off the ground. As the Spartacists were being annihilated in Berlin their newspaper *Rote Fahne* asked in incredulity, "Where are the Workers' Councils, the organs called to lead the revolutionary masses? They do not exist. They are not even meeting".[9] But the Councils, as Muller and Barth realised, were not ready to support the Spartacists.

Kautsky, one of the founders of the USPD, was appalled that the Spartacists had divided the forces of the democratic left at a crucial moment and gifted the far-right a perfect excuse to mobilise against the new Republic. "There can be no doubt about the result", he wrote in 1919:

> There was no doubt from the very beginning of the movement, at least amongst those who had preserved the capacity to view the real relation of forces clearly. On the one side stood a minority of the proletariat, on the other its majority in the Reich and the entire bourgeois world, together with the remains of the apparatus of military power that survived the period of the war.

This was not an endorsement of Noske, whom Kautsky loathed, but an acknowledgment that through their adventurist tactics the Spartacists had allowed Noske to inject the poison of the Freikorps into German political life. Of the new socialist government, Kautsky lamented "its ability to defend itself against bourgeois and military influences, which was slim to begin with, have been further reduced. The bourgeois elements and professional officers have acquired new energy. The danger of counter-revolution is becoming real".[10]

Two months after the only genuine attempt to repeat the

Bolshevik insurrection in a major European country went down in flames, the preliminary meeting of what would become the Third International took place in Moscow. In March 1919 this consisted of about 40 representatives from small foreign socialist parties and groups. To the Bolsheviks, cut off from Western Europe by the Civil War, these visiting socialists appeared as harbingers of the revolution they hoped would rescue them. Greeting the small gathering, Lenin told them:

> Not only in Russia, but even in the most advanced capitalist countries in Europe, for instance in Germany, civil war has become a fact. Revolution has begun and is gaining strength in all countries. The Soviet system has won not merely in backward Russia, but even in Germany, the most developed country in Europe, and also in England, the oldest capitalist country.[11]

Even allowing for the temporary surge of hope provided by the formation of the Hungarian Soviet Republic in March 1919, this was pure fantasy. The Soviet system died in Germany along with Luxemburg and Liebknecht. It never even existed in England. The spasms of revolution in post-war Britain were real but fleeting. In June 1917, enthused by the Russian Revolution of February 1917, the Leeds Convention brought together 1,150 delegates from British trade unions and socialist groups to discuss and offer support to the revolutionary process in Russia, attracting Labour leaders like MacDonald and Snowden, trade union leaders Tom Mann and Bob Smillie, and intellectuals such as Bertrand Russell. MacDonald exhorted the convention to emulate the February Revolution and to "lay down our terms, make our own proclamations, establish our own diplomacy, see to it that we have our own international meetings". The Convention's Fourth Resolution, passed by a large majority, called for the assembled delegates to "establish at once in every town, urban and rural district, Councils of Workmen and Soldiers' delegates for initiating and co-ordinating working class activity in support of the policy set out in the forgoing resolutions".[12]

This was excitable rhetoric. The only ones to genuinely attempt to put it into practice were the militant shop stewards of the Clyde Workers Committee (CWC) in Scotland, who established democratic workplace forums outside the standard trade union apparatus. In January 1919 the CWC led a strike in Glasgow against the imposition of a 48-hour working week in the engineering industry. The stewards demanded a 40-hour week. Under their direction the entire Clyde Valley came to a halt. Gas, electricity and tramway workers joined the engineers in mass strike action which quickly spread to Edinburgh and Belfast. By 1st February over 100,000 workers were on strike and the CWC's newspaper boldly declared, "We British Bolsheviks have the Russian precedent to guide us". So did the government. That night thousands of troops arrived by train and Glasgow woke up to find itself surrounded by a ring of machine gun nests and tanks, with battleships sitting off the docks.[13] This show of force intimidated the engineering union leaders into backing down, leaving the stewards isolated.

Despite the unrest in Glasgow and the agitation of British

soldiers for faster demobilisation and against deployment to Russia (the former being as strong a motivation for the latter as solidarity with Russian workers), it is not the case that the country was, in the title of Chani Rosenberg's study of that year, "on the brink of revolution". Rosenberg and others exaggerate the extent to which strikes in Clydeside and soldiers' protests against delayed demobilisation reflected wide-spread revolutionary sentiment. On the contrary, the General Election of November 1918, the first in which all men over 21 and all women over 30 could vote, returned a landslide majority for the wartime Tory/Liberal (Lloyd George) coalition. Labour secured 57 seats, but candidates known to have been anti-war or to favour a non-punitive peace treaty with Germany were defeated. Parties to the left of Labour secured less than 1% of the overall vote.

Proletarian revolution may have simmered briefly on Clydeside and in the Welsh mining valleys, but not elsewhere in Britain. Nor did it spread, as Lenin and Trotsky fervently hoped it would, from Budapest to Vienna and Berlin. Lenin's mishandling and misunderstanding of the two most important parts of his political project, transforming the Russian economy and inspiring European revolution, reveal a truth about the man which is often overlooked – he was a complete amateur in the field in which he operated. He laid down ambitious, impractical schemes and was surprised when they didn't work. Despite occasional reassessments of economic policy, he never once re-examined or questioned the monopoly of power exercised by the Bolshevik Party. On the contrary, he continued to delude himself that this constituted "Soviet power" and a "Commune State".

Martov never believed in Lenin's vision of the Commune State for an instant (not that he did not support such a project, he simply saw no correlation between the rhetoric and the reality). As early as 30th December, 1917 he wrote to his friend N.S. Kristi, who lived abroad, "What flourishes here is such a pseudo-socialism of 'trenches and barracks', founded on an all-out primitivisation of life and the cult of the fist [...] that one cannot help feeling guilty before every civilised bourgeois". He concluded, "We are undoubtedly moving through anarchy towards some sort of Ceaserism".[14] That Ceaserism slowly began to emerge, not from imperial triumph but from the depths of the party bureaucracy. The permanent installation in power of one party administering the Dictatorship of the Proletariat meant that there was no possibility of changing political administrations, no accountability through an independent media, no framework of law to hold state organs to account.

Without these safeguards the party-state grew into a vast network of interlocking governmental bodies staffed by an influx of new recruits to the Party. From 240,000 in October 1917, the membership of the Bolshevik (then Communist) Party skyrocketed to 732,000 by March 1921, although in response to complaints from ordinary workers at the abuse of power by party functionaries, the early 1920s saw a "purging" of new elements regarded as suspicious or careerist. The suspicions were justified. There was no mass conversion to Bolshevism after October 1917. Ambitious sons and daughters of the proletariat and peasantry saw the emergence of a new elite and wanted to be part of it. Brovkin records that "among workers, party membership was almost never associated with a set of political views or programmes. It was first and foremost a matter of moving into a different social world".[15]

A party card provided at least the minimum of housing, food and fuel, when most workers received even less. It also afforded some protection against the Cheka. Once they had their party cards new members were on the inside track, low-level functionaries of the only growth industry (aside from the Red Army) in Soviet Russia. As a cynical but popular limerick of the 1920s had it:

Party card, party card,
stick by us please
you're the one who'll earn for us
pretzels, sweets and tea[16]

In the early months of 1918, the number of state officials — meaning working directly for the Russian Communist Party (RCP) and its organs such as the Commissariats, the Vesenka and the Cheka — was a relatively modest 114,359. A year later the total was 559,841. By the end of the following year, 1920, it had ballooned to nearly six million (5,880,000) officials employed directly or indirectly by the state.[17] This was five times as many as the total number of workers employed in Russian industry.

Lenin grew incensed at the many examples of a slow-moving, inefficient bureaucracy weighed down with red tape. In 1921 he wrote to the Deputy Chairman of the Public Works Committee, "The Departments are shit. The Decrees are shit. To find men and check up on their work—that is the whole point".[18] Yet "checking up on their work" required more layers of bureaucracy. In 1919 he created the Workers' and Peasant Inspectorate (Rabkrin) to do just that. Rabkrin, with its remit to investigate and remove state officials, was the perfect power base for an emerging leader. Lenin chose the loyal yet efficient Stalin as the head of the Inspectorate. Within a year he had turned it into "his private police within the government".[19]

The futility of Lenin's approach to combating bureaucracy was lost on him. The only way to solve the problem was to dissolve the entire structure of one-party rule. That was not going to happen. On the contrary, the organs of central control continued to grow. The Eighth Party Congress in March 1919 formalised the role of the five-man Politburo, which would take all immediate decisions on implementation of policy and report periodically to the Central Committee. The Congress created two other important bodies: an Organisational Bureau (Orgburo) to "conduct the whole organisational work of the party", and a Secretariat for the CC, which would organise party congresses, CC meetings, agenda, minutes, rule changes, etc. To avoid the danger of overlapping responsibilities, it was decided that one of the Politburo should also sit on the Orgburo and head the Secretariat. Stalin was again chosen for what looked like dull administrative work.

Power inevitably flowed to these smaller bodies. Between March and December 1919 the Central Committee met only six times, whereas the Politburo met 29 times and the Orgburo 110 times. Under Stalin's direction, the Secretariat expanded in size from 15 staff in March 1919 to 80 staff by November 1919. Between March 1920 and March 1921 its total staff jumped from 150 to 602, including its own military detachment. One of the Secretariat's responsibilities was the appointment and transfer of party members. Stalin reported to the Tenth Party Congress in March 1921 that in the previous year the Secretariat had been responsible for appointing and transferring 42,000 members.

Stalin knew exactly what he was doing. Between 1919 and 1922 he assiduously cultivated new regional and provincial party leaders – often workers and peasants overawed by Marxist theorists like Trotsky and Bukharin – and placed them in influential positions within the ever-growing machine. They owed him. When they came to Moscow to take part in Party Congresses and elect the Central Committee they looked to him for guidance and carried out his wishes. Trotsky, on the other hand, was often so bored by the slow, inane bureaucracy of CC meetings that he sat at the back reading French novels. The small-town delegates did not fail to notice the difference between the Jewish intellectual Trotsky, who told them Russia was "backward" and "uncultured" in comparison to Western Europe, and the rough Georgian Stalin, who avoided abstruse Marxist theory and talked robust common sense about building socialism in the motherland.

1919 was a crucial year. The Mensheviks, taking advantage of the partial freedom granted them in 1918, began to win local and Soviet elections. So too did the Left SRs. Kevin Murphy records that in May 1919 the Left SRs won a majority on the Factory Committee of Moscow's Hammer and Sickle

Metal Works, explaining that "the Left sr electoral success derived in part from the persistence of democracy in the factory elections", a democracy being killed off elsewhere. In Petrograd there were fewer alternatives. As the Whites closed in on the city, over a fifth of Petrograd Bolsheviks were ordered to report for service at the front. Those that went tended to be the veterans of 1917, those who believed in autonomous Soviets and Factory Committees. Those that remained saw the Soviets as just another organ of one-party rule.[20] Party cells grafted themselves on to Factory Committees and used them as transmission belts for party directives. The number of workers taking part in Soviet elections plummeted. Working-class engagement with the party-state began to dry up. Even the editors of *Pravda* expressed concern that workers were too afraid to write to the paper without first securing approval from their local party.[21]

The Bolshevik Party had justified the fears of those who predicted that the concept of a vanguard party would lead to "substitutionism", i.e. the party organisation would replace the class it was supposed to serve. The standard Leninist explanation for this is that during the Civil War the best working-class activists had gone to the front or taken up administrative tasks within the new state bodies, leaving a "declassed" residue behind. Many militant workers had, of course, volunteered service—some for noble reasons, some not. The Party and the Red Army offered career and other rewards. But the mass of workers who did not move into Party or Army positions remained where and what they had always been. They remained workers. By 1919 the

Bolsheviks were becoming exasperated with them. Many Communist Party functionaries considered that, in the words of a Communist cell leader in the Duks factory in Moscow, "the majority of workers had counter-revolutionary views".[22]

The legendary Left SR leader Maria Spiridonova was particularly well received when she visited factories in Petrograd. Spiridonova had a long history of revolutionary heroism. In 1905, after her home province of Tambov was subject to brutal repression by the troops of General Luzhenovsky, she had walked up to the general at a railway station and shot him in the face. She was brutally beaten by his soldiers, became an international *cause célèbre* and was sentenced to exile in Siberia. After eleven years in the women's prison of Chita she was released following the February Revolution. She ordered the entire prison blown up. Its ruins behind her, she set out for Petrograd to continue SR agitation. Initially she had some sympathy with the Bolsheviks, but the suppression of the Soviets and the activities of the Grain Requisition Squads turned her against them. Following the Left SR uprising of July 1918 she was arrested and imprisoned.

Such was Spiridonova's fame on the Russian left that she was granted amnesty a few months later. She returned to the factories to hold rallies and to support the strikes against the regime that erupted at the beginning of 1919 (or as the pro-Bolshevik historian Kevin Murphy described the activities of the Left SRs at the time, "to fan the flames of labour discontent"). Frightened by her immense popularity, the government re-arrested Spiridonova at the end of February. A Revolutionary Tribunal charged her with slandering Soviet, i.e. government, power and she was sentenced to one year's isolation in a "hospital". After this she was periodically in and out of prison. In 1937 she was sent permanently to the Gulag. In 1941 she was executed, with many others, in an arctic forest.

At the end of February 1919 working-class discontent exploded in a strike at the Aleksandrovskii railway workshop, caused by failure to honour back-pay. A 3,000-man rally demanded the pay and also asked for rations equal to that of Red Army soldiers. After a few days the Cheka swept in and arrested the strike leaders. This escalated the strike as workers demanded the release of their comrades. The strike coincided with elections to the Moscow Soviet. Not surprisingly the Aleksandrovskii workers elected Menshevik and SR delegates to represent them. The Bolsheviks' response was to send in troops to occupy the plant, evict the strikers and sack the entire workforce. Strike leaders were tried by Revolutionary Tribunal and exiled to Murmansk. *Pravda* announced that new workers were to be hired and the sacked workers could reapply. From then on any meeting of workers at the plant had to be approved by the Cheka in advance. If a meeting took place the minutes had to be submitted to the Cheka.[23]

The strike at the Aleksandrovskii was followed in March by protests at what had been the beating heart of Bolshevik Petrograd, the huge Putilov Works. By 1919, the Putilov workers' anger with the regime was so intense that when Zinoviev tried to address them he was physically ejected. On 10th March the factory convened a mass meeting and passed by a huge margin a Resolution which began:

> We, the workmen of the Putilov works and the wharf, declare
> before the laboring classes of Russia and the world, that the
> Bolshevik government has betrayed the high ideals of the
> October Revolution, and thus betrayed and deceived the
> workers and peasants of Russia; the Bolshevik Government,
> acting in our name, is not the authority of the proletariat and
> the peasants, but the authority of the dictatorship of the Central
> Committee of the Communist Party, self-governing with the
> aid of Extraordinary Commissions, Communists and police.

The Resolution put a series of demands: the immediate transfer of authority to freely elected Soviets; immediate reestablishment of freedom of elections "at factories and plants, barracks, ships, railways, everywhere"; transfer of management to the trade unions; transfer of food supply to workers' and peasants' cooperatives; immediate release of arrested Left SR members; and immediate release of Maria Spiridnova.[24] The Resolution sparked off a strike wave that spread throughout Petrograd, resulting in nearly half of the city's workforce coming out on strike. Lenin himself personally came to Petrograd to address workers, but he was greeted with heckling and calls for his resignation. Workers demanded the Putilov Resolution be printed in communist newspapers. Street clashes with the Cheka escalated. For a few days it seemed that the workers of Petrograd might rise up and depose the Bolsheviks.

On 14th March the Bolsheviks used their majority in the Petrograd City Soviet to pass a resolution that resolved to "clear the Putilov of the White Guardists and bagmen". Any workers who refused to work would be fired. All workers' meetings were banned. Any worker found with a copy of the Putilov Resolution would be arrested. Any workers who stayed on strike would be evicted from their homes and have their ration cards removed. After this, those strikes still running (at the Putilov, the Truegolnik rubber factory and the Rozhdestvenskii trampark) were put down by force. When the Putilov workers barricaded themselves in, the factory was stormed and occupied, with several workers shot on the spot. Over three hundred were arrested. Executions followed after a summary trial.[25] Estimates of the total number of strikers shot varies from dozens to hundreds. Gordon Leggett records that mass executions took place outside the city where blindfolded workers were put against a wall and mowed down by machine guns.[26]

Despite this, disturbances spread beyond Petrograd and Moscow, with more revolts occurring in Tula, Briansk, Tver, Sormorvo, Orel, Smolensk and Astrakhan. A strike at the armaments plant in Tula broke out in February after the arrest of workers who had complained that local commissars, and Cheka and Red Army men received better rations. Although it was repressed more strikes broke out again in March and these escalated to a general strike in the city. This was put down by the army who imposed military discipline in Tula's factories. Strike leaders were identified and sacked.

In June, workers from textile mills, tram lines, printing shops and rail car plants in the city of Tver took strike action to protest the forced conscription of 10% of Tver's workers into the Red Army. They also protested the lack of fair elections to the local Soviet. Unlike in Tula, the government decided to listen to the strikers, and the special commissar dispatched from Moscow to "liquidate" the strike, V.I. Nevsky, reported back that the strikers' demands were justified. He also found that Tver's local Communist Party commissars had been hoarding rations, accruing special privileges and behaving like petty tyrants. Nevsky negotiated with the elected representatives of the Tver strikers, conceded many of their demands were legitimate and recommended to Moscow that the local one-party dictatorship be ended. Because of this the rebellion in the town subsided.[27]

Tver proved that not every manifestation of worker unrest needed to be dealt with in the bloody manner of Tula or the Putilov Works. Sometimes, as in Briansk, Orel and Smolensk, emissaries from Moscow honestly reported back that strikes were not "counter-revolutionary" but arose from real grievances. At the Eighth Party Congress in March 1919 the senior Bolshevik Nikolai Ossinski, previously head of the State Bank and now one of the leaders of the "Democratic Centralists" who criticised the lack of democracy within the RCP and the Soviets, told delegates honestly, "Rebellions that are going on are not White Guardist, they take place because our commissars behave disgracefully".[28] Ossinski and other Democratic Centralists openly warned of the danger of a "bureaucratic dictatorship".

Tragically, this approach faltered in the provincial fishing town of Astrakhan. In spring 1919 it sat between Kolchak's forces on the Volga and Deniken's sweeping in from the northern Caucasus. If these had joined up they would have formed one united White Army front. This may explain the exceptional brutality with which a strike at Astrakhan's metal plants and a rebellion by unwilling conscripted soldiers were put down. Communists and loyal Red Army units surrounded strike rallies and opened fire. Workers then joined with rebellious soldiers and fought back. Between 10th and 12th March there was heavy fighting throughout the town, which finally died down as the Communists reasserted control. The Cheka then carried out mass executions.[29]

Writing in 1990 in the *Slavic Review*, Vladimir Brovkin, whose work on the 1918 and 1919 mass strikes against the Bolsheviks is invaluable to an accurate understanding of the period, considered that "the strikes of 1919 have remained a blank in Soviet history".[30] To a great extent they still are, yet they are the vital background to the 1921 Kronstadt uprising and proof that it did not arise from "anarchist elements" or a "monarchist conspiracy", but was the culmination of a consistent and continuous working-class struggle for civil rights. The struggle took political form, but in great part it arose from protest against an intolerable industrial regime. Central to that regime was the imposition of the model of "scientific management" created by the American engineer Frederick Taylor onto Russian industrial workers.

Lenin's passion for "Taylorism" said much about his conception of socialism. Taylor's use of time-and-motion studies to make the tasks of the factory more automated and mechanistic had been utilised ruthlessly by American employers to restrict freedom within the workplace and reduce workers to heavily monitored drones. In theory Taylor's ideas, explained in *The Principles of Scientific Management* (1911), were designed to increase efficiency by providing proper training for workers and ensuring they did not waste their time in boring, unproductive labour. In reality they were used by employers to squeeze every last atom of labour possible from their employees. In his major work, Taylor wrote,

> It is only through *enforced* standardisation of methods, *enforced* adoption of the best implements and working conditions, and *enforced* cooperation that this faster work can be assured. And the duty of enforcing the adoption of standards and enforcing this cooperation rests with *management* alone.[31]

This was meat and drink to the Bolsheviks. They were classic productivists, in thrall to a vision of increasing industrial production as the only route to economic development and social liberation. They did not question the value of unrestrained industrial growth, or demonstrate the distaste for its moral and aesthetic squalor found in the socialism of Morris, Carpenter and Kropotkin. Lenin, Trotsky and Stalin all saw the salvation and achievement of socialism in the development of the economy's productive forces. Therefore any system of management, such as Taylorism, that produced measurable growth in the forces of production was by definition a good thing. Decentralised, grassroots control of production, as found in Factory Committees, self-managed firms or independent cooperatives, which all offered a different perspective on growth and on economic and social development, were deemed irrelevant at best and petty-bourgeois at worst.

The Bolsheviks were of their time. Socialist rhetoric

aside, their conception of work reflected the Protestant Work Ethic and unquestioning acceptance of the need for daily, routine, compulsory work performed in order to secure the means of subsistence. Sadly, these attitudes define the work experience of 2017 as much as that of 1917. The zero-hours contract, to take the worst example, is designed for the employers' convenience, with no regard for "work–life balance". It is a concept rejected by the growing "Refusal of Work" movement, itself linked to a positive conception of "degrowth" as the necessary route out of social and ecological collapse.

The anarchist writer Bob Black's influential essay "The Abolition of Work" (1985) argued that *work itself* is as much a source of exploitation, domination and hierarchy as the capitalist system or the state, and in a libertarian society would become voluntary "productive play". Black argued that for most people (with the exception of a lucky few whose work corresponds to their vocation and talent) work consists of getting up in the morning at a time they would rather not, travelling in unpleasant conditions to a place they do not wish to be, spending most of their day doing something they do not enjoy in the company, and under the control of, people they have not chosen to be with. This usually involves little to no creativity or control of the work process. Marx had proposed the concept of alienated labour based on the lack of genuine consent in the work contract with the employer. Black claimed that *all* non-voluntary work was alienated.

In *The Problem with Work: Feminism, Marxism, Antiwork Politics and Postwork Imaginaries* (2011), Kathi Weeks added a feminist perspective to Refusal of Work by suggesting that whilst feminist campaigners had, rightly, fought for equal pay and the recognition of women's unpaid work as a form of labour, they had thereby "depoliticised" work itself. In Weeks' view feminism had unconsciously accepted a patriarchal concept of work as a moral duty and acknowledged that the employment relationship is how income is and should be distributed. David Graeber, the author of *Debt: The First 5,000 Years* (2011) also questioned the value of work as conventionally defined. His popular blog on "Bullshit Jobs" has disinterred Keynes' belief that with technological advancement there is no need to work more than 15 hours a week, with free-time devoted to enjoyment and self-improvement.

Weeks and Graeber explicitly challenge that work, or compulsory labour of any kind, should define one's identity and self-worth, or that refusal to engage in it should lead to social stigma or poverty. In the 1980s André Gorz laid out a conception of a "post-work" society. In *Paths to Paradise* and *Critique of Economic Reason* he claimed there was no longer any connection between increased productivity and the satisfaction of society's needs. Computerised mass production made long hours superfluous. In a sane society people would work less for the same reward. But capitalism is not a sane society. Trade unions should recognise this and cease to be capitalism's mirror image. In Gorz's view, "Trade unionism cannot continue to exist as a *movement* with a future unless it expands its mission beyond the defence of the particular interests of waged workers".[32] The reduction in the amount of labour required should not mean furious and doomed attempts to preserve the handloom or the coalmine, but new strategies to shorten paid work hours while maintaining equitable distribution of rewards.

This kind of thinking cannot remain the province of bohemians and anarchists. The mainstream left needs to develop concrete proposals for a post-work society and for better measures of "growth" than the GDP, indeed to redefine the very concept of growth. The Refusal of Work philosophy is useful and necessary as a statement of intent. Clearly we do not live in a utopia where work is productive play. Nor will the mists simply part one day to reveal it. The task for the left now is to create transitional spaces, structures and policies, such as workers' cooperatives run on egalitarian lines, a shorter working week with no loss of pay, remuneration for housework, non-hierarchical trade unions for freelance workers and a universal basic income for all.

Most of these solutions to the problem of compulsory work were not available in 1920 to a semi-industrialised country shattered by war. Soviet Russia's "debate" on work was whether to labour under the supervision and discipline of trade unions and fellow workers, or buckle under to the robotic dictats of Taylorism. Lenin claimed that a Taylorist regime overseen by a proletarian state would not replicate that of the US, that it would take the positive and reject the negative. But as one of the main critics of Taylorism in the Soviet Union in the 1920s pointed out, the system invariably meant "not the optimum use of labour, but the maximum use".[33] "Taylorist socialism" was a misnomer. In reality it meant turning workers into an army of labour, and an inevitable confrontation with the trade unions.

CHAPTER SIXTEEN

Trotsky and Martov

The relationship between Sovnarcom and the trade unions was fractious from the start, despite Bolsheviks securing leading positions in most of the major unions between February and October 1917. Whether they were Bolshevik, Menshevik or SR, trade union leaders reached their positions through different routes and with different skill-sets than party leaders. Keep's study of the revolutionary tumult of 1917-18 devotes more time than usual to the role of the unions, and found that "in this early period of Soviet history trade union officials were as a rule drawn directly from the working class milieu; they knew industrial conditions at first hand; and they owed their election to their personal qualities as activists and organisers, rather than their record for ideological rectitude".[1]

As such they reflected the desires of the Russian working class in a way that party activists did not. This, and the importance of the unions at the point of production, gave them an influence on the Bolshevik government that no other non-governmental body could match. Even after the

Vikzhel's failed attempt to form a post-October coalition government, it still assumed *de facto* management of the railway network. Sovnarcom's Commissar for Transport, Andrei Bubnov, had little choice but to work in uneasy alliance with it.

This dual-power could not last. Bolshevik militants in the Moscow and Petrograd branches of the union began to agitate against the Vikzhel, and the schism came to a head at the union's congress on 20th December, 1917. The congress, which ran from 20th December until 6th January, saw in miniature the process whereby the Bolsheviks had taken over the government – direct, sometimes physical action and a disregard for accepted democratic procedures. Bolshevik activists from Moscow and Petrograd formed a caucus, which they claimed represented over one million "railway proletarians". On the basis of their claim to be the largest faction, they asserted that they alone had the right to elect the congress's Presidium. This proposal was defeated by 216 votes to 192. After the congress, the majority voted in favour of the right of the Constituent Assembly to continue to exist, and the Bolshevik faction walked out and set up a new Executive. In the next few months, supporters of the Vikzhel were purged from local branches.

The same events played out in the Postal Workers Union and in the Union of Employees and Workers in Inland Waterways, who also opposed the establishment of a one-party state and threatened strike action against Sovnarcom. The Postal Workers Union's congress in late November passed a resolution by 52 votes to 8 to support the Constituent Assembly and take strike action should it be dissolved.

The government offered postal workers special bonuses and pay increases in order to defuse the situation, but as soon as the Assembly was dissolved and Sovnarcom's power more firmly established it increased the political pressure. The "industrial" unions, such as the metalworkers and engineers, were initially supportive of Sovnarcom and the Bolsheviks, taking active stands against the Constituent Assembly and attacking Mensheviks and SRs within their unions. Although these pro-Bolshevik unions were heavily dominated by their militant Petrograd vanguards, there is no reason to doubt their commitment to genuine Soviet power.

The role of the trade unions within a socialist society was debated at length at the First All-Russian Congress of Trade Unions, held from 7th to 15th January, 1918. As with the All-Russian Soviet Congresses of 1917, the delegates tended to come from the more militant north and central regions of the country. Their mandate to represent the estimated 2.5 million unionised Russian workers did not bear much scrutiny, although it is probable that in early 1918 – after the Decrees on workers' control and peace, but before War Communism and the suppression of the Soviets – most workers did support the Bolshevik government. The key issue was trade union independence. Speaking for the Bolsheviks, Zinoviev told the Congress they were in favour of trade union independence, "but only from the bourgeoisie". He considered that after October independence as such had no meaning. They now had to become organs of the state.

In early 1918 Martov was still allowed to address gatherings like the All-Russian Congress of Trade Unions. He told delegates that the transfer of power had not been as complete as Zinoviev claimed, and that in view of possible counter-revolution the trade unions needed to be built up, not diluted. He agreed the unions must play their part in preventing counter-revolution, "insofar as consideration of the actual forces available permit the union to modify the plans of the (state) power".[2] At the close the Congress voted on two resolutions: one from the Bolsheviks that advocated trade union absorption into the machinery of the state, and another from the Mensheviks that maintained the principle of independence. The result was 182 votes for the Bolsheviks and 84 for the Mensheviks.

The foundation of Soviet labour relations had been established. It constituted "an overweening commitment to production and to planning",[3] in which the trade unions would play a key collaborative role. It would now be trade unions and their local agents, the Factory Committees, who were responsible for promoting productivity and for ensuring discipline and attendance in the workplace.

By the end of 1919 this system was already cracking. Workers had taken strike action against the Bolshevik government, and thereby the workers' state, for a number of reasons, some industrial, some political. Strikes had been crushed. Trade unionists had been arrested, sometimes shot. Even Bolshevik trade unionists were angry with the interference and compulsion to which the government was subjecting the unions. At the same time the economy was in ruins. The transport infrastructure was shattered. Food and other essential supplies were hardly moving. In December 1919, Trotsky (now devoting less time to the Red Army as it became clearer that the Reds were going to defeat the Whites in the Civil War) turned his attention to economic policy.

On 17th December *Pravda* published Trotsky's "theses" on the problem of the transition from a war to a peace economy (the theses had been submitted to the Central Committee in secret but by "accident" they were published). The theses proposed that the Commissariat of War assume the duties of the Commissariat of Labour, and that the methods used to mobilise the Red Army be applied to labour and industry. In essence workers would be treated like soldiers, directed and compelled to go wherever the state decreed and fulfill whatever tasks they were given. The trade unions were not mentioned. Trotsky's proposals became known as the "Militarisation of Labour".

There was an immediate reaction from the unions. Trotsky and Lenin, who whole-heartedly supported the proposals at the time, were shouted down at party and union meetings. Only a minority of People's Commissars—Rykov, Miliutin, Nogin and Tomsky—were opposed. In January 1920 Sovnarcom issued a Decree which laid out general regulations for a universal labour service that would supply all branches of the economy on the basis of a general economic plan. The tenor of the Decree is revealed by an aside to the document, which revealed Sovnarcom now had cause to "regret the destruction of the old police apparatus" because it had "known how to register citizens, not only in towns but also in the country".[4]

On 12th January Lenin and Trotsky attended a meeting of the All-Russian Central Council of Trade Unions (ARCCTU) and urged upon them the general scheme of the militarisation of labour. Of sixty Bolshevik trade union leaders present, only two supported them. The leading Bolshevik trade unionist and Chair of the ARCCTU Mikhail Tomsky argued for the principle of "collective management", i.e. for a co–partnership role for the trade unions and for their right to make and influence managerial decisions. This was as far as leading Bolsheviks could go in overt criticism of Lenin and Trotsky. It was a clear challenge to their authority from the heart of working–class Bolshevism.

The controversy exploded at the Ninth Russian Communist Party Congress, held from 29th March to 4th April, 1920. The Congress debated Tomsky's call for "collegial management" in industry instead of the one–man management favoured by Lenin and Trotsky. Tomsky's proposal argued:

> The basic principle in building the organs for regulating and administering industry, the only one capable of guaranteeing the participation of the broad non–party working masses through the trade unions, is the presently existing principle of the collegial administration of industry, beginning with the Presidium of the Supreme Economic Council and concluding with the plant administration.[5]

The Seventh Congress of Soviets and the Central Trade Union Council had both supported Tomsky's call for collegial management, i.e. for the input and influence of the organised working class. This meant nothing to Lenin. He rejected the idea of collective workers' management as "utopian", "injurious" and "impractical".

Trotsky went even further than Lenin. He completely

rejected the views of the Soviet Congress and the Central Trade Union Council (both of which were dominated by Bolsheviks) and told the Congress:

> Elected collegia, composed of the very best representatives of the working class, but not possessing basic technical knowledge, cannot replace one technician who has gone to a special school and who knows how to handle a given job. Collegial management is an entirely natural reaction of a young, revolutionary, recently oppressed class, which rejects the individual commands of yesterday's masters, bosses, commanders, but this is not the last word on building the state economy of the proletarian class.[6]

Neither Lenin nor Trotsky seem to have considered the option of retaining the technician for technical advice only, whilst an elected collegia of workers gained administrative experience.

Trotsky openly mocked the idea of working-class independence. He bluntly told the Ninth Party Congress, "The working class cannot be left wandering all over Russia. They must be thrown here and there, appointed, commanded, just like soldiers". He added, "Deserters from labour ought to be formed into punitive battalions or put into concentration camps". He called this "the progressive essence of Taylorism".[7]

In *Terrorism and Communism*, written at the time, Trotsky explained his reasoning:

> The young socialist state requires trade unions not for a struggle for better conditions of labour, but to organise the working class

for the ends of production, to educate and discipline [...] to exercise their authority hand in hand with the state in order to lead the workers into the framework of a single economic plan.

He rejected the concept of collective management as "a Menshevik idea". In Diane P. Koenker's estimation, "Trade Union independence was the keystone of the alternative model of labour relations, which was embraced by the Menshevik Party".[8] Despite themselves, a *de facto* alliance between Bolshevik trade unionists and the Menshevik party was now established on the issue.

Lenin backed Trotsky to the hilt. He told the Ninth Party Congress,

The elective principle must be replaced by the principle of selection [...] The trade unions are going to be placed in gigantic difficulties. It is necessary that they approach this task in the spirit of a struggle against the vestiges of the notorious democratic procedures.

After hearing the arguments of those opposing the militarisation of labour and the removal of union democracy, Lenin responded with pure contempt. "All your words are nothing but verbalism pure and simple; 'self activity', the 'rule of appointees', etc.! But when does our centralism come in?"[9]

Despite challenges from a few trade union leaders, there was never any doubt what a party Congress, most of whose delegates were directly chosen by Stalin's Secretariat, would decide. At the close the Congress passed a resolution that decreed "no trade union group should directly intervene in industrial management". It made clear that "Factory Committees should devote themselves to the question of labour discipline, of propaganda and of education of the workers".[10] With this resolution Bolshevik activists who had spent most of 1917 passionately agitating for working-class power at the point of production voted to give it away and to become enforcers for one-man management imposed by the government.

After the Ninth Party Congress Trotsky was put in charge of the Commissariat of Transport (in addition to the War Ministry and Red Army). The railways had all but collapsed in the Civil War. Without them industry would grind to a halt. Trotsky chose to address the problem by re-organising the transport system along military lines. He unilaterally removed the heads of the transport workers' unions and replaced them with a Central Committee for Transport (Tsektran), a strict military-bureaucratic operation. Under Tsektran's edicts the railway network began to function to at least minimal efficiency. Tsektran "worked" in the literal sense – in the sense that Mussolini made the trains run on time. But it did great damage to the morale of Russian workers and the reputation of Soviet power. Its existence was a negation and rejection of any kind of workers' democracy.

With attention focused on Tsektran, few noticed that the Ninth Congress gave the Orgburo, set up the year before, unilateral power to carry out transfers and postings of party members without reference to the Politburo. Although Stalin's power and influence continued to grow, it was Trotsky who appeared to ordinary party members as the epitome of bureaucratic coercion. In 1920 Trotsky conveyed the impression of a brilliant man drunk with power. At the Third All-Russian Congress of Trade Unions held in April he replied to criticisms that his forced labour policy resembled the slavery of the Pharaohs by candidly admitting it. "Is it true that compulsory labour is always unproductive? This is the most wretched and miserable liberal prejudice [...] Compulsory slave labour was in its time a progressive phenomenon". He concluded that "labour, obligatory for the whole country, compulsory for every worker, is the basis of socialism".[11]

He expanded on the subject in a chapter of his *Terrorism and Communism* (1920). After an eloquent demolition of bourgeois moralists who criticised the Bolsheviks for "terrorism" whilst overlooking the terrorism of their own states, Trotsky analysed what he called "Problems on the Organisation of Labour". He lamented that Mensheviks and others "opposed the practical measures of our economic reconstruction" with "bourgeois prejudices and bureaucratic-intellectual scepticism".[12] He openly avowed:

> The only solution of economic difficulties that is correct from the point of view both of principle and of practice is to treat the population of the whole country as the reservoir of necessary labour-power—an almost inexhaustible reservoir—and to introduce strict order into its registration, mobilisation and utilisation.

Trotsky dismissed the "fiction of the freedom of labour" and concluded, "The crown of all this work is Taylorism, in which the elements of the scientific organisation of the process of production are combined with the most concentrated methods of the system of sweating".[13]

Trotsky thus advocated a militarised industrial regime combined with the most concentrated methods of sweated labour that science could devise. Of this grand scheme, unencumbered by democratic checks or trade union counter-power, Maurice Brinton concluded, "Trotsky's philosophy of labour came to underline Stalin's practical labour policy in the Thirties".[14] After Stalin's death a well-thumbed copy of *Terrorism and Communism*, annotated with scribblings of approval, was found among his private papers. The philosophy of labour that Trotsky laid out here was not just a suggested route to rapid industrialisation. It was the *preferred* route to and the foundation of the Soviet Union's future model of industrialisation.

Significantly, the "Workers' Opposition" movement was born from the trade unions. Its prime mover and organiser was the Bolshevik union leader and ex-People's Commissar of Labour Alexander Shliapnikov. He began his political career as an apprentice mechanic in St Petersburg where he was sacked and blacklisted in 1901 for union activities. In 1903 he joined the Bolsheviks and was one of their most important activists, writing articles for Bolshevik journals on trade union and industrial policy. During the war he was one of the main links between the Bolshevik CC abroad and its cadres within Russia. In 1917 he was one of the Bolsheviks' delegates on the Petrograd Soviet Executive. He supported Kamenev and Zinoviev's attempts to prevent the October Insurrection because, like them, he felt it would lead to political isolation and economic disaster. After October he ran the Commissariat of Labour for a year until he resigned the post to fight in the Civil War.

Shliapnikov had an intuitive understanding of the Russian working class that Lenin and Trotsky sorely lacked. He knew full well that the Bolshevik Revolution had disappointed many on the factory floor. After Trotsky's proposals to militarise labour, disappointment turned to anger. The Workers' Opposition reflected that anger. As well as Shliapnikov, it was led by leaders of the Metalworkers' Union Mikhail Vladimirov and Sergei Medvedev, Chairman of the Miners' Union Aleksei Kiselyov, Artillery Industry union leader Alexander Tolokonstev, Chairman of the Textile Workers Union Ivan Kutuzov, and Kirill Orlov, a senior member of the Council of Military Industry and a veteran of the battleship *Potemkin*. The Workers' Opposition argued for more influence and control by trade unions in the direction of industry. This meant a reassertion of workplace and industrial democracy, with the senior levels of the factories, Soviets and party cells all directly elected by the workers and replaceable by them.

The Workers' Opposition was an expression of authentic socialist democracy, but they were still dissenters *within* Bolshevism. They were thus constrained from developing their critique to its logical conclusion, namely that it was the entire basis of the Dictatorship of the Proletariat that led to abuse of power and the death of the Soviets. Martov, though, was not. In October 1920 he was invited to address the Congress of the German USPD in Halle, Germany. This was no ordinary Congress. After the crushing of the Spartacist uprising in January 1919 the German left realigned itself to adapt to the new reality of a German republic presided over by a right-wing SPD. Kautsky and Hilferding's Socialisation Commission had gone nowhere and its leaders resigned in protest. The only left parties who might have carried out its recommendations – the USPD and the KPD – were not in power.

Following the creation of the Comintern in 1919, the KPD affiliated to it and accepted its "21 Conditions". Some of the Conditions, such as support for anti-colonialist movements and opposition to social patriotism, were positive and progressive. Much less so were those which established that the party press must "consistently spread the idea of the Dictatorship of the Proletariat"; that all "reformists and centrists" be removed from party organs; that both legal and illegal work be conducted; that party cells in the army be created; that the party must support the Soviet Union at all times; and that it must conduct "periodic membership purges" to clean out "petit-bourgeois elements". Even in Tsarist Russia, many of the 21 Conditions were irrelevant or inoperative between 1905 and 1917. In 1917 the reason for the eventual triumph of the Bolshevik Party was its freedom to organise and campaign openly and legally. The 21 Conditions thus did not even apply to the country that had seen the triumph of Bolshevism, let alone a bourgeois democracy like Germany.

For the Comintern, and the Bolsheviks who controlled it, the prize was the USPD. Unlike the relatively small KPD it was a mass party of the German working class. It condemned Noske and the SPD but it also stood ready to participate in National Assembly elections and secure as much as it could for German workers from the newly established Weimar

Republic. Between November 1918 and March 1919 the German working class gave its verdict on the two socialist alternatives to the left of the SPD. While the KPD stood aloof in sectarian purity, the USPD attracted 200,000 new members.

In July 1920 it was proposed that the USPD affiliate to the Comintern. Should that happen a mass-based German socialist party with 800,000 members would be working for the overthrow of the German state and its replacement with a Dictatorship of the Proletariat. Despite the election of pro-Comintern radicals Walter Stocker and Curt Meyer to the USPD leadership, the party as a whole was split down the middle on the proposal. Meyer, Stocker and the left wanted to affiliate. Kautsky, Hilferding and others wished to reform the Second International – in their terms, return it to the internationalism it had repudiated in 1914. Still others wished for an alternative between a Third International run by Bolsheviks and a Second International terminally discredited by its collapse into social patriotism. The Halle Congress would debate the proposal to affiliate to the Comintern. There would be two guest speakers from Russia on either side of the question – Martov and Zinoviev.

Martov would speak against the proposal with all the rhetorical and intellectual ability for which he was famous. The Politburo had wanted to deny him permission to attend Halle but Lenin insisted he be allowed to go.[15] Zinoviev, who by 1920 had an international reputation almost on a par with Lenin and Trotsky, would speak for the motion. Second only to Trotsky as the Bolsheviks' supreme orator, Zinoviev was a man of severe personality defects. Unlike Kamenev, Rykov and Shliapnikov, he had not opposed Lenin over the launching of the October Insurrection from political principle. Once it became clear that the Bolsheviks had secured power, Zinoviev instantly morphed into a hardline party boss, notorious for ruthless persecution of socialists with whom shortly before he had wished to form a coalition. Of Zinoviev, Trotsky once quipped, "Luther said, 'Here I stand. I can do no other'. Zinoviev says 'Here I stand. But I can do otherwise'".

By the time of the Halle Congress, Martov was reaching the end of the line with Bolshevism. At the Seventh All-Russian Congress of Soviets in December 1919, the Mensheviks had been allowed to send delegates and speak. Theodore Dan welcomed a "single revolutionary front, in all that concerns the defence of the revolution".[16] Martov, whilst recognising the need to defend the revolution from the Whites and pledging the Mensheviks to do so, read a declaration to the Congress that called for "freedom of the press, of association and of assembly [...] inviolability of the person [...] abolition of executions without trial, of administrative arrests and of official terror". Lenin replied personally, criticising Martov's declaration as "back to bourgeois democracy, and nothing else", and concluding, "When we hear such declarations from people who announce their sympathy with us, we say to ourselves, 'No, both terror and the Cheka are absolutely indispensable'".[17]

Throughout 1920 the Mensheviks were allowed to hold meetings and print newspapers—in May a British Labour Party delegation to Soviet Russia was allowed to talk to leading Mensheviks and even attend their Central Committee meeting—but this freedom was constantly impinged. Their offices were frequently raided by the Cheka and their officials arrested. Their last industrial stronghold, the Moscow Branch of the Printers Union, was slowly squeezed into submission. When the British delegation visited Moscow, the board of the union exploited the brief slackening of control to call a "General Meeting" of printers, at which the union leader Kefali launched a blistering attack on the government. Far worse, the board arranged for SR leader Victor Chernov – a wanted fugitive – to come out of hiding and address the mass meeting. He received a rapturous welcome. Although the Cheka descended and many members of the board were arrested, the print shops remained covert Menshevik sympathisers well into the 1920s.

The Eighth All-Russian Soviet Congress of December 1920 was the last that Mensheviks were allowed to officially attend, and even then they were denied voting rights. Dan told the congress that with the stifling of popular initiative, "the whole system of Soviet democracy has ceased to function except as a mere façade for one-party dictatorship".[18] The brief opening to a "socialist opposition" promised in late 1918 had slammed shut. The debate between Martov and Zinoviev at Halle therefore represented two different philosophies of socialism and democracy. As Ben Lewis says in his invaluable study of Halle, "It was here, in the furor of partisan cheering and electrifying speeches, cut and thrust polemics and killer points, that the fate of the German, and perhaps the International workers' movement, was fought out".[19]

Zinoviev began by attacking his opponents for propping up the bourgeois order. "Who is saving the bourgeoisie?" he asked. "The so-called social democrats!" He excoriated

Millerand in France, Branting in Sweden and Modigliani in
Italy as betrayers of revolutionary socialists who would have
overthrown capitalism if not sabotaged by parliamentary
maneuvers. By contrast, he said, "The International does not
wish to be anything else but the leader of world revolution".
He admitted the struggle to create socialism in a shattered
war-torn country had been more difficult than the Bolsheviks
had imagined:

> Previously we studied socialism in books. We thought it could
> come about more easily. We had spoken of the concentration of
> capital, of the development of the productive forces. Everything
> would go forwards; electricity, nice houses etc. We thought we
> could bring the bourgeoisie to its knees through one strike and
> that everything would fall into our laps [...] Now, comrades, it
> hasn't turned out like this, history is taking other paths.

Having gained sympathy for an honest admission of
difficulties, Zinoviev, knowing the USPD had arisen from
the work of the Zimmerwald Union, compared the new
Comintern to Zimmerwald and suggested that from these
beginnings grew real revolutionary change. He finished by
rejecting the theoretical version of the Dictatorship of the
Proletariat in the SPD's Erfurt Programme, and asked, "But
we want you to tell us whether you are for the Dictatorship
of the Proletariat in the actual, real sense – already initiated
by the German working class in the January Days and by the
Hungarian working class". If so, Zinoviev offered the USPD
and the KPD and other Marxist groupings a place in a "United
Communist Party" fighting for proletarian revolution within

the Comintern.[20] It was a spectacular, seductive prospect.

Martov replied the next day. He attacked Zinoviev's contention that the choice before the Congress was that between revolution and reform. He told the delegates:

> Communist Bolshevism attempts in demagogic fashion to take advantage of the masses' feelings of despair and their elemental indignation, in order to arrive at social revolution at top speed. If the reformist faith, knocked to pieces by the war, manages to be reborn among the worker masses of Europe and America, due to a series of heavy defeats for the proletariat – for example, Finland, Hungary, Bavaria – the entire historical responsibility will be borne by Bolshevism.

He asserted that "the Third International was formed to unify a series of communist parties and sects around the Russian Soviet state". He asked the USPD to assess the record of that state:

> The question is not whether the repression of the Soviet government is a response to the counter-revolutionary actions of its enemies. Rather, the question is this: is it permissible for a socialist party to apply terror, that is, a policy of inspiring fear […] by the indiscriminate murder of the guilty and the innocent?

He laid out starkly the system of mass arrests, prohibition of the press and assembly, regular punishment and imprisonment for strikes, and denial of voting rights in the Soviets. At the close he declared:

Someday the time will come when it will be acknowledged that the highest glory of the Russian proletariat is the fact that, in a time when a utopian psychosis of a completely religious type dominates the socially backward masses, when anyone who dares a word of criticism risks lynching, when so many professional politicians, of the sort well known to you, bravely keep their mouths shut [...] there will still be found in Russia simple workers who have gone through years in Tsarist prisons, who are fathers of families, who, despite everything, despite the unheard-of measures of repression, will use Marxist methods to counter-balance the utopian madness and who have one answer to the terrorist threats: such is my conviction and I can do no other.[21]

The result of the vote was never really in doubt. The Bolsheviks and their sympathisers in the USPD and KPD were far better organised than their opponents. Zinoviev came wrapped in the romantic mythology of a socialist revolution fighting for its life against White armies and imperialist intervention. And although Martov himself argued for a new International, shorn of the Second International's social patriotism, that alternative did not actually exist. The Third International did. For these reasons the vote was 234 for a merger with the KPD and affiliation to the Comintern, and 158 against. When the result was announced the minority walked out and the USPD split down the middle.

The result appeared a clear triumph for Bolshevism over Menshevism, but it was a pyrrhic victory. It divided the largest radical socialist party of Germany and weakened both sides. On one side stood the new United Communist Party of Germany with its affiliation to the Comintern, whose political strategies led ultimately to the catastrophe of 1933 and Hitler's destruction of the entire German left. On the other the remains of the USPD rejoined the SPD and thus lost the radicalism that had distinguished it from its tired, morally compromised parent. Martov's "third way" – rejection of sectarian Leninism and formation of a new International not beholden to Moscow – was a road never taken.

The lamentable record of the SPD throughout the 1920s led to the eventual fall of the Weimar Republic. But the new German Communist Party played a role in driving the SPD down this road. In March 1921 it called a General Strike across Germany known as the "March Action". The KPD called for workers to arm themselves. Its daily paper's headline was, "Who is not with us is against us!" Excited by Zinoviev's rhetoric and the vision of October, it assumed mass working-class support which did not exist. Chris Harman's history of Germany in the crucial years from 1918 to 1923 admits that "the Communist Party leadership completely misjudged what was happening", and that "the class would not move".[22]

Even in Berlin, where the KPD secured 200,000 votes the year before, the strike stalled. A mass demonstration in Hamburg tried to seize the docks, giving the government the excuse to impose a State of Emergency. When SPD workers in Berlin's Krupp Works refused to heed the strike call, the KPD sent in unemployed supporters to physically eject workers from the premises. Fights broke out between SPD workers and KPD thugs. The result was the total collapse of the strike and the resignation of half the KPD's membership.

Despite this, Ben Lewis concludes that of the two main antagonists at Halle it was Zinoviev who had the best long-term strategy for the German left, and Martov who lacked a viable plan. But Martov did have a plan—establish and build a radical democratic socialist party, like the USPD before the split, to effect a socialist transition. We cannot know if it would have been successful, other than the successful introduction of a progressive and comprehensive welfare state, run in conjunction with the SPD and major German trade unions, after the defeat of Nazism in 1945. Conversely, we *do* know that the KPD was totally unsuccessful. Firstly, in its failure to stop the triumph of the Nazis, a failure that arose in great part from the tactics forced upon it by the Comintern. Secondly, that when it had a monopoly of state power handed to it by the Red Army in 1945, it proceeded to construct in East Germany a repressive police state that replicated the Soviet model.

Martov was not allowed to return to Russia. He settled in Berlin where he continued to write and campaign for his version of democratic socialism. He died of tuberculosis in 1923, aged 47. Although most of his writings on Marxism and the Russian Revolution remain untranslated, his major essays, particularly those written between 1919 and 1923, were translated and collated together as *The State and Socialist Revolution*, published in 1939.[23] These essays eloquently sum up his analysis of the Bolshevik Revolution and why, for him, it had strayed so far from the rationalistic, democratic Marxism which he practiced all his political life.

Martov felt that Russia in 1917 possessed neither

the economic base, nor the social structure, nor the mature working class necessary for a successful socialist transformation. In *The State and Socialist Revolution,* he wrote, "No less than mystic is the concept of a political form that, by virtue of its particular character, can surmount all economic, social and national conditions". The "political form" was the Bolshevik Party and the Dictatorship of the Proletariat. Martov's characterisation of these as essentially "mystic", i.e. a cocktail of utopian desire and adventurism lacking solid plans for creating a socialist society and likely to degenerate into its opposite, is a judgment supported by history.

Yet even Martov's sympathetic biographer Israel Getzler concluded of his political life, "Martov failed". In one obvious sense this is true. The Menshevik Party did not emerge, as the Bolsheviks did, as the victor in the struggle for state power. But it was not trying to achieve the same thing as Bolshevism. In Menshevism Martov tried to develop a political form that would provide the working class of Russia with the self-confidence and knowledge to transform capitalism into a more civilised and equitable society. He shared many of the intellectual weaknesses of 19th-century Marxists like Kautsky. He also failed to perceive that the state-led, productivist socialism of the Mensheviks had much in common with that of the Bolsheviks, although he supported policies such as mutualism in land ownership that were more democratic and inclusive. On the whole, though, his failure to think beyond the accepted Marxist categories, to merge Left Menshevism with other strands of democratic activism seen in the Factory Committees and a variety of anarchist-inspired social experiments, was a material reason for its eclipse.

One thing remains unarguable. For all his political inadequacies and strategic mistakes, since 1903 Martov had stood utterly opposed to Lenin's concept of socialism—of vanguardism, substitutionism and one-party rule imposed by violence and repression. He did so without reneging on radical socialism, and provided an inspiring example of political principle and personal integrity in the midst of war and social breakdown. If political leaders are to be judged by the intent, outcome and legacy of their work, then it was Lenin who failed, and disastrously. By this criteria Martov also failed—although as Orwell wrote posthumously of Gandhi, compared to his political contemporaries "how clean a smell he has managed to leave behind".[24]

CHAPTER SEVENTEEN

National Bolshevism

By 1921 the threat of White counter-revolution had been defeated and all foreign expeditionary forces in Soviet Russia had been withdrawn. After six years of war and Civil War the Russian economy was on its knees. Its transport infrastructure barely existed. Taking the last full year of peace, 1913, as the base, industrial production was down 80% by 1920. Production of coal had fallen 73%, textiles 62% and cast iron an incredible 97.5% (this was mainly due to the loss throughout most of 1917-20 of the coal, iron and steel that used to come from southern Russia). As the Civil War ended the Red Army demobilised, which led to two and a half million men with military experience returning to the villages. Rural uprisings were spreading, often led by trained soldier-peasants.

In early 1920 the brutality of the Grain Requisition Squads led to a mass peasant rebellion in the Tambov province. Led by the charismatic Left SR Alexander Antonov, the revolt involved over 50,000 peasants and spread rapidly to Samara, Tsaritsyn, Saratov and parts of Siberia. With the Red Army engaged in the Soviet-Polish War in an attempt to force Soviet power on unwilling Polish workers and peasants, it could not direct enough men to Tambov to force it on unwilling Russian workers and peasants. The rebellion took a year to suppress. Even then the Red Army had to use chemical weapons and a chain of concentration camps to re-impose Sovnarcom's authority in the region.[1]

Tambov was the flashpoint of a massive, simmering crisis across all Soviet-held territory. When the crop failed in 1920 there were no surplus stores to fall back on and famine re-emerged for the first time in thirty years. People left the cities to try to find food in the country. The population of Petrograd plummeted from 2,400,000 in 1917 to 574,000 in 1920. Of the winter of 1920-21, Victor Serge recorded:

> Winter was a torture for the townspeople: no heating, no lighting, and the ravages of famine. Children and feeble old folk died in their thousands [...] Inside Petrograds' grand apartments, now abandoned, people were crowded in one room, living on top of one another around a little stove of brick or cast iron, its flue belching smoke through an opening in the window. Fuel for it would come from the floorboards of rooms nearby, from the last stick of furniture, or else from books [...] People dined on a pittance of oatmeal or half-rotten horsemeat. The local Commune did everything it could to keep the children fed, but what it managed was pitiful.[2]

From 1917 to 1921 the population of Soviet Russia's major cities fell by an average of 33%, although Petrograd was a large part of that average. The number of the industrial working class – the ostensible basis of the Soviet regime – also fell. Tens of thousands of workers were killed in the Civil War. Many joined the Communist Party and were promoted into the administration. In 1921 the total number of the industrial working class actually engaged in industry had fallen from 3,024,000 in 1917 to 1,243,000, and these were increasingly resistant to the orders of the Bolshevik government. At the same time as mass peasant revolts broke out in Tambov, Samara, Penza, Belorussia and western Siberia, a wave of strikes erupted in Moscow and Petrograd. Sovnarcom's greatest fear was that sooner or later working-class and peasant opposition to War Communism would unite.

Sovnarcom also had to grapple, as had the Provisional Government, with the desire of Imperial Russia's "territories" for independence. In June 1917 Lenin had condemned the Provisional Government for not carrying out its "elementary democratic duty" and providing for "the autonomy and complete freedom of secession of Ukraine".[3] On 2nd November, 1917 Sovnarcom's "Declaration of Rights of the Peoples of Russia" established its nationalities policy. Its key principle was "The right of the peoples of Russia to free self-determination, up to secession and formation of an independent state". It added, "Concrete decrees stemming herefrom will be worked out immediately after the establishment of the Commission for the Affairs of Nationalities". It was signed by Lenin and the People's Commissar for Nationalities Affairs, J.V. Stalin.[4]

After the Ukrainian People's Republic declared independence in January 1918, several political factions fought for control. Following the overthrow of Hetman Skoropadsky and the defeat of Deniken's White Army – victories won in great part by Makhno's anarchist army – the People's Republic of Ukraine was re-established, along with the Free Territories of the Mahknovshchina. But the Bolsheviks had no time for either. With Deniken defeated the Red Army invaded Ukraine in full force. On 21st November, 1919 the Politburo discussed "theses" put to it by Lenin which established policy for the occupation of Ukraine. These mandated that Ukrainian ethnic traditions and language should be respected and that new structures should be created in the country to "intensify work on the class differentiation of the village".

Lenin had learnt from the first attempt to create Poor Peasants Committees. Accepting that the dubious category of "middle peasants" hardly existed, he stressed that food should be redistributed to poorer peasants only at the expense of the very richest Kulaks, and that fewer surpluses than usual be taken. But the relatively lenient approach to the Ukrainian villages was solely to create a base of peasant support for political action in the towns. Thesis 7 stated, "Treat the Jews and urban inhabitants of the Ukraine with an iron rod, transferring them to the front, not letting them into government agencies" (in the margin, next to "Jews", Lenin noted "Express it politely – Jewish petty bourgeoisie"). Thesis 8 said, "Place the Teachers Union, the cooperatives, and other such petty bourgeois organisations in the Ukraine under special surveillance, with special measures for their disintegration".[5]

By this process Ukrainian nationalist organisations, especially in Kiev, were "disintegrated" and replaced with specially bribed poor peasants and trained party cadres. The exclusion of Jews from Ukrainian government organs was partly because they were the most likely to play significant roles in nationalist organisations, partly to appease the notorious anti-Semitism of Ukrainian peasants. Even Makhno's forces, committed to genuine social liberation, were not immune from anti-Semitism, although Makhno took stern measures to eradicate it from the *Makhnovischina*, which in comparison to the rest of Ukraine was a relative haven for Jews.

He and his Revolutionary Council issued numerous proclamations and orders against anti-Semitism. If soldiers under his command committed anti-Jewish outrages, Makhno had them swiftly arrested and executed no matter their rank or record. There is no truth in later Soviet propaganda about Makhnovist anti-Semitic pogroms, and overwhelming evidence to refute it. Many of Makhno's leading advisors and publicists, such as Voline and Baron, were themselves Jewish, reflecting his own lack of native prejudice. Unlike Lenin he did not pander to Ukrainian anti-Semitism but confronted it head on, instructing his Cultural-Educational Commission to conduct teaching seminars with peasant supporters to explain the basic principles of internationalism and anarchist humanism.[6]

Although the Ukrainian army, aided by Makhno in the south, fought an intermittent war with the Red Army from late 1919 to late 1920, by mid-1921 it had been defeated. In 1922 the Ukrainian Soviet Socialist Republic was admitted to the USSR as a "sovereign" state. The level of sovereignty was demonstrated in the 1930s when Stalin's mass collectivisation policy led to the "Holodomor", or "Hunger-Extermination", of between three and seven million Ukrainian peasants, a policy now regarded as a genocide inflicted on Ukraine in order to crush the last vestiges of national independence. Following the Holodomor, many Ukrainian nationalist leaders were executed in the Great Terror of 1936–38.

Poland might have gone the same way, except that in Josef Pilsudski Polish nationalism had a leader as ruthless and determined as Lenin. Since 1895 Pilsudski had been leader of the Polish Socialist Party (PSP). The PSP did not shrink from using paramilitary forces to achieve its goal of national liberation. At the outbreak of war in 1914, Pilsudski took the Polish Legion to fight for Austria and Germany against Russia. In November 1918 he was appointed Commander-in-Chief of Polish forces and promptly declared an independent Poland. Although his government introduced progressive social reforms, it was primarily a nationalist coalition and it was as a nationalist force that it fought the Polish-Soviet War. After the fall of Ukraine to the Red Army, Pilsudski formed an alliance with Ukrainian nationalist leader Petliura. In May 1920 Polish-Ukrainian forces under Pilsudski's command invaded Ukraine and took Kiev. The response inside Soviet Russia was immediate. Many non-political Russian patriots such as General Brusilov joined the Red Army in order to repel Catholic Poland from "Little Russia", whose capital Kiev was regarded as the cradle of Russian civilisation.

It was the beginning of a new conservative movement labeled "National Bolshevism", in which Russian patriots, after the undeniable and total defeat of the Whites, rallied behind Sovnarcom and the Red Army as the force most likely to re-establish Great Russia and its Empire. Its two most prominent figures were Brusilov and Nikolai Ustrialov, a Slavophile intellectual who had been a right-wing Kadet fighting for Kolchak before he sensed which way the wind was blowing and defected to the Bolsheviks. In 1920 he wrote, with some prescience, "The Bolsheviks, by the logic of events, will progress from Jacobinism to Napoleanism".[7]

Ustrialov influenced other Slavophiles who saw beyond the surface rhetoric of the Dictatorship of the Proletariat to its more enduring features – a professional army, a political police and a strong centralised state. Although Ustrialov himself never achieved the position he sought, his ideas took hold. After Lenin's death Stalin's conception of "Socialism in One Country", with the inevitable national pride that accompanied it, reflected many of the themes of National Bolshevism and secured the support of Ustrialov's illustrious followers Aleksei Tolstoy and Ilya Ehrenburg.

The Red Army counter-attack ejected the Poles from Kiev and Ukraine, after which Lenin, against the views of both Trotsky and Stalin, ordered a swift advance on Warsaw. He dreamed of the Red Army implanting Soviet socialism in Poland and thereby establishing a bridgehead to Germany. Behind the Red Army stood a "Provisional Polish Revolutionary Committee" headed by Head of the Cheka and native Pole Felix Dzerzhinsky. This would be the core of a new Polish government, a Polish Sovnarcom, from which bourgeois nationalists and democratic socialists would be excluded.

But Dzerzhinsky never got the chance to line up his firing squads. Although the Red Army, under its brilliant young commander General Tukhachevsky, advanced quickly into Poland and reached the outskirts of Warsaw, it had over-extended its supply lines. More importantly there was no welcome for them from the Polish working class, who preferred Pilsudski's socialist nationalism to a Soviet state imposed on them by the Red Army and the Cheka. In an unexpected reverse known to Poles as "the Miracle on the Vistula", on 16th August, 1920 Pilsudski counter-attacked from the south and defeated the larger Red Army, forcing a rapid retreat.

The campaigns against Ukraine and Poland revived the sleeping virus of militaristic nationalism within Soviet Russia. It would gradually begin to define the entire system. From 1921 it was the Red Army, not ranks of factory workers, who led major ceremonial parades in Moscow and Petrograd, "thus signaling a certain heroic and moral hegemony of the armed forces over civilian society".[8] After Lenin's death in January 1924, the trend to transform revolutionary leaders into revered nationalistic symbols took off in style with the 1924 May Day procession in Moscow. Rows of tanks and troops filed past Lenin's recently constructed tomb, in which lay his embalmed corpse, whilst a squadron of airplanes flew overhead. In 1941, when the Nazis invaded the Soviet Union, Stalin would unambiguously call on Soviet citizens to fight a "Great Patriotic War". The subsequent post-war expansion of Soviet power into Eastern Europe under the Warsaw Pact was a source of nationalistic pride to many Russians, especially the state elite, most of whom by the 1950s and 1960s could be described as National Bolsheviks.

With the close of the Civil War and the Polish–Soviet War Sovnarcom turned its attention to establishing Soviet

Republics in the west (Latvia, Estonia and Lithuania), in Transcaucasia (Armenia, Azerbaijan and Georgia) and in the eastern borderlands and Central Asia. The "Conference of the Peoples of the East", held at Baku in Azerbaijan in September 1920, opened up a new phase of Bolshevik policy towards former colonial possessions. The Conference was called by the Comintern and was attended by 1,900 representatives of Communist and anti-colonial parties from Persia, Turkey, Armenia, Azerbaijan, Georgia, Chechnya, and a variety of central Asian regions. It was addressed by Zinoviev, Radek, Bela Kun and John Reed. The "Manifesto of the Peoples of the East" adopted at the conference was intended mainly for the ears of Indian and other independence movements struggling against Western imperialist powers. It had less application to the USSR's own subject territories, as the fate of the independent Republic of Georgia testified.

The Democratic Republic of Georgia was created in May 1918 when Georgia availed itself of Sovnarcom's right of national self-determination and declared independence. In national elections held in February 1919 the Georgian RSDLP (i.e. the Mensheviks) won 81% of the vote and proceeded to establish a democratic socialist republic. Georgia's Menshevik government rejected the Bolshevik route to socialism. It held multi-party elections. It allowed a free press and independent trade unions. The Mensheviks implemented in Georgia the land policy they had not had the chance to apply in Russia due to their minority status within the Provisional Government before October 1917, and the dissolution of the Constituent Assembly after it. The Georgian government broke up large estates and allowed Georgian peasants to buy up plots at generous prices. It also introduced the kind of progressive labour reforms that had gained Pilsudski the loyalty of Polish workers, and with the same result. In its brief life the Democratic Republic of Georgia secured the support of Georgian peasants and most of the working class of Tiflis.

In April 1920 Georgian Bolsheviks, following tactics successful in Armenia and Azerbaijan, attempted a coup in Tiflis that was intended to act as the pretext for the Red Army to invade Georgia to liberate its workers. But the coup had virtually no internal support and was easily defeated. Ronald G. Suny's examination of the Georgian Menshevik government concludes that the reason the Mensheviks secured the loyalty of a majority of the population was because they adopted an approach entirely different from that of the Bolsheviks in Russia, which was "to mediate rather than intensify social conflicts, to keep as open as possible a political forum, both in the press and in elected institutions, and to use force minimally".[9]

The independent Republic of Georgia had wide support on the international left. This was one reason why Sovnarcom signed the Treaty of Moscow in May 1920 with the Georgian government, guaranteeing its independence. Despite this, senior officials of Stalin's Nationalities Commissariat in the Caucasus, including his friend and sidekick Sergei Ordzhonikidze, continued to plan a coup in Georgia. Although Trotsky was strongly opposed to this, he was in a minority of one on the Politburo. The majority feeling was that the existence of a viable, popular democratic socialist government led by the Menshevik

Party on Russia's doorstep was intolerable.

Stalin and Ordzhonikidze continued to work covertly with Georgian Bolsheviks to stage a series of "uprisings" in outlying Georgian towns in early 1921, and give Moscow a pretext to intervene. On 14th February the Central Committee met and approved an invasion, with only Karl Radek dissenting. Trotsky, away at the time, was not informed of the meeting by the Secretariat. With the excuse that it was coming to the aid of Georgian workers, the Red Army invaded on 16th February. Trotsky was not even told the operation was about to commence. The small Georgian army, with the support of most of the Georgian working class, resisted the invading force for a fortnight, but it stood no chance against the much bigger Red Army.

The social and political system subsequently imposed upon Georgia was so severe that on 7th August, 1921 an appeal was issued signed by 3,449 Georgian workers, titled "The Appeal of the Tiflis Workers to All the Workers of Western Europe". It read:

> From the very first days Georgia was conquered, we were placed in the position of and treated as slaves. We were deprived of freedom of speech, assembly and the right of free association. A regime of military labour service has been imposed upon all the workers of Georgia, irrespective of their occupation. Everywhere Extraordinary Committees (Chekas) have been set up and summary arrests of workers for innocuous remarks have been taking place.

After cataloging the oppression being visited upon Georgian

workers, the Appeal finished by proclaiming:

> Human life has become of no value. Innocent people are shot,
> even those who never mixed into politics, who never took
> part in any political struggle. People were shot because they
> served the democratic government and the state, because in
> open war they defended their native country from the invasion
> of foreign troops.[10]

The Western powers who intervened in Soviet Russia
to assist the Whites greeted the suppression of a democratic
socialist republic in Georgia with indifference. Karl Kautsky,
who visited Georgia in late 1920 for three months, spoke for
the democratic left with his book *Georgia: A Social-Democratic
Peasant Republic: Impressions and Observations* (1921). Despite
the immense difficulties under which it laboured – Georgia
was at roughly the same level of social and economic
development as Russia in 1917 – Kautsky was impressed with
the efforts of the Georgian Mensheviks to effect a social
revolution: "It was left for the revolution to take the land
from the feudal nobles, to provide the poor peasant with land,
and to change the leaseholder into a freeholder. This was no
socialistic but a middle-class revolution, but the conditions
rendered it necessary, and it took place". In Kautsky's view,
the course of the Georgian Revolution confirmed that the
entire political and economic programme of the Bolsheviks
was premature and excessive and could not be imposed
except by state coercion.

By contrast the Georgian Revolution, which did not
shrink from expropriating all large landowners' estates,

proceeded to create a mixed economy of peasant small holdings with state-owned enterprises, overseen by the state and local municipalities. The main strategic industries were nationalised with about a third of the economy left in private hands. A new economy of consumers' and workers' cooperatives was introduced to provide the space for different forms of ownership and economic management. Suggesting a slower but more practical route to socialism, not unlike that of Venezuela's Solidaristic Economy, Kautsky suggested, "In those spheres where the monopolistic character of capital has scarcely made itself felt, the production carried on by organisations of consumers can create socialistic conditions of production, if these consumers' organisations are dominated by the socialist outlook".

Kautsky ended by considering what the invasion meant for future socialist progress. He drew a parallel between the corruption of the Russian Revolution by the Bolsheviks and the degradation of the French Revolution by Napoleon:

The close parallel which exists between the course which the Russian Revolution has hitherto followed and that of the great French Revolution must not blind us to the differences between the two events [...] Although French Bonapartism constituted a strong reaction from the Republic, its policy of expansion brought many improvements to the rest of Europe. The present Moscow Bonapartism is not only reactionary in relation to the proletarian revolution of Russia, out of which it arose, but even more so in comparison with the proletarian movements of the rest of Europe, which it seeks to fetter.[11]

Within a few years Trotsky would advance the concept that in the 1920s Soviet Russia had undergone a form of "Thermidor" (the period of the French Revolution in which the conservative Thermidorians ousted Robespierre and the Jacobins, presaging the emergence of Bonapartism) as an explanation of the rise of the Stalinist bureaucracy. It was therefore no small irony that Trotsky was given the task of responding to Kautsky. The resulting work, *Between Red and White: Social Democracy and the Wars of Intervention* (1922), was not his finest. Most of *Red and White* avoids the question of the nature and policies of the Menshevik regime and the extent of its support by the Georgian working class. It concentrates instead on the wider canvass of foreign intervention in the Russian Civil War and the hypocrisy of social democrats like Henderson or Vandevelde to criticise the Soviet Union and the Third International. It was a dazzling display of intellectual pyrotechnics, but in a bad cause, and Trotsky knew it.

The attempted military expansion of the Revolution, whether in the form of the march on Warsaw, the revolutionary proclamations made at Baku, or the invasion of Georgia, was partly to offset its complete collapse at home. Many working-class activists were now bitter and disenchanted. As soon as she arrived in Petrograd in early 1920, Emma Goldman escaped her official Soviet minders and went in search of the real Russian working class. Taken at night to a secret meeting of Petrograd's few surviving anarchists, she heard "a recital of the betrayal of the revolution by the Bolsheviki". She reported that:

Workers from the Baltic factories spoke of their enslavement, Kronstadt sailors voiced their bitterness and indignation against the people they had helped to power and who had become their masters. One of the speakers had been condemned to death by the Bolsheviki for his anarchist ideas, but had escaped and was now living illegally. He related how the sailors had been robbed of the freedom of their Soviets, how every breath of life was being censored.[12]

Goldman initially refused to believe this. After travelling around Soviet Russia and encountering crushed Soviets and persecuted Mensheviks and anarchists, she returned to Petrograd in late 1920 to find disillusion had spread to her friends in the Communist Party itself. "Whenever they called on me they repeated their determination to get out of the party", she recorded. "They were suffocating in an atmosphere of intrigue, blind hatred and persecution". When she visited the headquarters of Sovnarcom, she recalled her "surprise on finding there were two separate restaurants in Smolny, one where wholesome and sufficient food was served to important members of the Petrograd Soviet and the Third International, while the other was for the ordinary employees of the party".[13] This was no freak occurrence. In 1919, when workers at the nationalised print shop of Ostrogozhsk in Voronezh complained about loss of back pay and lay-offs at the plant without explanation or reason, the Chair of the town's Revolutionary Committee responded, "Shoot every tenth man, and the rest will be silent".[14]

This was the social reality that created the Workers' Opposition. The chasm between ordinary workers on one side and Sovnarcom officials on the other grew wider and wider. Jonathan Aves records that "in the first six months of 1920 strikes had occurred in 77% of middle-sized and large works", and finds that these strikes were a direct protest against "intensification of War Communist labour policies, the militarisation of labour, the implementation of one-man management, as well as food supply difficulties".[15] In her study of militant Russian printers, Koenker concluded that the division between "productivists" and "workerists" ran right through the working class, "shattering the class-based sense of purpose that had contributed to the Communists' victory in October 1917".[16]

All these undercurrents exploded at the Tenth Party Congress, 8th-16th March 1921. The touchpaper was lit by the publication on 25th January of the Workers' Opposition "Theses on the Trade Union Question", followed in March, on the very eve of the Congress, by the "Platform of the Workers' Opposition". The platform was written by Alexandra Kollontai, the only member of Sovnarcom to take an explicit stand with the Opposition. Even before the publication of its programme, Lenin called the Workers' Opposition "the greatest danger to our continued existence". On 21st January he wrote in *Pravda*:

We must combat the ideological confusion of those unsound elements of the opposition who go the lengths of repudiating all militarisation of the economy, of repudiating not only the method of appointing, which has been the prevailing method up to now, but *all* appointments. In the last analysis this means repudiating the leading role of the party in relation to the non-party masses.

What most worried Lenin was that the Opposition was not a faction of left intellectuals based around a low-circulation newspaper. It was led by senior Bolshevik trade unionists and it had strong working-class support in the Metal Workers Union, the Printers Union, the miners of the Kuban and Donetz Basin regions, and swathes of the engineering and railway industries. In Samara the Workers' Opposition actually controlled the local party. In Moscow most members supported it, although they were kept out of official positions. The challenge came from those supposed to be the bedrock of the regime.

The Theses on the Trade Union Question was submitted to the Tenth Party Congress as the basis for general debate, although it ranged beyond just the issue of the role of the unions. Kollontai, whose libertarian political philosophy had deeply influenced the work of the Zhendotel, was already regarded with suspicion by hardline Leninists. Nonetheless her status within the party was high. She had forged a new path in a vital area of social revolution, had written groundbreaking works of Marxist feminist theory, and was married to ex-Commissar for the Navy and legendary Red Army commander Pavel Dybenko.[17] An organised grouping led by her and Shliapnikov was a serious threat.

Kollontai's pamphlet disposed of the idea that the only matter at issue was the role of the trade unions: "The break goes deeper". Having explained that it intended to focus on "cardinal political and economic questions", it criticised the role and privileges of the "specialists" within industry, and the departure from collective management for one-man management. In a section titled "Who has gained from the revolution?", Kollontai answered that the peasants gained directly from land redistribution and the bourgeoisie managed to adjust itself to the new government by claiming specialist knowledge that needed to be protected, but the workers had not seen any benefit. She dismissed the view of Lenin and Bukharin that the trade unions should be "schools of communism" and a "transmission belt" for instructions from the state to the workers, even though this was a step back from Trotsky's proposals for the militarisation of labour.

Kollontai explained that the Workers' Opposition wished to form a body made from the workers themselves to administer what she called "the peoples' economy". This should be overseen by trade unions working in conjunction with elected Factory Committees. In itself this was not a departure from the initial programme for industry advanced by Sovnarcom immediately after October 1917. It was not an anarcho-syndicalist programme or one that advocated the independence of autonomous workers' committees at plant level, even if these were linked together in a federated structure to ensure coordinated national production. But in the context of 1921 it was a loud call for more socialist democracy.

Even more so was the demand that the "elective principle"—the principle scorned by Trotsky in the Red Army and Tsektran but supported by Lunacharsky in education—be re-established "at every level" and that it replace the system of appointment by which the Orgburo had established its grip on the party. Kollontai finished with a call for political initiative and activity to once again reside with he working class:

> Finally, the Workers' Opposition has raised its voice against bureaucracy. It has dared to say that bureaucracy binds the wings of self-activity and creativeness of the working class; that it deadens thought, hinders initiative and experimenting in the sphere of finding new approaches to production – in a word that it hinders the development of new forms of production and life.[18]

Lenin, who in a crisis could be more tactically adroit than Trotsky, had already sensed that the proposals advanced by Trotsky, Dzerzhinsky and Bukharin to militarise labour and impose new leaders on trade unions were providing the Workers' Opposition with ammunition to attack the government. Trotsky argued that his proposals flowed from the nature of the Soviet state and had been endorsed by Lenin and the Politburo. He described any objections as a "manifestation of Kautskyian-Menshevik-SR prejudices".[19] But Lenin now backed off. He looked for a middle course between Trotsky and the Workers' Opposition, one which would restrain the former and undermine the latter. He therefore proposed the "Platform of the Ten" (the ten being Lenin, Zinoviev, Kamenev, Tomsky, Stalin, Kalinin, Lozovsky, Radzutak, Petrovsky and Artem). Whilst the Platform reiterated the need for one-man management and privileges for specialists, it stressed that the unions still needed to fulfill their function of protecting and representing workers.

In a speech on 30th December, 1920, published as "The

Trade Unions, the Present Situation and Trotsky's Mistakes",
Lenin said that the trade unions were

> an organisation of the ruling, dominant, governing class, which
> has now set up a dictatorship and is exercising coercion through
> the state. But it is not a state organisation; nor is it one designed
> for coercion, but for education. It is an organisation designed
> to draw in and to train; it is, in fact, a school: a school of
> administration, a school of economic management, a school
> of communication.[20]

This reserved for the unions a particular role and gave
them some latitude to implement it, but it was a far cry
from the economic democracy for which the Workers'
Opposition was arguing.

The Workers' Opposition never stood a chance. The
Control Commission which organised party congresses was
overseen by the Orgburo, run by Stalin. His apparatchiks
instructed local party officials to send only Lenin-loyalists
to the Congress, despite the sympathy for the Opposition
amongst the rank and file. At a conference of the large
Moscow branch of the party held in November 1920,
124 delegates out of 278 openly declared support for the
Opposition (more would have done so if not for immense
pressure from the leadership), which probably reflected the
level of support across the whole party. Yet at the Tenth
Party Congress there were only about 50 pro-Opposition
delegates out of a total of 694.[21]

The Congress was conducted in "an atmosphere of near-
hysteria"[22] in which Opposition speakers were shouted down.

Trotsky, sensing he had lost on the main proposals, turned his fire on the Opposition's calls for more internal democracy and a loosening of party control. It was here that he slated the Opposition for making a "fetish of democratic principle" and said it had "placed the workers' right to elect representatives above the party", something that was deplorable given the workers' "transitory mood".

The Workers' Opposition platform did not explicitly criticise one-party rule, but that criticism was implicit in its strictures on unaccountable, undemocratic power. As Robert Daniels's classic work on "Communist Opposition" within the Bolshevik/Communist Party put it, "Their programme of unfettered democracy and control of the economy by an 'association of producers' would mean an attempt at immediate introduction of the forms of social organisation which in 1917 the revolutionaries had generally agreed upon as the ultimate institutions of the communist society".[23] But this was not 1917. Mass strikes, the heckling of Bolshevik leaders at trade union meetings, and the uprising at Kronstadt – all this, Lenin knew, was a submerged iceberg of discontent within the party.

Lenin and many other speakers therefore launched a savage attack on the Opposition, especially Shliapnikov and Kollontai. It was only on the first morning of the Congress that Lenin obtained a copy of Kollontai's pamphlet, and he read it as he came in and sat down. "I hurriedly distribute my pamphlet", Kollontai wrote later in her diary:

The atmosphere is tense and strained. The Kronstadt uprising was only a few days before […] Now my pamphlet is in

Lenin's hands. He leafs through it irritably, shaking his head in disapproval. Then the storm burst. For three quarters of an hour Lenin fulminated against the Workers' Opposition and my pamphlet.[24]

Lenin did not baulk at crude sexist insults which were lapped up by a congress composed mainly of men chosen by Stalin's Secretariat. Slyly referencing what many delegates would have known from internal party gossip (that the aristocratic Kollontai and the working-class Shliapnikov had once had a personal relationship), Lenin from the rostrum joked, "Well, thank God, Kollontai and Shliapnikov are a 'class united'". The delegates laughed and Kollontai was suitably humiliated.

Lenin then turned to the Workers' Opposition platform itself. He condemned its call for workers' self-management as petty bourgeois, syndicalist and deriving from elements in the party who had not "fully adopted the Communist world-view". With the Kronstadt sailors declaring an independent Soviet just across the Gulf of Finland, he was in no mood to tolerate internal dissent. "I contend there is a connection between the ideas and slogans of the petty bourgeois counter-revolution and the slogans of this opposition, which although it doubtless has its honest and misguided supporters, is nevertheless inspired by disrupters who choose to add to the chaos of the Kronstadt rebellion", he told the congress. "People writing pamphlets like these should be exposed and eliminated".

Kollontai's biographer Cathy Porter conveys the hysteria of a Congress in which the debate was "ostensibly about the unions but more fundamentally about the function and unity of the party".[25] After vicious personal attacks on her from Lenin and Bukharin (whose over-emotional nature often betrayed him), Kollontai responded calmly that the anger and vituperation of her colleagues stood in stark contrast to the limited programme for democratic reform the Workers' Opposition had actually proposed. "The workers know there's something wrong", she told the congress, "but instead of running to Vladimir Ilyich's office for a chat, as so many of our more timid comrades did, we proposed a series of practical measures for cleansing our ranks and reviving our mutual relations with the people".[26] But for Lenin and Trotsky the working class has ceased to be a proper proletariat, and therefore any programme to devolve decision-making to them was politically dangerous. The Theses on the Trade Union Question was overwhelmingly rejected.

The crushing of the Workers' Opposition led to a fatal decision, one that ended whatever internal democracy still existed within the party. On the final day of the Congress, as the scars of the battles with the Opposition and the Kronstadt sailors were still live and raw, Lenin introduced two new resolutions – one on "Party Unity" and one on "Anarchist and Syndicalist Deviations in the Party". The first resolution declared that as part of a struggle against factionalism, "every organisation of the party must take strict action to prevent factional actions". It ordered "immediate dissolution of all groups without exception formed on the basis of one platform or another (such as the Workers' Opposition Group, the Democratic Centralists group, etc.)". Failure to comply or enforce this resolution would result in instant expulsion from the party.

The second resolution hammered the final nail in the coffin of the Workers' Opposition by targeting it specifically as an "anarchist and syndicalist deviation" and declaring that "the propaganda of its ideas" was "incompatible with membership of the Russian Communist Party". Out of over 600 delegates at the Congress, only 25 voted against the first resolution and 30 against the second.[27]

The ban on factions landed on the party like a fist. Trotsky told the congress that the ban and the proscriptions were temporary, but they were never to be repealed. Having passed his resolutions and gifted the bureaucracy the power to destroy any organised opposition, Lenin sought to ameliorate the policy with a few concessions. He acknowledged the validity of the Workers' Opposition's case against "bureaucratic perversions" and suggested that if an issue such as the Treaty of Brest-Litovsk arose in the future, "it is possible that it will then be necessary to elect by platform". He may even have meant this. But in the context of one-party rule enforced by the Secretariat, the Orgburo and the Cheka, Lenin's concessions vanished in the wind.

Some sensed the shadow that now hung over them. Karl Radek told the congress he had "a feeling that a rule is being established here which has left us still uncertain as to whom it will be applied [...] Although I am voting for this resolution I feel that it may even be turned against us." He finished by admitting:

Regardless of who this sword may be turned against—at such a moment it is necessary to adopt this resolution and say: Let the

Central Committee at the moment of danger take the sternest measures against the best comrades, if it finds this necessary. A definite line by the Central Committee is essential. The best Central Committee may make a mistake, but this is less dangerous than the wavering we see now.[28]

Radek and the party had now conceded the principle that, no matter the actual facts of the case, the Central Committee was always right.

In 1936-38 Radek, along with Rykov, Tomsky, Zinoviev, Kamenev, Bukharin and Shliapnikov—and thousands of other Old Bolsheviks—would all be purged from the party, arrested and executed. One of the reasons used to justify their infamous Moscow Trials was the "factionalism" (mixed with sabotage, espionage and other alleged crimes) of the accused, and how any such activity was, objectively, counter-revolutionary. The other charges were false, supported by manufactured evidence and confessions extracted by torture, but the claim that any opposition to Stalin, and to a Central Committee dominated by Stalin, was *inherently* counter-revolutionary had a twisted logic derived from the ban on factions. Those who had supported the ban, like Radek and Bukharin, stood helpless before these accusations. Their dilemma was captured perfectly in Arthur Koestler's *Darkness at Noon* (1940), a novel which expresses more about the grim logic of Leninism than the entire army of Lenin apologists then and since.

Stalin began the purge with the arrest and execution of Zinoviev and Kamenev and others classed as a "Trotskyite-Kamenevite-Zinovievite-Leftist-Counter-Revolutionary Bloc", and expanded it to take in tens of thousands of people accused of political crimes. NKVD Order 00447 authorised mass arrests of all whom the NKVD considered anti-Soviet elements, such as most of the intelligentsia, "ex-Kulaks" and non-Russian nationalists. These were divided into those to be immediately shot and those sent to the Gulag. The order also authorised execution of those already held in work camps on the grounds of "continuing counter-revolutionary activity". Unlike previous purges, this one annihilated the party itself. Of 1,966 delegates to the Seventeenth Communist Party Congress in 1934, 1,108 were arrested and most of these were executed. Of 139 members of the Central Committee of 1934, only 29 were still alive by 1939, the rest having been shot or driven to suicide. By its end point the Great Terror saw between 600,000 and 1.2 million people executed.[29]

Trotsky himself offered the ultimate capitulation at the Thirteenth Party Congress in 1924, the first after Lenin's death, which Stalin's Secretariat organised so well that not a single Oppositionist attended as a delegate. Faced with a storm of condemnation of his *The Lessons of October* (1924), which had made criticisms of the "Triumvirate" of Stalin, Kamenev and Zinoviev, Trotsky had to bend the knee. "The party in the last analysis is always right, because the party is the sole historical instrument given to the proletariat for the solution of its basic problems", he told the Congress. "I know that one cannot be right against the party. It is only possible to be right with the party and through the party, for history has not created other ways for the realisation of what is right".[30]

The National Bolsheviks had won. Of all the "oppositions" within the Bolshevik Party, only Shliapnikov and Kollontai could honestly claim that they had opposed the termination of internal party democracy and the subsequent fast-track to Stalinism. And even they were as complicit as all other Bolshevik leaders in establishing the one-party state and the denial of civil and democratic rights to non-party oppositionists in 1917-18. With hardly any exceptions, they all forged the weapons which killed them.

CHAPTER EIGHTEEN

Meet the New Boss

In comparison to the Workers' Opposition, the Left Opposition of 1923-24 and the "United Opposition" of 1927, though later lauded as the authentic Bolshevik opposition to Stalinist bureaucracy, were internal splinter groups easily suppressed. By the time Trotsky stirred to overt opposition the battle was already over, and Trotsky himself had played a leading role in disarming all who might have defeated Stalin – the trade unions, the Workers' Opposition and, most especially, the Kronstadt sailors. The Kronstadt rebellion of 1921 did not spring from nowhere, nor was it an anarchist-monarchist conspiracy (as some on the Marxist left, even today, maintain). It was a genuine, mass-based and popular working-class revolt against an oppressive state in favour of a system of radical socialist democracy.

The Fortress and the city of Kronstadt were situated on Kotlin Island, 20 miles west of Petrograd in the Gulf of Finland. A series of sea forts ran across the gulf to further protect Petrograd. In winter the sea between the mainland and Kotlin Island froze. Onto this unique and enclosed location – close to revolutionary Petrograd yet isolated enough to create a great sense of camaraderie and professional pride – were thrown some of the most independent-minded and instinctively rebellious workers and peasants in the Russian Empire.

Once inducted into the massive Baltic Fleet they were given a level of technical training and professional responsibility denied most production-line factory workers. The sailors of the Fleet were temperamentally anarchist and politically syndicalist, instinctively resistant to the hierarchy and discipline imposed by their aristocratic officers. Between the formation of the SR Party in 1901 and the 1905 Revolution, they soaked up the political propaganda of the SRs that reached them across the ice from Petrograd, and formed mini-Soviets of their own to discuss politics and organise around their own grievances.

The Kronstadt Soviet established in the February 1917 Revolution was virtually independent from 1917 to 1921. The unique nature of Kronstadt, where the sailors both lived and worked, made it more of a mass commune than a political forum. Inside the base were mini-communities where sailors, workers and bourgeois intellectuals laboured together on urban garden plots. Unlike the chaotic property sequestrations of Petrograd, Kronstadt distributed property according to family size. The sailors – recipients of the "special rations" that went to party cadres and militias – shared their portions with the rest of the city. Not for nothing has the Kronstadt commune been called "one of the most vivid utopian socialist experiments to surface in the revolution".[1]

After the suppression of the 1921 revolt, the Bolsheviks

claimed the sailors who had rebelled were not the same individuals as "the pride and glory of the revolution" hailed by Trotsky in 1917. Yet Kronstadt as a city, a workplace and a forge of revolutionary sentiment was basically the same in February 1921 as in October 1917. Three quarters of the sailors serving in the Baltic Fleet in 1921 had been serving in March 1918. It is true there had been a "churn" of sailors during those years as some went to fight on various fronts of the Civil War, but the nature of the Fleet (i.e. it consisted of warships that departed and returned to a fixed base) meant there was a definite degree of continuity. Nor were new recruits depoliticised. Israel Getzler's history of Kronstadt from 1917-21 found that "by the end of 1919 thousands of veteran sailors, who had served on many fronts of the civil war, and in the administrative network of the expanding Soviet state, had returned to the Baltic Fleet and to Kronstadt, most by way of remobilisation".[2]

If anything, the experience of the Civil War gave the sailors a sharper sense of the surrounding political environment than they had possessed in 1917, when their actions were driven more by visceral anti-government emotion rather than conscious political ideology. The record of the Kronstadt sailors and the Baltic Fleet bears out Paul Avrich's conclusion that "throughout the Civil War of 1918-1920 the sailors of Kronstadt, and the Baltic Fleet as a whole, remained the torchbearers of revolutionary militancy".[3]

The source of the fracture between the Bolsheviks and the Kronstadt sailors was that the latter did not fit the Bolshevik notion of "advanced" workers, i.e. schooled in Marxism, disciplined, productivist and loyal to the vanguard party. To the extent they had a specific ideology it was a localist, libertarian socialism. Their proximity to the labour movement of Petrograd kept them politically attuned and their military skills gave them enormous leverage when it counted. In his introduction to Ida Mett's classic work on the uprising, Murray Bookchin characterised the social milieu of the Kronstadt base, noting that "Its living traditions and its close contact with 'Red Petrograd' served to anneal men of nearly all strata into revolutionaries".[4] Right up to 1921 no one questioned this. In October 1920, five months before the rebellion, the sailors of "Red Kronstadt" led the third anniversary celebrations of October 1917 in Petrograd.

Yet Petrograd was now lost to the Bolsheviks. Jonathan Aves records that by early February 1921 "strikes were becoming an everyday occurrence", so much so that the Bolsheviks responded with a military clampdown and mass arrests.[5] General Strikes also broke out in Moscow, Saratov and Ekaterinoslavl. These were not simply work stoppages. They were mass social unrest that encompassed "factory occupations, 'Italian Strikes', demonstrations, mass meetings, the beating up of Communists and so on".[6] Striking railway workers sent emissaries along the tracks to spread the action. The strikers' demands expanded to holding free Soviet elections in which other socialist parties could stand. Red Army units sent to crush the railwaymen refused orders to fire on them and were replaced by reliable RCP detachments.

On 23rd February Moscow was placed under martial law, with RCP units putting factories under 24-hour guard.[7] After a General Strike in Saratov was suppressed it too was placed under martial law. Petrograd had been under unofficial martial law for some time. In Avrich's estimation, in February 1921 "an open breach occurred between the Bolshevik regime and its principal mainstay of support, the working class".[8]

The sailors had their own specific grievances. On 15th February, 1921 the Second Conference of Communist Sailors of the Baltic Fleet, composed of 300 delegates, passed a resolution which condemned the work of the Political Section of the Baltic Fleet (Poubalt) and decreed, "Poubalt has not only separated itself from the masses but from the active functionaries". In the latter half of 1920 over 20% of RCP members in the Fleet resigned from the party. The resolution stated, "The cause is to be found in the very principle of Poubalt's organisation. These principles must be changed in the direction of greater democracy".[9] The RCP ignored the sailors. As a result they turned against those who had been their idols and leaders in 1917 – Trotsky and their former leader Raskolnikov, now a senior party figure with a lifestyle to match. In February 1921 a further 5,000 sailors left the RCP in protest.

Alexander Berkman, who had arrived in Russia with Emma Goldman in late 1919, was in Petrograd at the time, desperately trying to maintain his faith in the revolution. He recorded in his diary that on 23rd February a strike broke out at the large Trubotchny Mill. Even though Zinoviev sent RCP students to break the strike, it spread to the Baltisky and Laferma tobacco factories, the Skorohod shoe factory, the Baltic and Patronny metal plants, and on 28th February to the enormous Putilov Works itself. The strikers' economic demands included more efficient food supply, the withdrawal of roadblocks around the city and freedom to travel outside the city to a radius of 30 miles. Their political demands included freedom of speech and the press, and the freeing of working-class and socialist political prisoners. The response was immediate. On 24th February an RCP-convened "Committee of Defence" declared a "state of siege" in Petrograd, imposing an 11pm curfew and a total ban on any political meetings indoors or outdoors. Strike leaders were arrested.

On 26th February the Kronstadt sailors sent emissaries to Petrograd to investigate. They found factories surrounded by troops. One of the sailors' leading activists, Chief Quartermaster of the battleship *Petropavlovsk* Stepan Petrichenko, an experienced seaman who had joined the navy in 1912 and played a key role in 1917, wrote, "One might have thought that these were not factories but the forced labour prisons of Tsarist times".[10] On 28th Februaru they returned to the naval base with a report of the suppression of the strikes. After hearing the report, the sailors of the *Petropavlovsk* called a mass meeting and passed a resolution which would function as the core programme of the Kronstadt rebellion.

The resolution demanded new Soviet elections by secret ballot and accompanied by free election propaganda; freedom of speech and of the press for all workers and peasants, as well as for "anarchists and left socialist parties"; freedom of assembly for trade union and peasant organisations; the organisation by 10th March of a conference of non-party workers from Kronstadt, Petrograd and the Petrograd District; immediate liberation of all political prisoners from the socialist parties and those belonging to workers' and peasants' organisations; election of a commission to investigate the cases of all detained in prison and concentration camps on political charges; equalisation of rations for all workers; granting of "freedom of action" to peasants on their own land; and abolition of all political sections within the armed forces.[11]

Aside from one, none of the grievances even touched on navy matters. They were written to reflect the needs and wishes of the mass of workers and peasants. Bookchin concluded that "the demands of the Kronstadt sailors were not formulated in the fastness of an isolated island in the Gulf of Finland; they were developed as a result of close contact between the naval base and the restless Petrograd workers, whose demands the 15-point programme essentially articulated". They were, in fact, no more than the minimum the Bolsheviks had promised Russian workers and peasants when they assumed power in October 1917. They also, though there had been no collusion between them, chimed perfectly with the "industrial" demands of the Workers' Opposition. Between them the Kronstadt sailors and the Workers' Opposition proposed a programme of renewed working-class democracy that sought to lessen and eventually supersede the one-party dictatorship of the RCP.

The Kronstadt sailors set up a "Provisional Revolutionary Committee" consisting of militant sailors of long service (i.e. service began before 1917), with a remit to administer both the town and the fortress of Kronstadt. Petrichencko was elected Chair. Amongst the Committee were Arkhipov, Chief Engineer of the battleship *Sebastopol*; Ossosonov, a boilerman of the *Sebastopol*; Perepelkin, an electrician on the *Sebastopol;* Romanchenko, a dock maintenance worker; Valk, a sawmill worker; Pavlov, a worker in the Marine Mining Shop; Kilgast, a Harbour Pilot; Boikev, head of the Building Section of the Kronstadt Fortress; Koupolov, the head male nurse at Kronstadt; and Yakovenko, the liaison telephonist to the Kronstadt Section.

The first thing the Committee did was submit a proposal to the Anchor Square assembly to hold new Soviet elections. On 2nd March a conference was held to conduct the elections, with 300 delegates attending, two from each ship, military unit, factory and trade union. The procedures were scrupulously democratic. Communists were not allowed to dominate proceedings or to weight the delegates in their favour. On 3rd March the Revolutionary Committee started to publish its own newspaper. In the first edition, Petrichenko wrote, "The task of the Committee is to organise in the city and fortress, through friendly and cooperative effort, the conditions for fair and proper elections to the new Soviet".

The Bolsheviks' response to the Kronstadt sailors' 15-point programme was a mix of hostility and panic. Two senior Bolsheviks, Mikhail Kalinin and N.N. Kuzmin, were sent to speak to the sailors and persuade them to withdraw their demands. But when Kalinin and Kuzmin delivered inflammatory speeches to a mass meeting of 15,000 people in Anchor Square, during which they called the Kronstadt programme counter-revolutionary and threatened those who supported it with severe reprisals, they were driven off the platform by a chorus of booing and had to hurriedly leave the city. The breakdown of the meeting put Kronstadt and the government on a collision course.

On top of this the situation in Petrograd was deteriorating.

Berkman recorded in his diary that in Petrograd on 1st March, the day Kalinin and Kuzmin were threatening the sailors, "Many arrests are taking place. Groups of strikers surrounded by Chekists, on their way to prison, are a common sight".[12] Calls for the convocation of the Constituent Assembly were heard once more throughout working-class districts of Petrograd. By 4th March the entire city was under martial law.

Faced with a mass working-class rebellion, the Bolsheviks responded with accusations that the Mensheviks and SRs were behind it all, plotting "counter-revolution". But the Mensheviks and SRs followed, not led, mass action. Menshevik sympathisers in the Printers Union helped them produce a series of leaflets supporting the strikes. On 27th February an unsigned manifesto that almost certainly originated with the Mensheviks appeared around the city, declaring

> a fundamental change is necessary in the policies of the government. First of all, the workers and peasants need freedom. They do not want to live by the decrees of the Bolsheviks. They want to control their own destinies. Comrades, support the revolutionary order. In an organised and determined manner demand: liberation of all arrested socialists and non-party working men; abolition of martial law; freedom of speech, press and assembly for all who labour; free elections of factory committees, trade unions and Soviets. Call meetings, pass resolutions, send delegates to authorities, bring about the realization of your demands.[13]

By early 1921 the Mensheviks had regained the mass support they had lost between February and October 1917, yet they still did not advocate the violent overthrow of the Bolshevik government. Instead they asked workers to organise legally to secure political and economic reforms.

The Mensheviks had limited opportunity to organise behind these demands. Few of their leaders were still at large. Those that were, like Rozovsky and Dan, were arrested in early March. In the first three months of 1921 approximately 5,000 Mensheviks were arrested by the Cheka, including the entire Menshevik Central Committee that the British Labour Party delegation had been allowed to visit six months before. By contrast, the SRs issued leaflets that called for a mass uprising, the overthrow of Sovnarcom and the recall of the Constituent Assembly. The Kronstadt sailors themselves did not want that, nor any restoration of bourgeois rule. The "Red Sailors" had been amongst those who closed down the Constituent Assembly in January 1918, when they still believed the Bolsheviks best represented their vision of the future society. They did not backtrack now. Even after the Bolshevik military force attacked on 7th March, the sailors continued to build their democratic socialist commune, dismantling the despised RCP apparatus in the city and preparing for genuine trade union and Soviet elections.

On 8th March the Kronstadt Revolutionary Committee published a statement in its paper called "What we are fighting for". It explained:

By carrying out the October Revolution the working class had hoped to achieve its emancipation. But the result has been an even greater enslavement of human beings. The power of the monarchy, with its police and its gendarmerie, has passed into the hands of the Communist usurpers, who have given the people not freedom but the constant fear of torture by the Cheka.

After condemning the dictatorship of the party, one-man management and Taylorism, the statement finished by decrying

the moral servitude which the Communists have also introduced. They have laid their hands on the inner world of the toiling people, forcing them to think in the way that they want. Through the state control of the trade unions they have chained the workers to their machines […] To the protests of the peasants, expressed in spontaneous uprisings, and those of the workers, whose living conditions have compelled them to strike, they have answered with mass executions […] The Russia of the toilers, the first to raise the red banner of liberation, is drenched in blood.[14]

The clock was now ticking down. Once the ice sheet between Petrograd and Kotlin Island thawed, the naval base would be virtually impregnable. It might then become a focus for other anti-Bolshevik forces such as Makhno's anarchist partisans, the peasant army of Tambov or the strikers of Petrograd and Moscow. The danger was so tangible that the Bolsheviks unleashed a torrent of hostile propaganda about the Kronstadt rebels, some of which is still repeated today by their staunchest defenders. None of it was true.

The sailors were not *déclassé* elements; not depoliticised since 1917; not led by anarchists; not backward peasant recruits from Ukraine replacing the good proletarians of a few years before. On the two main foci of the rebellion, the battleships *Petropovlovsk* and *Sebastopol*, 94% of their crews had been recruited before and during the 1917 revolutions. 59% of the crews had joined the navy between 1914 and 1916.[15] The rebels had no counter-revolutionary programme. They had no connections with White émigrés or foreign agents, and received no money or aid from them. On the contrary, they vehemently rejected that which was offered. Getzler quotes a Red Cross representative (who, towards the end, the rebels allowed in) as confirming that Kronstadt "will admit no White political party, no politician, with the exception of the Red Cross".[16] There were no secret White generals inside Kronstadt directing the revolt. The senior ex-imperial officer at the base, General Kozlovsky, was a military advisor to the Soviet in the same manner that thousands of other ex-imperial officers were advising the Red Army. The accusation that the sailors were discredited by the presence of Kozlovsky, who played no part in the fighting, when the Bolshevik forces sent against them were commanded by the ex-imperial officer General Tukchachevsky, was hypocrisy of a high order.

On 4th March the Petrograd Soviet, consisting entirely of RCP delegates, "mostly youngsters, fanatical and intolerant" (as Berkman, watching from the gallery, recorded), condemned the Kronstadt rebels. Representatives from Petrograd factories attempted to support the sailors but were shouted down. Kalinin claimed that Kronstadt was the centre of a plot orchestrated by Kozlovsky. After a short "debate" the Soviet declared the sailors were counter-revolutionary and demanded their immediate surrender. Trotsky, who had been called back to Petrograd to direct operations, sent the sailors one short communication.

Grimly titled "Ultimatum: March 5th, 1921, 1400 Hours", Trotsky's message said, "The Workers and Peasants' Government has decreed that Kronstadt and the insurgent battleships must be restored to the jurisdiction of the Soviet Republic without delay". After demanding the rebels immediately lay down their arms and release the commissars held at the base, it concluded:

> Only those who surrender unconditionally can count on the mercy of the Soviet Republic. I am issuing orders to quell the mutiny and subdue the mutineers by force of arms. Total responsibility for whatever calamities may befall the civilian population in this operation is on the heads of the White Guard insurrectionists. This is the last warning.[17]

The warning was ignored.

On 7th March the assault began. The ice in the Gulf of Finland had not yet thawed and so the 50,000 soldiers of Tukchachevsky's 7th Army could advance by foot and armoured car all the way to Kotlin Island. Although the epic battle lasted nearly two weeks, the outcome was never in doubt. Fire from the fortress blew great holes in the ice, which sent thousands of soldiers to icy deaths, but when a snowstorm came up they had cover to advance to the island's defences. On 16th March they broke through. Fierce fighting ensued inside the fortress and throughout the city, but in the end force of numbers won out.

Once the outpost had fallen retribution was swift. Prisoners were transported to Petrograd. On Zinoviev's personal orders, 500 of the sailors were immediately shot. When some of the regular Cheka units refused to carry out the order, teenage Komsomol cadres were used for the mass execution.[18] Over the next few weeks about 2,000 more were summarily executed without trial. The remainder were transported to Solovetsky concentration camp in the White Sea. About 7,000 sailors escaped across the ice to Finland, including Petrichencko, who wrote an invaluable memoir that confirmed the rebellion had been a reassertion of Soviet democracy, not a challenge to it.

For many on the libertarian left the violent suppression of Kronstadt was the final straw, a devastating and bitter irony that the Bolsheviks did not seem to comprehend. On 18th March, two days after Kronstadt fell in blood and smoke, the Tenth Party Congress closed with solemn remembrance of the Paris Commune and the 30,000 Parisian workers murdered by the French army after its fall. After watching captured Kronstadt sailors paraded through the streets on their way to either execution or Solovetsky camp, Berkman made one last entry in his diary. "The victors are celebrating the anniversary of the Paris Commune of 1871", he wrote bitterly, "Trotsky and Zinoviev denounce Thiers and Gallifet for the slaughter of the Paris rebels". Although he continued his translation work for the Comintern, he left Russia a few months later.

The last outpost of the workers' democracy born in February 1917 was extinguished in March 1921. After the suppression of the revolt, Kollontai's Workers' Opposition pamphlet was officially banned. The entire text was published in the British socialist newspaper *Workers' Dreadnought*, edited by Sylvia Pankhurst, a constant thorn in the side of Lenin and Sovnarcom. Pankhurst and Kollontai—Marxist feminists whose socialism was inextricable from sexual, social and cultural liberation—had much in common. Pankhurst had been expelled from the suffragette Womens' Social and Political Union in 1913 for sharing platforms with trade union and Irish independence leaders. She went on to support Anton Pannekoek's "Council Communist" movement in the 1920s and thereafter put her energies into anti-colonialism. Kollontai entered twenty-five years of diplomatic service for the Soviet Union, although for unfathomable reasons of his own Stalin never had her killed.

Kronstadt destroyed the Bolshevik Revolution, politically and morally. Even the Bolsheviks knew it. Their public responses verged on the hysterical. Trotsky, usually precise and eloquent, descended into violent crudity. In an article published in *Pravda* on 23rd March, 1921, he quoted a report from a French right-wing newspaper that linked the Kronstadt events and the possible fall of the Soviet regime to the prospects of renewed capitalist profits in Russia. He claimed this discredited the entire programme of the Kronstadt sailors and revealed the real motivations of all who had supported it. It was a desperate and dishonest argument, wrapped up in fear and hatred:

The counter-revolutionary riff-raff, the SR blowhards and simpletons, the Menshevik garbage, and the rip-roaring anarchist daredevils—all of them, whether consciously or unconsciously, out of guile or stupidity, perform one and the same historical function: they support every attempt to establish the unlimited sway of the bandits of world imperialism over the workers. The economic, political and national independence of Russia is possible only under the dictatorship of the Soviets. The backbone of this dictatorship is the Communist Party. There is no other party that can play this part, nor can there be. You wish to break this backbone, do you, dear sirs of the Menshevik and SR parties? Go ahead and try. We are ready to add to your experience.[19]

Trotsky was right in one regard. The forces that fought on the ice before Kronstadt had diametrically opposed political values. Whatever they told themselves, the Bolsheviks stood for hierarchical state capitalism imposed by dictat, with minimal to no influence on this process by trade unions or the wider working class. The Kronstadt sailors wanted to revive the vision of the February Revolution and the localised democratic structures that had emerged from it. This did not always accord with the political and economic programme of social democrats like the Mensheviks, but the period 1917-21 had taught hard lessons. By the middle of 1918 it was clear to many, probably most, workers that the Mensheviks' commitment to civil liberties and non-coercive government would have given them the greatest space and freedom to organise and to build structures of self-government. But by then it was too late.

Even the most hardline Bolsheviks acknowledged how badly wrong things had gone. On 8th January, 1921 Dzerzhinsky had written to Lenin to report on the current security threat. "The prisons are packed", he told him, with a hint of weary sarcasm, "mostly with workers and peasants instead of the bourgeoisie".[20] In one memo he summed up the entire procession of events from the dispersal of the democratic Soviets in 1918 and 1919, to the breaking of anti-government strikes, to the crushing of the sailors of Kronstadt. Contrary to left mythology, still powerful today, the Stalinist counter-revolution did not begin in 1921. It began on 25th October, 1917, although there were other elements within Bolshevism that it had to contend with before it was triumphant. With the destruction of Kronstadt and the banning of oppositional elements in the Bolshevik Party it was complete.

At the close of the Tenth Party Congress Lenin accepted the inevitable and called a halt to War Communism. In February Bukharin had visited Tambov and reported back to the Politburo that the Soviet regime was doomed unless it conceded peasant demands for greater economic freedom. It was essential to restore an exchange of products between town and country, to kickstart agricultural production as soon as possible and to defuse peasant discontent. Lenin determined that the best way to do this was to institute a "tax-in-kind" on the peasants. This was an agreed percentage of requisition of the harvest on all peasant producers (originally half the amount of the 1920 requisition, eventually reduced to 10% of the total harvest), while allowing them to retain the surplus and sell it as they chose. At the same time the state monopoly on commerce was reduced, with small-scale private manufacturing and commercial enterprises allowed to operate.

Lenin introduced the tax-in-kind policy as a resolution

to the Tenth Party Congress on its last full day, after many delegates had already left. He spoke for three hours, during which he conceded that War Communism—what he called an attempt to create socialism by "administrative fiat"—had been a utopian dream. He stressed the urgent need to appease the peasants lest the entire Soviet regime crumble. He admitted the failure of revolution in Western Europe left the Bolsheviks with little choice but to lessen state control of the economy, to allow the market to operate, and to seek foreign aid and investment to build up the forces of production. He reassured delegates that as long as the state owned the major sectors of the economy (heavy industry, the banks, transport, foreign trade) then the market would still be regulated and controlled. As Avrich observed, by his admission that War Communism had failed, "Lenin tacitly conceded an argument of his Menshevik critics, who in 1917 had warned against any premature attempt to plunge their backward agrarian country into socialism".[21]

The tax-in-kind was the beginning of a series of new policies that collectively became the New Economic Policy (NEP). The NEP emerged in stages over the next year or so, guaranteeing the peasants tenure of land and allowing them to hire labour and lease plots. Within six months, as Cohen records, "The principles of NEP came to permeate the whole economy".[22] Reciprocal buying and selling of goods swept across Soviet territory. The dominance of the state sector in industrial production was retained—state-controlled heavy industry still employed 84% of the labour force—but private capital circulated around the rejuvenated retail and merchandise sector.

Crucially, the rural economy and peasant industry was set free of the iron control of War Communism. By the mid-1920s there were 25 million small holdings in the countryside. Whilst these produced small fortunes for some, they supplied the towns and cities with the food and resources they had sorely lacked before the NEP. The Soviet economy during the heyday of the NEP (roughly 1922 to 1927, although it survived until Stalin began mass collectivisation in 1929) was a form of "mixed economy", albeit with a very powerful and politically illiberal state.

Victor Serge recorded that within a few months the NEP "was already giving marvelous results. From one week to the next the famine and the speculation were diminishing perceptibly". Restaurants re-opened and food that had been unobtainable shortly before made a reappearance. On the other hand, "the confusion among the party rank and file was staggering. For what did we fight, spill so much blood, agree to so many sacrifices?"[23] Many of the party cadres did not directly benefit. If they worked in heavy industry they had no more money than before and could not afford the new luxuries appearing in the shops. Although party membership still conferred privileges these tended to be at the higher levels, with lower orders no more likely to secure special goods than the peasantry.

A new species of private entrepreneur, middle-men who bought surplus product in the country and sold it at a profit in the cities, pre-empted the fledgling system of barter and exchange that NEP was supposed to create. These "Nepmen", often well-dressed and with glamorous women on their arms, became familiar figures in the 1920s and were deeply resented by hardcore Bolsheviks and the less privileged working class. When Stalin turned on them in 1929 he did not lack for supporters in the party.

Lenin explained his conception of the NEP in a major article "The Tax in Kind: The Significance of the New Policy and its Conditions". In it he referred back to a 1918 article, "The Chief Tasks of Our Day: Left Wing Childishness and the Petty-Bourgeois Mentality", in which he had assumed the transition phase from capitalism to socialism would last about a year. He admitted the timescale "turned out to be longer than was anticipated at the time". Lenin claimed it was solely the Civil War and foreign intervention that had forced the Bolsheviks on to the path of War Communism and that any assertion to the contrary by "Mensheviks, SRs and Kautsky and co" were those of "lackeys of the bourgeoisie".

Forgetting that his first pronouncement after 25th October, 1917 had been "We will now proceed to construct the socialist order", Lenin now wrote that the only alternative to the failure to do so was "not to try to prohibit or put the lock on the development of capitalism, but to channel it into state capitalism". He claimed that state capitalism and the Dictatorship of the Proletariat were perfectly compatible. As long as the state controlled concessions and leases to foreign and private capital then the transition to socialism was still on course. He waxed lyrical about the paramount need for mass electrification of the far-flung Soviet provinces and village economy, which in his view was an essential precondition for the transition to socialism. Although Lenin claimed, in a famous mantra, that socialism would consist of "Soviet power plus electrification", he never explained how a new form of energy supply would have such seismic political consequences.

The most telling part of the "Tax in Kind" article was its assault on the programme of the Kronstadt sailors and its reaffirmation of political repression. Lenin condemned Martov for claiming "in his Berlin journal" that "Kronstadt not only adopted Menshevik slogans but also proved that there could be an anti-Bolshevik movement which did not entirely serve the interests of the White Guards, the capitalists and the landowners". Although the Kronstadt programme had proven exactly that, Lenin considered that there was no difference, no space at all, between the Miliukovs of the world, who wished to restore capitalism to Russia, and what he called "a proletarian vanguard that is capable of governing". Tactical concessions aside, Lenin had learnt nothing from the disasters of 1917-21 or the mass alienation of workers and peasants from his regime.

The "Tax in Kind" article – relatively unknown and yet as crucial to an understanding of Lenin as the April Theses – demonstrated beyond doubt that the NEP, whilst bringing economic liberalisation, did *not* herald a lessening of political control and repression. After urging yet more promotion of workers from the rank and file "to the work of economic administration", Lenin finished,

As for the non-party people who are only Mensheviks or SRs disguised in fashionable non-party attire *a la* Kronstadt, they should be kept safe in prison, or packed off to Berlin, to join Martov in freely enjoying the charms of pure democracy and freely exchanging ideas with Chernov, Miliukov and the Georgian Mensheviks.[24]

The article was published and distributed in May 1921 in the magazine *Krasnaya* and distributed throughout Soviet territory.

And yet both workers and peasants continued to resist, to strike and rebel. Even after Kronstadt and the promulgation of the NEP strikes continued. Aves records that in 1922 there were 538 strikes with 197,000 participants, but the real total must be higher as this derives from official statistics. These occurred in tandem with what were known as the "Green" rebellions, i.e. those in the countryside. The best-known was that centred on Tambov, but there were many others. Some of these had clear political goals. Others took the form of roaming bandit armies, particularly in the deep south, where peasants and Cossacks found common cause in mutual hatred of the Bolsheviks. In the Caucasian Mountains a rebel army of 30,000 peasants almost matched Antonov's in size. The first six months of 1921 saw the entire province of western Siberia lost by the Soviet regime as an army of approximately 60,000 peasant rebels held the Omsk, Tiuman, Tobolsk, Ekaterinburg and Tomsk regions.

The Green rebellions were systematically put down throughout 1921-22 by a mixture of military action, famine, and a slackening-off of peasant discontent as the tax-in-kind policy fed through. Tambov, in particular, went down hard. In April 1921 Tukchachevsky arrived with 100,000 men, a fleet of armoured cars and his own small airforce to drop poison gas on rebel hideouts. By June 50,000 peasants had been rounded up and placed in newly constructed concentration camps. Figes reports estimates that 100,000 peasants were imprisoned or deported while 15,000 were shot.[25] By summer the rebellion was effectively over, with famine in the region delivering the literal death blow. Antonov and a small core of rebels evaded capture and continued to harry the authorities until summer 1922 when they were trapped, surrounded and eliminated.

Makhno also fought to the bitter end. After the Red Army's invasion of Ukraine in 1919 he had formed a temporary alliance with Bolshevik forces to defeat Denikin's armies. Despite Sovnarcom's attempt to impose its authority on the Free Territories, that alliance held throughout the summer of 1919. Makhno's Insurrectionary Army was instrumental in stopping Denikin's drive towards Moscow and in pushing him back to the Black Sea. At the end of 1919 Makhno was ordered by Trotsky to transfer his forces to the Polish front, an order he refused. The Bolsheviks then turned on the Makhnovists.

A Makhnovist proclamation of June 1920 entitled "Pause! Read! Consider!", aimed at Red Army soldiers, some of whom were native Ukrainians, attempted to subvert Bolshevik discipline. "They tell you that the Makhnovists are bandits and counter-revolutionaries", it began, before explaining,

> We, the revolutionary insurgent Makhnovists, are also peasants and workers like our brothers in the Red Army. We rose against oppression. We are fighting for a better and brighter life. Our frank ideal is the achievement of a non-authoritarian labourers' society without parasites and without commissar-bureaucrats.

Our immediate goal is the establishment of the free Soviet order, without the authority of the Bolsheviks, without pressure from any party whatsoever.

The proclamation ended, "Comrade! Think about it, who are you with and who are you against? Don't be a slave — be a man".[26]

Hostilities between the Red and Insurrectionary armies continued until October 1920, when the Bolsheviks again asked Makhno to assist them in throwing back the last White offensive of the Civil War, Wrangel's drive north to Moscow from the Crimea. Again Makhno fought the Whites and helped defeat Wrangel. His reward was that on 25th November his senior commanders in the Crimea were arrested and shot. Simultaneously Trotsky ordered a mass attack on Gulyai-Polya, which destroyed the core of his army and seized control of the Free Territory.

Makhno himself escaped with a few men and spent the next year wandering the Ukrainian steppes fighting a last-ditch guerilla war. Wounded and ill, in 1921 he crossed to Romania. He ended his days working on the production line of the Renault car plant in Paris, where he died of tuberculosis in 1934. Yet some things are not forgotten. In 1953, upon hearing of the death of Stalin, a vast insurrection took place across the camps of the Gulag. It is reported that after seizing control the prisoners of Norilsk camp in the Arctic Circle, 70% of whom were Ukrainians serving the standard 25-year sentence for political prisoners, hoisted the black flag of Nestor Makhno to the top of the flagpole.

The Bolsheviks were lucky in the timing of the peasant

rebellions. The food shortages that caused them also prevented them from developing into a unified national movement. Peasants in many regions were simply too weak to battle the Red Army. The great famine of 1921-22 devastated the Volga region and spread to the Urals Basin, the Don, southern Ukraine, Kazakhstan and western Siberia. Its direct cause was a crop failure in 1920 followed by severe draught that reduced the area to a dustbowl. Even then the peasants might have survived from reserve stocks, but these stocks had been taken by the Grain Requisition Squads. There was nothing to fall back on and no government willing or able to direct food to where it was most needed. Desperate peasants tried to escape the wasted regions but the roads were closed. There was no transport to the towns. Whole villages died and were later found empty but for corpses. It is estimated that nearly five million people died of starvation over 1921 and 1922.

Although the NEP era was very different from that of War Communism, one thing remained constant—the privileges to be had from party, especially inner-party, membership. The system of privilege started at the top, with the 5,000 senior Bolsheviks and their families who lived in the Kremlin or the special party hotels, the Metropole and the National, in the centre of Moscow. The hotels had been restored to their pre-war opulence and after 1920 were well-stocked with luxuries that most workers could not afford. The Kremlin had a staff of 2,000 servants and its own shops and restaurants. In Petrograd the party elite lived in the former Astoria hotel, now the First House of the Soviets. Chekists in leather jackets kept the masses away, who could only watch in awe as Zinoviev, the local party boss, went back and forth in his limousine, "with his Chekist bodyguards and a string of assorted prostitutes".[27] This was a side of the struggle he had forgotten to mention at the Halle Congress.

In June 1921 Berkman had occasion to visit the Hotel Luxe in Moscow, where delegates to the Comintern from foreign communist parties were quartered. He recorded that the street outside was lined with Rolls Royces. "The brilliant banquet hall is crowded", he wrote. "The velvety cushions and bright foliage of the smoking room are restful to the delegates of the western proletariat". He was allowed to observe the full Congress of the Comintern, marveling at the naivety of newly arrived delegates:

> With glowing fervor they dwell on the wondrous achievements of Communism. Like a jagged scalpel their naïve faith tears at my heart where bleeding lie my own high hopes, the hopes of my first days in Russia, deflowered and blighted by the ruthless hand of dictatorship.

After reports of the imprisonment of Mensheviks and anarchists, some foreign delegates began to ask difficult questions. "Some of the Germans, Swedish and Spanish members are perturbed by the general situation", Berkman recorded on 9th July. "They have been in contact with the actual conditions; they have sensed the spirit of popular discontent and caught a glimpse of the chasm between Communist claims and the reality".[28]

Soviet citizens themselves knew the reality very well, and adapted to it. Once the Civil War was over and the danger of seeing military service had declined, membership of the RCP shot up, from 430,000 at the beginning of 1920 to 600,000 six months later. Lenin sensed what was happening but couldn't admit what had caused it. "It was absolutely inevitable", he wrote in June 1919, "that adventurers and other pernicious elements should hitch themselves to the ruling party. There has never been, and never can be, a revolution without that". In July 1921 he oversaw a purge of about a fifth of the RCP's members, designed to clear out those who had joined solely out of self-interest. In the long run it made no difference. In April 1922 Lenin approved the creation of a new post at the apex of the party, the General Secretary, to oversee and control the entire party bureaucracy. Over some objections, his preferred candidate, Stalin, was duly appointed.

At the same time Lenin finished, for good and all, the quarrel between the Bolsheviks and the Mensheviks. In *Memoirs of a Revolutionary*, the anarchist turned Bolshevik Victor Serge recalled of Lenin's long-standing opponents in 1919:

> The Mensheviks seemed to me admirably intelligent, honest, and devoted to socialism, but completely overtaken by events. They stood for a sound principle, that of working class democracy, but a situation such as the state of siege, fraught with such mortal danger, did not permit any functioning of democratic institutions.[29]

This was honestly meant, but naïve. The democratic institutions, and the Menshevik party itself, had been suppressed in early 1918, before the Civil War and the state of siege in Petrograd. When the siege and war were over, democratic institutions and working-class democracy did not return.

If it had ever been the intention to restore them, the first beneficiaries would surely have been the Mensheviks. With a few exceptions they had been the Bolsheviks' "loyal opposition", socialists and trade unionists who had never campaigned for the forcible removal of Sovnarcom and had tried, through reasoned criticism and what little input they had to Soviet and other congresses, to expand the sphere of democratic freedom in the new system. None of this mattered. On the contrary, most of the Menshevik Party was now in jail. After the arrest of thousands of Menshevik activists in early 1921, Zinoviev had petitioned Lenin for permission to execute them for complicity in the Kronstadt uprising. But mass executions at that time would have damaged Sovnarcom's attempts to re-establish diplomatic relations with Britain and France. Therefore, in January 1922 many of the imprisoned Mensheviks were deported to Germany.

By 1923 the battle begun at the RSDLP Congress of 1903 was finally over. In June 1923 the Bolshevik CC issued a circular, "On Measures of Struggle with Mensheviks", which accused them of consciously supporting counter-revolution. The GPU rounded up many of their remaining activists, more than 1,000 in Moscow alone. Most would die in the Gulag. After Martov's death the Mensheviks faded into a dusty corner of Russian history.

The SRs and the Bund went the same way. The physical resistance of many SRs to the Bolshevik regime – in the south under Komuch, in the Left SR rising of July 1918 and at the time of Kronstadt – sealed their fate. With leading Mensheviks deported, and in any case too well known on the international left to publicly arraign and execute, the SRs became the focus of the first "show trial" of the Soviet Union, a precursor of the Moscow Trials of 1936-38. In June 1922 twelve SR leaders were put on trial for counter-revolutionary activity. All were found guilty and sentenced to death, but following protests from the emigrant Russian community in America, the regime commuted the sentences to imprisonment. The trial, allied to the final suppression of the Green rebellions, destroyed the SRs as a political force inside the Soviet Union, although exiled leaders established a vibrant SR presence in Prague and kept alive the tradition of a populist, democratic socialist alternative to Marxism and Bolshevism.

At the same time the Bund also ceased to function as a mass-based political party. Since 1917 it had lost members to both the Zionist Poalei Zion and to the Communist Bund (Kombund), a breakaway group of Left Bundists that supported the Bolsheviks in the Civil War. In 1920 the Bund officially split into the Communist Bund and the Social-Democratic Bund. In 1921 the Kombund dissolved itself and its members sought admission to the RCP. The mainstream Bund, led by Abramovich, staged a demonstration against the trial of the SRs in 1922, but under pressure of state persecution it gradually disappeared. The Polish Bund, more numerous and better organised, survived intact in Pilsudki's Poland and continued to organise on behalf of Jewish workers. Bundists helped organise and lead the 1943 Warsaw Ghetto uprising against the Nazis, and fought to the last as it was crushed.

The last independent Russian trade union expired in October 1921. Somehow, until then, the Chemical Workers Union had preserved its independence. Its "Presidium" included two Mensheviks, one Right SR, one Left SR, one anarchist and other non-party activists. At a regional conference in March 1921, Bolshevik delegates proposed that Lenin be elected "Honorary Chair" of the union, but when put to a vote the majority of delegates voted for Martov instead. The contested position then went to a national conference in October, at which twice the number of delegates than usual turned up, the extras being Bolshevik "members" not elected or mandated. A resolution put by the Bolsheviks on the tasks of the trade unions was rejected by 123 votes to 113. At this the Bolsheviks walked out and formed a new union, the "Congress of Red Chemical Workers", which promptly announced its submission to the state. The old union closed its conference knowing it would be its last. Shortly after, its leaders were all arrested.[30]

As early as 1919, in response to the increase in the Menshevik vote in the Soviets and the strikes at former Bolshevik industrial strongholds, Lenin had written, "The industrial proletariat [...] has become declassed, dislodged from its class groove, and has ceased to exist as a proletariat". In early 1921 he wrote, "Since the war the industrial workers of Russia have become much less proletarian than they were before, because during the war all those who desired to avoid military service went into the factories. This is common knowledge".[31] He cited, without evidence, an influx of peasants, ex-students and ex-shopkeepers into the remaining factories. Yet before 1914, when the main base of Bolshevik support had been workers fresh from the village and new to the factories, and it was the Mensheviks who attracted the organised proletariat of the trade unions, this distinction had been unimportant. Possibly Lenin was displaying, once again, his dialectical genius.

By 1922 his political mystique was beginning to wear thin. At the Eleventh Party Congress in March 1922 the party – or, at least, those few delegates who still had independent views and the courage to express them – debated if the Russian working class could be said to anymore exist, and if not what that meant for a "dictatorship" based upon it. Lenin made very clear what input and influence the organised workers, such as they were, could have over their working lives. He told the congress:

> It is absolutely essential that all authority in the factories should be concentrated in the hands of management. Under these circumstances any direct intervention by the trade unions in the management of enterprises must be regarded as positively harmful.[32]

In a remarkable speech Lenin dismissed the working class of 1922 as people who had migrated to the factories to avoid the Civil War, although it was unclear why a peasant would migrate from the country where there was, supposedly, a grain and food surplus, to starving Petrograd under siege by the Whites. He also, by implication, dismissed the entire Russian working class in whose name his party retained power. Asking if "real proletarians" came to Russia's factories and plants, he answered,

> It is true in Marx's terms, but Marx was not writing about
> Russia. He was writing about all capitalism as whole, starting
> from the 15th century. Over the course of six hundred years it
> is true, but for present day Russia it is not true.[33]

Alexander Shliapnikov, shortly after to be sent on diplomatic missions where he could cause no more difficulties, responded with the bitter sarcasm of a veteran working-class Bolshevik who had seen all the party's promises of 1917 betrayed and reversed. "Vladimir Ilyich said yesterday that the proletariat as a class, in the sense that Marx meant, does not exist", he told the Congress. With restrained but obvious contempt he addressed Lenin directly. "Permit me to congratulate you", he said, "on being the vanguard of a nonexistent class".[34]

New and Surpris

I pondered all these things, and how
battle, and the thing they fought for c
their defeat, and when it comes turns
meant, and other men have to fight f
under another name.

—William Morris, *A Dream of Jo*

In 2013, Noam Chomsky comn
blows to socialism in the Twe
Bolshevik Revolution".[1] It wa
inside and outside Soviet Russia
swift and immediate suppression
political parties in the weeks foll
the denial of press and other p
since the February Revolution,
encircle, choke and eventually d
political parties. Beyond Russia, t
of the Bolshevik Revolution and
a disaster to the prospects of a ur

ng Worlds

en fight and lose the
mes about in spite of
ut not to be what they
what they meant

n Ball

ented, "one of the great
tieth Century was the
a blow delivered both
. Inside Russia, after the
f conservative and liberal
wing October 1917, and
litical freedoms gained
he Bolsheviks moved to
estroy the remaining left
e influence and example
the Bolshevik Party was
fied and popular socialist

Bolshevik Revolution hit all the right buttons. Inconvenient details, such as the persecution of other socialists, state control of trade unions and suppression of strikes and Soviets, were brushed aside. All critical faculties were suspended in the inspirational light of what many socialists perceived as an authentic working-class revolution. For example, the adulation of militant Minnesota miners for Lenin and the Bolsheviks in 1918 was intense, with one activist admitting, "In mystic silence, almost in religious ecstasy, did we admire everything that came from Russia".[3]

The widespread support across the left for Lenin and the Bolsheviks was a classic instance of what Maurice Brinton called "the irrational in politics", specifically that "those aspiring to a non-alienated and creative society based on equality and freedom should 'break' with bourgeois conceptions only to espouse the hierarchical, dogmatic, manipulatory and puritanical ideas of Leninism".[4] Some Marxists did of course support Lenin's version of the Dictatorship of the Proletariat with full understanding of what it meant, because they believed that it promised the best route to socialism and because social, civil and democratic rights were not a priority for them. They were commissars and proud of it. But most socialists did not think like this. They did not support Bolshevism because of ruthless pragmatism, nor from an objective analysis of class forces, nor because "the dialectic" revealed that a higher synthesis would emerge from the contradictions of the present crisis. They believed because they wished to believe.

Many still do. Even now it is a standard argument of those defending Lenin and the Bolsheviks that by 1921 the

Russian working class that achieved the October Revolution was "atomised", "declassed", had in effect disappeared. This is not so. The Russian working class of the 1920s had political consciousness, it was collectively organised and it fought the Bolshevik state apparatus. In July 1923 alone more than one hundred enterprises employing a total of 50,000 workers were on strike. In August this nearly doubled. Brovkin records the pattern of worker action and government reaction. "The Bolsheviks acted with the explicit purpose of routing out the possibility of further progress. They tried to condition workers that labour protest was futile".[5] Despite this, John B. Hatch's study of labour conflict in Moscow in the 1920s records that between 1921 and 1926 all branches of industry and transport experienced wildcat strikes, run by spontaneously organised strike committees and "parallel factory committees".[6]

Aside from pure numbers – and Petrograd excepted, the exodus of workers from town to country has been exaggerated, with the bulk of women workers, for example, staying put – there is little evidence to support the "deproletarianisation" thesis. Daniel R. Brower records that "average decline in the north (167 towns in all, excluding the capital cities) amounted to 24% between 1917 and 1920".[7] Diane P. Koenker found that military mobilisation of young male workers and the flight to the countryside of unskilled recent migrants, servants etc., actually left "an older, more female and more urbanised working class population".[8] In these circumstances working-class survival and adaptation was demonstrated by "a strong sense of neighbourhood and district loyalty" and an increase in freely available civil marriages, something that in itself indicates a secular, urban working class, not backward peasants drifting to the city.

Examining two examples of strong and cohesive Russian working-class occupational groups, Moscow's printers and the miners of the Don Basin, Lewis Seigelbaum and Ronald Suny point out that although their professional and social milieu were poles apart—one urban, literate, disciplined; the other living in tight-knit mining settlements, mostly illiterate and politically volatile—they both fell back on traditions of community self-reliance and workers' self-management during the Civil War, and in its aftermath stood up for their interests against the new regime. As a result, they both "failed to conform to the party's productivist, self-sacrificing vision".[9]

The Mensheviks' émigré journal was kept well informed of industrial relations matters by its remaining underground activists. In 1924 it published a detailed report on the Moscow printers: its leaders were in exile or prison; Factory Committees had become junior partners of the GPU; workers who spoke up were sacked; those who complied were given special privileges. A once-vibrant working atmosphere, full of political debate, was now mostly silent and defeated.[10] In the end, due to the unrelenting criticisms of shopfloor printers, "the union opted for better stage management rather than more genuine democracy".[11] One method of ensuring difficult issues were not discussed openly was to fill meetings with ideological lectures, from which workers took refuge in absenteeism, sarcasm and satire. In 1924 the "Union Organisers' Dictionary" of the Print Union defined "activism" as "…the ability to sit through a report on the international situation to the end".[12]

The anger and incomprehension with which Bolshevik leaders greeted the Workers' Opposition, Menshevik trade unionists and non-party workers derived from their heroic-simplistic conception of an "advanced" or "conscious" worker. As Sheila Fitzpatrick astutely observed, "a 'conscious' worker was a worker who fitted the intellectuals' idea of what a worker ought to be",[13] and Bolshevism, for all its rhetoric, was led by intellectuals. For Lenin, Trotsky and Bukharin the disappearance by 1921 of conscious or advanced workers—all, apparently, either killed or promoted—meant there was no longer a Russian working class worth speaking of. But as Koenker's investigations suggest, its class consciousness "did not so much disappear as migrate from the workplace to the home, the neighborhood, and such proliferating cultural facilities as libraries, schools, and the theatre".[14]

This was real class consciousness, of the kind examined by E.P Thompson in *The Making of the English Working Class*, a work that valorised the life experience of a young proletariat at the beginning of the 19th century which—like its Russian counterpart one hundred years later—did not slot neatly into Marxist theoretical categories. In a later work Thompson dismissed these categories, observing "Classes do not exist as separate entities". Class, he suggested, is a relationship, a process, a mutual inter-action within specific social circumstances. In that sense, "Class eventuates as men and women live their productive relations....and as they handle these experiences in cultural ways"[15]. The class consciousness of the Russian working class of 1917 to 1930 was rooted in the productive relations of a revolution gone wrong. It lived and breathed in a world of tenements, street vendors, deserters, black markets and pubs as much as Rosta Windows, Red Guards and Soviets. It resisted being turned into Soviet marble. In 1926 the Bolshevik economist Preobrazhenski noted of the party's failed attempts to divert off-duty workers, especially young workers, away from the wildly popular Foxtrot craze towards politically elevating activity, "Our clubs are empty but the pubs are full".[16]

The Dictatorship of the Proletariat predictably failed, but was there ever a realistic chance of a successful democratic socialist settlement in Russia in 1917? It is not as impossible as many claim. The policies of the liberal Kadets and moderate Mensheviks of the Provisional Government were often inept and badly communicated, above all the decision to remain in the war as a form of "revolutionary defencism" against the Kaiser's imperialism. Kerensky's offensive of June 1917 was doomed to failure and was perhaps the major reason for the Provisional Government's eclipse. Postponing immediate elections for a Constituent Assembly also provided the Bolsheviks with an excuse to accuse the government of soft-peddling on democracy and allowed the reactionary right led by Kornilov time to mobilise. Caught in between, the Kadets and Mensheviks seemed paralysed.

Yet the policies of the Bolsheviks after October 1917 emphasised what intractable problems had faced the Provisional Government. Sovnarcom's decision in March 1918 to take any peace offered led to the loss of great swathes of vital territory and a mass rebellion on the left that was, in essence, the same revolutionary defencism assailed the year before. The closure of the Constituent Assembly after a national election in which the SRs emerged as the majority party, and the suppression of Soviets that did not return Bolshevik majorities, also put the efforts of the Kadet-Menshevik-SR alliance of 1917 in a more positive light.

The hypothetical scenario of a more inclusive and disciplined democratic left government before and after October 1917 bears examination. Had one existed from April 1917, when the conservatives departed the Provisional Government, October may never have occurred. At various moments in 1917 the SRs led by Chernov, the Menshevik-Internationalists led by Martov and the Bolshevik "centre" led by Kamenev, Zinoviev, Rykov and Lunacharsky almost reached agreement. After October 1917 there was a widespread feeling that the best way to safeguard the Soviet system and protect the Constituent Assembly, bodies which need not have been mutually exclusive, was to form a socialist coalition government. Most delegates at the Second Congress of Soviets voted for this. Most trade unions supported it.

To have any chance of legitimacy and longevity any democratic left government that emerged from the revolutionary process, either from the overthrow of Tsarist autocracy in February 1917 or post-October 1917, would have had to integrate and protect large parts of the social revolution that had swept Russian society. Above all it would have needed to find a compromise solution, a governance model or constitutional settlement that allowed the Soviets, urban and rural, significant control over policy. Significantly, in his one speech as President of the Constituent Assembly in January 1918, Victor Chernov indicated that such a settlement was acceptable. With good will and necessary compromise it could have been reached. Had it been, the worst of the Civil War might have been avoided and some form of democracy retained.

As Russia veered from autocracy to autocracy, the political space in which a progressive democratic government could survive quickly shrunk to nothing. Not until 1927 did Trotsky advance a rounded critique of the Soviet system of the mid-1920s, and even then it was an attack on bureaucratic degeneration and lack of centralised economic planning, not a call for political pluralism. The Declaration of the United Opposition of Trotsky, Zinoviev and Kamenev, in Tony Cliff's words, "embraced the essential principles of the Opposition case for the whole period 1923-27".[17] The Declaration identified "bureaucratism", not the political system which had produced it, as the cause of the crisis within the party. It also called for rapid industrialisation to offset what it saw as the damage inflicted on Soviet society by the NEP and the revival of the Kulaks.

In late 1927 the Opposition's Platform, whilst it demanded "working-class democracy", made clear that the Opposition "will fight with all our power against the idea of two parties, because the Dictatorship of the Proletariat demands at its very core a single proletarian party".[18] Stalin could live with that. Despite a few supportive rallies in the factories of Moscow and Petrograd, the Opposition was easily dispersed and Trotsky was sent into internal exile. External exile followed in 1929.

Trotsky never rejected the concept of central planning carried out on a grand scale. One of his key allies in the

Opposition, the economist Evgeny Preobrazhenski, advocated a policy of "Primitive Socialist Accumulation". He argued that capitalism in England took off during the Industrial Revolution of 1770–1830 through the rapid accumulation of surplus value and excess capital. Socialism, especially a socialism that had arisen in an economically backward country, must do the same. Because a socialist country could not (in theory) exploit the working class, the resource to drive this process had to come from the economic surplus produced by the peasants. This meant maintaining the state's monopoly of trade and artificially fixing prices to drain resources from agriculture and concentrate them in industry. The massive Soviet industrialisation of the Five Year Plans, the first of which began in 1928, rested on this concept.

Socialist Accumulation was the antithesis of the NEP that had delivered Soviet Russia relative prosperity and stability since 1921. For that reason, the NEP's primary advocate, Bukharin, completely opposed it and assumed that Stalin, his partner in the leadership between 1925 and 1928, did also. Between 1921 and 1926 the NEP had restored Russia's productivity to its pre-war years. It had also spread wealth, though not equitably. The notorious "Nepmen" skimmed off a lot of it, to the anger of urban workers whose wages did not keep pace. But Bukharin, traumatised by the mass alienation of the peasantry from the regime during the Civil War, was convinced that the Soviet Union could not survive unless it accommodated the majority of its population in this way. He believed that after the enormous wounds inflicted on the social fabric of the country by the Civil War, socialism must now avoid "catastrophic programmes" and must "proceed upon an evolutionary path".[19]

As the Twenties progressed Bukharin worried more about the emergence of a new ruling class based on "monopolistic" power and privilege than about the supposed threat to socialism posed by private producers. He stated plainly:

> To fulfill the economic functions of the small producers, small peasants etc., requires too many employees and administrators. The attempt to replace all these small figures with state *chinovniki* (Tsarist bureaucrats) [...] gives birth to such a colossal apparatus that the expenditure for its maintenance proves to be incomparably more significant than the unproductive costs which derive from the anachronistic condition of small production.[20]

Between 1925 and 1928 Bukharin and Stalin seemed to agree on this. But in 1928 the Central Committee, controlled by Stalin, approved the first of the Soviet Union's Five Year Plans – what Bukharin called a "Genghis Khan Plan". It was to run from 1928 to 1933 and concentrate on the expansion of heavy industry and intensified requisition of surplus from the peasants. In 1929 Stalin revised it to include the complete, forced collectivisation of agriculture. It was Socialist Accumulation gone nuclear.

Although Trotsky did not endorse every aspect of Preobrazhenski's concept, Deutscher conceded that in essence "it was still the same case they were both defending".[21] Hence many of his followers, including Preobrazhenski, abandoned the Opposition in 1929 once Stalin embarked on collectivisation of the peasantry. It seemed to them that Stalin, having disposed of Bukharin and the NEP, had adopted the economic programme of the Opposition, and that it was their duty as Bolsheviks to help him carry it out. It encompassed not just the complete collectivisation of Russian agriculture but the elimination of all Kulaks and private traders.

Tens of millions of peasants were forced into "Kolkhoz" or "Sovkhoz" collective farms, with the result that in 1933 alone nearly four million people died of famine. Huge new engineering plants were created. Mining in the Don Basin and the Urals expanded ten-fold. The White Sea–Baltic Canal was blasted into existence. The industrial workforce rose from 3.12 million in 1928 to over 6 million in 1932 and to 12 million by 1937. A mass literacy drive enabled new peasant employees to participate. With the removal of bourgeois "specialists" some workers secured more prestigious positions and rewards. These newly empowered functionaries formed Stalin's social base, although there was no thought given to production of consumer items for the wider masses.

The Plan's goals were for more machinery, coal, iron and steel. In the "long wave" of history this was what counted. Despite the drama, violence and suffering of the Bolshevik Revolution and the Civil War, when the dust settled the Russian state pulled itself back together and continued its 19th-century pattern of industrialisation. It was a more coercive and dictatorial process than that overseen by Count Witte, but the massive industrialisation delivered in the 1930s was the long-term economic policy of Stalin *and* Trotsky.

Stalinism reached its dark culmination in the Main Camp Administration, or GULAG. The first seed of the Gulag was planted in 1918 with the special "inner prison" inside Cheka

HQ on Lubyanka Square, and then expanded to other prisons such as Butryka, which held political prisoners, mainly socialists and anarchists. In 1920 the first Special Purpose Camp was opened on Solovetsky Island in the White Sea, to which thousands of Kronstadt sailors were sent after the mutiny. In 1923 approximately 300 socialist prisoners were transferred to Solovetsky. By 1925 it held 6,000 prisoners, topped up by White Guard officers, aristocrats, landowners and "speculators". It is indicative of the conditions on Solovetsky that a quarter of these died in the winter of 1925-26.[22] In 1930 the fledgling Gulag system was expanded to contain a flood of new prisoners. By 1932 the camps contained 200,000 prisoners. By 1935 they held 800,000. Then came the Great Purge of 1936-38.

The physical liquidation of huge numbers of the ruling party, government officials and the Red Army were Stalin's own psychotic policies, but the tracklines of the Gulag were laid by Lenin. Just six weeks after October 1917 the mission of the Cheka established that it was not what a person had done (i.e. specific evidence of a crime or treasonable activity) that determined their guilt, but their supposed sociological position and political opinion as defined by the state police. The Decree on the "Socialist Fatherland" of February 1918 made that explicit and gave the Cheka the right of execution without trial. In June 1919, on the recommendation of Lenin and Dzerzhinsky, the first camps with the express purpose of using prisoners for industrial slave labour were opened. Stalin did not pervert this system. He simply enlarged it.

None of this should have come as a shock. In 1939, when considering the rise of Stalin, George Orwell wrote, "The essential act is the rejection of democracy—that is, of the underlying values of democracy; once you have decided upon that, Stalin—or at any rate someone *like* Stalin—is already on the way".[23] Lenin candidly admitted that the Dictatorship of the Proletariat was force unrestrained by law. After October 1917 he labeled all who opposed the Bolshevik Party counter-revolutionary. By 1921 he leveled that accusation at opponents within the party. He had been open about his aims from the formation of the RSDLP. The first Russian edition of *What Is To Be Done?* reproduced on its frontispiece Ferdinand's Lassalle's aphorism, "The Party strengthens itself by purging itself". Lenin lived by that edict and his political heirs took it to heart.

Trotsky was easily the most impressive of those heirs. Despite his many flaws, follies and crimes, the attraction of the man is obvious. He could write like an angel. He was a supple and provocative thinker and a courageous fighter for his version of social emancipation. Many believe his greatest achievements were during the revolution, in October 1917, and the building of the Red Army shortly after. But these were also the seeds of his downfall, of the hubris that led him to advocate the militarisation of labour and to dismiss any opposition, even socialist opposition, as unnecessary. Martin Amis in *Koba the Dread* and Clive James in *Cultural Amnesia* condemned him unreservedly as a mass murderer and criminal. But judgments from Amis, James or historians such as Robert Service are one-sided. They do not condemn Western statesmen like Churchill or Eisenhower or Reagan—whose political policies and military interventions caused far more innocent deaths than those of Trotsky—in the same manner, or hold them to the same standards.

The greatness of Trotsky derives from his struggle against Stalinism in the 1930s, his prescient and insightful warnings about German fascism, and his unflagging resistance, even as friends and family were murdered around him, to Stalin's enormous corruption of socialism. In that time, most especially in his work with the American liberal John Dewey on exposing the criminal frame-up of the Moscow Trials, he achieved the moral stature of a Cicero, a Luther, a Bertrand Russell or a Noam Chomsky, of a truth-teller who could "do no other". Many of his works—especially *History of the Russian Revolution, Literature and Revolution, My Life* and his writings on Germany and Britain—repay rereading today and contain food for thought for socialists struggling with the "forces of conservatism" on both left and right. Yet he, as much as Lenin, was responsible for introducing the structures and institutions of the Dictatorship of the Proletariat, for the "substitutionism" against which he warned in 1903.

After Khrushchev's "Secret Speech" in 1956 and the acknowledgement of Stalin's crimes, the myth of the Soviet Union took a severe blow. The New Left which emerged in the early 1960s drew intellectual sustenance from a diverse range of thinkers, such as the neo-Marxist philosopher Herbert Marcuse, the sociologist C. Wright Mills, the cultural theorist Stuart Hall, and E.P. Thompson. In 1959 Thompson described this new young generation of leftists as a

generation which never looked upon the Soviet Union as a weak but heroic Workers' State; but rather as the nation of the Great Purges and Stalingrad, of Stalin's Byzantine Birthday and of Khruschev's Secret Speech; as the vast military and industrial power which repressed the Hungarian Rising and threw the first Sputniks into space [...] The young people are enthusiastic enough. But their enthusiasm is not for the Party, or the Movement, or the established Political Leaders [...] They prefer the amateur organisation and amateurish platforms of CND to the manner of the left wing professional.[24]

In the 1960s and 1970s Marxism and Leninism—sometimes enmeshed in the new quasi-religious cult of Maoism— underwent an unexpected intellectual resurgence, at least amongst the student and academic left. But it had a limited impact on the labour and trade union movement. The main reason for the failure of the 1960s New Left to sustain itself was its inability to understand or connect to working-class struggles. In 1968-69 it seemed for a brief moment that a genuine alliance between the radical elements of the New Left and the trade union movement, especially in France and Italy, might emerge. But it was not to be. The unions had more realistic goals than revolution in mind and the New Left preferred its social and intellectual wonderland.

By the end of the 1960s New Left thinking had bifurcated. On one side there was the beginning of Cultural Theory and "the long march through the institutions", a march that usually ended up in the tutor's common room and a villa on Lake Como. On the other, in reaction to this, there was a reassertion of a heavily intellectualised Marxism that reproduced the worst aspects of Leninism under the guise of Structuralism. In Britain the leading lights of the *New Left Review* produced long, scintillating and insightful essays on British Labour and British culture, skewering and damning both, but never turned their analytical weapons on the record of the Bolsheviks during 1917-21. Small wonder that the Whitehall-Oxbridge Stalinist E.H. Carr praised the intellectual mandarins of the *NLR* and strongly endorsed his friend Isaac Deutscher's attack on George Orwell and *1984*. Orwell's crime was not only to have seen through Leninism and the Soviet myth long before New Left intellectuals eventually woke up but to have also, in *Animal Farm*, delivered it an artistic death blow.

The same dynamic played out in America. The popular base and promise of the American Socialist Party was shattered by the Bolshevik Revolution and the attempts of American Leninists to re-orient the party towards Moscow and the Comintern. The American New Left of the 1960s, although it stemmed from democratic and inclusive movements such as Students for a Democratic Society (SDS) and the Student Nonviolent Coordinating Committee (SNCC), also took a futile detour into Leninism and Maoism, which meant it had absolutely no attraction to American workers. By 1971 SDS organisers with a base in the working class, such as Jack Newfield, could write with justification, "in its Weathermen, Panther (White) and Yippee incarnations, the New Left seems anti-democratic, terroristic, dogmatic, stoned on rhetoric and badly disconnected from everyday reality".[25]

At the same time the libertarians of the European left, such as Daniel Cohn-Bendit, went their own way. In *Obsolete Communism: The Left Wing Alternative* (1968) Cohn-Bendit attacked the new fashion on the left to uncritically revere Lenin and Trotsky. Drawing instead from Luxemburg,

Kollontai and Reich, he condemned Lenin and the Bolshevik Party as an exploiter and then a fetter on the revolutionary energies unleashed by the February 1917 Revolution. For him, October represented "the point where the action and aspiration of the masses co-incided with those of the temporarily de-Bolshevised Bolshevik Party". He disinterred the struggles of Makhno and the Kronstadt sailors and concluded, "it was not in 1927, nor even in 1920, but in 1918 and under the personal leadership of Trotsky and Lenin that the social revolution became perverted—a fact Trotsky could never understand, simply because he himself was one of its prime architects".[26]

Yet, incredibly, Leninist theorists continue to churn out the same discredited arguments in various tomes—*Lenin Reloaded*, *Lenin Rediscovered*, *Lenin Reconstructed*, *Unfinished Leninism*, etc. Although these works vary in quality, they display the same historical blindspots, the same refusal to directly address the record of rigged Soviets, suppressed strikes, the EAD and the Cheka, and how early in the revolutionary process these appeared. Even the admirable Paul Foot, whose *Red Shelley* and *The Vote* are outstanding radical histories full of passion and intelligence, can casually mention in the latter book "The destruction of the Russian Soviets in the 1930s",[27] when the Soviets as functioning democratic organs were stone dead by 1920.

The attempted resurrection of Leninism is doomed to failure. Mass resistance to vicious austerity and galloping inequality has found expression in a variety of new movements and campaigns such as Occupy, the *Indignados*, Climate Camp, *Comunilidad*, the Bolivarian Revolution, the

Arab Spring, Syriza, Podemos and the campaign to elect and re-elect Jeremy Corbyn as leader of the Labour Party. These campaigns—some successful, some stalled—have all eschewed the authoritarian, top-down programmes of the traditional Leninist and/or Social Democratic Party. They have taken the path suggested by Hilary Wainwright in 2015, that of "the need to abandon purisms and single perspective politics—whether pure anarchism, pure parliamentarianism, pure syndicalism or any other one-track approach—and instead to urge a hybrid and experimental politics where collaboration is the guiding method".[28]

The strength of this kind of broad, experimental radicalism—and one reason it has had more impact than all the "revolutionary socialist" groups combined—is that it does not ground its political activity on an exclusionary and anachronistic notion of the working class. In post-industrial capitalist societies the working class is now so heavily stratified, fragmented and lacking in common social and cultural referents that the concept itself can hinder as much as liberate. This does *not* mean that "we are all middle-class now". On the contrary, we are, if anything, all working-class now, if the working class is defined as the vast majority of the population outside the charmed circle of the political and economic elite—the 99% as opposed to the 1%.

Trotsky often referred to the "molecular movements" of the masses. But molecules mutate and evolve. When Murray Bookchin wrote of "class decomposition", he meant it not solely as an economic process, nor as a process that would have a depoliticising effect, but as one that offered liberation from cultural prisons constructed by the elite. He considered that "the process of decomposition embraces not only the traditional class structure but also the patriarchal family, authoritarian modes of upbringing, the influence of religion, the institutions of the state, and the mores built around toil, renunciation, guilt and repressed sexuality".[29] If this were the end result of the dissolution of the proletariat, it could be welcomed as a necessary step towards broader social emancipation, as obviously progressive as women's liberation or racial equality.

Sadly, capitalism is not so kind. Guy Standing's identification of the "precariat" reveals a harsher truth. The precariat is the working class stripped of trade union protection or regular employment, frequently laid off or working to zero-hours contracts in unregulated areas of the fast-food industry, cleaning, retail, marketing, etc. The precariat is not an underclass – it encompasses workers with families and mortgages, single young people in rented accommodation or multi-occupancy homes, and educated migrants willing to take any job. It takes the process of working-class decomposition and finds instead "recomposition", i.e. marginalised, exploited people tied to economic serfdom by the logic of the neoliberal economy but not, as was once the case, centralised in big industrial complexes run by identifiable owners and opposed by visible trade unions.

There are still significant areas of full-time working-class employment outside the precarious service sector and the gig economy, i.e. in manufacturing, engineering, construction and transport. But as the examples of the Grangemouth oil refinery in Scotland and Port Talbot steel works in Wales demonstrate, "full-time" and "secure" are now relative terms. Neoliberalism has introduced precarity right across the working class. A steel worker is at the mercy of corporate outsourcing as much as a shared services provider. Whatever class de(re)composition has occurred or is occurring in the global economy, trade unions remain essential to defend workers from exploitation in the workplace and to provide a better quality of life outside it. But they cannot reset the clock to the days of mass industry or preserve every existing job regardless. Nor should they want to.

Protecting public services and local communities from the ravages of austerity is vitally important, but ultimately it is still laagering the wagons. Lasting social emancipation consists in campaigning for and helping to create new, innovative, high-quality work that provides not only good pay, decent pensions and early retirement, but freedom from coercion and hierarchy, from the fate of becoming a cog in the machine of corporate capitalism. In 1982, André Gorz wrote, "Protecting jobs and skills, rather than seeking to control and benefit from the way in which work is abolished, will remain the main concern of traditional trade unionism. That is why it is bound to remain on the defensive". [30]

It is still on the defensive. For many years now, the left and the trade unions have failed to articulate a convincing narrative of an alternative, better and fundamentally different society, of the kind suggested by earlier Marxists like August Bebel, William Morris and Alexander Bogdanov, a community in which democratic ownership of natural resources means a reduction in compulsory labour in favour of greater leisure, creativity, altruism and public welfare. For most people there are no funds, no social framework, no moral endorsements or financial inducements to reject the work ethic in favour of the full development of one's personality and potential, to participate in a process in which, as Trotsky put it in the conclusion to *Literature and Revolution*, "Social construction and psycho-physical self-education will become two aspects of the same process".[31] We are a fair way from that, but not as far as defeatists and cynics suppose.

New models of work are emerging within the folds of a dysfunctional, dying capitalism. These range from large collaborative business models such as the Spanish Mondragon Federation of Workers' Cooperatives, to small non-profit social enterprises that rely on unpaid voluntary work to achieve definite social goals. The Mondragon Federation is Spain's seventh-largest company, employing 75,000 people in 257 companies covering retail, industry, finance and knowledge products. Because it has its own financial support structure (local banks, mutual funds, etc.) it responds to recession differently than do traditional companies. It does not lay off workers but reassigns them, it accepts a temporary lack of profit, it provides workers for whom it cannot for the moment find work with non-monetary rewards. With wages determined by Mondragon's worker-owners, the ratio between those who perform "executive" functions and the average worker is only 5:1, compared to 475:1 in large capitalist corporations.

In 2009 Mondragon signed an agreement with the us United Steelworkers Union (USW) to create worker cooperatives in the United States. In 2012 the USW, Mondragon and the Ohio Employee Ownership Center launched a "Union-Co-Op Model" to rescue and reinvigorate declining rust-belt industries. The model is part of a budding alternative economy in the US. Already over 13 million Americans work in 11,400 Employee Stock Ownership Plan Companies (ESOPs), with many more in a variety of not-for-profit enterprises. Extrapolating this trend, the socialist SF writer Kim Stanley Robinson's visionary novel *2312* suggests that three hundred years hence the basis of the solar system's entire economy (beyond an Earth devastated by climate change) will be a vast co-operative network run by quantum AIs called "the Mondragon".

That network is reaching out, building on experiments begun decades ago. The town of Marinaleda in Andalusia is a successful "cooperative municipality" run on communist lines. After the death of Franco, the citizens of Marinaleda rejected mainstream political parties and elected members of the Workers' Unity Collective to oversee their town and surrounding rural area. After buying up vacant landed estates the town merged all of its agriculture, industries and services into one integrated cooperative in which all citizens work and reward is distributed equitably. Although private enterprise is permitted (there are private bars and cafes run by locals, but a Starbucks would not be allowed), most people work for the cooperative. All workers receive the same salary and profits are re-invested to create more jobs. Its priorities and plans are decided in the town's General Assembly, a democratic forum similar to those of the Occupy movement or the Kronstadt Soviet.

Marinaleda has no police force because there is no crime. Once a month volunteers perform necessary municipal tasks such as cleaning and maintenance. Alone in post–2008 Spain, wracked by economic depression and austerity, it has full employment (from 60% unemployment in the 1970s) and no poverty. Speaking of Marinaleda's "communist utopia", the town's mayor Juan Manuel Gordillo said, "We have learned that it is not enough to define utopia, nor is it enough to fight against the reactionary forces. One must build it here and now, brick by brick, patiently but steadily, until we can make the old dreams a reality [...] We sincerely believe that there is no future that is not built in the present".[32]

Mondragon and Marinaleda exemplify the real, protracted transition from capitalism to socialism, not the Leninist fantasy version. Other examples are micro-enterprises with social aims, credit unions, mutuals, ESOPs and workers' cooperatives, supported by the use of labour-saving technology to reduce working hours with no loss of pay. The over-riding characteristic of such organsations is that they are value-driven, motivated by social goals rather than distribution of profit. From them to become firmly established – to succeed, connect and grow – the entire structure of privatised, corporate-led neoliberalism must be replaced by an enabling economy of intelligent regulation and state-sponsored support. With this in mind a growing number of left thinkers such as Paul Mason, George Monbiot and Nick Srnicek argue that one of the 21st century left's central tasks is to foster new value systems, new business models, new working patterns, new relations of production, and insert these into the DNA of capitalism, reconfiguring its operating code, mutating the system from within, liberating knowledge, information, creativity and labour-time.

The Bolsheviks dallied with this alternative economy in the 1920s. Before the enormous wrong turn of 1929 that force-fed Russian workers into a titanic state capitalist machine, Bukharin had advocated a "wager on the cooperatives". He suggested the best way to satisfy the small-producer instincts of the peasants and to move the Soviet economy towards socialism was to expand the cooperative sector, supported by government credit and state-managed markets. This would constitute "the continuous and systematic growth of the cells of the future socialist society".[33] In this Bukharin – far more than Lenin, Trotsky or Stalin – followed in the footsteps of Marx.

In his Inaugural Address to the First International in 1864, Marx spoke of the British workers' cooperative movement. "The value of these great social experiments cannot be over-stated", he declared,

> By deed, instead of by argument, they have shown that production on a large scale, and in accord with the behests of modern science, may be carried on without the existence of a class of masters employing a class of hands; that to bear fruit, the means of labour need not be monopolised as a means of dominion over, and extortion against, the laboring man himself; and that, like slave labour, like serf labour, hired labour is but a transitory and inferior form, destined to disappear before associated labour plying its toil with a willing hand, a ready mind, and a joyous heart.[34]

In like vein, Mark Fisher, the author of *Capitalist Realism* and an acute cartographer of the social and cultural reality wrought by neoliberalism, echoed this when he wrote of the socialist alternative, "Our struggle must be towards the construction of a new and surprising world, not the preservation of identities shaped and distorted by capital".[35]

Fisher saw that the primary strategic goal of any serious left should be to foresee and shape the future. The essential thing is not just to create the political vehicle to help deliver it—in my view, either radically transformed left parties operating more like social movements than traditional political parties, or entirely new cross-class progressive alliances—but to germinate the seeds of an alternative society within the decimated shell of the existing one. We have already seen this process in action in the creation of Greece's "Solidarity Economy", an unofficial sub-culture of free exchange and alternative currencies that is providing the necessities of life—food banks, soup kitchens, legal aid, free education and medical care—to those who can no longer afford them.

Thessaloniki's Micropolis, which emerged out of the disintegration of Greece's formal economy after the 2008 crash, is a voluntary "community" which includes a daycare centre, workshops, a library, a kitchen that serves cheap food, and a farmer's market where farmers not only sell produce but teach others to be self-sufficient. It also has a Wild Animals Team that rescue and support abandoned and injured animals. Micropolis reaches out to its equivalents in other countries, buying its coffee from Zapatista liberated zones and its sugar from the Brazilian Landless Workers Movement. It is run via direct democracy and a weekly General Assembly.

Micropolis has been called "an example of how alternative institutions can meet our collective needs in the short term while prefiguring the self-managed society".[36]

Similar examples exist all over the world. To take just one, the Mousai House in the heart of Afro-American Washington D.C. is a communally owned music venue, studio, school and community centre that exists outside the conventional money economy. Providing peer-led cooperative education, the Mousai House has been converted from an abandoned warehouse to "a self-sufficient, self-determined artist-led cooperative incubator". Its membership pays minimal fees to take part and run the enterprise, but the fees are optional and can be replaced by other input such as teaching aspiring musicians. It is just one segment of a growing national network of democratically owned enterprises providing life opportunities and dignified employment to an excluded black underclass. Of this network, the political economist and specialist in community-based asset building Jessica Gordon Nembhard wrote, "The theory of change behind this model of a cooperative solidarity commonwealth is that the more people that practice economic democracy, collective ownership, and economic transparency, the more they will come to expect to see these practices in the rest of their lives".[37]

This impulse to what Irving Howe called "a world more attractive" finds expression at all levels. The bourgeoisie are not immune. After the decline and decay of the elevated tracks that used to feed New York's meatpacking district, a group of local residents formed a not-for-profit group called the Friends of the Highline and lobbied to convert the disused track to an urban greenway running for two miles through central Manhattan. In response the New York City government committed $50 million of public funds to assist the conversion of the Highline into an elevated urban park. The Highline is an example of how collective voluntary endeavour, assisted by imaginative support from local government, can turn the discarded structures of industrial capitalism into free green spaces for public use and enjoyment.

If neoliberalism is the undiluted logic of capital, the marketisation of every aspect of our lives, then projects like Micropolis, the Mousai House and the Highline are the *de-marketisation* of capitalism, the organic emergence of a Solidarity Economy. By its very nature an economy of this type can only be run on democratic lines, with the continuous input of the citizens it services. Murray Bookchin—a man raised in the Bronx by his exiled SR grandmother—championed the model of the popular general assembly, as practiced in Kronstadt, Rojava and by Occupy. There are logistical issues with a General Assembly representing an area (e.g. a city) beyond a certain size and population, but these could be solved by a mixture of local assemblies reporting upward and continuous digital inter-connectivity.

Such a model would also require acknowledgement there is only so far consensus-oriented decision-making can go, and that ultimately decision-making has to be based on democratic debate and majority vote. This model is a modern variant of the Council Communist philosophy rejected by the Bolsheviks. In Noam Chomsky's view,

> some form of Council Communism is the natural form of revolutionary socialism in an industrial society. It reflects the belief that democracy is severely limited when the industrial system is controlled by any form of autocratic elite, whether of owners, managers, technocrats, a 'vanguard party' or a State bureaucracy.[38]

New economic forms and emergent social structures arise spontaneously, but they can fail and fall back. Contrary to John Holloway's assertion that the left can "change the world without taking power", a lasting transformation to a carbon neutral post-capitalism will require progressive governments to pave the way. But who and what will form these governments? Regurgitating the classic social–democratic party is a non-starter. Its traditional social base – the organised industrial working class – has eroded, along with its instinctive sense of identity, community and solidarity. This is a grievous loss, one the old left continues to pathologically deny. And yet, if it is to achieve political victory, it will have to re-create that solidarity in other forms, other communities, other identities, other networks. It will also have to re-create *itself* as the champion of political pluralism, free information, participatory democracy and eco-socialism.

We have seen the beginnings of this process in new political formations such as Podemos in Spain, Die Linke in Germany, the Parti de Gauche in France and the Five Star Movement in Italy. The next stage is for these parties to put aside nationalism and marginal policy differences, and to form a functioning transnational alliance to support and protect each other from Empire's attacks. Even so, it will not be easy for them to be elected or to implement transformative policies once in office. Like Syriza in Greece, they will face ruthless opposition. Nonetheless they must aim for, and deliver, democratic public ownership of key utilities, strong regulation of the financial sector, a real increase in affordable social housing, free higher education and a significant redistribution of wealth. Equally important is the provision of a Universal Basic Income to all citizens. Sufficiently generous, it would deny the neoliberal economy the army of cheap labour on which it depends whilst simultaneously creating space for social, economic and cultural experimentation.

It does not matter if the social framework in which this takes place is called Socialism, or Council Communism, or Social Ecology, or Communalism, or a Solidarity Economy. What matters is that it survives and thrives. Its language, song, poetry, slang, gifs, memes, shops, community centres, websites and fashion are emerging right now. A sprawling, rich, overlapping smorgasbord of anti-capitalist campaigns—Reclaim the Streets, Justice for Janitors, Earth First!, Greenpeace, CodePink, Avaaz.org, Brazil's Landless Workers' Movement, the Zapatistas, Adbusters, UK Uncut, Occupy and many more—mix politics, PR, art and design together. These campaigns, ideas and values are beginning to form a genuinely counter-hegemonic culture. In Britain it finds its best voice in campaigns to defend public services, such as Focus E15, Sisters Uncut, Take Back the City and the People's Assembly, to demand tax justice and to democratise the state. It is based on the recognition, as Russell Brand wrote of the neoliberal capitalist model, that "it's fucked and it's fucking us and it's obsolete".[39]

Lenin and the Bolsheviks also felt capitalism was fucked, but their prescription to end it was, in Rosa Luxemburg's words, "worse than the disease it is meant to cure". At the end of his life Trotsky, politically isolated, examined two awful possibilities: that the Russian Revolution had failed irrevocably and degenerated into "bureaucratic collectivism"; and that the historic mission of the proletariat might never be successfully carried out. In an article written on 25th September, 1939, he pondered, "If the present war will provoke not revolution but a decline of the proletariat, then there remains another alternative [...] the further decay of monopoly capitalism, its further fusion with the state, and the replacement of democracy wherever it still remained with a totalitarian regime".

He acknowledged that if the Stalinist bureaucracy was not "an abhorrent relapse" in the process of socialist construction, then the bureaucracy "would become a new exploiting class". In that scenario,

> if the world proletariat should actually prove incapable of fulfilling the mission placed upon it by the course of development, nothing would remain except openly to recognise that the socialist programme, based upon the internal contradictions of capitalist society, ended as a Utopia.[40]

Trotsky could hardly have expressed more stoic fatalism and romantic despair had he been sitting in "one of the dives on 42nd St" with W.H. Auden, composing the greatest poem of the 1930s. For both men,

> Exiled Thucydides knew
> All that a speech can say
> About Democracy,
> And what dictators do,
> The elderly rubbish they talk
> To an apathetic grave;
> Analysed all in his book,
> The enlightenment driven away,
> The habit-forming pain,
> Mismanagement and grief:
> We must suffer them all again.[41]

Must we suffer them all again, or can the radical left now finally bury the elderly rubbish of Leninism?

Democratic, libertarian socialism existed before Leninism and will outlive it. It has been richly expressed in the work and thought of socialists and anarchists such as Robert Owen, William Morris, Edward Carpenter, Sylvia Pankhurst, Jean Jaurès, Emma Goldman, George Orwell, Aneurin Bevan, Murray Bookchin, Irving Howe, E.P. Thompson, Noam Chomsky, Tony Benn and Pablo Iglesias. This tradition encompasses libertarian Marxists such as Rosa Luxemburg, Anton Pannekoek, Raya Dunayevskya and Maurice Brinton, as well as Marx himself in some of his work, such as the *Economic and Philosophical Manuscripts* and the *Grundisse*. There is no internally consistent doctrine here. In important respects – most obviously, the role of the state – some of these writers contradict each other. But that is the point. Their work is a path to social and political liberation, a route map and general guide, not a doctrine that is omnipotent because it is true.

Leninism and the Bolshevik Revolution are a cautionary tale, a warning from history, an example of how *not* to overturn power and privilege and establish a healthy democratic alternative. Everything that was inspiring and positive about the Russian Revolution – the lively democracy of the Soviets and the Factory Committees, the seizure of landed estates by the peasant *Volosts*, the spirit of the Petrograd working class fighting to defend the city from the Whites, the progressive educational and social experiments, Kollontai's work on female emancipation – sprang from deep values of autonomy and liberation that had very little to do with Marxist or Leninist theory, and were in some respects oppositional to them.

Those values were exemplified by two members of the Russian feminist punk band Pussy Riot, Maria Alyokhina and Nadya Tolokonikova, jailed for two years by the oppressive state machine of Vladmir Putin, who as an ex-KGB chief is literally the political heir of the Cheka, Dzerzhinsky and Lenin. At their trial for a direct-action propaganda protest, Maria Alyokhina said in her closing statement:

Because all you can deprive me of is 'so-called' freedom. This is the only kind that exists in Russia. But nobody can take away my inner freedom. It lives in the word, it will go on living thanks to openness [*glasnost*], when this will be read and heard by thousands of people. This freedom goes on living with every person who is not indifferent, who hears us in this country.

With everyone who found shards of the trial in themselves, like in previous times they found them in Franz Kafka and Guy Debord. I believe that I have honesty and openness, I thirst for the truth; and these things will make all of us just a little bit more free. We will see this yet.[42]

Endnotes

Introduction: Because It's True

1   A colleague of mine, a well-read and politically literate member of the Socialist Party, upon reading in my first book a positive reference to the Menshevik leader Julius Martov, exclaimed with indignation that Martov was an imperialist and supporter of the First World War. Yet Martov was as opposed to the war as were Lenin and Trotsky. He was the prime organiser of the Zimmerwald anti-war conference in 1915 and, after the February 1917 Revolution, the leader of the "Menshevik-Internationalists" who opposed their own party colleagues in the Provisional Government who supported continuation of the war.

2   Christopher Hill, *The Century of Revolution* 1603-1714, Abacus, 1961, p.13

3   For Rosa Luxemburg's "The Russian Revolution" see https://www.marxists.org/archive/luxemburg/1918/russian-revolution/ch01.htm

4   Bertrand Russell, *The Practice and Theory of Bolshevism*, Arc Manor, 2008 (first published 1921), p.43. Russell's short book, written in 1920, is an astonishingly perceptive analysis of early Soviet Russia. Amongst its many insights it predicted that "Asiatic empire with all its pomps and splendours may well be the next stage of development" (Ibid, p.67).

5   Russell, Ibid, p.96

6   Julius Martov, *State and Socialist Revolution*,
     International Review, New York, 1940 (first
     published 1919), p.18

7   Alexander Berkman, *The Bolshevik Myth*, Pluto
     Press, 1989 (first published 1925). Berkman's
     memoir is an indispensable starting point for those
     who instinctively side with the process of socialist
     revolution and the heroic ambition of Bolshevik
     slogans but are not blind to the failure and
     corruption of that ambition. It is written by a brave
     and principled libertarian socialist who devoted
     his life—before and after the Bolshevik detour—to
     those principles.

8   Emma Goldman, *My Disillusionment in Russia*,
     Dover, 2003 (first published 1923/24), p.vii

9   Goldman, Ibid, p.200

10   Noam Chomsky, "Noam Chomsky on Violence,
     Leninism and the Left after Occupy", interview
     with Christopher Helali, 11th September, 2013, at
     http://www.thenorthstar.info/?p=10111

11   Diane P. Koenker, *Labour Relations in Socialist Russia:
     Printers, Their Unions and Soviet Socialism,* National
     Council for Soviet and East European Research,
     1991, p.177

12   Alexander Rabinowitch, *The Bolsheviks in Power:
     The First Year of Soviet Rule in Petrograd*, Indiana
     University Press, 2007, preface, p.x

13   Georg Lukács, *Lenin: A Study in the Unity of his
     Thought*, Verso, 2009 (first published 1924), p.63

14   Lukács, Ibid, p.84

15   Isaac Deutscher, *The Prophet Armed: Trotsky* 1879-1921, Oxford, 1954; *The Prophet Unarmed: Trotsky* 1921-1929, Oxford, 1959; *The Prophet Outcast: Trotsky* 1929-1940, Oxford, 1963.

16   Deutscher, Ibid, p.504

17   E.H. Carr, *The Bolshevik Revolution* 1917-1923 *Volume* 1, Pelican, 1950, p.36

18   Lucio Colletti, *From Rousseau to Lenin*, NLB, 1972, p.236

19   Ernest Mandel, "The Leninist Theory of Organisation", *International Socialist Review* 31, 1970

20   Marcel Liebman, *Leninism under Lenin*, Merlin, 1975, p.428

21   Liebman, Ibid, p.448

22   Lars T. Lih, *Lenin*, Reaktion Books, 2011, p.181

23   Kevin Murphy, *Revolution and Counterrevolution: class struggle in a Moscow metal factory*, Haymarket Books, 2005, p.4

24   Vladimir N. Brovkin, editor and translator, *Dear Comrades: Menshevik Reports on the Bolshevik Revolution and the Civil War*, Hoover Institution Press, 1991, p.16. Brovkin's important collection of previously unpublished Menshevik documents is drawn from the Boris I. Nicolaevsky collection in the archives of the Hoover Institution, Stanford University. It provides evidence of how the Menshevik Party was violently suppressed soon after October 1917, and of how urban and rural Soviets that turned to the Mensheviks during 1918 and 1919 were also suppressed. As well as hitherto

unpublished letters from key figures like Martov, Dan and Axelrod, it includes reports from regional and local Menshevik parties to the Menshevik Central Committee and to party and trade union meetings, appeals to socialists abroad to counter Bolshevik propaganda, and snippets of individual stories. The cumulative picture is a damning one and stands in comparison with the best journalistic reports of the persecution of socialists and trade unionists by state police and military thugs.

25   Gordon Leggett, *The Cheka: Lenin's Political Police*, Oxford University Press, 1981, p.313

26   Murphy, Ibid, p.2, p.x. Tony Cliff was also apparently unaware of the wave of anti-Bolshevik, pro-Soviet strikes in 1918-19. Volume 3 of his life of Lenin, covering the period 1917-23, does not mention them. His sole reference in the book to the suppression of the Soviets by the Bolsheviks, much of which took place in March-June 1918, before the Civil War began, is to note that "the civil war undermined the operation of local Soviets". This meant that "much of the influence of the local Soviets was taken over by the party. One reason was that the local Soviet administration was often backward and corrupt". He does not further substantiate this, although he repeats without criticism a report from Stalin that blames local Soviets for military setbacks in the civil war and the consequent need for the party to "supervise the unreliable Soviets". Tony Cliff, *Revolution Besieged:*

Lenin 1917-23, Bookmarks, 1987, p.150-51

27 *Lenin Reloaded: Towards a Politics of Truth*, edited by
    S. Budgen, S. Kovalakis, S. Žižek, Duke University
    Press, 2007.

28 Paul Le Blanc, *Unfinished Leninism*, Haymarket
    Books, 2014.

29 Le Blanc, Ibid, p.11, p.23

Chapter One: The Spark

1 Christopher Read, "Russian Intelligentsia and
   the Bolshevik Revolution", *History Today*, Vol. 34,
   Issue 10, 1984

2 http://www.counterpunch.org/2006/03/07/
   noam-chomsky-on-the-hopeful-signs-across-latin-
   america/

3 Orlando Figes, *A People's Tragedy: The Russian
   Revolution* 1891-1924, Penguin Books, 1996, p.108

4 See Derek Offord, *The Russian Revolutionary
   Movement in the* 1880s, Cambridge University
   Press, 2004, p.65-81 for a fascinating discussion of
   the Narodniks' views on post and alter-capitalist
   economic relations, derided at the time as
   insufficiently modernist but strangely relevant today.

5 Richard Pipes, *Struve: Liberal on the Left,* 1870-1905,
   Harvard University Press, 1970, p.37-40

6 V. Vorontsov, *Sud'by Kapitalizma v Rossii*, 1882

7 Karl Marx, Letter to Vera Zazulich, 1881, cited
   in David McLellan, *The Thought of Karl Marx*,
   Papermac, 1971, p.111

8 Preface to Second Russian Edition of *Communist*

Manifesto, 1882, in Karl Marx and Frederich Engels, *Selected Works* Vol. 1, Moscow, 1962.

9   Leszek Kolakowski, *Main Currents of Marxism (The Founders; The Golden Age; The Breakdown)*, Norton, 2005, p.270

10 Joan Robinson, *An Essay on Marxian Economics*, Macmillan, second edition, 1966 (originally published 1942), p.xi

11 The entire text of Murray Bookchin's "Listen, Marxist!" is at http://theanarchistlibrary.org/library/murray-bookchin-listen-marxist

12 Sean Michael Wilson & Carl Thompson, *Parecomic: The Story of Michael Albert and Participatory Economics*, Seven Stories Press, 2013, p.147

13 Wilson & Thompson, Ibid, p.161

14 Rudolf Bahro, *Socialism and Survival*, Heretic Books, 1982, p.63

15 André Gorz, *Farewell to the Working Class*, Pluto, 1982, p.15

16 Karl Marx, *Capital Volume III*, New York: Vintage, p.949

17 Karl Marx, *Capital Volume I*, Moscow, 1954, p.302

18 Sal Englert, "The Rise and Fall of the Jewish Labour Bund", *International Socialism* Issue 35, Summer 2012

19 The rich socialist culture of the Bund was disinterred in Paul Mason's *Live Working or Die Fighting* (2006). Mason's book is a superb example of how to make the history of labour and trade union struggle relevant to today's anti-capitalists without boring them with postmodern jargon

and Marxist slogans. It uncovered episodes
and personalities of lost struggles—lost because
they did not fit a narrow conception of class
struggle centered on the Party and the urban
proletariat—and drew lessons from them for the
21st century. In the words of its left-wing publisher,
Haymarket Books, "It is a story of urban slums, self-
help cooperatives, choirs and brass bands, free love,
and self-education by candlelight".

20   Richard Pipes, *Social Democracy and the St Petersburg
        Labour Movement* 1885-1897, Cambridge, 1963, p.60
21   Israel Getzler, *Martov: A Political Biography of a
        Russian Social Democrat*, Cambridge, 2003 (first
        published 1967), p.26. Martov has never received
        the historical and literary monument that, in my
        opinion, he deserves. In the absence of a full-scale
        first-rate biography this study of his political life
        will have to do.
22   G.V. Plekhanov, *On the Tasks of the Socialists in the
        Russian Famine*, Geneva, 1892, p.58
23   Tony Cliff, *Lenin: Building the Party,* 1893-1914,
        Bookmarks, 1986 (originally Pluto, 1975), p.46
24   Cliff, Ibid, p.58

Chapter Two: Mensheviks and Bolsheviks

1   Francis King, *The Narodniks in the Russian
        Revolution: Russia's Socialist Revolutionaries in 1917,
        a Documentary History*, Socialist History Society
        Occasional Paper No.25, 2007, p.4
2   David Shub, *Lenin: A Biography*, Penguin Books,

1948, p.91

3   Ironically, the Tsarist Ministry of the Interior's attitude was not very different from Lenin's after October 1917. Although the Bolsheviks sought to raise literacy levels amongst the peasantry they did not do so in order to bring literature to the masses, much less to promote critical thinking. "The purpose of 'liquidate illiteracy'", said Lenin in 1922, "is only that every peasant should be able to read by himself, without help, our decrees, orders and proclamations. The aim is completely practical. No more" (quoted in Robert Conquest, *Lenin*, Fontana Modern Masters, 1972, p.30).

4   Maureen Perrie, *The Agrarian Policy of the Russian Socialist-Revolutionary Party: From its Origins through the Revolution of 1905-07*, Cambridge University Press, 1976, p.9

5   For Sergei Semenov see Figes, Ibid, pp.233-38

6   The intervention of Chase Manhattan Bank in the Zaptatista uprising at Chiapas in January 1994 and Roett's injunction that the Mexican government crush the rebellion are documented at http://www.hartford-hwp.com/archives/46/025.html

7   Subcommandante Marcos' speech quoted in Staughton Lynd and Andrej Grubacic, *Wobblies and Zapatistas: Conversations on Anarchism, Marxism and Radical History*, PM Press, 2008, p.8

8   Cliff, Ibid, p.87

9   Shub, Ibid, p.75

10   V.I. Lenin, *What Is To Be Done?*, Progress Publishers,
      1947 (first published 1902), p.31, taken from Volume
      5 of the English edition of Lenin's *Collected Works*,
      Progress Publishers.

11   Lenin, Ibid, p.78. Although Lenin is brutally clear
      in *What Is To Be Done?* about the inadequacy of
      the working class as an independent force in the
      formulation of a socialist alternative to capitalism,
      some of his earlier work in the 1890s — when
      he was, for the first and only time in his career,
      personally engaged in grass-roots industrial
      struggle — indicate otherwise. In his 1899 "On
      Strikes", he wrote, "Every strike brings thoughts
      of socialism forcibly to the worker's mind [...]
      A strike teaches workers to understand what the
      strength of the employers and the strength of
      the workers consists in; it teaches them to not
      to think of their own employer alone and not of
      their own immediate workmates alone but of all
      the employers, the whole class of capitalist and the
      whole class of workers. A strike, moreover, opens
      the eyes of the workers to the nature, not only of
      the capitalists, but of the government and the laws
      as well". This was essentially the argument of "On
      Agitation" and those, like Martov, who had taken
      this strategy to the Marxist Study Groups of the
      1890s and turned them into effective agitational
      bodies leading industrial actions. At the time Lenin
      saw its efficacy, but once in exile in Switzerland he
      seems to have lost touch with the complex reality

of working-class struggle and regressed to the Marxist dogmatism of his earlier days.

12 Eric Hobsbawm, *The Age of Empire:* 1875-1914, Cardinal, 1987, p.298

13 Conquest, Ibid, p.37

14 Manuel Castells, *Networks of Outrage and Hope: Social Movements in the Internet Age*, Polity Press, 2015, p.15

15 For an examination of one particular Occupy action, and how it creatively used social media to generate publicity and support, see my article for the Institute of Employment Rights (IER) on OccupySussex, in which students at Sussex University occupied a campus building to protest the privatisation of the facilities provided by the campus and the transfer of the employees providing them to the private sector – http://www.ier.org.uk/blog/privatisation-and-%E2%80%98pop-unions%E2%80%99-occupy-sussex-fights

16 http://www.redpepper.org.uk/the-case-for-radical-modernity/

17 Castells, Ibid, p.7

18 Lih, Ibid, p.65

19 The dramatic story of the Second Congress of the RSDLP has been translated into film, TV and theatre. Snippets of what is presumably meant to be the Congress are portrayed in the film *Nicholas and Alexandra* (1971). An entire episode of *Fall of Eagles*, the epic 1974 BBC historical drama about the fall of the pre-WW I European dynasties, written by the socialist playwright Trevor Griffiths, was

devoted to the Congress, with Patrick Stewart
as Lenin, Michael Kitchen as Trotsky and Edward
Wilson as Martov.

20   Getzler, Ibid, p.68

21   Getzler, Ibid, p.70

22   Martov, Second Congress, quoted in Abraham
      Ascher (Editor), *The Mensheviks in the Russian
      Revolution*, Thames and Hudson, 1976, p.47

23   Robert Service, *Lenin: A Biography*, Pan, 2000, p.155

24   Theodore Dan, *The Origins of Bolshevism*, Schocken
      Books, 1964 (originally published in Russian
      1944), p.244

25   Pavel Axelrod, "The Unification of Russian Social
      Democracy and its Tasks", *Iskra* No 55, December
      1903, p.15

26   *The Mensheviks in the Russian Revolution*,
      "Documents of Revolution" series, edited by
      Abraham Ascher, Thames and Hudson, 1976, p.11

27   Irving Howe, *Trotsky*, Fontana Modern Masters,
      1974, p.22. An elegantly written, concise and
      insightful introduction to Trotsky's life and politics.
      In the 1930s Howe was a gifted young Trotskyist
      who had many bruising encounters with the
      Stalinists of the CPUSA at City College, New York.
      In later years he created the democratic socialist
      magazine *Dissent* and wrote fine literary and social
      history, including *World of our Fathers*, a massive
      and sensitive recreation of the life experiences and
      cultural world of Eastern European and Russian
      Jews who settled in America (mainly New York's

Lower East Side) between 1880 and 1920. After 1917 there was an influx of Mensheviks fleeing the persecution of the Bolsheviks, many of whom then became active in the American trade union movement. The best biography of Howe is Gerald Sorin, *Irving Howe: A Life of Passionate Dissent*, NYU Press, 2005.

28   The entire text of Luxemburg's article is at https://www.marxists.org/archive/luxemburg/1904/questions-rsd/ch01.htm

29   Rosa Luxemburg, *Leninism or Marxism?*, I.L.P publications, 1935 (first published 1904), p.14

Chapter Three: 1905–The First People's Revolution

1   Cliff, Ibid, p.119

2   V.I. Lenin, *One Step Forward, Two Steps Back*, Progress Publishers, 1948, p.28

3   Cliff, Ibid, p.129

4   Cliff, Ibid, p.130

5   Pavel Axelrod, Letter to RSDLP organizations, November 1904, reprinted in Ascher, Ibid, p.53-56

6   George Gapon, *The Story of My Life*, New York, 1906, p.144

7   Englert, Ibid

8   Figes, Ibid, p.182

9   Viktor Chernov, *Revoluyutsionnaya Rossiya* No 67, May 1905, p.3

10   Perrie, Ibid, p.108

11   Baruch Knei-Paz, *The Social and Political Thought of Leon Trotsky*, Oxford University Press, 1978,

p.53. Knei-Paz's work is in my opinion the most considerable and interesting examination of Trotsky as a writer and thinker. Ernest Mandel dismissed Knei-Paz's scrupulously fair and comprehensive work because of his "failure to understand Trotsky's more daring dialectical combinations" (Mandel, *Trotsky: A Study in the Dynamic of His Thought*, NLB, 1979, p.150), a common problem with daring dialectical combinations.

12   Liebman, Ibid, p.87

13   Cliff, Ibid, p.161

14   Liebman, Ibid, p.88

15   Liebman, Ibid, p.85

16   Cliff, Ibid, p.230

17   Carr, Ibid, p.59

18   Lenin, *Collected Works*, Vol. 8, p.325, cited in Shub, Ibid, p.102

19   In a priceless comment, Tony Cliff concludes the 1905 Revolution failed "in spite of Lenin's correct tactics and strategy" because "the proletariat was insufficiently developed". But if this were so should not Lenin have taken it into account when formulating his tactics and strategy? Cliff, Ibid, p.234

20   Hugh Seton-Watson, *The Russian Empire 1801-1917*, Oxford University Press, 1967, p.61

21   Cliff, Ibid, p.275

22   Cliff, Ibid, p.277

23   A.S. Izgoyev, *Russkaya mysl'*, December 1907

24   Barbara Tuchman, *The Proud Tower: A Portrait of the*

World Before the War 1890-1914, Papermac, 1966, p.410

25   Paul Foot, *The Vote: How it was Won and How it was Undermined*, Penguin, 2005, p.404

26   Karl Kautsky, "Nochmals unsere Illusionen", *Die Neue Zeit* No 23, 1914, p.268

27   The Erfurt Programme, Berlin, 1965, p.112, quoted in Salvadori, Ibid, p.34

28   Friedrich Engels, Introduction, *Class Struggles in France 1848-1850* (Marx), International Publishers, 1964, p.20, p.27.

29   Eduard Bernstein, *Die Neue Zeit*, January 1898

30   For a detailed account of how the Bolshevik faction within the RSDLP financed itself, and the sometimes dubious individuals and schemes it used to keep up the secret funding stream to the Bolshevik "Centre", see David Shub, *Lenin: A Biography*, p.125-37.

31   Shub, Ibid, p.112

32   Figes, Ibid, p.218

33   Getzler, Ibid, 115

Chapter Four: Stop the War

1   Liebman, Ibid, p.56

2   Russell Brand, *Revolution*, Century, 2014, p.301

3   H.G. Wells, *History of the World*, Pelican, 1960, p.157

4   www.truthdig.com/avbooth/item/russell_brand_socialism_is_christianity_politicized_20140120

5   *The Authorised King James Version of the Bible*, New Testament, Book of James, Chapter 5, Verse 1-6.

6   Read, Ibid.

7   Camilla Gray, *The Russian Experiment in Art* 1863-
        1922, Thames and Hudson, 1962, p.31

8   Sheila Fitzpatrick, *The Commissariat of Enlightenment:*
        Soviet Organisation of Education and the Arts under
        Lunacharsky October 1917-1921, Cambridge
        University Press, 1970, p.5

9   Lenin, *Materialism and Empirio-Criticism*, Moscow,
        1909, p.257.

10   Robert Conquest, *Lenin*, Fontana Modern Masters,
        1972, p.66

11   Murphy, Ibid, p.26

12   Shub, Ibid, p.149

13   Isaac Deutscher, *The Prophet Armed,*
        *Trotsky:*1879-1921, Oxford, 1954, p.212

14   Tuchman, Ibid, p.449

15   Hobsbawm, Ibid, p.324

16   Donald Sassoon, *One Hundred Years of Socialism:*
        The West European Left in the Twentieth Century, I.B.
        Taurus, 1996, p.30

17   Hobsbawm, Ibid, p.326

18   J. Martov, *Golos* No 19, 3rd October 1914

19   Rosa Luxemburg, "The Junius Pamphlet", *The Rosa*
        Luxemburg Reader, Monthly Review Press, 2004,
        p.312–13

20   Lenin, letter to A. Shliapnikov, Quoted in Shub,
        Ibid, p.162

21   Deutscher, Ibid, p.226

22   Quoted in Shub, Ibid, p.168

23   V.I. Lenin, *Collected Works*, Fourth Edition, Vol. 23, p.96

24   V.I. Lenin, Ibid, Vol. 19, p.357

**Chapter Five: February 1917 –
The Second People's Revolution**

1   Although written in 1935 and therefore not reflecting later research, George Dangerfield's *The Strange Death of Liberal England* is still the best account of those years. For literary flair and impressionistic flavour it is unmatched by more academic work on the period.

2   Murphy, Ibid, p.25–26

3   Figes, Ibid, p.252

4   Ascher, *The Russian Revolution*, Ibid, p.57

5   Edward Acton, *Rethinking the Russian Revolution*, Oxford University, 1990, p.102

6   Cited in Shub, Ibid, p.182

7   Shub, Ibid, p.184

8   Ascher, Ibid, p.67

9   Barbara Evans Clements, "Working Class and Peasant Women in the Russian Revolution, 1917-1923", *Signs* Vol. 8, Winter, 1982, p.225

10   Leon Trotsky, *History of the Russian Revolution*, Haymarket Books, 2008 (originally published 1932), p.75

11   A.I Rodionova, "Semnadtsatyi god", *Zhenshchiny goroda Lenina*, Lenizdat, 1963, p.89

12   Trotsky, Ibid, p.91

13   Orlando Figes, *Revolutionary Russia, 1891-1991*, Kindle edition.

14   Trotsky, Ibid, p.111

15   Castells, Ibid, p.27

16   Stephen M. Walt, "Why the Tunisian Revolution won't spread", ForeignPolicy.com, 16th January, 2011

17   Paul Mason, *Why It's Still Kicking Off Everywhere: The New Global Revolutions*, Verso, 2013, p.14

18   Castells, Ibid, p.77

19   Ronald Grigor Suny, "Social Democrats in Power: Menshevik Georgia and the Russian Civil War", in *Party, State and Society in the Russian Civil War: Explorations in Social History*, edited by Diane P. Koenker, William G. Rosenberg and Ronald Grigor Suny, Indiana University Press, 1989, p.327

20   Interviewed by Mark Bray and quoted in Bray, *Translating Anarchy: The Anarchism of Occupy Wall Street*, Zero Books, 2013, p.87

21   Bray, Ibid, p.3, p.5, p.28, p.29

22   The Bolshevik government was not so generous. In April 1918 it removed Nicholas and his family (and a few retainers) to Ekaterinburg. After the February Revolution he had applied for asylum in England. The British government was initially minded to accept but Nicholas' cousin George V vetoed the idea as it could prove embarrassing for the Windsor (formerly Saxe-Goburg Gotha) dynasty. On 17th July, 1918, as the Russian Civil War was escalating, Nicholas and his family (wife, mother, son and daughters) were all shot to death by a hastily assembled firing squad in the basement of the house in which they had been detained.

The Bolsheviks said in explanation that the White Armies attempting to overthrow them would have used Nicholas as a rallying totem for monarchists and conservatives. The hereditary principle meant this applied to his close relatives as well. There was a brutal logic to this, although it fails to explain why they also shot the family doctor, maid and dog.

23   Isaac Deutscher, *The Prophet Armed, Trotsky*: 1879-1921, Oxford University Press, 1954, p.251.

24   Abraham Ascher (Editor), *The Mensheviks in the Russian Revolution*, Thames and Hudson, 1976, p.91

25   An extremely useful analysis of the Factory Committees arising from the February Revolution is to be found in Chapter 1 of Carmen Sirianni, *Workers Control and Socialist Democracy: The Soviet Experience*, Verso, 1982; and for a breakdown of their sometimes amorphous procedures see pp.29-32.

26   Maurice Brinton, *The Bolsheviks and Workers' Control 1917-1921: The State and Counter Revolution*, Black Rose Books, 1975, introduction, p.i

27   Sirianni, Ibid, p.17

28   Ronald Grigor Suny, "Revising the old story: The 1917 Revolution in light of new sources", *The Workers Revolution in Russia, 1917: The View from Below*, edited by Daniel H. Kaiser, Cambridge University Press, 1987, p.7

29   Sirianni, Ibid, p.26

30   Resolution of the workers of the Old Parvianan metal and machine factory, 13th April, 1917, reported in *Izvestiia* No 41, 15th April, 1917, p.3

Chapter Six: Coalition Governments

1   Paul Mason, *Post-Capitalism: A Guide to Our Future*,
     Penguin, 2015, p.58

2   Stephen F. Cohen, *Bukharin and the Bolshevik
     Revolution: A Political Biography,* 1888-1938, Oxford
     University Press, 1973, p.25

3   Michael Hardt and Antonio Negri, *Empire*, Harvard
     University Press, 2001, p.19

4   Hardt and Negri, Ibid, p.xv

5   V.I. Lenin, *Imperialism, the Highest Stage of Capitalism*,
     Progress Publishers, 1978 (first published 1916), p.83.

6   Karl Kautsky, *Bernstein und das sozialdemokratisches
     Programme*, Eine Antkritik, 1899, p.43

7   Massimo Salvadori, *Karl Kautsky and Socialist
     Revolution* 1880-1938, NLB, 1979, p.15

8   Thomas Friedman, "Manifesto for a Fast World",
     The New York Times, 28/02/99

9   Lenin, Ibid, p.118

10   V.I. Lenin, *Philosophical Notebooks*, Volume 14
     of Fourth Edition of *Collected Works*, Progress
     Publishers, p.259-60.

11   Lenin, Ibid, p.109

12   Karl Marx, "Critical Notes on the King of Prussia
     and Social Reform", 1844

13   Figes, Ibid, p.358

14   N.N. Sukhanov, *The Russian Revolution* 1917: *A
     Personal Record*, edited, translated and abridged by
     Joel Carmichael, Princeton University Press, p.280

15   Shub, Ibid, p.216

16   V.I. Lenin, *April Theses*, Kindle Edition

17   The full text of the proclamation from the
      Okulovsky Paper Factory, 21st May, 1917, is in Mark
      Steinberg, *Voices of Revolution 1917*, Yale University
      Press, 2001, pp.99-100. A fascinating collection of
      informal reports, resolutions, complaints, petitions,
      letters and poems of 1917 translated from the
      Russian and taken from originals held in the State
      Archive of the Russian Federation in Moscow,
      formerly the Central State Archive of the October
      Revolution. Steinberg's collection is especially
      interesting in that it features the seldom-heard
      voice of semi-literate peasants and workers, some
      politicised by events, some not, some idealistic,
      some cynical, but all authentic and direct.
18   SR journal *Dela Narodo*, No.45, May 1917, quoted in
      King, Ibid, pp.30-31
19   Vero Broido, *Lenin and the Mensheviks: The
      Persecution of Socialists under Bolshevism*, Gower
      Publishing, 1987, p.15
20   E.H. Carr, Ibid, pp.40-41
21   V.I. Lenin, Vol. 19 of the Fourth Edition of *Collected
      Works*, English version, Progress Publishers,
      1960-70, p.429
22   V.I. Lenin, Vol. 20, Ibid, p.45
23   Trotsky, Ibid, p.289
24   "A Flame of Gold Ablaze", Pyotr Oreshin, 14th
      May, 1917, *Delo Naroda* No 49, p.2
25   Keep, Ibid, p.388
26   V.I. Lenin, *Tasks of the Proletariat in our Revolution*,
      Selected Works, Vol. 6, pp.62 and 85-6

27   Brinton, Ibid, p.5

28   "Argentinean Worker–Taken Factories: Trajectories of Workers' Control under the Economic Crisis", Marina Kabat, in *Ours to Master and to Own*, Haymarket Books, edited by Immanuel Ness and Dario Azzellini, 2011, pp.369–77

29   Gregory Wilpert, *Changing Venezuela by Taking Power: The History and Policies of the Chavez Government*, Verso, 2007, p.76

30   Brinton, Ibid, p.2

31   Castells, Ibid, p.11

Chapter Seven: All Power to the Soviets

1   Trotsky, Ibid, p.315. Despite his honestly expressed ideological bias Trotsky's data is usually sound.

2   Deutscher, Ibid, p.266

3   *Izvestia* number 84, June 1917, quoted in Ascher, Ibid, p.97

4   Liebman, Ibid, p.158

5   Liebman, Ibid, p.148

6   Getzler, Ibid, p.154

7   Getzler, Ibid, p.151

8   Figes, Ibid, p.417

9   Figes, Ibid, pp.420–21

10   Figes, Ibid, p.428

11   Getzler, Ibid, pp.155–56

12   Trotsky, *Results and Prospects*, 1907, London, 1962, pp.246–7

13   Liebman, Ibid, p.127

14   Trotsky, *History of the Russian Revolution*, Ibid, p.155

15   Adam Ulam, *Lenin and the Bolsheviks*, Fontana/ Collins, 1965, p.462

16   Frederich Engels, *Anti-Duhring: Herr Eugen Duhring's Revolution in Science*, 1884, Third German Edition, p.303

17   V.I. Lenin, *The State and Revolution*, 1918, Peking Foreign Language Press, first edition 1976, originally published 1918, p.122

18   Carr, Ibid, p.35

19   Lenin, Ibid, p.123

20   Ramsay MacDonald, *Socialism: Critical and Constructive*, Cassell and Company Ltd, 1921, p.vi, p.112, p.32. The problem with MacDonald's socialism was not his general analysis of capitalism—which is surprisingly radical—or faith in a more rational, cooperative alternative, but lack of any realistic plan to get from one to the other. In that respect he and Lenin, alike in no other way, were two sides of the same coin.

21   Wilson & Thompson, Ibid, p.164

22   Derek Wall, *Economics After Capitalism: A Guide to the Ruins*, Pluto, 2015, p.103

23   Andrew Fisher, *The Failed Experiment: And How to Build an Economy that Works*, A Radical Read, 2014, p.123

Chapter Eight: October 1917

1   Marc Ferro, *The Bolshevik Revolution: A Social History of the Russian Revolution*, Routledge and Kegan Paul, 1976, p.38

2   N. Podvoysky, "The Military Organisation of the
     Central Committee of the Bolshevik Party in
     1917", *Krasnaya Letopis* No 9, Leningrad, 1923, p.34

3   Abraham Ascher, *The Russian Revolution*, 2014, One
     World, p.100

4   Steve A. Smith, *Petrograd in 1917: The View From
     Below*, in Kaiser, Ibid, p.7

5   Leon Trotsky, *The Lessons of October*, 1924,
     Bookmarks (1987), p.40

6   Deutscher, Ibid, p.298

7   V.I. Lenin, *The Bolsheviks Must Assume State Power:
     a Letter to the Central Committee and the Petrograd and
     Moscow Committees of the* RSDLP, Progress Publishers,
     Collected Works, English Edition, Vol. 26, p.19

8   V.I. Lenin, *Advice of an Onlooker*, Progress Publishers,
     Collected Works, English Edition, Vol. 26, pp.179-81
     Proletarskaya Revolyutziya No 10, Moscow, 1922,
     p.462

9   Trotsky, Ibid, pp.44-45

10   Rabinowitch, Ibid, p.3

11   Trotsky, Ibid, p.51

12   P.A. Sorokin, *Volya narado* No 116, September 1917

13   Howe, Ibid, p.50

14   Sukhanov, Ibid, p.578

15   Deutscher, Ibid, p.310

16   Trotsky, Ibid, p.1074

17   Shub, Ibid, pp.274-75

18   Sukhanov, Ibid, p.628

19   Sukhanov, Ibid, p.630

20   Figes, Ibid, p.493-94

21 P.N. Maliantovich, "In the Winter Palace, October 25-26 1917", *The Past* No 12, 1918, p.117-19. Antonov-Ovseenko would later discover just how interesting the social experiment would become. A principled Bolshevik, he was appalled at the rise of the Stalinist machine in the 1920s and was a prominent member of the Trotskyist opposition until Trotsky's exile in 1929. He was sent to Spain in the 1930s to work for the Comintern but on his return to the Soviet Union in 1938 he was executed in the Great Terror. Thus Stalin murdered the Bolshevik who had led the storming of the Winter Palace.

22 Sukhanov, Ibid, p.635

23 Figes, Ibid, p.494

24 John L.H. Keep, *The Russian Revolution: A Study in Mass Mobilization*, W.W Norton & Company, 1976, p.255

Chapter Nine: Sovnarcom

1 Trotsky, *History of the Russian Revolution*, Ibid, p.838

2 Trotsky, Ibid, p.839

3 Sukhanov, Ibid, p.636

4 Boris Nicolaevsky, "Pages from the Past", *Sotsialisticheskii vestnik*, No 77-78, 1958, p.150

5 Oleg Budnitskii, *Russian Jews Between the Reds and the Whites* 1917-1920, University of Pennsylvania Press, 2012, p.65

6 T.H. Rigby, *Lenin's Government: Sovnarkom* 1917-22, Cambridge University Press, 1979, p.3

7   For the complete translated texts of Sovnarcom's most important Decrees between October 1917 (November in the subsequently adopted Gregorian calendar) and July 1918 see *First Decrees of Soviet Power: Acts of Legislation November 1917-July 1918*, compiled with an introduction and explanatory notes by Yuri Akhapkin, Lawrence and Wishart, 1970. Most of the Decrees published in Akhapkin were translated from *Decrees of the Soviet Government* Volumes I and II, 1957 and 1959, prepared by the Institute of Marxism–Leninism of the Central Committee of the Communist Party of the Soviet Union and the Institute of History of the USSR Academy of Sciences.

8   Brinton, Ibid, p.12

9   Diane P. Koenker, "Labour Relations in Socialist Russia: Class Values and Production Values in the Printers Union 1917-1921", in *Making Workers Soviet*, Ibid, p.171-72

10   Cited in Carr, Ibid, p.152

11   V.I. Lenin, *Collected Works*, Fifth Edition, Vol. 37, p.245; Lenin, Ibid, Vol. 41, p.383

12   Rabinowitch, Ibid, p.26

13   Broido, Ibid, p.22

14   The full text of the resolution of the Baltic Shipbuilding Works, 2nd November, 1917, is in Steinberg, Ibid, p.274

15   Getzler, Ibid, p.168

16   Rabinowitch, Ibid, p.31

17   Tony Cliff, *Revolution Besieged: Lenin* 1917-1923,
      Bookmarks, 1987, p.25

18   *The Debate on Soviet Power: Minutes of the All-
      Russian Central Executive Committee of Soviets, 2nd
      Convocation, October 1917-January* 1918, Oxford
      University Press, 1979, translated and edited by
      John L.H. Keep, contains "a composite text,
      reconstructed according to published primary
      sources, of the proceedings of Soviet Russia's first
      quasi-legislative assembly" between 27th October,
      1917 and 6th January, 1918. It thus records the only
      period of free and uncensored debate in the CEC
      after 25th October, 1917, when Sovnarcom had
      not yet consolidated its power and all strands of
      socialist opinion could argue about the political and
      economic make-up of the regime, whether there
      should be a broad socialist coalition government,
      how accountable it should be to the CEC, and if
      the executive and legislative functions should be
      united or divided. As Keep summarises the matter
      of the arguments, "very few of these representatives,
      or the men for whom they spoke, were in favour
      of unlimited dictatorship by a single revolutionary
      party, the form which 'Soviet power' quickly
      assumed" (Keep, Preface, p.v). Ibid, pp.50-53

19   Keep, Ibid, p.63

20   Quoted in Shub, Ibid, p.310

21   See Shub, Ibid, pp.311-12 for a breakdown of
      all socialist newspapers forcibly closed down
      in late 1917.

22   Keep, Ibid, pp.68–74

23   Keep, Ibid, pp.77–78

24   Quoted in Pipes, Ibid, p.523, drawn from the
      Minutes of the All-Russian Central Executive
      Committee of Soviets, 4th November, 1917

Chapter Ten: No Power to the Soviets

1   The most forensic examination of the Constituent
      Assembly general election, Oliver H. Radkey's
      *Russia Goes to the Polls: The Election to the All-Russian
      Constituent Assembly* 1917, first published in 1950,
      found that although the electoral statistics were
      in "a deplorable condition" it was still possible,
      with great care, to reconstruct them and establish
      reliable results. Radkey's definitive totals, while
      clarifying and improving some regional returns,
      were surprisingly not that far from those published
      at the time. In all the controversy surrounding the
      Constituent Assembly elections it is significant that
      no party, not even the Bolsheviks, seems to have
      questioned the overall statistical accuracy of the
      result, and there is no reason to do so now.

2   Sheila Fitzpatrick, Introduction to Radkey, p.2

3   See Radkey's chart on pp.18–19 of *Russia Goes to the
      Polls* (1977 version) for a breakdown of the electoral
      returns. Chapter 2 considers the returns by regions
      and provinces, and also other segments of the vote
      such as soldiers still at the front.

4   Liebman, Ibid, p.233

5   Leninist arguments about a misleading united SR

Party list have some validity but miss the main point. Most SR voters, before and after the SR split, did not differentiate between Left SR and Right SRs. The vast bulk of their peasant supporters saw the historic SR programme as a whole, and voted for it. There is no evidence that any of those who voted the main SR slate did so because of a hidden desire for an urban-based dictatorship of the proletariat overseen by another party. Additionally, if a united SR electoral list was misleading it was no more misleading than a united Bolshevik party list. The Bolsheviks, too, had vast and fundamental internal differences, although these had been disguised. And the Bolsheviks, in any guise, had not gone to the electorate offering what became their actual programme for the land. The peasant electorate would never get another chance to pronounce on this programme as there were no further national elections.

6   Radkey, *Russia Goes to the Polls: The Election to the All-Russian Constituent Assembly,* 1917, Cornell University Press, 1950 (updated edition 1977), p.16

7   V.I. Lenin, "Theses on the Constituent Assembly", *Pravda,* 13th December, 1917

8   Cliff, Ibid, pp.35–36

9   Steinberg, Ibid, pp.267

10   *Novaya Zhizn* No 4, 6th January, 1918, p.3

11   Maxim Gorky, *Novaya Zhizn* No 6, 9th January, 1918, p.5

12   Liebman, Ibid, p.235

13   T.E. Novitskaya, compiler of Constituent Assembly records, *Uchreditel'noe Sobranie*, 1918, Nedra, pp.158–59, quoted in King, Ibid, pp.95–96

14   Shub, Ibid, p.326

15   Broido, Ibid, p.26

16   Brinton, Ibid, p.16

17   A. Lozovski, *Rabochii Kontrol*, Socialist Publishing House, Petrograd, 1918, p.10

18   Sirianni, Ibid, p.102

19   David Mandel, "The Factory Committee Movement in the Russian Revolution", in *Ours to Master and to Own*, Ibid, p.119

20   V.I. Lenin, *Collected Works*, Vol. 22, Moscow, p.215

21   William G. Rosenberg, "Russian Labour and Bolshevik Power: Social Dimensions of Protest in Petrograd after October", originally published in *Slavic Review* Volume 44, 1985, reprinted in Kaiser, Ibid, p. 98–131

22   Quoted in Brinton, Ibid, p.26

23   Quoted in Brinton, Ibid, p.27

24   *Kommunist*, No 2, April 1918, p.5

25   Alexander Rabinowitch, "The Petrograd First City District Soviet during the Civil War", in *Party, State and Society in the Russian Civil War: Explorations in Social History*, Indiana University Press, 1989, p.153

26   Rabinowitch, Ibid, p.134–36

27   Vladimir Brovkin, "The Mensheviks' Political Comeback: The Elections to the Provincial City Soviets in Spring 1918", *Russian Review* Volume 42, Issue 1, 1983, p.1

28   V.I. Lenin, *Collected Works*, Vol. 27, p.133

29   Brovkin, Ibid, p.6

30   *Kostromskoi Guberni*, May 1918, p.305–06

31   Brovkin, *Dear Comrades: Menshevik Reports on the Bolshevik Revolution and Civil War*, Ibid, p.83–85

32   Brovkin, *Russian Review* 42, Ibid, p.11, p.13, p.14

33   A. Lockerman, *Les Bolsheviks a l'oeuvre*, Paris, 1920, p.54

34   Quoted in *Novaia Zaria* No 1, 22nd April, 1918, p.34

35   Leonard Schapiro, *The Origins of the Communist Autocracy: Political Opposition in the Soviet State, First Phase,* 1917-22, Palgrave Macmillan, 1956, p.191

36   Rosenberg, Ibid, p.118

37   Rabinowitch, Ibid, p.226

38   Quoted in Broido, Ibid, p.77

39   Quoted in Rabinowitch, Ibid, p.255

40   Akhapkin, Ibid, p.147–53 for the full text of the Decree on Nationalisation, 28th June, 1918.

41   K. Radek, "After five months", *Kommunist* 1, April 1918, p.3-4

42   V.I. Lenin, *The Immediate Tasks of the Soviet Government*, originally published in *Izvestia*, 28th April, 1918; Progress Publishers, 1970, p.19, p.21, p.25, p.35, p.46

43   Leon Trotsky, *Terrorism and Communism: A Reply to Karl Kautsky*, originally published 1920, Verso, 2007, p.104

Chapter Eleven: Surveillance State

1   Howard Zinn, *A People's History of the United States*,
     Harper Perennial, 2001, p.372

2   Sharon Smith, *Subterranean Fire: A History of
     Working-Class Radicalism in the United States*,
     Haymarket Books, 2006, p.95

3   For a detailed breakdown and analysis of the
     FBI's secret COINTELPRO memoranda, some of it
     redacted, see Ward Churchill and Jim Vander Wall at
     http://archive.is/YJA4m

4   Tim Weiner, *Legacy of Ashes: The History of the CIA*,
     Penguin, 2007, p.556

5   John Pilger's documentary *The War on Democracy*
     is a detailed exposé of the CIA and US State
     Department's involvement in the attempted coup in
     2002 against Hugo Chavez's democratically elected
     socialist government, which unlike the Bolshevik
     government maintained freedom of the press and
     political pluralism.

6   Isaac Deutscher, *The Prophet Unarmed, Trotsky:* 1921-
     1929, Oxford University Press, 1959, p.109

7   J.O. Martov, letter to P.B. Axelrod, 1st December,
     1917, Hoover Institution Archives, Nicolaevsky
     collection, series no 17, box 511, files 1-12

8   Ulam, Ibid, p.550

9   Quoted in Donald Rayfield, *Stalin and His
     Hangmen*, Penguin, 2004, pp.65-66. Rayfield's
     work is full of detail on individual Chekists and
     Stalin's inner circle, but it hardly touches on the
     mass killings of the White Terror, which on most

evidence exceeded its red counterpart. His source evidence – drawn not only from the Russian State Archive of Social-Political History (formally the Communist Party Archives) and the State Archive of the Russian Federation, but also from the Georgian Central State Archive and the Russian State Archive of Literature and Art, as well as formerly (until 2004) inaccessible Cheka and NKVD documents, correspondence, interrogation records etc. – is impressive but unbalanced.

10   Legget, Ibid, p.17

11   *Golos Truda*, 3rd November, 1917, p.1

12   N.I Pavlov, "Party Blindness", *Golos Truda*, 18th November 1917, p.4

13   Richard Stites, *Revolutionary Dreams: Utopian Vision and Experimental Life in the Russian Revolution*, Oxford, 1991, p.56

14   For the complete chapter on Makhno in Avrich's *Anarchist Portraits* (1988), see http://www.ditext. com/avrich/7.html

15   The entire text of the Declaration can be found in the Appendix to Peter Arshinov, *History of the Makhnovist Movement* 1918-1921, Freedom Press, 2005 (originally published 1923).

16   Michael Mallet, *Nestor Makhno in the Russian Revolution*, MacMillan, 1982, p.124

17   Cited in Arshinov, Ibid, p.103-04

18   Figes, Ibid, p.533

19   V.I. Lenin, "How to organise competition", December 1917, *Collected Works* Vol.35, p.204

20   "'The Socialist Fatherland is in Danger!': Decree
       of the Council of People's Commissars, 21st
       February, 1918", in *First Decrees of Soviet Power: Acts
       of Legislation November 1917 - July 1918*, ed. Yuri
       Akhapkin, Lawrence and Wishart, 1970, pp. 108-09

21   Carr, Ibid, p. 169

22   I.N. Steinberg, *In the Workshop of the Revolution*,
       New York, 1953, p. 145

23   Dzerzhinsky's report of 17th February, 1919 and the
       Soviet Central Executive Committee's resolution
       on concentration camps are quoted in Richard
       Pipes, *The Russian Revolution* 1899-1919, Collins
       Harvel, 1990, p. 834

24   Karl Kautsky, *The Dictatorship of the Proletariat*,
       Manchester, 1918 (re-issued by Ann Arbor
       Paperbacks, University of Michigan Press,
       1964), pp. 4-5

25   Salvadori, Ibid, p. 257

26   V.I. Lenin, *The Proletarian Revolution and the
       Renegade Kautsky*, 1918, text in *Selected Works*,
       Foreign Languages Publishing House, Moscow,
       1952, p. 11, 20

27   Kautsky, Ibid, p. 23, pp. 6-7

28   Lenin, Ibid, p. 25, 24

29   V.I. Lenin, *Collected Works*, Vol. 26, Moscow,
       1964, p. 303

30   Karl Marx, "The Civil War in France", in *Selected
       Writings*, Ibid, p. 542

31   Karl Kautsky, "Demokratie und Demokratie", *Der
       Kampf*, XIII, 1920, p. 209

Chapter Twelve: Civil War

1   L. Trotsky, "Work, Discipline, Order", *Sochineniya* XVII, p.17

2   Isaac Deutscher, *The Prophet Armed: Trotsky 1879-1921*, Oxford University Press, 1954, p.406

3   Quoted in Deutscher, Ibid, p.421

4   Figes, Ibid, p.579

5   Rabinowitch, Ibid, pp.288-89

6   Figes, Ibid, p.649

7   *Weekly of Kazan Cheka* No 1, November 1918, reprinted in *Pravda* No 281, 25th December, 1918

8   Shub, Ibid, pp.360-61

9   This telegram, and others of similar ilk, are contained in *The Unknown Lenin: From the Secret Archive*, Yale University Press, 1996, edited by Richard Pipes. The volume was prepared with the aid of the Russian Centre for the Preservation and Study of Documents of Recent History of the State Archival Service of Russia. When published it contained dozens of hitherto unreleased documents (letters, telegrams, memoranda, etc.). Whilst the contents are primary sources of the first importance it should be noted that Pipes himself has an extra-academic agenda. He was not just Baird Research Professor of History at Harvard University but also a former Director of East European and Soviet Affairs for the US National Security Council, and a consultant to the CIA. Pipes' immense hostility to Lenin heavily colours his historical work, to its detriment. His selection in *The Unknown Lenin*

must be seen in that light. That said, it appears to reflect the totality of the unpublished material and there is no question as to their authenticity.

10   The full text and a scanned facsimile of Lenin's memorandum to N.N. Krestinsky is in Pipes, Ibid, p.56

11   Both decrees are quoted in Gregory Petrovich Maximoff, *The Guillotine at Work, Vol. 1: The Leninist Counter-Revolution*, Black Thorn Books, 1979 (first published Chicago 1940 by the Alexander Berkman Fund), pp.76–77

12   Lyuobov Krassin, *Leonid Krassin: His Life and Work*, Skeffington & Son Ltd, 1929, p.98

13   https://www.marxists.org/archive/luxemburg/1918/russian-revolution/ch01.htm

14   *The Manchester Guardian*, 13th July, 1920

15   Victor Serge, "During the Civil War", *Revolution in Danger: Writings from Russia 1919-1921*, Redwords, 1997, p.11

16   Quoted in Figes, Ibid, p.677

17   Cliff, Ibid, p.18

18   Vero Broido, *Daughter of Revolution: A Russian Girlhood Remembered*, Constable, 1998, p.114

19   Figes, Ibid, p.604

20   Keep, Ibid, p.429

21   Sovnarcom Decree of 9th May, 1918 quoted in Cliff, Ibid, p.135

22   J. Sverdlov to Russian Communist Party Central Committee, as reported in the *Protocols of the RCP CC May 4th-20th* 1918, Moscow, 1920, p.294

23   V.P. Miliutin, *Agrarnaia Poilitika SSSR*, Moscow, 1929, p.106

24   Keep, Ibid, p.435

25   Quoted in Cliff, Ibid, p.137

26   Quoted in Shub, Ibid, p.371

27   Victor Serge, *Memoirs of a Revolutionary* (1951), New York Review Books, 2010, p.135

28   V.I. Lenin, *Collected Works*,Vol. 33, Moscow, p.421-2

29   Nikolai Bukharin, *The Economics of the Transition Period*, 1920, p.56, quoted in Cohen, Ibid, p.90

30   Bukharin, Ibid, quoted in Cohen, p.91

31   Cohen, Ibid, p.94

32   Serge, *Revolution in Danger*, Ibid, p.67

33   Resolution of the Menshevik Party Central Committee of 2nd August, 1918, reprinted in *Rabochi Internatsional*, 7th August, 1918, Petrograd

34   Getzler, Ibid, p.183

35   "The International Situation and the Tasks of the Russian Revolution", *Partiinoe soveshchanie*, October 1918, pp.10-11

36   Serge, "During the Civil War", Ibid, p.11, 14

37   Serge, Ibid, p.27

38   Serge, *Memoirs*, Ibid, p.107

39   Leon Trotsky, *My Life: An Attempt at an Autobiography*, Penguin, 1975, p.44

40   Quoted in Deutscher, Ibid, p.445

41   Serge, Ibid, p.109

Chapter Thirteen: Sex-Pol

1   Fitzpatrick, Ibid, p.15

2   Cited in Stites, Ibid, p.76

3   Serge, Ibid, p.13

4   Stites, Ibid, p.78

5   Liebman, Ibid, p.331

6   For background on the Venezuelan government's successful "Mission Robinson" programme to combat mass illiteracy see http://venezuelanalysis.com/news/7402

7   Richard Stites, *The Women's Liberation Movement in Russia: Feminism, Nihilism and Bolshevism* 1860-1930, Princeton University Press, 1978, p.162

8   Stites, Ibid, p.244

9   "The Social Basis of the Woman Question", *Selected Writings of Alexandra Kollontai*, edited Alix Holt, W.W. Norton and Company, 1977, p.58, p.68

10   Stites, Ibid, p.363

11   Norton Dodge, *Women in the Soviet Economy*, Johns Hopkins University Press, 1966, p.141

12   Alexandra Kollontai, *Autobiography of a Sexually Emancipated Woman*, Irwin Fletscher, London, 1972 (originally published 1926), p.43

13   Clements, Ibid, p.228

14   "Make Way for Winged Eros: A Letter to Working Youth", 1923, Kollontai, *Selected Writings*, Ibid, p.277

15   Kollontai, Ibid, p.288, p.282

16   Data from http://ukfeminista.org.uk

17   For the full text of Eve Mitchell's challenging article see https://libcom.org/library/i-am-woman-human-marxist-feminist-critique-intersectionality-theory-eve-mitchell

18   https://www.theguardian.com/
      commentisfree/2016/nov/17/trump-brexit-
      minorities-working-class

19   Dawn Foster, *Lean Out*, Repeater Books, 2016, p.11

20   V.I. Lenin, "The Tasks of the Working Women's
      Movement in the Soviet Republic", *Collected Works*
      Vol. 30, Moscow, p.40, p.42

21   Clara Zetkin, *Reminiscences of Lenin*, International
      Publishers, 1924, p.44

22   Wilhelm Reich, *The Mass Psychology of Fascism*,
      Penguin Books, 1970 (originally published
      1934), p.78

23   Reich, Ibid, pp.25-26

24   Reich, Ibid, p.89

25   Wilhelm Reich, "Dialectical Materialism and
      Psychoanalysis", in Wilhelm Reich, *Sex-Pol Essays*
      1929-1934, Verso, 2012, p.73

26   Reich, "Politicising the Sexual Problem of Youth",
      Ibid, p.274

27   Cited in Maurice Brinton, *The Irrational in Politics*,
      Black Rose Books, 1974, pp.58-59

Chapter Fourteen: Proletkult

1   Filippo Marinetti, "The Foundation and Manifesto
      of Futurism", 1909, in 100 *Artists' Manifestos: From
      the Futurists to the Stuckists*, edited Alex Danchev,
      Penguin, 2011, pp.4-5

2   Gray, Ibid, p.94

3   Leon Trotsky, *Literature and Revolution*, Redwords,
      1991 (originally published 1924), p.172

4   Stites, Ibid, p.44

5   Aude Lancelin, *Le Nouvel Observateur*, 2001

6   Harry Cleaver, "Marxian Categories, the Crisis of
       Capital, and the Constitution of Social Subjectivity
       Today", in Werner Bonefeld, *Revolutionary Writing:
       Common-Sense Essays in Post-Political Politics*,
       Automedia, 2003, p.203

7   Derek Wall, *Economics after Capitalism*, Pluto Press,
       2015, p.97

8   Hardt and Negri, Ibid, p.xiii

9   Hardt and Negri, Ibid, p.295

10   Cited in Fitzpatrick, Ibid, p.89, p.93

11   Lynn Mally, *Culture of the Future: The Proletkult
       Movement in Revolutionary Russia,* University of
       California Press, 1990, p.42

12   I. Eventov, *Mayakovsky-Plakatist*, Iskustvo, 1940, p.25

13   Liebman, Ibid, p.327

14   Stites, Ibid, p.71–72

15   Quoted in "Intellectuals in the Proletkult: Problems
       of Authority and Expertise", Lynn Mally, in *Party,
       State, and Society in the Russian Civil War*, edited by
       Koenker, Rosenburg and Suny, Ibid, p.299

16   Trotsky, Ibid, p.130

17   Sheila Fitzpatrick, *The Cultural Front: Power and
       Culture in Revolutionary Russia*, Cornell University
       Press, 1992, p.5

18   Leon Trotsky, *Problems of Everyday Life: Creating the
       Foundations of a New Society in Revolutionary Russia*,
       Pathfinder Books, 1973 (originally published 1924),
       p.20, p.76

19   Pablo Iglesias, "Understanding Podemos", *New Left Review* 97, May–June 2015

20   Iglesias, Ibid

21   Victoria E. Bonnell, "The Iconography of the Worker in Soviet Political Art", in *Making Workers Soviet: Power, Class and Identity*, ed. Lewis H. Siegelbaum and Ronald Grigor Suny, Cornell University Press, 1994, p.343.

22   Stephen White, *The Bolshevik Poster*, Yale University Press, 1988, p.32

23   White, Ibid, p.22–23

24   Leon Trotsky, "Vodka, the Church and the Cinema", *Pravda*, 12th July, 1923

25   V.I. Lenin, "Party Organisation and Party Literature", *Novaya Zhizn* No 12, November 1905

26   Leon Trotsky, *Class and Art*, New Park Publications, 1974 (originally published 1924), p.7

27   N. Berdyaev, *The Philosophy of Inequality*, 1925, quoted in Burbank, Ibid, p.199

28   Fitzpatrick, Ibid, p.43

29   A.V. Lunacharsky, quoted in Solomon Volkov, *The Magical Chorus: A History of Russian Culture from Tolstoy to Solzhenitsyn*, Vintage, 2009, p.72

30   See Chapter 3 of Trotsky's *Literature and Revolution* for an eloquent and fascinating analysis of Blok's work.

31   Clive James, "Transparent Petropolis", *From the Land of Shadows*, Picador, 1982, p.235

32   Dzerzhinsky's note cited in Vladmir Brovkin, *Russia after Lenin: Politics, Culture and Society* 1921-1929, Routledge, 1998, p.23

33   Leon Trotsky, *Pravda*, 27th September, 1922

34   Inaugural Congress of Soviet Writers, Stenographic Record, Moscow, 1934, pp.479-503, pp.573-77

Chapter Fifteen: The Transitory Mood of the Workers' Democracy

1   Karl Marx, *Critique of the Gotha Programme*, in *Selected Writings*, ed. D. McLellan, Oxford, 1977, p.564

2   Quoted in Deutscher, Ibid, p.508

3   Goldman, Ibid, p.247, p.246

4   Cohen, Ibid, p.55

5   V.I. Lenin, *Collected Works* Vol. 33, Moscow, p.58

6   Goldman, Ibid, p.32

7   Deutscher, Ibid, p.449

8   Donny Gluckstein, *The Western Soviets: Workers' Councils versus Parliament* 1915-1920, Bookmarks, 1985, p.147

9   *Rote Fahne*, Berlin, 9th January, 1919

10   Karl Kautsky, *Das Weitertreiben der Revolution*, Berlin, 1919, p.4

11   V.I. Lenin, *Collected Works* Vol. 28, Moscow, pp.443-44

12   *Daily Herald*, June 1917, report of Leeds Convention

13   Gluckstein, Ibid, p.85

14   J. Martov, letter to N.S. Kristi, 30th December, 1917

15   Brovkin, Ibid, p.41

16   *Krokodil*, October 1929

17   Statistical data on the number of state officials cited in Liebman, Ibid, p.321

18   V.I. Lenin, *Collected Works* Vol. 36, Moscow, p.557

19   Deutscher, Ibid, p.47

20   Murphy, Ibid, p.161

21   *Pravda* no.2, Editorial, Moscow, 4th February, 1919

22   *Vosmaia konferentsiia* RKP, Moscow, 1961, p.221

23   Rabinowitch, "The Petrograd First District Soviet During the Civil War", Ibid, p.150

24   Text of Putilov workers' Resolution in "Putilov Meeting", *The Times*, London, 4th April, 1919

25   Vladimir Brovkin, "Workers' Unrest and the Bolsheviks' Response in 1919", *Slavic Review*, Vol. 49, Issue 3, 1990, p.361, which cites multiple contemporary reports from *Pravda*, *The Times*, the *Bulletin Russe* (Lausanne), the *Proletarskaia Revoliutsiia* 55 (1926) – based on reports from a Baltic Fleet Commissar who refused to follow orders to suppress the Putilov workers – and several *Bulletins of the Russian Liberation Committee* of May 1919, as well as US Consul Imbrie's Dispatch 86100 4323 18th April, 1919.

26   Leggett, Ibid, p.313

27   Brovkin, Ibid, p.356

28   Brovkin, Ibid, p.367, also citing reports from Tambov and Smolensk that it was the abuse of power by local Communists that created working-class resistance.

29   Brovkin, Ibid, p.369, cites reports that reveal what
        actually happened in Astrakhan, despite the Soviet
        government imposing a complete news blackout on
        events in the town.

30   Brovkin, Ibid, p.371

31   The complete text of F.W. Taylor, *The
        Principles of Scientific Management*, is at http://
        nationalhumanitiescenter.org/pds/gilded/progress/
        text3/taylor.pdf

32   For a summary of Gorz's analysis and its
        implications for trade unions, see http://
        globalsolidarity.antenna.nl/gorz.html#top

33   Stites, Ibid, p.147

Chapter Sixteen: Trotsky and Martov

1   Keep, Ibid, p.289

2   Report in *I s'yezd*, Moscow, p.76

3   Diane P. Koenker, *Republic of Labor: Russian Printers
        and Soviet Socialism* 1918-1930, Cornell University
        Press, 2005, p.4

4   *Sobraniye Uzakonenii*, 1920, No 8, Article 49; in
        record of Third All-Russian Trade Union Congress,
        1920, 1, Plenum, p.50-51

5   "The Tasks of the Trade Unions", M. Tomsky, Ninth
        Party Congress, Appendix 13, p.534

6   Leon Trotsky, *Sochinenya*, Vol. 15, p.126

7   Leon Trotsky, Ninth RCP Congress, p.100, cited in
        Robert V. Daniels, *The Conscience of the Revolution:
        Communist Opposition in Soviet Russia*, Harvard
        University Press, 1960, p.121

8   Koenker, Ibid, p.165

9   V.I. Lenin, Ninth RCP Congress, Report of the
Central Committee of the RCP, Vol. 27, p.76, quoted
in Maximoff, Ibid, p.114

10   Ninth Party Congress, Resolutions, Appendix
12, p.532

11   Third All-Russian Congress of Trade Unions,
stenographic report, Moscow, 1920, p.87-97

12   Leon Trotsky, *Terrorism and Communism: A Reply
to Karl Kautsky*, Verso, 2007 (first published 1920),
p.124, p.125

13   Trotsky, Ibid, p.127, p.137

14   Brinton, Ibid, p.65

15   It is impossible to tease out Lenin's motivations for
allowing Martov to travel to Halle, when doing
so was an obvious threat to Bolshevik interests.
The Lenin-Martov relationship was a deep and
complex one, in some respects second only to
Lenin's relationship with Inessa Armand. Despite
their intense political differences, which Lenin
never soft-pedaled, he seems to have felt a genuine
affection and respect for Martov. When Martov
was ill in 1919 he sent him one of the best doctors
in Petrograd. Lenin's insistence that Martov be
allowed to travel abroad, with the likelihood he
would not be allowed back, may have been an
attempt to remove him from harm's way. After 1920
Martov would not have survived much longer in
Soviet Russia and it is certain he would never have
compromised his principles. In 1923, when Lenin

lay incapacitated by a severe stroke, he is said to have told his wife with obvious sadness, "They say Martov too is dying".

16   Record of Seventh All-Russian Soviet Congress, 1919, p.20

17   Record of Seventh All-Russian Soviet Congress, 1919, pp.60–63

18   Record of Eighth All-Russian Soviet Congress, 1920, pp.55–57

19   Ben Lewis and Lars T. Lih, *Martov and Zinoviev: Head to Head in Halle*, November Publications, 2011, p.27

20   The entire translated text of Zinoviev's speech is in Lewis and Lih, Ibid, pp.117–58

21   The entire translated text of Martov's speech is in Lewis and Lih, Ibid, p.167–79

22   Chris Harman, *The Lost Revolution: Germany 1918-1923*, Bookmarks, 1982, pp.196–201, contains a very useful examination of the "March Action".

23   Martov's *The State and Socialist Revolution* consisted of several essays. "The Ideology of Sovietism" first appeared in the Menshevik journal *Mysl* in 1919; "The Conquest of the State" in the exile Menshevik journal *Sozialsticheski Vestnik* in Berlin in 1923. The main essay, "Marx and the Problem of the Dictatorship of the Proletariat", was published originally in 1918 in *Workers International of Moscow*.

24   George Orwell, "Reflections on Gandhi", *Partisan Review*, January 1949

Chapter Seventeen: National Bolshevism

1   See Robert Conquest, *The Harvest of Sorrow:
    Soviet Collectivisation and the Terror-Famine*, Oxford
    University Press, 1996, for a complete account of
    the Tambov Rebellion.

2   Victor Serge, *Memoirs of a Revolutionary* (1951), New
    York Review Books, 2010, p.136–137

3   V.I. Lenin, *Collected Works*, Vol. 20, Moscow,
    pp.539–41

4   "Declaration of the Rights of the Peoples of
    Russia", Sovnarcom, 2nd November, 1917, in
    Akhapin, Ibid, pp.31–32

5   "Draft Theses of the Central Committee RPK(b)
    Concerning Policy in the Ukraine", entire text in
    Pipes, Ibid, pp.76–77

6   See Paul Avrich and Michael Malet for two
    excellent accounts of Makhno's politics, and a
    thorough demolition of the claims that he and his
    movement were anti-Semitic – https://libcom.org/
    history/anti-semitism-makhnovists-michael-malet
    and https://libcom.org/history/nestor-makhno-
    man-myth

7   M. Agursky, *The Third Rome: National Bolshevism in
    the USSR,* Boulder, 1987, p.185

8   Stites, Ibid, p.99

9   Ronald Grigor Suny, "Social Democrats in Power:
    Menshevik Georgia and the Russian Civil War",
    in *Party, State and Society in the Russian Civil War*,
    Ibid, p.345

10 Text of the Appeal cited in Maximoff, Ibid, pp.171–72

11   The full text of Kautsky's book on Georgia, which
      is one of his leanest, clearest and most personally
      engaged works, is at https://www.marxists.org/
      archive/kautsky/1921/georgia/index.htm

12   Goldman, Ibid, p.12

13   Goldman, Ibid, p.174

14   Cited in Diane P. Koenker, *Republic of Labor: Russian
      Printers and Soviet Socialism,* 1918-1930, Cornell
      University Press, 2005, p.52

15   Jonathan Aves, *Workers against Lenin: Labour Protest
      and the Bolshevik Dictatorship* 1920-1922, I.B Tauris,
      1997, p.69, p.74

16   Koenker, Ibid, p.53

17   Dybenko later became a Stalin loyalist who led the
      purging, torture and murder of his old commander
      Marshall Tukchachevsky and other Red Army
      leaders in 1937. Like many who led the first wave of
      the Great Terror, Dybenko perished in the second.
      In 1938 Stalin had him arrested and executed.

18   Alexandra Kollontai, *The Workers' Opposition*, First
      Prism Key Press Edition, 2011 (first published 1921),
      full text.

19   Leon Trotsky, "The Trade Unions and their
      Further Role", Tenth Congress of the RCP, appendix
      10. p.786

20   V.I. Lenin, *Collected Works,* Vol. 32, Moscow, p.20-21

21   Brinton, Ibid, p.79

22   Cathy Porter, *Alexandra Kollontai: A Biography,*
      Virago, 1980, p.369

23   Daniels, Ibid, p.135

24   Anna Itkina, *Revolutionary, Tribune, Diplomat:*
      A Brief Life of Alexandra Mikhailovna Kollontai,
      Moscow, p.213

25   Porter, Ibid, p.370

26   Itkina, Ibid, p.193

27   Resolutions of the Tenth Party Congress "On
      the Unity of the Party" and "on the Syndicalist
      and Anarchist Deviation in our Party", CPSU
      in Resolutions, pp.527-30 and p.531, as cited in
      Daniels, Ibid, p.468

28   K. Radek, record of Tenth Party Congress, p.540,
      cited in Daniels *op cit*

29   The total number of people who perished in the
      Great Purge is contested and ranges from the "low
      hundreds of thousands" to 1.2 million, depending
      on the criteria used to establish "murder", i.e. direct
      execution by the NKVD or a range of other deaths
      brought about by the conditions in the Gulag
      camps. Anne Applebaum points out that as terrible
      as the Great Purge was and the high level of deaths
      in 1936-38, the death rate in the Gulag in the
      periods before and after the Purge, at the time of
      the state-directed rural famine of 1932-33 and again
      in 1942-43, was much higher.

30   Leon Trotsky, Thirteenth Congress of the RCP,
      pp.166-67, cited in Daniels, Ibid, p.240

Chapter Eighteen: Meet the New Boss

1   Stites, Ibid, p.55

2   Israel Getzler, *Kronstadt 1917-1921*, Cambridge University Press, 1983, p.212

3   Paul Avrich, *Kronstadt 1921*, Princeton University Press, 1970, p.6

4   Ida Mett, *The Kronstadt Uprising*, Black Rose Books, 1971, Introduction by Murray Bookchin, p.2

5   Aves, Ibid, p.113, p.120

6   Aves, Ibid, p.112

7   Richard Sawka, *Soviet Communists in Power: A Study of Moscow during the Civil War 1918-1921*, Palgrave, 1988, p.94–95

8   Avrich, Ibid, p.35

9   Resolution of Second Conference of Communist Sailors of the Baltic Fleet cited in Mett, Ibid, p.36

10   S.M. Petrichenko, *Pravda o Kronshtadtskikh Sobyittakh*, 1921, p.6

11   Mett, Ibid, pp.40–41, for the Kronstadt resolution and political programme of the Kronstadt rebellion.

12   Alexander Berkman, *The Bolshevik Myth: Diary 1920-1922*, Pluto Press, 1989 (first published 1925), p.292

13   *Kornatovskii miatezh*, p.26, cited in Avrich, Ibid, p.43

14   *Pravda o Kronshstade*, 8th March, 1921, pp.82–8

15   Samuel Farber, *Before Stalinism: The Rise and Fall of Soviet Democracy*, Polity Press, 1990, pp.192–93

16   Getzler, Ibid, p.235

17   The "Ultimatum" to the Kronstadt sailors was issued in Petrograd by Trotsky as People's Commissar of War. Its full text can be found in *Kronstadt by V.I. Lenin and Leon Trotsky*, Pathfinder Press, 1979, p.67

18   Figes, Ibid, p.767

19   Leon Trotsky, "Kronstadt and the Stock Exchange", *Pravda* No 63, 23rd March, 1921

20   Cited in Broido, Ibid, p.66

21   Avrich, Ibid, p.224

22   Cohen, Ibid, p.124

23   Serge, Ibid, p.172

24   The entire text of Lenin's "The Tax in Kind" article is at https://www.marxists.org/archive/lenin/works/1921/apr/21.htm

25   Figes, Ibid, p.768, and references to support the estimation of the total imprisoned and shot during the suppression of the Tambov rebellion.

26   "Pause! Read! Consider!" proclamation cited in Appendix to Arshinov, Ibid

27   Cited in Figes, Ibid, p.683

28   Berkman, Ibid, p.310, p.311, p.314

29   Serge, Ibid, p.88

30   V. Alexandrovna, *Perezhitoe* (1917-21) (Past Life), Paper No 12, "Inter-University Project on the History of the Menshevik Movement", pp.69-82

31   V.I. Lenin, *Collected Works* Vol. 33, Moscow, p.65

32   V.I. Lenin, *Collected Works* Vol. 32, Moscow, p.412

33   Record of the Eleventh Party Congress, CPSU in Resolutions, 1, p.607, p.610

34   Record of the Eleventh Party Congress, Ibid, pp.103-04

Conclusion: New and Surprising Worlds

1   "Noam Chomsky on Violence, Leninism and the Left after Occupy", interview with Christopher Helali, 11th September, 2013, at http://www. thenorthstar.info/?p=10111

2   Eric Hobsbawm, *Age of Extremes: The Short Twentieth Century* 1914-1991, Michael Joseph, 1994, p.69

3   Peter Koivisto, "The Decline of the Finnish-American Left 1925-45", *International Migration Review* 17, 1983

4   Maurice Brinton, *The Irrational in Politics*, Black Rose Books, 1968, p.11

5   Vladimir Brovkin, *Russia after Lenin: Politics, Culture and Society* 1921-1929, Routledge, 1998, pp.174-75

6   John B. Hatch, "Labour Conflict in Moscow 1921-1926", in *Russia in the Era of NEP: Explorations in Soviet Society and Culture*, edited by Sheila Fitzpatrick, Alexander Rabinowitch and Richard Stites, Indiana University Press, 1991, pp.62-67

7   Daniel R. Brower, "The City in Danger: The Civil War and the Russian Urban Population", in *Party, State and Society in the Russian Civil War*, Ibid, p.61

8   Diane P. Koenker, *Journal of Modern History*, Ibid

9   Lewis H. Siegelbaum and Ronald G. Suny, "In Search of the Soviet Working Class", in *Making Workers Soviet: Power, Class and Identity*, Ibid, p.16

10 *Sotsialistichenskii vestnik* No 18, 20th September, 1924

11   Diane P. Koenker, *Republic of Labour: Russian Printers and Soviet Socialism* 1918-1930, Cornell University Press, 2005, p.170

12   Koenker, Ibid, pp.166–67

13   Fitzpatrick, Ibid, p.21

14   Diane P. Koenker, "Urbanisation and Deurbanisation in the Russian Revolution and Civil War", *Journal of Modern History* 57, 1985, pp.424–50

15   E.P. Thompson, "Eighteenth Century English Society: Class struggle without class?", *Social History* 3, May 1978, p.147-8 and 149

16   Cited in A.V. Lunacharsky, *Vpadochrye Nastoeniya Molodezhi*, p.56-7

17   Tony Cliff, *Trotsky: Fighting the Rising Stalinist Bureaucracy* 1923-1927, Bookmarks, 1991, p.149

18   https://www.marxists.org/archive/trotsky/1927/opposition/

19   Articles by Bukharin cited in Cohen, Ibid, p.159

20   Articles by Bukharin cited in Cohen, Ibid, p.140

21   Deutscher, Ibid, p.234

22   Anne Applebaum, *Gulag: A History of the Soviet Camps*, Penguin, 2004, pp.44-45. Although Applebaum is a classic product of the Anglo-American ruling class (educated at Yale and Oxford, Foreign and Deputy Editor at the *Spectator*, on the editorial board of the *Washington Post* and married to the Polish Foreign Minister) her history of the Gulag, based on state and personal records

previously unearthed or inaccessible, is definitive and irreproachable.

23   George Orwell, *New English Weekly*, 12th January, 1939

24   E.P. Thompson, "The New Left", *The New Reasoner* No 9 (Summer 1959), pp.1-2

25   Jack Newfield, "A Populist Manifesto: The Making of a New Majority", *New York Magazine*, 1971, pp.39-46

26   Daniel Cohn-Bendit, *Obsolete Communism: The Left-Wing Alternative*, AK Press, 2000 (first published 1968), p.197, p.221

27   Foot, Ibid, p.448

28   http://www.redpepper.org.uk/my-support-for-jeremy-corbyn-is-about-much-more-than-reclaiming-labour/

29   Bookchin, Ibid

30   Gorz, Ibid, p.7

31   Leon Trotsky, *Literature and Revolution*, Ibid, p.284

32   Victoria Burnett, "A Job and No Mortgage For All in a Spanish Town", *The New York Times*, 25th May, 2009

33   Bukharin's articles on the cooperative sector are cited in Cohen, Ibid, p.196

34   Karl Marx, *Inaugural Address to the First International Working Men's Association*, 1864, cited McLellan, p.178

35   "Exiting the Vampire Castle", *Our Kingdom* blog, 24th November, 2013

36   Bray, Ibid, p.257

37   For a fascinating analysis of the Mousai House,
      see http://www.truthdig.com/report/item/
      the_mousai_house_--_a_grassroots_model_for_a_
      cooperative_economy_20160702

38   Noam Chomsky, "Notes on Anarchism", *New York
      Review of Books*, May 21st, 1970

39   Brand, Ibid, p.342

40   Leon Trotsky, "The USSR in War", *Byulleten
      Oppositzii*, October 1939, p.9, p.15

41   W.H. Auden, "September 1st 1939"

42   See http://criticallegalthinking.com/2012/08/20/
      pussy-riot-maria-alyokhinas-closing-statement/

Acknowledgments

For almost three years, like Elvis Costello, "Every Day I Write the Book". So first and foremost to my wife Sue, who said it would be nice, when it was finished, to have me back on the sofa watching the TV as used to be the case. I owe her much more than these words can say.

This book is not a work of original primary research, except to the extent that neglected works of forgotten socialists and anarchists can be found in old pamphlets in the second-hand sections of left-wing bookshops and online. Although my academic background is in history and I have done professional research work for the British trade union movement and for my first book on the Labour Party in the mid-1970s, I am an amateur historian. I have had neither the time nor resources to visit the archives of Moscow, St Petersburg or Harvard University, and I am glad that others have so that I can mine their work. In that respect I have stood on the shoulders of giants, most especially Diane Koenker, Richard Stites, Vladimir Brovkin, Sheila Fitzpatrick and Alexander Rabinowitch. I must also thank my friend Valerie Phillips for loaning me some of her collection of Russian revolutionary agitprop posters and prints.

On the other hand, I have one small advantage that, I imagine, nearly all historians of the Russian Revolution lack. Since the mid-1980s I have continuously been a trade union activist, an elected representative at Branch and National level, and then a full-time union official. In these capacities I have negotiated with local and national management on numerous issues, represented members personally in grievance and discrimination cases, run recruitment and other campaigns, led strikes, organised picket lines and argued the case for public services and public ownership within Westminster and the EU. I found in writing this book that my personal experience of the socialist and trade union milieu was helpful in understanding the pressures and dilemmas of socialists who also worked outside the political mainstream, also organised congresses, meetings, motions, rallies, demonstrations, etc., while trying to ensure these efforts had some connection to what could be achieved.

I must thank Repeater Books, in particular Tariq Goddard, Mark Fisher and Josh Turner, who have been incredibly generous and supportive. First at Zero Books and now with Repeater, they have been almost alone in UK publishing in giving first-time authors a voice and platform. With Repeater they have again provided a much-needed space for radical, questioning and non-generic work that avoids the double pitfalls of Tory-lite metropolitan narcissism and predictable, self-satisfied leftism.

Lastly, a word of thanks to friends and colleagues who see more merit in Leninism and Trotskyism than I do. In my experience they are better socialists in practice than the doctrine I criticise here—more Alexander Shliapnikov than Vladimir Lenin. I know they will disagree with most of this book, but maybe not all of it.

John Medhurst
November, 2016

Repeater Books

is dedicated to the creation of a new reality. The landscape of twenty-first-century arts and letters is faded and inert, riven by fashionable cynicism, egotistical self-reference and a nostalgia for the recent past. Repeater intends to add its voice to those movements that wish to enter history and assert control over its currents, gathering together scattered and isolated voices with those who have already called for an escape from Capitalist Realism. Our desire is to publish in every sphere and genre, combining vigorous dissent and a pragmatic willingness to succeed where messianic abstraction and quiescent co-option have stalled: abstention is not an option: we are alive and we don't agree.